Frederick W. Seward

Reminiscences

of

A War-Time Statesman and Diplomat

1830—1915

By

Frederick W. Seward

**Assistant Secretary of State during the Administrations of
Lincoln, Johnson, and Hayes**

Illustrated

G. P. Putnam's Sons
New York and London
The Knickerbocker Press
1916

The Knickerbocker Press, New York

PREFACE

My long life is drawing toward its close. The portions of it that will have interest for those who are to come after me, I suppose are chiefly those which illustrate the character of the times and the characteristics of the persons concerned in them. So I set down my recollections of some of them here. Some of them have already been narrated in my *Life and Letters of William H. Seward.*

F. W. S.

Montrose-on-Hudson
1914

iii

CONTENTS

PART I

BEFORE THE WAR

PART II

DURING THE WAR

Contents

Contents

PART III

AFTER THE WAR

Contents

ILLUSTRATIONS

Reminiscences

of

A War-Time Statesman and Diplomat

Reminiscences

of a

War-Time Statesman
And Diplomat

PART I

Before the War

1833.

First Recollections.   Here is the first scene of which I
have any vivid and connected remembrance.

My brother and I, sleeping together in the trundle bed,
are suddenly awakened at night, and find the candles all
lighted.   My father is kindling a fire in the small box stove.
Then my mother takes me up to be dressed.   From the
talk between her and the nurse, I learn that we are about
to start on a journey, and that it is three o'clock in the
morning.   Peering out of the window I see that it all
looks dark, except that the ground is covered with snow.
At the gate are two bright lanterns, and horses are stamp-
ing in the snow.   This, I am told, means that the sleigh-
stage is there, in which we are to travel.   The whole
scene is novel and exhilarating, but suddenly changes,
when we get inside of the dark, cold stage, groping for
seats among the buffalo skins.   The curtains are fastened

down, the windows closed.   Shuffling of feet and subdued
voices are heard, from which I know there are other passengers, but can see nothing.   The stage starts and goes
sliding and bumping over the rough road.   Wrapped up
and in my mother's lap, I soon fall into a doze, and after
a series of naps, wake up again in daylight, to be told that
we have come twenty-six miles to Syracuse.

Two or three dreary, weary days and nights in the
stage now follow, varied only by stopping to change
horses, to get meals and occasional hours of sleep.   This
is the method of journeying from Auburn to Albany, in
the year 1833.

January, 1834.

Hotel Life in Albany.   Now we are living in a hotel at
Albany.   It is called "Bement's."   In front of it is a
broad, smooth, sloping road, covered with ice and snow.
This, I am told, is "State Street."   The sun is shining
through our frosty windows.   Sleigh bells are jingling
and people are walking briskly up and down the hill.
Everything looks bright and cheerful.   Indoors, our
rooms are light and warm.   There is a fire in the grate.
There are toys and pictures, and other children to play
with.   There are nuts and raisins and various sweet
things at dinner.   There is plenty of light and plenty of
noise.   On the whole, I like hotel life very much.

Many visitors come in, all polite to my mother, and
some very kindly to me.   There are three whose visits
are frequent.   These are my "Uncle Cary," my "Uncle
Tracy," and "Uncle Weed."   I am fond of all of them,
especially the latter.   He is a tall, dark-haired man, with
a very gentle voice, who takes long and vigorous strides
as he walks up the street.   They are not my "real"
uncles—not my father's brothers—but his intimate friends.
They often go with him up the hill, to the large building

William H. Seward

of red freestone, with a white cupola, having a statue on top. The statue represents "Justice," they tell me; and that is the Capitol, where my father goes to attend to his business in the Senate.

December, 1834.

Christmas. Christmas morning at Auburn! Everything is gay and full of fun. I do not remember much of other Christmases; nevertheless it seems to me a long established custom, and from what I have heard about it, I am expecting a joyous day. My mother says we must not get up to look at our stockings hanging by the fireplace, until each has counted, in French, the years of his age. It is a part of the general fun to discover that my age is equivalent to a cat (*quatre*), and that my brother's is wheat (*huit*). Then, a mad rush for the stockings, which of course are loaded with toys and candy. There is a red-coated soldier with a black shako. There is a dog that opens his mouth and barks and there are other marvels. I take mine down to show to my grandfather. "Merry Christmas, Grandpa!" "What!" he says, "is this Christmas? Then I must make you something." He picks up a piece of wood, and by deft and skilful use of his jack-knife has presently completed a miniature snow-shovel. In the kitchen, where the servants and children are congregated, an earnest debate arises over the question whether Santa Claus is a real person or not. My brother, with the wisdom and experience of eight years, cuts the argument short by saying, "Anyhow there is somebody. Things can't get into the stockings just of themselves." To this conclusion we all agree.

My Great-Grandmother. She is sitting by the window, not far from the blazing woodfire on the hearth. Behind her rocking chair is the high corner cupboard, containing her treasures, into which we are not allowed to pry. She is an erect, stately little body, notwithstanding her eighty-four years, with white hair and neat prim lace cap and collar, silk neckerchief, and grey dress. Her kind old eyes beam through gold-rimmed spectacles upon the children, for whom "Grandma's Room" is always a favourite resort.

The wood fire needs frequent replenishing, and so at intervals, Peter, the "hired man," comes in with an armful. To save the carpet, there is a little pathway of rag carpeting, running from door to chimney, for him to walk on; which we also try to walk on—when we don't forget it.

We are telling Grandma that it is bitter cold outside, and that our fingers are "most frozen" in our mittens. The snow is four feet deep, and when I am in the shovelled path, I can see nothing but the sky. A rooster is crowing somewhere and Peter, who is tall enough to see, tells me he is on the top of the snow-drift. Roads are gone and fences are covered.

Then Grandma tells us of "the hard winter" in the time of the Revolution, when cannon were dragged across the Hudson River on the ice. She has plenty of stories, but we especially like to hear those about "the War." We are always ready to lay aside even *Puss in Boots* and *Mother Hubbard* with their beautiful pictures, to draw our stools up around her chair and listen,—for Grandma's stories are "real" ones.

She tells us that when she was a girl, her name was Paulina Titus until she grew up and married Josiah Miller, who soon became a Captain in the Continental Army. She tells us of the little village of Bedford, where they used to live, and how people there began to talk of "bad times coming." How some said King George was crazy, and others said his ministers were fools. How folks saw great displays of "Northern lights" with flashes of blue and red, in rows, marching toward each other, like armies in battle. Then, how ships began to come into New York harbour loaded with soldiers and cannon. How there were rumors of riots and prisoners in New York. How the farmers began to get together their old muskets and swords and cartridge-boxes and powder-horns, and to hide them in barns. How they began to cast bullets in their kitchens out of odd pieces of lead. How they had secret meetings and drills, and "committees of safety." And, at last, how riders came post haste down the Boston Road, with the news that there had been fighting at Lexington. And so began the long years of battles and sieges and hardships.

Then she tells us how Bedford awoke to the discovery that it was in the midst of "war's alarms." It was in the "Neutral Ground," which neither side could hold,—so it was plundered and ravaged by both. One morning the hen-roost would be found robbed of all its fowls. Another, all the hams and beef would be stolen from the smoke-house. Then the corn would disappear from the crib, and the cow from her stable. Occasionally a bullet from some unseen gun would crash through a window pane. These were supposed to be the deeds of two gangs of marauders, one of which was known as the "Cowboys" and the other as the "Skinners." The "Cowboys" were said to be in sympathy with the British, and the "Skinners" with the Americans. But one was about as bad as the other. More to be feared than either, were the raids of "Tarleton's Dragoons," and "Delancey's Horse," their purpose being, not merely to plunder, but to burn and kill.

Most thrilling of all is the story of how she sat by the window one morning and saw two horsemen galloping down the road. As they passed the house, one shouted, "The Regulars are coming!" Then they went on over the hill. Presently the sound of firing was heard; and soon after one horse came galloping back with the saddle empty.

Then the heads of an advancing column appeared. One glance was enough to perceive that they were the dreaded dragoons of Colonel Tarleton. They came slowly, as if anticipating resistance. But there was none. All the able-bodied men were with the army. Only women, children, invalids, and a few negro slaves remained in the village. The troopers halted in the middle of the broad street. Then, in obedience to some order of the commander, several of them dismounted and entered the nearest houses. Seizing the burning brands from the kitchen fires, they scattered them about the rooms, where they would set things in a blaze. From one roof after another, smoke began to pour out, and flames appeared at the windows. The inmates, hastily gathering their children and such clothing as they could lay hands on, fled for their lives,—some to distant friends, some to the woods.

As the conflagration approached her home, old Mrs. Titus (Paulina's mother) went out into the street, and taking hold of the bridle of the commanding officer, said something to him. He bent down, and they conversed in low tones. Then, raising his head, and pointing toward Mrs. Titus's home, he gave the order: "You need not burn that house." What was said can only be conjectured, but it was presumed that she told him that she was a loyal subject of King George. Probably she did not mention that her son-in-law, Captain Miller, was just then engaged in harassing Tarleton's flanks and rear. When night fell, all that was left of Bedford was one dwelling, and a dozen or two of heaps of smoking ashes.

"And when was the war done and over, Grandma?"

ask her impatient little hearers. The old lady pauses in her knitting, to count up. "Four years later," she says. Then she describes how the British marched out of New York, as the Americans marched in, and how different the two armies looked. The British, with their neat uniforms, scarlet coats, and gleaming muskets, moving at regulation step, through silent or scowling crowds. The Americans, swinging cheerily down the road, with every kind of shot-gun and rifle, some well clad and some in rags and tatters, and woefully deficient in shoes. Some had their feet bound up in bloody rags to protect them from the frosty ground. But how the people cheered, and cried, and laughed, and wept, as they saw them come marching in! Grandma wipes her spectacles now, at the remembrance of it.

There is also another tale, now become a family tradition. But like other family traditions, it is open to cavil or doubt, on account of lacking corroborating evidence. So far as I recall it, the substance of it was this.

About a year after the burning of Bedford, Captain Josiah Miller came home one day, and said: "Paulina, you can't live here any longer. We must go north and get inside of Putnam's lines." A few days later the whole household, with such effects as they could carry, started on horseback toward Fishkill.

The journey was long, and the roads were bad. When night came on, they had only reached Crompond. They bethought themselves of a cousin, Andreas Miller, living there, who sometimes "entertained travellers."

Andreas met them at the door, and greeted them cordially, but said: "I can't give you very good accommodation, for I have two travellers staying here, already."

When they went in to supper, the two travellers were there. One looked like a farmer, in a rough grey coat; the other was a handsome young gentleman in dark clothes, who laid aside a long riding cloak.　Both were taciturn, and retired early.

The next morning Andreas said: "The other travellers were earlier than you.　They have started already for Pine Bridge."

The Millers duly reached their destination "inside of Putnam's lines."　A few days later, she was startled by her husband's announcement:

"Well, Paulina, that handsome young man you met at Crompond turns out to be a British spy, and General Washington is going to hang him!"

.　　　.　　　.　　　.　　　.　　　.

Half a century passes.　Sons and daughters have been born to the Millers, have grown up, married, and scattered far and wide.　Captain Josiah is sleeping in the churchyard.　His widow, Paulina, is now a great-grandmother, and is living at Auburn, with her son, Elijah.　He is a Judge, and is my grandfather.　To us, he looks almost as old as his mother.　We often hear the two talking over the events of "the War."

"Yes, Elijah," she says,　General Washington was a good man—a great and good man—and he did a great deal for the country.　But I never liked his hanging Major André."

"But, mother, André was a spy.'

"No, Elijah, Major André did not mean to be a spy. It was that wicked traitor, Arnold, who brought him into his trouble.　If Arnold had been hung, I should say he richly deserved it."

"But, mother, Washington hadn't got Arnold, and he had got André.　He tried to exchange them, but Sir Henry Clinton wouldn't do it.　They were conspirators —and such conspirators deserve hanging.　They generally get it too, when they are caught."

"It surely was a conspiracy, and a great crime, Elijah, —but I have never approved of the hanging of Major André."

"Well, mother, if he hadn't been caught and hung, I think you and I wouldn't be here to-day, to talk about him!"

1835.

A Carriage Journey. "A journey! A long journey, in a carriage with my father and mother. Going miles away from home, seeing new places and meeting strange people. Won't it be fun?" So I say to myself and to my companions.

On a mild May morning, the journey actually begins. In my new green jacket and cap, I am sitting on the front seat of the carriage, by the side of William Johnson, the coloured driver. Before us are two stout grey horses one of whom William calls "Lion," and the other "the Doctor." On the back seat are my father and mother. The baggage and clothing are mysteriously stowed away beneath the seats and behind. There is an extension top, to put up when it rains, a fishing-rod to catch mountain trout, a pail to water the horses, and a tin drinking cup for use at wayside streams.

The greys trot off briskly, as if they liked the prospect of travel. Soon we are climbing and descending hills on the way to Cayuga Lake. The first two or three days are over roads we have known about. We stop to visit cousins, uncles, aunts, and old friends, at Seneca Falls, Aurora, and Ludlowville. Then we strike off into regions heretofore unknown. We follow the banks of the Cayuga Creek down to the valley of the Susquehanna.

Now we are in the Pennsylvania mountains, following the valleys of the Lycoming and the Susquehanna. The rugged and narrow roads wind along the mountainsides, crossing wild gorges, over dangerous looking bridges. There are rocky cliffs stretching far up on one side, while deep abysses open on the other. There is apparently impenetrable forest in each direction, and we seem to be out of sight of civilization.

We spend the nights in such rustic taverns as the region affords. In the morning William recounts to us such tales as he has heard overnight, about wolves and robbers and rattlesnakes. Of robbers and snakes we see none, but we hear the wolves howling high up in the mountain forest. When I inquire as to the possibility of their coming down, I am reassured by the reply that they are probably chasing the deer, and are not looking for little boys.

We lunch under shady trees, gather wild flowers, and fish for trout. Rhododendrons, scarlet and crimson, dot the valley and mountain. My father and mother talk to each other about the "scenery." The term is a vague one to me, but I understand it to refer to the mountains, hills, woods, and waters that they evidently admire. For my own part, I think I prefer the roads near the villages, where the children are playing, and the dogs run out to bark, and the chickens scurry across the roadway, and people come along in farm wagons loaded with wood, or hay or produce. Sometimes a young colt will be accompanying the farmer's team; and I am in great hopes that we can persuade one to change his mind and follow us.

Most of the men we meet nod their heads, and some say, "Good-morning," as we pass. I ask my father if they are all acquaintances of his. He says, no, but that it is the custom of the country to exchange salutations in passing, and a very good custom it is. My mother adds that travellers should be pleasant to those they meet, if they want others to be pleasant to them,—a maxim that I think I will treasure up for future use.

Names of places do not mean much to persons of my

age, but a few of those of the largest towns stick in my
memory—Athens, Towanda, Williamsport, Milton, and
finally Harrisburg, the State capital.

Next we are traversing a less mountainous and more
thickly settled region. The roads are broader and more
level. There are cultivated farms, large barns, fields of
grain, herds of cattle and sheep. There are towns with
hotels and mills and shops. There are many more coloured
people both in town and country.

Every day we meet more and more of summer. Red
cherries and ripe strawberries abound, and melons are
ripening in the sun. So we pass on through southern
Pennsylvania and northern Maryland, pausing a day or
a night at Carlisle, Chambersburg, Hagerstown, Boones-
borough, Shepherdstown, and Harpers Ferry.

Even a small boy could appreciate and remember the
magnificent panorama of scenery at Harpers Ferry—
the towering hills and meeting valleys, that mark the
junction of the Shenandoah with the Potomac.

As we enter the "Old Dominion" and pursue our way
through the "Valley of Virginia," my father tells us of
the historic events that occurred in the region we are
traversing, of Washington's early campaigns, of Braddock's
defeat, and of the battles and skirmishes of the "French
and Indian War." That was a long while ago. It all
belongs to the past. If any prophet should arise to tell us
that even in our own lifetime, we shall again see this peaceful region become the scene of war, and of advancing and
retreating armies and bloody battles, we certainly should
not believe him.

"You will not find towns and hotels in the Valley like
those in your own State." So our friends at Harrisburg
had warned us. Certainly travel here is very different.
The roads are muddy and stony, the fields neglected and
overgrown with weeds. Thickets abound on either side

of us. We meet few carriages or wagons, and only occasionally travellers on horseback. Dwellings are seldom
in sight. The planters' houses stand back from the road,
and the negro cabins huddle near them.

Such a day's ride might lead us to expect that our night's
lodging would be in some dilapidated old town or noisy
tavern. But nothing of the sort is before us. We drive
up an avenue of spreading trees. The carriage stops at
the door of a large, low, comfortable looking house, with
wide porches or veranda, covered with vines. Evidently
it is the house of a gentleman. The owner meets us at
the door with hospitable greeting, directs his servants to
take charge of our horses, and ushers us into the parlour,
where his family give us an equally cordial welcome.
They are well dressed, well bred, and not at all inquisitive,
though ready to hear the latest news and talk on the topics
of the day. The table is loaded with the luxuries of the
season. Our bedrooms are neat and comfortable, and
there is an abundance of black servants, patient, gentle,
and polite. In a word, it is a typical planter's home.

If there is at times a lack of neatness or dispatch, we
should hardly observe it, if we did not sometimes hear
the master or mistress speak of one of our smiling attendants as a "lazy, no account," or "trifling nigger." When
we take our departure, it seems as if we were parting from
old acquaintances, and the pressing invitations to come
again are evidently sincere. Our host asks no compensation, but will sometimes accept it, in a way that seems
to imply that he does so to please us, as much as himself.

My mother remarks that she has often been told that
she could not travel in Virginia with any pleasure, because
the taverns were so poor. But she finds it just the reverse.
Not only are the planters so hospitable, but even the few
little taverns we meet are neat and quiet, without noise
or bustle or dram-drinking,—and one is not annoyed with

the crowd of lounging topers so frequent at the country taverns of New York.

My father replies that the Virginians have had the reputation for a hundred years of being a frank, hospitable, vigorous people, justly proud of their State as the "Mother of Presidents." But, he adds, Virginia is now deteriorating, materially as well as politically, since she became the breeder of slaves for the Southern and Western markets. And the worst is that the people are unconscious of the cause of the decay, and in a great degree ignorant that other parts of the country enjoy greater prosperity.

Much of this talk is beyond my comprehension until recalled by later events. I think I am the one who enjoys the journey most. When we come to what William calls an "ole Virginny bridge," I like to see "Lion" and the "Doctor" plunge into the clear stream, and to watch the water coming up to the hubs of the wheels. That we are travelling chiefly in the woods is no hardship, since there are so many shady trees, wild flowers, birds, colts, and chipmunks. Then there is always the prospect of coming across another "cake and beer" shop by the roadside. The beer I do not care for, but the cake (usually fresh gingerbread) is always welcome.

The humble, submissive black race that we meet everywhere seem so loyal to the white, that it is a surprise to find that apprehensions of harm from them are entertained. William, our coachman, comes to say that he is stopped in the road, whenever he goes out after sundown.

"But you are a free man, William?"

"I told them so, but they say it don't make any difference,—that I have got to have a pass."

So it proves. There seems to be a sort of general understanding, that no coloured man is allowed to be out after dark, without a written permit from some white man, presumably his employer, and that anybody may stop him and demand to see it.

．　　．　　．　　．　　．　　．　　．

Arriving in the afternoon at a large plantation, I stray out of the parlour to a sort of gallery or shed, adjoining the house. There I find a group of twenty or more little "darkies," playing and chattering like so many monkeys. Some are older than I am, some younger. All have only very scanty clothing and some none at all. They stop their play, and surround me, though at a little distance away. Yet I instinctively perceive that their looks imply no dislike or fear, but rather pleasure and admiration.

Somewhat abashed by the circle of bright eyes and gleaming teeth, I turn to stroke the back of the old cat, reposing on the gallery rail,—saying "Poor Pussy—poor Pussy!" Instantly, there is an outburst of joyous laughter from the whole group, as if I had made the finest jest in the world. "Lil' mas'r say 'po' Puss!'" they repeat. Then one by one they timidly advance to stroke the cat, in imitation of me, until she jumps down and runs away. Then very gently and wonderingly, they touch my bright buttons and lace collar, evidently regarding them as something very fine. My childish vanity is awakened, by finding myself the centre of so much deferential and admiring regard. I hasten to the parlour to tell my mother of it. Her only comment is "Poor things!" I do not know why she should pity them. But that I am to find out later.

．　　．　　．　　．　　．　　．

At an inn, where we stop to rest one morning, my mother observes a woman, blind and decrepit with age, turning the ponderous wheel of a machine on the lawn. Going out to speak with her, she says:

"Is not that very hard work?"

"Why, yes, mistress; but I must do something and this is all I can do now, I am so old."

"How old are you?"

"I don't know; past sixty they tell me."

"Have you a husband?"

"I don't know, mistress."

"Have you ever had a husband?"

"Yes, I was married."

"Where is he now?"

"I don't know, mistress, he was sold."

"Have you children?"

"I don't know, mistress; I had children, but they were sold."

"How many?"

"Six."

"Have you never heard from any of them since they were sold?"

"No, mistress."

"Do you not find it hard to bear up under such afflictions?"

"Why, yes, mistress; but God does what He thinks best for us."

A still sadder sight is presented at a country tavern on the way, where the carriage arrives just at sunset. A cloud of dust is seen, coming slowly down the road, from which proceeds a confused noise of moaning, weeping, and shouting. On reaching the gate of the stable yard, it discloses itself. Ten naked little boys, between six and twelve years old, tied together, two and two, by their wrists, are all fastened to a long rope, and followed by a tall, gaunt, white man, who, with his long lash, whips up the sad and weary little procession, drives them to a horse trough to drink, and thence to a shed, where they lie down on the ground, and sob and moan themselves to sleep.

These, we are told, are children gathered up at different plantations by the "trader," and are to be driven down to Richmond, to be sold at auction and taken South.

We push on southwards, winding up and down the mountain roads in the bright sunshine. But I intuitively feel, as children do, that somehow we are not so merry and cheerful a party as when we first set out. William sits by my side sober and silent. My father and mother converse in low tones, on the back seat.

When at night they mention their plans, I am rather sorry to hear that we are not going to Richmond, as everybody seems to expect, but glad to know that we are to see the two great natural wonders—Weyer's Cave and the Natural Bridge.

Arriving one morning at the foot of a mountain we slowly climb up to "the Cave," which it seems is near the top instead of the bottom of the mountain. There are guides with tallow candles in tin sconces, to show it to visitors. William and I go with the others, far enough into the interior to see some of the glittering and fantastic stalactites and stalagmites, rising like curved pillars and lost to sight high up in the darkness.

But a brief view of these satisfies our curiosity, and we are content to go outside and sit on a bench in the sunshine, while awaiting the return of my father and mother who are exploring the farther recesses of the cavern. When they come out they tell of the marvels they have seen. I think I should like to have seen the things that look like statues and animals, but I am not desirous to go through "Washington's Chamber" and the thirty other realms of darkness.

Now we pass through Staunton and Lexington, then over more rocky hills and mountain roads. Finally we come in sight of the Natural Bridge. Here we pause, for some hours, to wonder and admire. The great rocky arch looks as if it had been excavated by human hands, yet none have ever laboured at it. We drive across it in our carriage. We walk under it by the side of the creek which it spans, and at last we leave it reluctantly.

And now we turn our faces northward. Lion and the Doctor trot off merrily, as if they knew they were going home. We do not return by the way we came, but strike by an easterly route, stopping to look at Jefferson's home at Monticello and Washington's at Mount Vernon.

We end our Virginia pilgrimage at Alexandria at night-fall, and are to cross the Potomac in the morning to visit the national capital.

1835.

First Visit to Washington. On board the horse-boat in our carriage, we are transported across the Potomac from Virginia to Georgetown. Thence we drive at a leisurely pace down into Washington.

Seen from this direction the city looks like a jumble of unfinished and unpaved streets. Here and there a brick building on a corner lot marks the intersection of some street and avenue. Between these brick buildings are long vacant spaces, with occasionally some old-fashioned village residence, having its shade trees, fences, and garden.

Pennsylvania Avenue seems to be the only one that is compactly built up. It looks to me longer and broader than any that I have ever known. On the hill at one end stands the magnificent white Capitol; at the other the President's mansion is surrounded by a grove of trees.

We arrive at Gadsby's, which is said to be the best hotel, and one much patronized by members of Congress. Several gentlemen and some ladies call during the evening, and talk over the latest news and gossip of the government and the city.

.   .   .   .

Morning comes, and my mother tells me that Governor Dickerson, the Secretary of the Navy, is coming to take us up to see the President.   I have heard (as who has not) of General Jackson, "the Hero of New Orleans," and I am quite ready to make his acquaintance.   But when my mother brings out the little coat I am to wear, I demur to the colour of it.   "If I wear a red coat, won't General Jackson take me for a Britisher?"   However, this objection is overruled.

In due time Mr. Secretary Dickerson arrives in a carriage, and we are whirled over the macadamized avenue to the Executive Mansion.

We ascend the stairs and are ushered into the President's room, where he sits at a writing table with a great pile of commissions before him, to which he is appending his signature.   He is tall and thin, with iron grey hair brushed stiffly back from his forehead, and is dressed in a black suit.   At first glance he reminds me of my grandfather Seward.   He rises and greets us with stately courtesy, invites us to be seated, and takes me on his knee.

The conversation opens with polite inquiries about our travels and my mother's health.   Then it turns to governmental topics, which I do not understand; and I amuse myself by looking round the room.   It is a library, for there are bookshelves on each side.   But its most noticeable feature is that there are so many portraits and busts of General Jackson himself all around.   They are all different, yet each is an unmistakable likeness.

When the talk reverts to our journey again, and our visit to Monticello, he seems much interested.   Presently I observe that his voice is growing louder and his face getting redder and the arm round me is quivering with excitement.   Evidently he is getting angry with somebody, but who?   I am relieved to find that it is not with any of us, but somebody whom he calls "the Senate," and speaks of with scorn. It seems there is some question about a statue, but the merits of the case are beyond my comprehension; and when Mr. Dickerson essays a word in behalf of the offending body, he is summarily silenced by the remark, "That is no argument, sir."

But he soon calms down, and the conversation goes on smoothly again. He is emphatic though not irritable when he tells my father that "a frank and vigorous policy is the best, in dealing with foreign nations, as with men." When the interview is closing, he again rises and bids us "good-bye," with the same stately courtesy as when he received us.

As we drive away down the avenue, I keep thinking of the General and his pictures and busts. Only two portraits of Presidents are within my remembrance, those of Washington and Jefferson. Mentally comparing these I decide that all Presidents are tall, grey-haired, and stern looking and always dressed in black. By the time I have reached this sage conclusion, we are at the door of Gadsby's. And so ends my first visit to the White House.

1835.

"Colonel John." In my visits to my grandfather's home in Orange County, I found there were some old residents still living, who remembered my great-grandfather, Colonel John Seward, of Revolutionary memory. They had stories or traditions to tell about him.

He lived in New Jersey, and was one of the earliest to take part in the struggle for independence. In command of a company, he fought under Washington, at the battle of Long Island, shared in the experiences of the subsequent retreat, and afterwards was in the battle at White Plains.

The next year he was engaged in the battle at Princeton, and in 1778 in the battle of Monmouth. In 1779, he had been promoted to the colonelcy of a New Jersey militia regiment, and with a part of it joined in the pursuit of Brant with his Tories and Indians, after the bloody massacre at Minisink.

The Tories in his neighbourhood heartily hated and feared him; and a reward of twenty pounds was offered for his capture "dead or alive."

His home in Sussex County was an occasional stopping place for Washington, in his frequent journeys between the New York and New Jersey encampments. "Seward's Home" is noted on one of the campaign maps in Irving's *Life of Washington*.

One story illustrative of his energetic character was in regard to an attempt to decoy him into an ambuscade. Colonel Seward was sitting on his front porch, toward evening, when an ill-looking fellow, mounted on a cadaverous horse, which he guided with a rope halter, rode up, and delivered to him what purported to be "a message from General Washington." Colonel Seward, suspecting some treacherous design, after questioning the messenger, said sharply: "General Washington never sent you on such a horse as that, with a message to me." Turning round, he took down his rifle, which hung over the doorway. The spy, seeing himself discovered, started quickly to escape, whipping up his beast, in order to warn his confederates. But before he had reached the gateway, a bullet from the Colonel's rifle brought him down.

Another tale was that, in one of the Jersey battles, the colonel captured, with his own hand, a Hessian soldier, and brought his prisoner home with him. The soldier, being a sensible German peasant, thought life on a gentleman's country place much preferable to service under the Prince of Hesse-Cassel, who had sold him, and King George, who had bought him, as "food for powder." So he proposed to remain with his captor, and proved to be a faithful and capable servant, for many years. His name was not remembered, but he was popularly known in the neighbourhood as "Colonel John's Hessian."

1837.

The Panic of 1837—Shinplasters. My first lesson in finance came in 1837. Like other boys, I had my little "money-box" as my savings-bank, into which to put an occasional big copper cent or a battered Spanish sixpence.

Then one summer came "Hard Times," when sixpences and shillings and even pennies suddenly disappeared from general use. Some people said that President Van Buren was to blame for it. Others laid the blame on Congress and the banks. Of the crash of corporations, the suspension of payments, and the wreck of merchants, I was happily ignorant. I only knew that nobody had any "change" and nobody could tell me why or wherefore. Or, if they could, the reasons were beyond my comprehension.

But presently there began to appear in use little square tickets of paper, like those of the circus or the baker and milkman. On these was printed, "Good for 5 cents," or "Good for sixpence," or "Good for 1 shilling," and they bore the name of some merchant or tavern-keeper. These I was told were "shinplasters." They seemed to pass from hand to hand as easily as any other money. But when I got one and proposed to put it in my "money-box," I was told it would not do for that, as it might prove worthless any day. The only thing to do was to get rid of it as speedily as possible,—which was always easy at the candy store and toy shop.

Then later I was told that some of the men who issued them were "calling them in" and burning up whole handfuls of them, which seemed a great waste of good money.

When silver and copper began to appear again, I inquired why those paper things were called "shinplasters."

No one seemed to know until I asked my grandfather, who laughed and said he supposed it was because people hated them as much as they did the shinplasters they used to have when he was a boy. But what were they? So he went on to tell me.

In the days when he was young, every gentleman wore knee breeches and long silk stockings on his legs. When he went out to ride on horseback or to walk through mud and snow, he put on long riding boots over them. On coming in chilled and cold, he pulled off the boots and sat down in front of the open fire, where everybody drew up their chairs to get warm. Of course the knees were the parts nearest the blaze. These frequent and sudden changes from cold to heat and heat to cold made the shin tender, and "sore shins" were a prevalent winter complaint. Various salves, ointments, and plasters were prescribed for their cure.

Said he: "I never was so glad of any change of fashion as I was when pantaloons came in. The three-cornered hats and ruffled shirts and buckled shoes were well enough, but I hated the knee breeches as much as I did the pigtails tied with eelskin. People said the fashion would change again, and go back to the short breeches, but I do not believe it ever will, in this country, whatever the British and French may do."

1839.

" Henry Clay at Auburn." "Henry Clay is coming to Auburn. He is to stop over night at Governor Seward's." This is the joyful news. The great Kentucky statesman is making a "tour" through several States this summer, and at Cayuga Bridge a delegation from Auburn on horseback and in carriages meet him and escort him to town. All the Whig boys and most of the Whig men are on the *qui vive* to welcome him.

He arrives in the afternoon, in a barouche and a cloud of dust. He is received and welcomed at the hotel with flags, music, cheering, speeches, and much handshaking. His tall form and commanding air, his winning smile and resonant voice rouse the public enthusiasm. After the public reception, he comes over to spend the night at our house. All the evening the parlor is thronged with ladies who are captivated by his courtly manner, and men who eagerly drink in his words of political wisdom. This is still going on when I am sent up to bed.

Early in the morning I am up and out to play in the dooryard. In the woodshed I find a young and very well-dressed coloured man, who is polishing a pair of boots. I venture to ask him if he is "Charles." "Yes, I'se Charles, sure enough. And what may your name be?"

I tell him, and then ask him if he has been long with Mr. Clay.

"Ever sence I was born," he says. "And I 'spect I'm going to stay with him, too. Some of them fool fellers down to Boston tried to get me to leave him, and come there to live. But I said to 'em, 'No, sir,' says I, 'I'm going to stick to Mas'r Clay, and going back with him to Ole Kaintuck. Henry Clay and Ole Kaintuck are good enough for me any day.'"

Then, contemplating the boots, he continues: "My ole man he wakes me up right early and tells me to get these boots. Now, I'm going to wake him up right early and tell him to get up and get his breakfast."

So, with a laugh and a flourish, he departs to the house, leaving me to ponder over the new phase of the Abolition question, which his words have presented to my mind.

1839.

The Governor's Mansion. "Kane's Walk," on Westerlo Street in Albany, was a fine old residence, which had been occupied in former years by Governors Clinton, Tompkins, and Yates.   It was now selected as my father's "Executive Mansion."   It stood at some distance back from the roadway, and was a spacious two-storied brick edifice, painted in the Colonial style, yellow with white blinds.   The grounds were large, but had been shorn of some of their former grandeur.   A street had been cut through what was originally the lawn in front of the house, and the remains of the old avenue extending from South Pearl Street were visible.   But there were still two or three acres of land and a grove of trees surrounding the house, with ample space for stable, carriage house, and outbuildings, and on the south side was the formal garden, whose beds and walks were now overgrown with grass.

A broad hall extended through the middle of the house from the front door to the rear one.   This was carpeted and furnished as a sitting-room, and was well adapted for the reception of deputations, committees, and casual visitors.   On one side of it were two parlors connected by folding doors and opening into a great dining-room, fifty feet long, which was also used as a ballroom.   On the other side were three or four family rooms, and there were half a dozen more above.

In the wing nearest to Westerlo Street was the library or office, which the Governor could use as a study, or for the reception of confidential visitors, as it had a separate entrance.   A room for his private secretary adjoined it.

Below, a spacious basement contained two kitchens, several servants' rooms, and cellars.   Here were the coloured servitors, old and young—some of whom had traditions of the days when they lived with Governor Clinton or Governor Tompkins.   In fact the house seemed especially well adapted to its uses.   There was plenty of light and air.   Heat was supplied by Nott-stoves and grate fires, to burn Liverpool coal—anthracite was still scarce—and there were wood stoves in the family rooms. Furnaces and heaters for household use were not yet in vogue.

Light for evening entertainments was supplied by sperm candles, in chandeliers, mantel and table candelabra, brackets and silver gilt candlesticks—making the rooms brilliant but entailing much care. As the guests of the first evening party were taking their leave, the stately head-waiter, William, presented himself with a bow, to say: "Governor, shall we begin to blow?"—and receiving permission commenced extinguishing the candles.

The grounds gave ample space for children to play, and our neighbours and friends joined us there for ball games, marbles, and "follow my leader" in the summer, and for snow forts and sliding downhill in winter. In these sports we had as companions various dogs and, at one time, "Jenny," a tame fawn.

It was the fashion for the Governor to entertain generously. On New Year's Day he was expected to keep open house for all comers. Through the winter there were numerous dinners and evening parties with dancing. The usual dinner hour in Albany then was two o'clock, but on state occasions it was put off till four or five. Evening parties began promptly at eight, and were usually over at or soon after midnight.

The old Albany families, the State officers and members of the Legislature, especially the Whig ones, met on these occasions, and distinguished visitors to the city were also guests. In their long procession during four years came Washington Irving, Daniel Webster, General Scott, Josiah Quincy, Ambrose Spencer, John Davis, John J. Crittenden, Hugh S. Legaré, Francis Granger, Dr. Eliphalet Nott, Lewis Gaylord Clark, Sir Charles Bagot, Lord Morpeth, and others of well-known memory.

John C. Spencer, the Secretary of State, and Rufus

King, the Adjutant-General, were frequent callers to discuss questions of administration. Three or four prominent New York Whigs, Richard M. Blatchford, James Bowen, Simeon Draper, and Moses H. Grinnell, with Thurlow Weed and Lewis Benedict of Albany, were said by the New York *Herald* to constitute the "Governor's Clique," since they were in such frequent consultation with him.

Delegations from charitable, religious, and scientific societies occasionally appeared, to urge the Governor to take official action, or make recommendations to the Legislature, in their behalf. But to me those of especial interest were the young pupils of the blind or deaf and dumb asylums, who, having exhibited their proficiency to the legislative committees, came to spend the evening at the Governor's and invoke his help.

The office or library with its separate entrance was used by the Governor in the morning to dispose of his correspondence. That finished, he would go up to the Capitol and spend several hours in the Executive Chamber in receiving visitors and attending to official work. When some important state paper or message was to be prepared, he would go to work on it in the "office" with the help of his private secretary, and often protract the labour all the evening and far into the night. Samuel Blatchford was his first private secretary, and afterward Henry Underwood.

As the office was lighted and warmed even when not occupied, I found it a quiet and comfortable place to read or study my lessons. On the bookshelves were Irving, Shakespeare, and Charles Lamb, and once a month came *Oliver Twist* or *Nicholas Nickleby* or Ainsworth's lurid *Tower of London*, while the *New Yorker* and the *Mirror* came every week, so there was no lack of good reading. In my corner, I listened sometimes to the discussions over the state papers, and though rather difficult as political problems, I found them more interesting than the Greek grammar or Daboll's Arithmetic.   Thus I acquired a smattering of knowledge and an opinion as to the merits of the Virginia Controversy, the Georgia Controversy, the Canal Debt, the School System, the Registry Law, the McLeod Case and the "Helderberg War," and other topics supposed to be beyond my years.

But in 1840 came a whole box full of interesting reading. The Legislature had made an appropriation for School District libraries, and Harper & Brothers had prepared a library of fifty or a hundred duodecimo volumes, arranged in a neat little pine case.   A sample set was sent up to the Governor for his inspection, history, travels, and fiction in such attractive form became immediately popular.   Thurlow Weed borrowed the *Life of Franklin*, the Adjutant-General the concise story of Napoleon's campaigns.   Gulian C. Verplanck found amusement in a little volume on Chinese manners and customs, and when he came to dinner, greeted us with "chin-chin" and announced that he had come to "eat rice under the light of our countenance."   For my own part I was deep the first day in Dana's *Two Years before the Mast*.

There was other fascinating literature in the proof sheets, sent for the Governor's inspection, of the successive volumes of the Natural History of New York.   The Geological Survey begun during Governor Marcy's term had now expanded into the great quarto volumes dealing with Ornithology, Zoölogy, Ichthyology, and Crustacea, illustrated by engravings in the best style of art.   Those volumes to this day are invaluable works of reference in scientific libraries.   Occasionally the professors in charge of the respective portions of the work would call to explain matters to the Governor, who was to write an introduction to the whole series.

The fine arts also found a foothold in the office. When a sculptor or painter desired to get a likeness of the Governor, he was invited to set up his easel or his clay in the office, where he could study the Governor's features and expression. As there was no time for sittings, this had to be done while he was at work. Here Frankenstein made his bust and Carlin his portrait.

Most marvellous of all were some curious pictures brought by Gavit, the engraver, one day to show to the Governor. They were about six inches square, taken on metallic plates, resembling engravings, except that the polished plate reflected objects like a looking-glass. It was necessary to hold them at an angle, in order to see what the subject was. On one was an accurate though faint representation of State Street and the Capitol; on another a view of the Museum on the corner of North Market Street. But objects were reversed and the signs read backward. These, we were told, were the results of a new process devised by a Frenchman named Daguerre, and were the imprint of light itself through a camera. Various comments were made on the new scientific discovery. Some saw in it the beginning of a revolution in art, but others insisted that it was all a fraud; that it was simply the transfer of engravings to the plates; and that even if it was the effect of light, the invention would never amount to anything because it would be transient. They observed, "You can't see much of anything in them now, except your own face." These prophets were fortified in their opinion when, a few weeks later, the pictures grew indistinct and seemed fading out entirely.

1839-40.

New Year's Day in Albany. Albany still observed New Year's Day in accordance with old Dutch traditions and customs. It was the favorite day for gifts and greetings, public and private hospitality.

Every gentleman was expected to call on that day upon the families with whom he was socially intimate. This had been easy enough when the town was small, but it was getting to be rather an arduous task when one's acquaintance had grown larger. Some still made their peregrinations on foot; others found it desirable to use sleighs and cutters. Frequently four or five would club together to so make their rounds. At every house they would find the ladies in their parlor, arrayed to receive them, and usually a table of refreshments awaiting them in the dining-room. When there were sixty or eighty calls to be made, they were necessarily short, and often would be only the exchange of greetings and good wishes, with little or no time to sit down and converse, or to accept the hospitable invitation to the table. Every guest was expected to take a New Year's cake, sweetened and spiced with caraway seeds and stamped with ornamental figures or inscriptions. Of course he could not eat them all, and so he frequently put them into a basket or bag in his sleigh, to be sent up later in the day to the Orphan Asylum or other benevolent institution. Those young men who incautiously accepted too many of the hospitable glasses of wine or punch were occasionally incapacitated for continuing their round of calls long before the day was over.

The Governor was expected on New Year's Day to keep "open house" for all comers. The carpets were taken up and the furniture removed from the great hall and the adjoining rooms. Long tables were set out with refreshments. Seven barrels of New Year's cakes were placed so that every caller might take one. The boys of the family had the pleasure of handing them out of the window to such of the throng as could not get in.

The day began with a serenade at midnight by "Johnny Cook's band," and the stream of callers continued all day, varied occasionally by the advent of a military organization.

Albany was still small enough and decorous enough to do without any uniformed police force. One constable with two assistants were deemed sufficient to maintain order about the mansion.

1839–40.

A Political Caricature. There is still extant a political caricature of this period, showing both wit and artistic skill. Its humorous points were so well taken that friends and foes had to join in the merriment it created. It was a lithograph purporting to represent a drill of the new Whig State officers in the vacant square in front of the Governor's residence. It presented Thurlow Weed as drummer, striding in advance, cigar in mouth, and vigorously beating a tune, to which the others were trying to keep step. Behind him came the diminutive Governor, also smoking, vainly trying to follow the footsteps of the long-legged drummer and unconsciously imitating the movements of his hands. The Adjutant-General followed, arrayed in most gorgeous and bewildering regimentals. Then came the Secretary of State and Comptroller, the former of whom evidently would not, while the latter could not, keep step. The Treasurer had fallen out of line, and, with a determined air, sat down on his strong box to protect it; while the Attorney-General, sitting under a tree, was diligently conning his first lesson in Blackstone's *Commentaries*.

Of this lithograph, Weed wrote to the Governor: "I send you a picture. The shop at which I found it was the scene of capital fun. The salesman proposed to furnish a key. 'This,' said he, 'is the Attorney-General. This fellow is Weed, who was a drummer in the last war, and an excellent likeness.' By this time a third person who was standing by very quietly inquired whether I considered it a likeness. The man stared and the others laughed. I stipulated for a reasonable abatement of nose, and agreed that the thing was admirable. They have got that jockey great coat that Lee made you. But the Adjutant looks magnificently. The figure intended for Haight is a striking likeness of Holley. I found the 'Premier' in good humour and presented him a copy. He talked it all over with Dr. Nott."

Years afterward, the story of the origin of this caricature was told. One evening at the house of ex-Comptroller Flagg, the popular young artist Freeman was making a call. The family circle were laughing over a burlesque article in the *Argus*, purporting to describe a "drill of the State Officers." As Freeman sat listening, he took out his pencil and commenced sketching on a sheet of paper the scene described. While thus engaged ex-Governor Marcy came in, looked over his shoulder, and recognizing the likenesses, said sharply and indignantly:

"That's libellous, sir. Do you know, sir, that the man who makes such a picture can be prosecuted for libel?"

"Yes," said Freeman, looking up—"Yes, and what shall be done with the scoundrel who wrote the article?"

The general laugh that greeted this reply, showed Governor Marcy that he was known to be the author. Freeman's sketch was pronounced so good that next day it was taken to be lithographed.

1839–40.

The Pearl Street Academy. It was decided that I should go to school in Albany during the winter, and the Pearl Street Academy was the one selected. This was in the northern portion of the street, near Patroon Street, and facing the square. Mr. L. Sprague Parsons was the principal.

This required a pretty long walk daily, but my parents believed the walk would be beneficial to my health, and I was of an age when any amount of time spent in the streets seemed preferable to the same time spent in the confinement of a schoolroom.

The Academy had rather an imposing classic front with a portico of large Doric columns. The schoolroom extended across the whole width of the building on the second floor, and there were smaller rooms for classes and recitations.

On presenting myself as a pupil, I was assigned to a desk bearing the familiar ink stains and carved initials of previous occupants. As each boy had a separate desk, it was certainly more convenient and comfortable than any I had had in my previous school experiences, but it had the drawback in boys' eyes that it made whispering difficult and surreptitious mischief almost impossible.

The boys occupying desks on each side of mine I was introduced to as Chapman and Williams. The roll-call of the school was by surnames only, so we fell naturally into the habit of calling each other by them instead of nicknames. I made the acquaintance of several boys as Lansing, Dix, March, Boyd, Lush, Stafford, and Vanderlip, and only accidentally learned afterwards what their other names were.

Some of my schoolmates were dull and heavy, but for the most part they seemed to me to be fine, clever, and good natured. There was an unwritten law amongst them that the bigger boys were not to tease the little fellows. This met my unqualified approval, as I was one of the little fellows myself.

I was set to work on Æsop's fables, though I thought the Latin version much more curt and involved, and therefore much less interesting than the English one I had at home. I also grappled with the Greek alphabet with a view to further struggles with the Testament at a later day. But the arithmetic, the "doing sums" on a slate, where they seemed to have a proclivity for "coming out wrong,"—that was the rub! I found my school-mates shared my own opinions that Addition and Sub-traction were useful arts, and we all had more or less acquaintance with the Multiplication table, and even Long Division had its uses. But "Vulgar Fractions" and "Reduction" of pounds, shillings, and pence into Federal money, these we felt sure we should never want to use when we were "grown up." Probably we would have had the same opinion in regard to "Extraction of the Cube Root," but none of us had got so far as that yet.

When my daily lessons had been learned and recited, either well or badly, I used to look out through a window which commanded a view of the two-steepled Dutch Church and the town clock thereon. The hands moved so slowly that I often wondered whether the clock had stopped. However, it did get at last to twelve o'clock, when we had a recess for lunch, and then finally to two o'clock, when we were dismissed for the day.

Mr. Parsons introduced some variations into the usual weekly afternoon for "declamation and compositions." Sometimes we were allowed to take part in dialogues on the stage. Sometimes the school was resolved into a de-bating society. Two of the older boys would lead on the "Affirmative" and "Negative" sides, and they chose their followers alternately, as in a ball game. A tall, serious-faced boy, who I was told was Morgan Dix, usually led on one side, and a smiling young giant named McElroy led on the other. The little fellows were not allowed to participate in the debate, but we had our opportunity at the end, when the vote was taken and we could shout "Aye" and "No" with the loudest. Occasionally the school became the scene of a spelling contest, the words

3

being given out, not from the spelling book, but from Webster's Dictionary. As there were seventy or eighty of us, each one's turn came but seldom, and each hoped he would get an easy one.

The old Academy lasted during two winters of my stay in Albany, and then it came down to give place to more modern structures.

1840.

Early Railroad Experiences. On arriving at Schenectady from the west, after a tedious stage-coach journey, the traveller would find there the cars of the "Mohawk and Hudson Railroad," the first link in the great chain that was ultimately to stretch across the State.

The cars were of the English pattern, short and divided into three compartments, each having two transverse seats for passengers. A narrow "running board" extended along the outside on which the conductor made his rounds to gather fares through the windows. The baggage was piled on top of the car.

One or two horses then drew the car for half a mile or more to the foot of a hill. Here was an inclined plane, up which the car was drawn by a heavy cable running over wheels, and worked by a stationary engine at the summit. Reaching the plateau, thickly covered with pine woods, the cars were next attached to one of two locomotives, named respectively the "John Bull" and "Brother Jonathan." Fifteen miles more of the journey were thus accomplished. Then the level ground ended, and the descent into the valley of the Hudson began, horses again taking the place of the locomotive. So the car reached State Street in Albany, and there entered the "car house" near the Capitol.

This was well enough for passengers going to places "on the hill," but not for passengers and freight going down to the lower town and the steamboat landing. So the railway company soon after established another inclined plane running down by way of Lydius Street.

The journey of sixteen miles was thus made more smoothly but not much more quickly than by the Turnpike, on account of the changes and delays. In fact, at Schenectady stages were in waiting by the side of the train, whose drivers shouted, "Take you to Albany quicker than the cars, for fifty cents. Right to the door of your hotel." Many chose that alternative.

The railway next constructed was that from Utica to Schenectady, where the track could follow an almost level grade along the banks of the Mohawk. This greatly shortened the journey.

Auburn and Syracuse, which were then two villages, each having about five thousand inhabitants, next determined that they would have railway connection. After some little delay in obtaining the charter, the funds, and the right of way, the road was completed. Desirous of getting it into operation as speedily as possible, the company laid down wooden rails to serve till the iron ones should arrive.

My father's family were invited to one of the early trial trips. Mr. Sherwood, the stage proprietor, and his family occupied the adjoining compartment in the one passenger car. Another was improvised by putting the body of one of Sherwood's stages on a platform car. Thus equipped, and drawn by horses, we made the journey to Syracuse in what seemed the marvellously short time of two hours and a half.

A few months later more cars were obtained, and two locomotives, the "Auburn" and the "Syracuse," which were objects of admiration and curiosity all along the line. The locomotive whistle was a novelty, and the boys were of the opinion that the engineer must have very strong lungs to be able to blow it so loudly.   To ride with him was a delightfully dangerous privilege granted to only a favoured few.

Some travellers still preferred to go by the packet boats of the Erie Canal.   The journey required no changes and was smooth and safe, except for the risk of having one's head knocked by a "low bridge."   The speed was about the same as that of the stage-coach, the three horses being kept on a brisk trot—though the locks caused some delay.

The long and narrow shape of the canal boat made it necessary to serve the meals on very narrow tables.   The sleeping arrangements were unique.   At nine o'clock in the evening the captain would take his stand at the door of the cabin with a list of the passengers in his hand.   He would then call out: "Mr. Jones."   Thereupon Mr. Jones would meekly rise and proceed to the cabin and go to bed.   Next "Mr. Brown" would be called and comply in like manner.   The berths were like shelves with no adequate passageway between, and the passengers would have to rise in the morning in the same order as they retired.   The last one to go down would be the first to get up—so as to make room for the others to get out.

1840–41.

Early Theatrical Memories.   Everybody, I suppose, remembers his first visits to the theatre.   Mine began at Buffalo, where, with my parents, I witnessed *Tom Cringle's Log*, a melodrama based upon a novel of that day.   The gay audience and brilliant lights, the enlivening music, the rapidly moving scenes of the story, and the reality of the dialogue on the stage were all-absorbing, and the illusion was so perfect that I needed to be reassured, between the acts, that the house which was struck by lightning did not really burn down, and that the wrecked sailors did not really drown, nor the pirates actually get killed, though I fully believed they ought to be.

Afterwards, at Auburn, I occasionally saw the moral or temperance drama at the Town Hall, and once a company of strolling players gave *Macbeth* and *Julius Cæsar*. They had not enough "supers" for the required armies, so the manager came over to the Academy playground, to ask if some of the taller boys would not come, and march in battle array armed with shields and helmets? Of course they would, and were delighted to do so. Those of us who were too small for Thespian honours envied Roscoe Conkling and burly Spencer and Pasco, whose stature gave them not only free entrance, but actual participation in the performance.

But it was at Albany that I now saw the drama in its glory. All the boys and girls in town eagerly watched the great red double tent, going up at the corner of Dallius and Westerlo streets. It was a circus enterprise, on a large scale, exciting an interest like that of Barnum in later years. It was so successful that in another year, Nichols, the proprietor, replaced it by a brick amphitheatre on the same ground. This contained both stage and ring. Usually equestrian and acrobatic feats in the ring were followed by a farce or melodrama on the stage.

Here Spartacus thundered through the voice of Forrest, and Richelieu called down the appalling "Cur-r-rse of Rome."

Occasionally there would be a spectacle in which stage and ring were used together. Then the wild horse would not only climb the canvas rocks and drink from the painted stream on the stage, but presently would be careering round the sawdust circle with Mazeppa lashed on his back.

When *St. George and the Dragon* was first performed the beautiful maiden was left tied to the stake on the stage, while the two combatants came down into the ring to have it out, under the eyes of the audience.   Unfortunately the first charge of the Saint was so fierce that it upset the Dragon, who lay helpless and kicking.   Evidently the boy who performed his insides could not get him up, and the "terrific combat" had not yet come off. Saint George was equal to the emergency.   Dismounting he ran to the prostrate monster, kindly lifted and set him on his legs again, and then remounting his patient steed, fought the combat out to a finish, amid the applause of an admiring audience.

One of the "properties" at the amphitheatre was a tame fawn, which Mr. Nichols afterward presented to the Governor.   She became a favourite playmate for the boys who named her "Jenny."   She was always ready for a romp or a race with us, in the grounds.   After a couple of years, however, she grew so tall and strong that gates and fences could no longer keep her in, when she chose to make one of her flying leaps.

One day when the table was set in the dining-room for a state dinner, Jenny saw through the open window a fine bunch of flowers on the centrepiece.   With a long leap she seized the flowers, but at the same time brought down the tablecloth, glass, and dishes in a grand crash, and then stood amid the débris, placidly wondering at the commotion she had caused.   So she had to retire from the Executive Mansion to private life in the North Woods.

Applicants for Pardons.   There is a "black care" that rides on the shoulders of every governor—that follows him by day, haunts him by night, and will not be shaken off.   This is the "pardoning power."

There are always a thousand poor wretches in prison, or on their way there, and hardly one of them but has a wife or child or friend to implore executive clemency.

Public opinion, which is an avenging Nemesis as long

as the culprit is at large, softens as soon as he is behind bolts and bars; and not unfrequently the turnkey who locks him in, the public prosecutor who arraigned him, the jurors who convicted, and even the judge who sentenced him, join in the appeal for his release.

Yet if the governor weakly yields to the pressure, the same instinct of self-preservation in the community which sent the criminal to jail is aroused with fresh indignation at seeing him at liberty in the streets.

But the suitors for mercy will take no denial. How can they? Then pleading letters come in every mail; their piteous faces are ever round the door of the executive chamber. They watch the governor's path; they wait in his hall; they sit on his doorstep, and try to gain the sympathy of his family. If he be of a kindly compassionate nature, disposed to listen to their "oft-told tale" of misery, he will have time neither to eat nor sleep, nor write messages, nor make appointments. The applicants and their applications are often unreasonable, grotesque, and absurd, yet always sad and always painful.

One of my father's early experiences of this sort was shortly after his inauguration. A well-dressed, ladylike woman, evidently in deep grief, was imploring the pardon of her brute of a husband, sent to prison for beating her. She stayed during the whole evening, exhausting her powers of argument and entreaty, and deaf to any answer but a favorable one. Growing excited and frantic over the ill-success of her plea, she threw herself on her knees, and with sobs and hysterics, refused to get up until her prayer should be granted. The Governor, while vainly endeavouring to calm her, was startled at seeing in the open doorway the sudden apparition of York Van Allen, his coloured waiter, arrayed in overcoat and cap, with a lantern in his hand.

"What do you want, York?"

"I beg pard'n, sir," replied York, with the dignified courtesy which distinguishes his race, "but I thought de time had arrived when you wanted me."

"Want you? What for?"

"Governor Clinton used to allers tell me I was to take 'em away, when dey began to go on like dat," pointing to the kneeling female, "and Governor Tompkins too, sir, allers."

Equally to the surprise and relief of the Governor, the lady seemed, like York, to take it as a matter of course. Rising and adjusting her shawl and bonnet at the mirror, she curtsied adieu, and went off to the hotel, under the escort of York and his lantern.

Yet there are many cases when the exercise of the pardoning power is not only judicious but is followed by beneficent results. Such a one was that of Catharine——. Her pardon was accompanied by a kindly letter of advice from the Governor, to return to her country home, and, by persevering assiduity in domestic duties, try to regain the respect and confidence of her friends and neighbours. A few years later one of the benevolent friends who had aided her happened to be journeying through a remote rural region, when he unexpectedly met Catharine there —now grown an industrious, respectable woman, regarded with esteem by her neighbours. She took from her bosom the letter of the Governor, and said it had saved her from ruin, and that she had carried it about with her ever since it brought her the welcome news of her release.

Both those who solicit pardons and those who grant them are apt to look at the case of the individual sufferer without bestowing much thought upon the interests of the community at large. Yet this is really of more extended consequence.

A forger had been convicted in Dutchess County on evidence which left no doubt of the crime. But he was a man of property, and his high standing in the community and the church had brought him the help of learned counsel and sympathizing neighbours, to whom the verdict of the jury was a surprise. So strong was the pressure of public opinion in his behalf, that the jury recommended him to the clemency of the Executive, and the court suspended sentence in order that the application might be made.

The Governor denied it, saying, as in other cases, that he could not yield under the impulse of feeling, or from respect to popular sympathy; and that to set aside the judgment of the courts where there was no injustice or doubt of guilt, would be to destroy public confidence in the certainty of punishment and that salutary respect for courts of justice which secures the peace and good order of society.

There was one case that had a ludicrous side in its unexpected ending. A Frenchman and his wife who had just emigrated to this country were accused of theft, locked up, tried, convicted of grand larceny, and sent, the woman to the prison for female convicts at Sing Sing, and the man to the prison at Auburn.

On review of the evidence, it turned out that the offence, on the woman's part at least, had some palliating circumstances, and that she had intended nothing worse than to make reprisals on neighbours who had plundered her. Ignorance of the language had prevented the case from being fully and fairly presented in court.

The Governor made out a pardon for the woman, and taking it with him on one of his visits to Sing Sing, handed it to the warden, who forthwith released her, handed her the pardon, and she went on her way rejoicing.

It happened that her name and her husband's (Françoise and François) differed only in a letter, and the engrossing clerk by mistake had written his for hers. When outside of the prison, she looked at the document which had been put in her hands, and found there her husband's name. , Not doubting that he had been pardoned also, she hastened up to Auburn, and presented it to the warden of the prison there.   It was in every respect correct, and so François was released also—and the pair started for Canada.

The mistake was discovered when the Governor next visited Auburn; but the worthy French couple never came back to have it rectified.

1840.

The " Morus multicaulis " Fever. A new form of agricultural enterprise suddenly arose in the spring of this year.   It had been demonstrated by experiment that the *Morus multicaulis* would thrive in New York and other northern States, and so it was assumed that silkworms could easily and profitably be raised.

Little capital was required.   Families could easily increase their income.   The owner of an acre of mulberry trees could at once embark in the enterprise, and his children could care for the worms in the intervals of their school hours.   A newspaper spread over an old table and plentifully supplied with mulberry leaves was all that was necessary.   The silkworms would not wander away from the table.   Nothing more would be needed, except to gather the cocoons when the worms began to spin, as they would do in a very few weeks.

I found that my schoolmates, as soon as the teacher dismissed us, hastened home, as I did, to climb fences and scale mulberry trees, in order to get the leaves to feed their new pets.

As this disposition spread, it of course enhanced the price both of mulberry trees and of silkworms' eggs, so that those who had begun early were now reaping handsome profits.

In New Jersey and Long Island, we were told, raw silk had been raised, exported to Europe, and received there with commendation. In Pennsylvania, Ohio, and Maryland farmers now began to engage largely in the business.

At Auburn the cultivation received special attention. There had long been a jealousy of prison labour among mechanics and manufacturers, who found or fancied they would find themselves in competition with it.

It was desirable to find some occupation for convicts, which would not compete with the trades, and yet would meet the prison expenses. It was now claimed that the manufacture of silk was such a one. When thus turned into a silk manufactory, the prison, instead of injuring the mechanics, would be benefiting them, and all the farmers of the surrounding country, by furnishing a steady market for all the cocoons they could raise.

The experiment was tried. Mulberry trees were set out in the prison grounds. A silk shop was established with reels and "throwing-mills," spindles, and dyeing kettles. In and around Auburn hundreds of acres were planted with mulberry trees. Cocooneries were built or extemporized out of farm buildings and rooms of dwelling houses.

The Legislature passed laws encouraging the cultivation, by bounties on cocoons. Agricultural societies offered premiums. Newspapers and periodicals teemed with advice about hatching and feeding silkworms, and calculations showing how easily one hundred bushels of cocoons per annum could be produced by every owner of an acre.

As a further illustration of the ease with which silk might be made in Central New York, a lady appeared in Ontario County, dressed in silk which had passed in all its changes from the leaf to the loom through her own hands.

An advertisement appeared in which the agents of the Auburn Prison offered cash prices for cocoons and raw silk. Both began to pour into the market thus established and for four or five years the manufacture went on.

But there were other things which had not entered into the calculations. Adult male convicts, however cheaply supported, or easily supervised, lacked the delicate touch of women and children, or the skilled experience of silk workers, which come by lifelong training. Worms and trees, though both may be raised with success in a northern climate, yet cannot be so cheaply raised as in a milder region.

So prices declined, and the enthusiasm for the new industry gradually waned. The "fever" passed, and in a few years more was entirely forgotten.

1840.

The Harrison Campaign of 1840. My boyish enthusiasm was all for Henry Clay, "Harry of the West," as the Whig Presidential candidate, and my disappointment at his failure to receive the nomination at Harrisburg was by no means assuaged by the present, soon after, of a handsome flag inscribed with the names in gilt letters of "Tippecanoe & Tyler Too."

But the campaign was a long and memorable one. Popular interest in it seemed to be increasing up to the day of election. The Whig leaders aided it with all the appliances that political skill or experience could suggest, and the Democrats found their arguments and even their ridicule of the Whig candidate turned to his advantage. Someone alluding to his pioneer western life had advised that Harrison be given a log cabin and plenty of "hard cider" to drink—implying that that condition of life was more fitting for him than the White House.

It was an unfortunate sneer for the Democrats, for it

supplied the spark that only was needed to kindle popular sympathy into a blaze. The Whigs fanned the flame. He became "the Log Cabin" candidate. The log cabin became the emblem of his pioneer life, of his military services, of his kindred feeling for the farmers, of his unrequited toil for his country. A log cabin sprang up in nearly every city—a club house and rallying place for Whigs. Log-cabin "raisings" and house-warmings were held, with music and political speeches. Log-cabin medals were struck, and passed from hand to hand. Miniature log cabins were carried in processions and displayed on platforms. Log-cabin pictures were hung in the bar-rooms and parlours. Log-cabin magazines and song-books found ready sale. Ladies made log-cabin fancy work for fairs, and children had little log cabins of wood, tin, and confectionery.

The Whig State Committee got up a campaign newspaper, published simultaneously in New York and Albany, and named it the *Log Cabin*, calling Horace Greeley to its editorial chair. For him it was the stepping-stone to fame and fortune, for the energy and skill displayed in it, and its wide circulation, opened a way for its successor the *Tribune*.

All the appurtenances of the log cabin came into favour; there was the barrel of hard cider standing by the door, there was the coonskin nailed by its side, there was the latch string to admit the welcome guest, and it was remembered that Harrison told his old soldiers that they would never find his door shut or "the latchstring pulled in."

But the log cabin was not the only *ad captandum* argument used by the Whigs. Taking a lesson from their own crushing defeats by the "Hero of New Orleans," they hoisted flags, fired salutes, and declaimed panegyrics on the "Hero of the Thames," the "Defender of Fort Meigs," and the "Victor of Tippecanoe."

"Tippecanoe," besides being the leading exploit of the military chieftain, was a good sonorous name for the orators to pronounce, and clubs to sing in swelling chorus. For by this time the popular enthusiasm had burst out in song. Campaign songsters, glee-clubs, and Harrison minstrels were now in vogue. Familiar old melodies were adapted to new words. But the "song of songs" was one which, having little music in it, everybody could sing, and nearly everybody did.

This was:

What has caused this great commotion, motion, motion, motion
              Our country through?
              It is the ball a-rolling on,

CHORUS

For Tippecanoe and Tyler too,
For Tippecanoe and Tyler too,
And with them we'll beat little Van,
Van, Van—Van is a used up man,
And with them we'll beat little Van.

This chant was hummed in parlours and kitchens—sung by the boys in the streets—marched to in processions, and was a grand finale at all Whig meetings, the whole audience shouting it through their thousand throats with as much fervour as Frenchmen sing the *Marseillaise* or Englishmen chant *God Save the King*.

Most presidential candidates have a nickname, and General Harrison, long before the summer was over, was universally known as "Old Tip." There were Tippecanoe banners, Tippecanoe clubs, Tippecanoe meetings. Steamboats were named after him, children christened for him. Dogs were called "Tip," and spans of horses were "Tip and Ty."

Political meetings took on a new character. They were no longer forced assemblages in club rooms, but spontaneous outdoor crowds overflowing with enthusiasm. Whole counties were called to assemble in "mass-meeting" —whole States were invited to meet in mass convention. Great meetings were held in cities, and obscure country towns became the gathering points for thousands. Held by daylight the mass-meeting made a holiday for the whole surrounding region. Farmers flocked in by all the country roads bringing their wives and children. Delegations came by rail and steamboat from distant points. Nothing attracts a crowd so rapidly as the knowledge that there is a crowd already—and when it was known that there was to be not only a crowd, but music and festivity, flags, decorations and processions, eloquence of famous men and keen political humour, few could resist the infection. Webster and Clay, Crittenden and Stanley, Corwin, Leigh, Legaré, Rives, Ogden Hoffman, Preston, and a hundred of lesser note were "on the stump." General Harrison himself made a speech at the Dayton Convention. "Are you in favour of paper money?" asked the multitude. "I am," was the reply, and then the shouts of applause were deafening.

Of course this was just the kind of campaign to strike the imagination of the small boy. I do not know how many meetings I attended, how many songs I sung, or how many log cabins I took part in erecting.

It seemed to be the natural culmination of such a campaign when I was permitted to sit among the pages at the meeting of the Electoral College at Albany, and saw that august body cast their vote, under the lead of two Revolutionary veterans, Colonel James C. Burt of Orange County and Peter B. Porter of Niagara.

The dramatic proceedings came to a sudden and tragic ending in April. I recall the popular grief when the news came that the newly elected President lay dead in the White House. Funeral and memorial services were held at Albany and other cities, and I especially remember the torchlight procession with which they closed, when the coffin of "Old Tip" was borne in red glare with solemn music, and followed by the riderless horse of the old hero.

The Helderberg War. The ancient Manor of Rensselaerwyck, which dated back to the time of the earlier Dutch settlers, had been handed down from father to son in the Van Rensselaer family through a long line of "Patroons."

While modern customs and innovations had gradually changed the aspect of the whole country, society, and government, the Patroon and his tenants were still continuing the old usages of feudal tenure, of perpetual leases, of rent payable in fowls and bushels of wheat, in personal service and in "quarter sales."

The Manor comprised a broad region of Albany and Rensselaer counties "extending on either side of the Hudson River backward into the woods twenty-four English miles." It is said the original grant meant to give the Patroon the choice of a manor on one or the other side of the river, but that the grantees took advantage of the ambiguity of language of the grant and construed the words "either side" to mean both sides of the river.

It had now become well settled, cultivated, and improved. The tenants had gradually come to think that their long occupancy of the lands and their improvements had at least vested a part of the ownership in themselves, and that the rents paid during so long a series of years more than compensated for the wild land which the first Van Rensselaers had sold to the original settlers.

This theory had been much strengthened by the neglect of the "old Patroon," General Van Rensselaer, to make collections of his rents. When he died in the early part of this year, the Manor had been divided between his sons, Stephen taking the part in Albany County and William that in Rensselaer County. A third brother, Courtlandt, took the real estate in New York City.

It was in Albany County that the troubles began. The young Patroon's lawyers advised him he might enforce his legal right to collect rents. When this claim was made in behalf of the heir, the tenants very generally resolved to resist it as illegal and unjust. Legal measures were taken to compel payment. But when the sheriff went out upon the farms, he was met by gatherings of angry men with threats and execrations. Alarms were given through the neighbourhood, horns sounded, tar barrels fired, and the obnoxious writs were seized and thrown into the flames. Shouts of "Down with the Rent" were heard from the gathering crowd of rural rioters who, with brandished sticks and arms, and with threats of personal violence, compelled the official to turn his horses' heads towards home.

Such was the news received in Albany. Thereupon the Sheriff resolved to resort to a *posse comitatus*. He summoned six or seven hundred citizens to appear at his office in Albany on Monday morning at ten o'clock.

Great was the excitement, and much the merriment in the crowd that gathered round his office, and high was the delight of the small boys who flocked around to watch the marching of this novel force. The merriment increased when Sheriff Archer came out on the sidewalk and commenced to call the roll. It showed that he was no respecter of persons, for among the names were those of ex-Governor Marcy, Recorder McKoun, John Van Buren, the presidents and cashiers of the banks, the Patroon's lawyers, and the Patroon himself.

The posse proceeded on horseback, on foot, and in carriages, with the sheriff in command, twelve miles from

4

the town, till he reached a small hamlet at the foot of the Helderberg. But here the posse summoned according to law met another posse, not summoned at all, and defiant of any law whatever. The unlawful gathering outnumbered the lawful one, for it mustered fifteen or eighteen hundred men, and furthermore it had clubs while the sheriff's posse had none. The sheriff became satisfied that his force was "entirely inadequate to overcome the resistance," an opinion in which his whole force unanimously concurred. So they endeavoured to retreat to Albany in as good order as they came out of it. A second posse comprising a hundred or more armed men did not have a greater success. A rainstorm rendered the roads almost impassable, and this time the rioters resorted to the expedient of barricading all the places where the sheriff and his posse could find food or shelter from the storm.

Only one alternative remained to vindicate the majesty of the offended law. That was to apply to the Governor for a military force, to enable the sheriff to execute his process. It was evident that the time had come for executive action. The messenger from the Sheriff arrived late at night, and Mr. Blatchford, the private secretary, was sent to summon the Secretary of State, Comptroller, and Adjutant-General, to a midnight council of war in my father's office.

The council remained in session all night, and the dawn of day found them there round the table strewed with papers, and with candles still burning.

Hitherto I had only seen my father's military staff in their holiday attire on parade occasions; now I found them suddenly transformed into an active and resolute group of young men quite ready to assume soldierly duties. Adjutant-General Rufus King proved his West Point education of value, in enabling him to accomplish that greatest proof of military skill, of massing an effective body of troops at the shortest possible notice. Colonels Amory, Bowen, and Benedict were sent "to the front," with orders to attend to the movement of troops; the commissariat was supplied by wagon loads of bread and meat, blankets and tents. Major William Bloodgood was assigned to the command of a battalion, consisting of the Burgesses Corps, the Van Rensselaer Guards, the Union Guards, the Republican Artillery of Albany, besides three Troy companies, the Citizens' Corps, the Independent Artillery, and the City Guards. The various bodies of troops were ordered to move at once and reinforcements from the Mohawk Valley were held in readiness to arrive if needed.

In the morning a proclamation was issued by the Governor enjoining upon the people of the country "to aid and assist the officers of justice in performing their duty," and appealing to all who had taken part in the unlawful proceedings to reflect upon their consequences and remember that organized insurrection, in our republic, is absurd and unnecessary. The lawful means to obtain relief from any injuries or grievances are to appeal to the courts and the Legislature, which are open to all the citizens of a self-governing State. He further added: "I assure them that they shall receive every facility which the executive department can afford in bringing their complaints before the Legislature. I enjoin upon them to conduct and demean themselves as orderly, peaceable, and well disposed citizens, justly estimating the invaluable privileges they enjoy, and knowing that the only security for the preservation of their rights consists in the complete ascendancy of the laws."

As I heard this proclamation copied and read by the secretary, and was permitted to affix the privy seal to it, it seemed to me so simple and plain that any American schoolboy ought to have known as much as that. I wondered at the ignorance of the country people. It was my first experience—often repeated since—of discovering that even American citizens do not always remember the fundamental principles of their own government.

The troops moved with a celerity worthy of veterans. It was on Tuesday morning that their orders were issued, and before noon the Troy companies passed through Albany on their way "to the front," and were furnished with two field pieces from the arsenal. The proclamation was published in all the newspapers and copies were struck off in handbill form, which the troops scattered broadcast in the insurrectionary regions.

While the Governor was sitting at breakfast on Thursday morning a bearer of military dispatches dashed up to his door, and handed him a packet from Major Bloodgood. It was dated at the headquarters of the expeditionary force at Rensselaerville. It stated that he had met a large assemblage of people at Reidsville. Halting on the hill and forming his force in solid column, he had marched into the midst of them, and told the Sheriff to do his duty. The Sheriff had done so, served his process, and had taken one prisoner, who had been sent to the rear, greatly to his relief, as he had begged for quarter, under the impression that he was to be instantly shot. The Major stated that the appearance of the troops and the knowledge of reinforcements hurrying forward had made such an impression upon the inhabitants that there was no longer danger to his command, that the troops would continue with the Sheriff and enable him to execute his process as they passed through the country.

Meanwhile there came to the Executive Mansion a letter, from Azor Taber and Henry G. Wheaton, saying that leading citizens of the towns where the disturbance existed had come in, to ask those gentlemen to make representations in their behalf to the Governor. They were desirous to avail themselves of the occasion presented by his proclamation to end the difficulties. They requested Messrs. Taber and Wheaton to assure the Governor that all resistance to the Sheriff should cease, and that the assemblage of people should quietly disperse.

Dispatches continued to come during Thursday and Friday and Saturday of similar tenor.

Sunday morning there was a heavy snowstorm. In the midst of it, and while the bells were ringing for church, the sound of drums was heard approaching on the hill beyond the Capitol. It was the returning force who, wrapped in their blankets, had marched twelve miles since daybreak, plodding through the drifting snow and bringing their three prisoners in a wagon.

The Governor sprang into his sleigh, taking me with him, and drove up State Street. He met, received, and welcomed the troops, under the shelter of the Schenectady Railway Depot, and thanked them for their good conduct and patriotism. They cheered him in return, and marched to their respective armories. So ended the first campaign of the "Helderbarrack."

1843.

An Artistic Contest. The Governor's Room in the City Hall of New York is so called, because, in accordance with time-honoured custom, it has been used as an official reception room for governors of the State when they visit the city, and has been the repository of portraits of former governors from George Clinton down.

The Common Council, in 1843, desired to add to this collection a full-length portrait of my father. But no artist had been designated, there being divided opinions as to their respective merits.

So, after visiting many different studios, a committee

consisting of Messrs. Minturn, Draper, Ruggles, Grinnell, Blatchford, and others concluded to gratify all the conflicting preferences by inviting five artists—Inman, Harding, Huntington, Page, and Gray—each to paint a portrait of the ex-Governor. The Common Council might select whichever it chose, and his personal friends would themselves take the others.

In accordance with this arrangement, Chester Harding was to begin; he arrived at Auburn early in March and was a guest at my father's house, where he was also a genial and hearty companion.

His studio on Main Street became a favourite resort for the little circle at Auburn who were interested in art. His pictures and his conversation won the esteem of the villagers, and parties were made in his honour. Harding's massive figure seemed as if fitted for athletic exercise. It would have befitted a commanding general; he was six feet three inches high, with a large face, hands too large for ordinary gloves, eyes too broadly separated for ordinary spectacles. He was a fine looking man, of evident vigour and energy, but the last person a casual observer would suspect of delicate handling of palette and pencil. Harding completed his work in July, and took his leave.

A few days later Henry Inman arrived, to enter upon his work. He was high in public esteem, occupying the first rank among American artists. He showed in every look and action the fruits of a life of artistic culture, ease, and taste. Graceful and engaging in his manners, fluent and imaginative in his conversation, he had almost a boyish fondness for fun, and a keen eye for the beauties of nature.

He had not been an hour in the house before it seemed as if he were an old acquaintance. He told me that he would go out with me into the morello cherry trees, whose fruit was just hanging red and ripe, and promised my brother that he would go with him to the Owasco Lake for boating and perch fishing, both of which promises he fulfilled before the week was out.

"Music, Mr. Seward," said he, as he was sketching the outlines of my father's face in crayon, "music I think must be the vernacular in Heaven. They may have some other language for grave, intellectual, and religious topics, but for the small talk I think they probably use music—now, Mr. Seward, wait one moment before you answer. I want to catch that expression I see on your face, before you move a muscle."

The Episcopal Convention of the new diocese of Western New York held its session in Auburn during August. For a week the village was full of clergymen. It happened also to be the anniversary week of the Presbyterian Seminary, and it was remarked that nearly every other man you met in the streets had spectacles or a white cravat. Said one, "I see, Governor, that you are being painted in a white cravat; are you adopting the theological custom?"

"No," said he, "that is the artist's taste." Inman added: "I never paint a man in a black cravat if I can help it. On canvas, especially with a dark background, it looks as if his head was cut off."

Inman remained two or three weeks in Auburn and finished the "study," from which the full-length portrait for the City Hall was to be painted. This "study" still hangs in the parlour at Auburn, in its original place.

Sometime later the committee of the Common Council met, who were to decide about the portrait, but they were divided in opinion between that of Harding and that of Inman. Both were so excellent that, after careful examination and comparison of views, they declared themselves unable to say that either was better than the other.

When this was announced to the artists, Inman with his usual cheerful vivacity laughed and said to Harding:

"Well, we shall have to settle this ourselves. Let us toss up for it?"

Harding assented, and Inman, drawing a half dollar from his pocket, threw it up in the air, saying, "Heads or tails?"

Heads came up and Inman won.

His picture was formally turned over to the Common Council, and it still hangs in the Governor's Room.

The friends who had originated the competition had already determined that whichever picture was not taken by the city, they would purchase, and present to my father's children; they did so, and Harding's portrait was intrusted to the care of Seth C. Hawley until the children should grow up.

In due time it was delivered according to this arrangement.

It hung in my house at Albany during my residence there. When I moved to Washington, the Rev. Dr. Campbell, on behalf of the trustees of the State Library, asked that it might be left at Albany until my return. For many years it occupied the central place in the row of portraits at the library.

When the old library building was finally torn down to make room for the new Capitol, it was transferred to the Executive Chamber in that building, and there it still hangs.

1843.

John Quincy Adams at Auburn. In the summer of 1843, John Quincy Adams was visiting Niagara Falls. When news came that the venerable ex-President would return through Western New York, my father, who had been for so many years one of his political disciples, suggested that he should be received with suitable demonstrations of welcome. The suggestion, however, was hardly needed, for the western part of the State was full of his admirers, some dating back to the time when he was a presidential candidate; others more recently enlisted under his banner as defender of the Right of Petition.

At Buffalo he was received with a public demonstration and an address by Mr. Fillmore, at Rochester with a procession, and at Canandaigua with an address by Francis Granger.

My father and grandfather went over there to meet him. Arriving at Auburn in the evening he was met by a torchlight procession, which escorted him to our house, where he was introduced to the people and addressed them briefly from the steps. Much fatigued, he declined eating, drank a glass of wine, and retired to his room as soon as prepared. At five o'clock the next morning he rose, and at six went over to visit the State Prison, returning to breakfast at eight.

The conversation turned naturally upon the condition of public affairs and the political outlook. The question of slavery having been broached, the customary opinion of the times was expressed by one of the guests, that the institution was a colonial inheritance from Great Britain, incongruous with our republican system, which must eventually disappear. To this Mr. Adams seemed to assent. One of the gentlemen said: "But do you not think, Mr. Adams, that it will be peacefully and legally abolished —perhaps twenty, perhaps fifty years hence?" Mr. Adams had sat with head bent forward, apparently in reverie. The inquiry roused him in a moment. With a keen glance at the speaker, he said: "I used to think so, but I do not now. *I am satisfied that it will not go down until it goes down in blood!*"

A pause ensued and then somebody remembered that it was time to proceed to the church, where Mr. Adams was to have a formal public reception at nine o'clock. The citizens of Auburn and their families had already filled the church to overflowing.

The ceremonies at the church were simple. An address of welcome by my father, in behalf of his townsmen, was followed by suitable response from Mr. Adams, expressing his thanks for the courtesy shown him, his good wishes for the future of the village and its citizens, but without touching upon any of the public questions of the day. A short time was then spent in introductions, shaking hands, and conversation. The hour fixed for his departure drew near, and at eleven he left the railroad station in a special train, amid the acclamations of the gathered crowd.

"Governor," said a friend, a short time afterward when some allusion was made to the startling remark in regard to slavery, "Mr. Adams is a very great man, but he is growing old. Don't you think he is rather despondent, —discouraged perhaps, by what he sees at Washington?"

"I think," was the answer, "that he is wiser than any of us on that subject; but I shall not give up my hope of a peaceful solution, so long as any such solution is possible. At any rate it is our duty to labour for such a one."

Mr. Adams, after leaving Auburn, was received with ovations along the entire route. The Whigs hoisted flags in honour of his coming and had special ceremonies of reception at Herkimer, Little Falls, and Schenectady. He reached Boston three or four days later.

A characteristic expression of a steamboat captain with whom he travelled illustrated the popular feeling. He said: "Oh, if you could only take the engine out of the old Adams, and put it into a new hull!"

1845.

Entering College. There is a fascination to every boy in the idea of "going to college." However pleasant his home, he has a natural desire to enter into the life of that microcosm which is supposed to separate boyhood from manhood. Usually, it is neither the studies nor the sports which are the chief attraction, but rather the indefinable longing to mingle with others, each of whom is also learning how to be "a man among men." At least that was my case. My lot in childhood had been cast in pleasant places, guarded with sedulous care, and cheered by every reasonable indulgence; and yet I was quite ready, when the time came, to go out to seek adventures in college halls. At the age of fifteen, I had accompanied the pious Æncas in his voyages to the end of his twelfth book of hexameters, had dipped into the Greek Testament, and pursued the Arabic numerals as far as the Rule of Three— and so believed myself fit to be a freshman.

Union College had been my father's Alma Mater. Dr. Nott, who was his preceptor there, and had been his guide, philosopher, and friend ever since, was still hale and vigorous and, as President, was still dispensing instruction and discipline to another generation. So I was sent to become a student at "Old Union."

I well remember the thrill of pleasurable excitement when I donned my first frock coat, put on my first high hat and standing collar, and heard myself accosted as "Mr. Seward." No more "roundabouts," no more of the enforced tedium of the schoolroom, or the noisy fun of the playground. *Majora canamus.*

My father accompanied me on the train to Schenectady. On the way down the Mohawk Valley various passengers came to talk to him. Among them was a young man who, like myself, had a very youthful face surmounted by a very elderly hat, with standing collar and frock coat like my own. He introduced himself as a son of Senator Hard, and I was not surprised to learn that he was also on his way to the college. We speedily became intimate friends.

He was in the senior class, and his superior wisdom and experience enabled him to give me much useful information in regard to my fellow students and instructors, and the routine of college life. When we arrived at Schenectady, he was surrounded by a group of other students at the station, whose jocose remarks to each other, and easy self-possession in the presence of their elders, seemed to me quite worthy of emulation.

We proceeded leisurely up Union Street, my father pointing out scenes recalling incidents of his own college days, and arrived at last at the grey old buildings "on the Hill." Our first visit was to President Nott, and our next, by his advice, to Professor Reed, at whose house the Examining Board was in session. Both the venerable President and the genial Professor of Greek had been frequent visitors in Albany. The examination proved satisfactory and not very severe. As one of my new college friends had told me, "A freshman isn't expected to know much at the beginning of his year, but he'll know lots more at the end of it."

Presenting my certificates and paying the entrance fee to the Registrar, Alexander Holland, my name was entered in the great book, and I was informed that I was duly "matriculated." A key was handed me as that of a room on the second floor in the South College, thenceforth to be my home. Brick flooring and heavy oak stairs led up to it. The walls were whitewashed, the floors bare, and the woodwork of the plainest kind, but abundantly ornamented by the carved initials of previous tenants, which were also inscribed on some of the panes of glass in the window. So far from regarding these as defects, it pleased my fancy to believe that they indicated "fellows" having a good time, and not subjected to overmuch inspection or restraint.

A cot and bedding, a table and chairs, a washstand and

its appurtenances, an oil lamp and a small looking-glass were speedily purchased at a shop in the town. The shop-keeper promised to send them up immediately. My father told him to send the larger articles, adding that we would carry up the small ones ourselves. So, taking the pitcher in his hand, he gave me the lamp and looking-glass, and we marched up Union Street again. On the way we met Professor Reed, driving out with his family. "Why, Governor," said he, "you look as if you were going to housekeeping."

"No, I am not," was the reply, "but Frederick is, and I thought that if he saw me carrying things through the street of Schenectady, he would probably never be afraid or ashamed to do it himself."

We spent the next day in Albany, and when I returned in the evening, after taking leave of my father, I entered my room, and found all my new furniture piled up in a heap in the centre. I had not provided such trivial necessaries as oil and matches, and so, groping in the dark for enough to make a bed on the floor, I slept soundly till daybreak.

At half-past five a loud knocking at the door roused me. Opening it, I met the good-humoured face of an Irishman who informed me that he was "Pat," and that he had charge of the rooms. He gave me the further information that the chapel bell at the West College would ring at six, and a second time twenty minutes later, and then be immediately followed by the roll-call. As the West College was down in the town, and nearly a mile away, I hastened my toilet, to arrive in time.

The West College, I found, was a substantial old brick building, that had once been a school, and once served as a town hall. It was now the abode of the freshmen and sophomores—the buildings on "the Hill" being entirely filled by the senior and junior classmen. In a large and rather dingy-looking chapel I saw my future classmates ranged in a row. There were but eighteen of us in all. But on the other side of the chapel there was a larger row of sixty or seventy sophomores. Some had the dress and air of cultivated young gentlemen; others had not yet discarded the look of rustic schoolboys.

We all listened intently to the roll-call, not only to answer to our own names, but to learn the names of the others. I think we hardly gave due attention to the brief religious services, as we were eagerly scanning the ranks, and wondering what sort of fellows we should find each other to be. All things seem possible to the youthful imagination; so I suppose that if I had that morning been told that one of my fellow-students in that chapel was destined to be a general, another a senator, another a judge, another a bishop, another to be a cabinet minister, and another to be president of the United States, I should not have been at all surprised. But we all should have been much surprised, if we had been told upon which ones those destined honours were to fall.

A short recitation followed, and then we dispersed to our respective breakfasts, and on the way began our mutual acquaintance, without much formality of introductions.

As my room was on "the Hill" and my class at the West College, it necessitated walking three times back and forth between them. But this six-mile walk I soon learned to consider no hardship, and it doubtless largely contributed to my rapid improvement in health, strength, and growth, for, having been rather a puny lad, I was now attaining a height of nearly six feet.

. There was a further advantage in the fact that I was thus thrown into relations with the freshmen and sophomores during part of the day, and with the juniors and seniors during the other part, thus enlarging my acquaintance, and allowing me to profit by the experiences of the men of all classes.

The professors and tutors treated us all courteously, and gave us instruction in their respective departments. But matters of conduct and discipline were left almost wholly to the President—or "Old Prex," as we used to call him. We believed then, and I am of the same opinion still, that for this work he was peculiarly gifted and qualified. His profound and sympathetic knowledge of human nature, his wise judgment, good humour, and good sense, enabled him to win not merely respect but affection. His chief aim seemed to be to cultivate and encourage the student's self-reliance and sense of personal responsibility—so as to fit him to become a good citizen and a practical man of affairs. Doubtless he watched over us with paternal care, but if there was espionage we never knew it; if there was advice, it was sound; if there was reproof, it was deserved. Discipline there was, but never harsh or unjust.

Not only the curriculum of our studies, but our organization of societies, debates, meetings, and elections were no bad preparation for similar work in later life.

The tone of the student body was such as might be expected. We felt ourselves to be no longer schoolboys. Mischievous pranks were tolerated, but not applauded nor imitated. There was a strong *esprit de corps*. Newcomers were treated with kindness; old graduates with high regard. Of course there were students who were inclined to dissipation and idleness; but these were the exceptions, not the rule. There was a sort of latent feeling that it behooved a student at "Old Union" to act like a man and behave like a gentleman.

Athletic games and sports were not yet in fashion. Yet we thought we had plenty of opportunity for outdoor exercise, whether walking, riding, rowing, swimming, boxing, or fencing.

It was my good fortune to have a seat at Dr. Nott's table, and to that extent I became an inmate of his family circle. It was a large one, comprising not only his family, but the sons of several of his intimate friends. As he sat benignly at the head of the table, there was nothing of the stern pedagogue or the morose invalid in his manner. He was rather the genial host, the wise and kindly grandfather, always cheerful and interesting. Our undergraduate talk was naturally of college themes and gossip, but we were speedily lifted out of that, to the discussion of the broader topics of the day. He would say:

"Clarkson, what do the papers say this morning about the revolutionists in Paris? Are the students there still singing the *Marseillaise,* and throwing up barricades in the streets?"

"Howard, my son, how are they getting on at the Novelty Works, with that newly invented cut-off valve for the steam engine?"

"Mr. Perry, your German friends seem to be announcing some almost incredible theories about the connection of electricity with animal life."

"Mr. Whitridge, have you noticed those remarkable discoveries of paintings in the recent excavations at Pompeii?"

"Frederick, what do you hear from your brother with the army in Mexico? I hope they are going to make peace down there before long."

"Yes, John, *tirosh* is the Hebrew word for the unfermented juice of the grape. But you won't find any of it in the Schenectady bar-rooms. They only sell the intoxicating *yayin,* and even that I believe is adulterated."

I think he liked to draw out our crude opinions on these and kindred topics. There was an amused twinkle in his eye as he listened to them, but there was no parade of superior knowledge in his comments. His sound maxims and humorous illustrations would illuminate the whole subject, and, unconsciously to ourselves, we were gaining as much instruction at every meal as from any recitation in the classroom.

We did not realize then, as we have since, that we were being led up from the realm of small talk to that of intelligent observation of the world's progress in civilization and enlightenment.

The study at Union that was of prime importance in those days was known as "Kames." It was the afternoon lecture or recitation of the senior class, in which Dr. Nott was the preceptor. It was based upon Kames's *Elements of Criticism*. But Lord Kames himself would have rubbed his eyes in astonishment, if he could have seen and heard the use that was made of his book. He would have found it so amplified and expanded that, instead of a compend of æsthetics, it had become a comprehensive study of human nature, ranging over the whole field of physical, moral, and intellectual philosophy, and applied to practical use in business, politics, and religion. Usually this afternoon session took the form of a monologue by Dr. Nott, replete with wit and wisdom, but varied occasionally by question or dialogue, to keep up individual attention in the class. We were taught the analysis of human emotions and passions—how to control our own, how to deal with the manifestation of them by others, how to choose the modes of expression and the rules for conduct of life that would enable each to use his natural powers to the best advantage. Quotations from authors and illustrations from history and from the Doctor's own experience lent the whole a fascinating interest.

There was a pocket pamphlet surreptitiously printed and circulated in the class, that was called "Little Kames."

5

It contained an abstract of each chapter, thus saving the indolent student the labour of studying.   Dr. Nott knew of the practice but never positively forbade it.   He used to say the big book was better than the little primer, but the little one was better than nothing.

He would say: "Someone in the class, I suppose, has a copy of it in his pocket.   Take it out, my son, and read what the author says on the point we have been discussing.   No, I don't want you to repeat his words by rote. If you do, you may think it is an infallible rule, and perhaps it isn't.   I want you to read it over carefully, and then think for yourself whether the author is right or wrong. You can get a good deal of instruction out of a book that you don't entirely agree with.   If you wish to commit universal truths to memory, take up your Bible or Shakespeare.   You will find more of them there than anywhere else."

The ringing of the chapel bell at five o'clock brought the lecture to an end.   But all graduates of that period remember their "Kames."   Many a clergyman, many an author, many a lawyer and statesman has found that Dr. Nott and "Kames" have given him the solution of some of the most perplexing problems of his life.

When the students among themselves spoke of " Old Prex," it was not in tones of disrespect, but rather those of friendly regard.   They looked after his stately figure whenever it appeared in chapel or on the campus with affectionate admiration, from the first day when they saw him driving his three-wheeled carriage, to the last one when he put on his three-cornered hat to distribute their diplomas on Commencement Day.

Leaving College.   The last days at college bring as vivid a memory to the mind of the "alumnus" as the opening ones.   Each period marks an era in his life.

When the inevitable "Commencement" (which is also the ending) of our college life begins to loom up in the near future, we of the senior class begin to realize that we are about to leave tried friends and familiar scenes, and may have to encounter others that may prove far less enjoyable.

We have reached the top of the present ladder, and are to begin at the bottom of the next one. Our studies are no longer onerous, and we no longer fear "exams." Having learned all that there is to know in the "curriculum," we feel that we have attained a state of wisdom and dignity almost, if not quite, equal to that of the Faculty. We are confirmed in this opinion by the high respect and deference shown to us by the members of the lower classes.

Contrary to what might be expected, we talk but little of our plans for our future lives and careers in the world of maturity. We have plenty of plans and projects but their details are hazy and uncertain. Our immediate topics of conversation are the things to be done at and about Commencement time. There is an undertone of regret at our approaching separation.

"Seward," said Charles Nott to me, one day, "these fellows are exchanging daguerreotypes, and promising to go to see each other, and to write each other once a fortnight. Of course they won't do it, or can't do it—at any rate, not long. Then coolness and distance will supervene, and they will drift apart. What shall we do about corresponding with each other?"

"Suppose," I answered, "that we make a promise that we can keep. Let us promise never to write to each other, except on business."

"Agreed," said he, and we shook hands on it.

Sixty years have elapsed since then, and the Chief Justice and I have continued our uninterrupted friendship. The mutual promise has been, on the whole, faithfully kept—though the "business" has sometimes been rather trivial. But such a promise is a sheet anchor for good understanding, since it furnishes an all-sufficient explanation for any apparent forgetfulness or lack of interest.

1849–50.

Washington in '49 and '50. *The Compromise Debate.* Fairly started as a law student, and endeavouring to master that abstruse science by the help of Blackstone, Kent, and divers and sundry other volumes bound in formidable "law-calf," and even trying my "prentice hand" at drawing papers for actual use in practice, the study of my profession occupied my days, until it was interrupted for the winter by a summons to Washington to become a private secretary of my father, who had now been elected a member of the United States Senate.

I found him ensconced in his new home on F Street. It was a respectable, unpretending red brick structure, and was one of a block of three ordinary city houses, each twenty-five feet wide and all just alike. Near the Patent Office, the General Post Office, and the shops on Seventh Street, it was a convenient place of residence, and within walking distance of the Capitol. Some books had been sent down from Auburn, with his old writing chair. His office, or study, was established in the basement.

Washington in 1849 had become a town of about forty thousand inhabitants, either connected with the business of government themselves, or engaged in supplying the needs of those who were. It was in its least attractive stage. The rural beauty of its youth was gone; the tasteful elegance of its maturity had not yet come. It was still the "City of Magnificent Distances." Little else about it was magnificent. The white fronts of the Capitol and the Executive Mansion gleamed through surrounding foliage at each end of "the Avenue," the substantial Post Office building and the long colonnade of the Treasury looked finished and imposing. The old brick edifices for State, War, and Navy Departments were still standing. The Smithsonian was gradually rising out of a chaos of brick and freestone. There was a maze of broad, unpaved streets, dusty in summer, muddy in winter, along which were scattered detached houses or straggling rows of buildings. Lamps were few. Houses were not numbered, and the visitor who wanted to find a residence had to depend upon the hack-drivers, whose method of memory seemed to be that each person lived "just a little way from" somewhere else.

Though the capital of the nation, it was in all social and industrial aspects a Southern town. The slave pen and the auction block were prominent on a public thoroughfare. Many families owned slaves, whom they used for domestic service or "hired out" to perform it for others, the owner receiving the slave's wages. Society looked upon "Abolition" with dread and disgust.

Not only in Washington but throughout the country it was realized that the coming session of Congress was likely to be a long and stormy one. Our great acquisition of territory from Mexico, after the Mexican War, had raised the question whether it should be used for slave-holding or free States.

The two great political parties had commenced to disintegrate on that issue. The Democrats had nominated General Cass and the Whigs General Taylor for the Presidency. But many anti-slavery men of both parties withdrew from their party affiliations, and held a formidable convention at Buffalo, where they organized a "Free Soil" party, nominating ex-President Van Buren for President and Charles Francis Adams for Vice-President. The three-sided contest thus begun resulted in the election

of General Taylor and a Congress embracing all the war-
ring elements.

Meanwhile the discovery of gold in California had attracted thousands of new settlers. These held a convention and adopted a "Free-State" constitution, which
Congress was now to approve or reject.

On Monday, the 3d of December, the flags were hoisted
on the two wings of the Capitol. The Thirty-first Congress began its session, destined to be a memorable one
in history. Of course I was a frequent visitor, to avail
myself of the opportunity to look down upon the proceedings from the galleries.

The Senate Chamber of that period was the room
afterwards occupied by the Supreme Court. Semicircular
in form, graceful in proportions, with its dark marble
columns and crimson hangings, it had an air of stately
dignity, more impressive to the spectator in the narrow
gallery than the spacious, easy, and comfortable Chamber
of the present day. Looking down upon the Senators,
one saw many that were already famous. On the right
of the main aisle were to be seen the massive head and
deep-set eyes of Webster, the tall and commanding figure
of Clay, the dark but genial face of Corwin, the white
head of "Honest John Davis," the calm and cautious
visage of John Bell, the scholarly looking head of Berrien,
the tall forms of Mangum and Dayton, and the merry
smile of John P. Hale; on the left, the portly form of
General Cass, the towering bulk of General Houston,
ex-President of Texas, the classic head and genial face
of Colonel Benton, the long, grey locks and sharp attenuated features of Calhoun, the erect, slender figure of
Jefferson Davis, the swarthy, foreign-looking face of Pierre
Soulé, the energetic, black-clothed "Little Giant" Douglas, the dark, curling locks of Hunter, and the silver-haired
familiar face of Daniel S. Dickinson.

As a new Senator, my father's choice among seats was limited to such as were vacant. He selected one on the Whig side, but soon after relinquished it to oblige Mr. Clay, and took the chair on Clay's right hand, at the extreme end of the back or outer row of chairs. This, however, had some advantages. It was remote from the noisy main entrance, and conveniently near the private door, for conferences with friends or visitors. The Senate Chamber was not so large but that every member could, without difficulty, catch the eye of the presiding officer and be heard in debate. He liked the place so well that he retained it during most of his Senatorial term.

Passing over now to the other wing of the Capitol, I entered the gallery of the House of Representatives. Here I looked down upon a busy, bustling scene, very different from the quiet dignity of the Senate. The House had commenced its session with a struggle over the Speaker-ship. The Whigs had nominated Robert C. Winthrop of Massachusetts. The Democrats had nominated Howell Cobb of Georgia. As a majority of the whole House was required to elect a Speaker, there was no choice. Anti-slavery men were baffled; Southern men were exultant.

The House as a whole contained many members whose names were then, or have since, become historic. Massachusetts had sent Horace Mann and Robert C. Winthrop; Pennsylvania had Thaddeus Stevens and David Wilmot; North Carolina, Edward Stanley; Georgia had sent Alexander H. Stephens, Robert Toombs, and Thomas Butler King; Alabama, Henry W. Hilliard; Mississippi, Albert J. Brown and Jacob Thompson; Louisiana, Charles W. Conrad; Ohio had Joshua R. Giddings, David A. Carter, Robert C. Schenck, Samuel F. Vinton, and Lewis D. Campbell; Kentucky had Linn Boyd; Tennessee had Andrew Johnson and Frederick P. Stanton; Illinois

had Edward D. Baker, John A. McClernand, and John
Wentworth; Wisconsin had Charles Durkee, and Minnesota, Henry K. Sibley.

The New York delegation was a strong one and pre-
sented many faces with which I was already familiar.
Of the thirty-four, the larger part were Whigs. Among
them were John A. King, Charles E. Clarke, Harvey
Putnam, Elijah Risley, O. B. Matteson, John L. School-
craft, William A. Sackett, Elbridge G. Spaulding, and A.
M. Schermerhorn. Among the Democrats was Preston
King.

Roll-call after roll-call followed each other in tedious
succession. Nearly three weeks were consumed in fruitless attempts to effect a choice. Sixty-two ballotings
were taken, and between them occurred heated debates
and recriminations. One day an Indiana member was
nearly elected by a hasty combination, which then col-
lapsed amid great excitement.

At last, on the 22d of December, it was decided to let
a plurality determine the result. This elected Howell
Cobb. So the Democrats had control of both Chambers.
The speakership contest having been settled on Saturday,
the President was informed that Congress would be ready
to receive his message on Monday.

President Taylor was a Southern man and a slaveholder.
But he was an old soldier, intensely loyal to the Union,
with the firmness of General Jackson, but without his
stormy temper. General Scott used to say that when he
spoke of General Taylor as "an upright man" his wife
quickly added, "Yes, and a downright one." My father
in one of his letters to Weed, said: "The malcontents of
the South mean to be factious, and they expect to compel
compromise. I think the President is as willing to try
conclusions with them as General Jackson was with the
Nullifiers."

Monday morning the message was received. Of course the part most eagerly listened to, as it was read from the Clerk's desk, was that which declared the President's policy in regard to the new Territories. This was sagacious and clear. Shortly after his inauguration he had sent out to the Pacific Coast Thomas Butler King, of Georgia, to invite the people of California and New Mexico to form State constitutions, and with them apply for admission to the Union. This was the "President's plan," and it seemed to be a more speedy and practicable plan than either the plan of "disunion" or the plan of "compromise," especially as California had already accepted the invitation, and was now ready to present herself at the door of Congress with a "free-State constitution." But for that very reason it was not satisfactory to those who deemed "an equilibrium" necessary, between free and slaveholding States, nor to those who wanted slavery extended. My father, having heartily concurred in the President's invitation when it was sent, was now even more heartily disposed to approve and defend its results.

The deep dissatisfaction which existed in the South in view of the possibility that slaveholders might be forbidden to take their slaves to California was manifested in both Chambers nearly every day. One representative said: "If slavery is to be abolished in the District, or prohibited in the Territories, I trust in God that my eyes have rested on the last Speaker of the House of Representatives." Another said: "I do not hesitate to own, before this House and the country, and in the presence of a living God, that if, by your legislation, you seek to drive us from the Territories, and to abolish slavery in this District, I am for Disunion." In one wing of the Capitol it was said: "The day in which aggression is consummated, this Union is dissolved," and in the other wing a Senator echoed that the Union was "already dissolved."

The Senate was believed to be conservative, and had among its members Clay, Webster, Calhoun, Benton, Cass, and Douglas—all ambitious to lead, and none of them desirous to follow anybody.

Mr. Clay believed the times were ripe for another great compromise like that of 1820. One day toward the close of January he rose from his chair in the Senate Chamber, and, waving a roll of papers, with dramatic eloquence and deep feeling announced to a hushed auditory that he held in his hand a series of resolutions proposing an amicable arrangement of all questions growing out of the subject of slavery.

Read and explained by its author, this plan of compromise was, to admit California, and to establish territorial governments in the other portions of the region acquired from Mexico, without any provision for or against slavery, to pay the debt of Texas and fix her western boundary, to declare that it was "inexpedient" to abolish slavery in the District of Columbia, but expedient to put some restrictions on the slave-trade there, to pass a new and more stringent fugitive slave law, and to formally deny that Congress had any power to obstruct the slave-trade between the States.

His speech was by turns impressive and courtly, imperious and sarcastic. He dwelt with pathos upon the country's "bleeding wounds" which he proposed to stanch.

The Senators listened in silence. Most of them were desirous of some compromise that would "finally settle the slavery question," but very few were disposed to accept this one in its entirety. The proposed admission of California and the abolition of the slave-trade in the District of Columbia were distasteful to the Southern Senators, while the assumption of the debt of Texas, the quasi opening of the Territories to slavery, and the proposed Fugitive Slave Law were equally objectionable to Northern ones. So began the long debate, lasting through winter, spring, and summer.

Meanwhile the newspapers and letters from constituents showed that elsewhere, as well as at the Federal capital, the proposed Compromise was an engrossing topic. Meetings were held in support of it. State legislatures took ground for and against it. Absurd rumours found credence in the lobbies. One day there was an alarm that the House of Representatives was "to be broken up by Southern men coming armed for contest." The next, the story was that there would be "no shooting," but that the Southern members "would withdraw in a body." California contributed to the excitement. Her new constitution was received, published, and commented upon. Dr. Gwin and Colonel Frémont, whom she had chosen as her Senators, were announced to be on their way to Washington.

Each of the leaders in Senatorial debate felt that the hour had come for him to define his position. Mr. Bell, of Tennessee, introduced a new series of resolutions, similar in principle but differing in detail.

Mr. Calhoun, though in failing health, obtained the floor for a speech. Everybody awaited it with great interest, regarding him as the acknowledged exponent of Southern opinion. He had already said briefly, in solemn tones, that he had "long laboured faithfully to repress the encroachment of the North," that he "saw where it would end, and now despaired of seeing it arrested in Congress." "What the South will do," he added, "is not for me to say. They will meet it, in my opinion, as it ought to be met."

When he rose to speak on the 4th of March, an expectant throng filled the Senate Chamber. His gaunt figure and emaciated features attested that he had risen from a sick bed; but his fiery eyes and unshaken voice showed he had no intention of abandoning the contest. In a few words he explained that his health would not permit him to deliver the speech he had prepared, but that "his friend the Senator behind him [Mason] would read it for him." Beginning by saying that he had believed from the first that "the agitation of the subject of slavery" would probably end in "disunion," the speech opposed Clay's plan of adjustment, attacked the President's plan, adverted to the growing feeling at the South that it could not remain in the Union "with safety and honour," pointed out the gradual snapping, one after another, of the links which held the Union together, and expressed the most gloomy forebodings for the future. When he closed, the general feeling in Washington was that it was Calhoun's last speech, and that it had rung the knell of the Union.

Three days later a similar or greater throng gathered to hear Daniel Webster's great "7th of March speech," which has ever since been regarded as marking a distinct era in his life. When he rose from his seat, in the middle of the Chamber, wearing his customary blue coat with metal buttons, he stood grave and sombre as a sphinx. He was listened to with eager curiosity. There had been much uncertainty as to his probable course, and his conversation had been reticent and guarded. He began slowly, calmly, almost judicially, without a gesture or movement for several minutes. Then, growing slightly more animated, he drew his hand out from his breast to emphasize a sonorous utterance. He was, as always, clear and powerful. His words, while they disappointed thousands of his friends at the North, lent new vigour to the "Compromisers," with whom, it was seen, he would thenceforth act. Washington society was delighted to gain such a champion, but as one of his colleagues cynically remarked: "Wait till you hear from Boston."

On the 11th of March, my father had the floor. There was no uncertainty about the position of "the ultra Senator from New York," who was deemed the head and front of the unpopular anti-slavery minority. No crowd filled the galleries, and there was but a slim attendance of Senators, though many of the newly elected Representatives came over from the other chamber to listen to him. The speech was elaborate and one of his best. He advocated the immediate admission of California, and the abolition of slavery in the District of Columbia, denounced the proposed fugitive slave law, and called up a picture of what would happen when the projectors of disunion should come to draw the lines of their new "republic of the South." He told them it would entail border warfare, stoppage of trade and travel and social intercourse, families and kindred separated and converted into enemies, new and onerous taxes and conscriptions to maintain an army and navy "under the new and hateful banner of sedition"; and all this done to secure the institution of African slavery. He said the question of dissolution embraced the fearful issue whether the Union should stand and slavery be removed by gradual, peaceful effort, with compensation—or the Union be dissolved, "*and civil war ensue, bringing on violent but complete and immediate emancipation.*" He closed by saying that the Union would survive even such a conflict—that it was the creature of necessities, physical, moral, social, and political, and "endures because some government must exist here and no other government but this can."

Every morning's mail now brought a pile of criticisms and commendations upon this speech from far and near. Warm, enthusiastic, and grateful letters came from the Pacific Coast. The boldness of its dissent from such honoured leaders as Clay and Webster called forth the censure of many of his own party as well as of the other.

His vivid description of what a civil war in the United States would be—and his prediction that it would inevitably bring sudden and violent emancipation, attracted less attention from either friends or foes than might have been expected—perhaps because neither of them, at that period, were disposed to believe that such events could actually happen.

Those who were seeking for a vulnerable point for attack in his argument thought they had found one in his declaration that the fugitive slave law was not only in contravention of the Constitution, but also of the higher law of justice and humanity. This mention of a "higher law" was denounced as certainly treason and little short of blasphemy. It was held that no law could be higher than the Constitution, even those of the Almighty,—for every good citizen was bound to obey the one; while the other he could think as he pleased about. The phrase "higher law" became a byword of political reproach and a theme of religious discussion. Press and pupit through the country divided in opinion over it. It was pronounced pernicious, immoral, and wicked. It was declared to be moral, philosophic and Christian. Nearly every public man of prominence found himself called upon to state what his views were in regard to the relative obligation of divine and human laws. Even those who disliked the provisions of the Fugitive Slave Law were required to say that it should be obeyed "because it was law," and also because it would please the South. Of course views varied with varying minds and tempers.

Beginning with criticism by the cautious, the debate ran into rancorous and abusive epithets by the zealous and violent. The phrase was repeated and quoted so often that it became associated with my father's name, and with that of his party. The wordy storm raged for months, and was not forgotten during his lifetime. Yet the most rancorous of his critics were all the while declaring that the right of disunion and secession was considerably "higher" than any constitution ever made.

Colonel Benton spoke more than once in the long debate. His commanding personality, his originality and independence, and his incisive sarcasm always secured attention. Although representing a slave State, he had no sympathy with disunion, and not much with the "Compromise" proposed to avert it. He moved to take up and pass the California bill without regard to other measures.

General Cass and most of the other Northern Senators followed the lead of Clay and Webster. There were only three anti-slavery dissenters, Seward, Hale, and Chase.

A select "Committee of Thirteen" was appointed, having six Northern Senators and six Southern ones and one to be chosen by the twelve. To this committee the resolutions were referred, and it was expected to mature some scheme that should solve "all pending differences growing out of the institution of slavery." Clay was chairman, and Webster, Cass, Bell, Dickinson, Berrien, Mangum, and Mason were among the members.

The death of Calhoun and the funeral honours to his memory occasioned a pause, but only a brief one, in the engrossing debate.

Winter passed away. Spring buds and blossoms came, and the hot summer sunshine began. But there was no talk of adjournment. Not only Congress but the country was absorbed in the great debate. Newspapers throughout the land were teeming with it. In May the Committee of Thirteen reported a scheme, embodying substantially all of Clay's propositions with the addition of one to make Utah a distinct Territory. This compound legislation soon gained the popular nickname of "the Omnibus Bill."

It proved an unwieldy vehicle, as it rumbled on through

more speeches and more debates, with an occasional test vote on some minor point.

On the Whig side, Senators Upham and Truman Smith took ground against it. On the Democratic side, Senators Douglas, Morton, and Shields said it would be defeated as a whole, but most of its measures might be taken up and passed separately. John Bell's speech was able and scholarly, and intended to be impartial, but seemed not even to satisfy himself. On the first day of its delivery, people in the galleries said, "Bell is for it." On the second day they said, "Bell will vote against it." On the third that he "cannot make up his mind."

My father made a second speech, in which he described "the Slaveholders' Dream"—a dream of new States surrounding the Gulf of Mexico, combined with the old slave States and constituting a Slave Empire with its metropolis in the Crescent City. This, he said, was woven of "the stuff that dreams are made of," and yet "nothing seems impossible to the slaveholders, after the advantages they have already gained."

As the summer wore on, Mr. Clay began to look wearied and haggard and to betray impatience and temper. The fiery sun beat down each day more pitilessly on the hot Capitol and its heated orators in the two chambers.

One of the recreations of Washington society was to gather in the grounds of the Executive Mansion, to sit in the shade and fan themselves, while listening to the strains of the Marine Band.

One Saturday afternoon, my father and I strolled from there across Lafayette Square, to call on Mr. Clayton, the Secretary of State. He received us with hearty Southern hospitality. His sideboard with decanters and glasses stood in the front hall, and every visitor was invited to refresh himself. He was tall, sturdy, white-haired, and of very genial presence.

In his easy chair, glass in hand, he gave us the latest gossip of the executive circle. The President was not going to budge from his position. The Queen of England was going to approve the Clayton-Bulwer Treaty, whether Nicaragua liked it or not. Sir Henry and Lady Bulwer were going to Staten Island for the summer, and later would receive higher diplomatic rank. The Queen of Spain wanted pay for the Amistad slaves, liberated by our Supreme Court. She would not get it. The King of the Sandwich Islands had sent his two sons to visit the United States, in charge of a missionary, Rev. Dr. Judd. They were educated, erect, graceful, and were royal princes. Washington society was disposed to adore their rank, but balked at their complexion. It was feared they might be "black." Most of the diplomats were out of town. Most of the Congressmen wanted to be, but couldn't. The South American republics were having their usual revolutions—none very sanguinary, but generally all ending in the dictatorship of some general.

The Secretary talked thus of the world's governmental problems with the freedom and ease of an expert chess player about the moves of a game. His conversation was a reminder that "there are more things in heaven and earth" —besides Congressional debates.

As had been foreshadowed, the "Omnibus Bill" was defeated as a whole, but the several measures composing the "Compromise" were taken up separately, and fresh debate on each ensued. In this complex contest the House of Representatives, the State legislatures, and the newspapers were now taking active part.

It had long been a custom at the Academy of the Visitation at Georgetown to ask the President to come as an honoured guest to the annual exercises, and bestow the prizes upon the members of the graduating class. General Taylor complied with the invitation, but the day proved very hot even for July. Returning much heated and fatigued to the White House, he ate freely of cherries and drank freely of milk. This was believed to be the incipient cause of an illness, news of which now alarmed the capital and the country. A long line of anxious inquirers besieged the doors of the White House.

A few days later it was announced that the physicians had given up hope. On the morning of the 10th, those who lived near the Executive Mansion were awakened by the solemn tolling of the bell on the old State Department. The dreaded calamity had happened. It was the second of that series of events, each of which has made an epoch in the history of the country.

There is always deep and sincere grief in Washington over the death of a President. Many have become his personal friends and admirers. Many more have been building hopes and aspirations upon his continuance in office. Then follows a brief period of curiosity and apprehensions in regard to the probable policies of his successor. Gradually the country settles down to acceptance of the inevitable, in accordance with the ancient maxim, "The King is dead, long live the King!"

Vice-President Fillmore proceeded to the House of Representatives, and there took the oath of office without any ostentatious ceremony.

When it was announced a few days later that the new President had invited Mr. Webster to become his Secretary of State, and that the invitation had been accepted, it became evident that the new Administration would discard "General Taylor's Plan," and instead would cast its influence in favour of "Clay's Compromise." The Compromisers themselves had almost lost heart when they found the Compromise had failed in its entirety, but they were now inspired with new zeal by the belief that it could be taken up and carried through piecemeal.

The tone of Congress began to veer, especially as the press and the country seemed to grow weary of the strife, and ready to accept any panacea that time-honoured leaders assured them would "finally settle the slavery question."

Looking down from the galleries, I saw the closing scenes of the great drama pass in rapid succession. The California Bill was taken up. Attempts were made by its opponents to remand her to a territorial condition, or to remit her constitution to a new convention, or to cut her in two by the line of 36° 30'. When these had all failed, she was at last admitted. The Senate doors opened and Dr. Gwin and Colonel Frémont entered to take their seats as Senators, amid much handshaking with their friends.

The other measures were ordered to their third reading. My father made a last attempt for emancipation in the District of Columbia, but of course his amendment was voted down, and slavery was left undisturbed there, except that the slave-trade was restricted. New Mexico and Utah were organized into Territories open to slave-holders. The "Texas Boundary Bill" was passed, taking ten million dollars from the Treasury to pay off the discredited "Texas scrip," large amounts of which were said to be in the pockets of members of Congress and their intimate friends. The "Fugitive Slave Law" was rushed through.

I happened to be in the Congressional Library that morning, when I saw many Northern members coming in, one by one, and aimlessly strolling about. Inquiring of one what was going on in the House, I was told that the Fugitive Slave Law was about to be voted on. These were the "dodgers," who did not want to vote for it, nor dare to vote against it.

I hurried over to the House gallery, in time to find

Thaddeus Stevens on his feet, and sarcastically moving that the Speaker might "send one of his pages to inform the members that they can return with safety, as the slavery question has been disposed of!"

1851.

The "Evening Journal" Office. A rather unpretending three-story brick building stood on the north side of State Street in Albany, about halfway down the hill, on the corner of James Street. This was the office of the Albany *Evening Journal*, a paper of wide political repute, and whose editor-in-chief was Thurlow Weed. All agreed as to Mr. Weed's sagacity and shrewdness, however they might differ as to his course. He was popularly regarded as a "Warwick the King Maker," who moved party magnates like chessmen, elevating or putting down legislators, State officers, governors, and even presidents. He was still in his prime, though his head was beginning to grow grey, and his shoulders to stoop a little.

After my admission to the bar I had entered upon the practice of the law. But a few months later I received an invitation from Mr. Weed to come and try my hand, for a time at least, in journalism.

The winter of 1851–1852 found me installed in the editorial room as one of the assistants. Everything there was simple, plain, and businesslike. Our editorial furniture consisted merely of a table, a chair, an inkstand and pair of scissors for each, and a shelf or two of books of reference, besides piles of exchange papers everywhere.

Adjoining this room was the long one where the foreman and compositors were setting type and making up the "forms," which were then sent down to the press-room in the basement. A counting-room on the first floor opened upon the street.

Mr. Weed introduced me to my future associates.

George Dawson, long his trusted lieutenant, was the "managing editor." He sat by one window and my table was placed at another. John Ten Eyck, the "city editor," had a small room by himself. There were legislative and other reporters, and occasionally E. Peshine Smith or some other unattached journalist would be called in for editorial work. Visscher Ten Eyck and his nephew Philip had charge of the counting-room and the books.

It was not a large editorial force, but a busy one. Giles Winne had for many years been the foreman in the composing room, and now his son, Jacob, reigned in his stead. Work began with the daylight, and continued with increasing activity until three, when the paper went to press. The scene of labour was then transferred to the press-room in the basement, the mail wagons, and newsboys in the streets.

The work of the journalist, like that of the housewife, is never done, and I found that it was often necessary or wise to devote some evening hours to preparation of the matter for "tomorrow's paper."

When I first took pen in hand Mr. Weed gave me two valuable maxims for my guidance: "*First*. Never write any article without some clear and definite point and purpose. *Second*. When written, go carefully over it and strike out every superfluous word or sentence, and then see how much you have improved it." As he remarked: "People have to sit and listen to a sermon or a speech that may be full of rambling repetitions. But when they find the newspaper growing dull or tedious, they simply lay it down, and don't take it up again."

Another thing that I speedily discovered was that there is little time in an editor's "sanctum" to study up a subject or to consult authorities. The editor, whether right or wrong, must be swift in decision and prompt in expression. His readers will be eager for any information he can give them about the topic they are interested in today.   But they care little about what happened day before yesterday, and less about his comments thereon, if deferred till day after tomorrow.   Furthermore he is expected to know something about everything, to say why things happen, and who is to blame for them.   Like every college graduate, I had fancied that I had accumulated a considerable amount of useless information on a variety of subjects.   But I soon learned that any scrap of knowledge that I possessed on any subject was likely to come into unexpected need, some day or other.   Reporters sometimes carry this doctrine to such extremes that when they cannot get facts, they accept rumours and then invent details to embellish them.   Even conjectures are only too readily believed when they are new.   This was just the reverse of the rule I had learned in my law office, that "you must assert nothing that you cannot prove."

As our staff was small, our work was not divided and apportioned, but was rather conducted on the plan that each was to give his aid wherever it was most needed at the time.   So, within a few weeks, I found myself assigned to proof-reading, reporting, news gathering, literary reviewing, editorial writing, and general management. Either editor might any day find himself in sole charge. The first time that event happened to me the responsibility seemed oppressive.   I felt as if the world would be out of joint if the *Evening Journal* should not get to press at the usual hour, through my labours, and the equally important ones of Jacob Winne, the foreman.

There are many visitors each day at the editorial room. The throng included dignitaries of Church and State, members of the Legislature and Congress, State and city officials, political leaders, editors of other journals, popular lecturers, bankers, merchants, managers of institutions,

hospitals, and places of amusement, each of whom had
something that he wished to say, or to have said, in the
Journal.   This procession of visitors would be interesting
and often instructive, if it did not continually interrupt
editorial work; which must go on, for the press, like "time
and tide," will wait for no man, and the *Journal's* hour
for going to press was 3 P.M.   So I found it was necessary
to acquire the arts of learning what was in a pile of papers
by merely skimming through them, of getting at the heart
of long disquisitions without reading them, and of writing
on one subject, while asking questions or answering them
about another.

Mr. Weed was tall, active, and vigorous, an indefatigable
worker in the office and out of it.   Although the *Journal*
was only twenty years old, it was already a recognized
political power in the State and the leading organ of its
party.   Desiring no official position for himself, he was
regarded as the wise and disinterested adviser of all aspi-
rants for place.   Besides his reputation for political sagacity, he had won esteem as a public-spirited citizen and a
philanthropist of wide though unostentatious benevo-
lence.   The word "boss" had not yet come into use as a
designation for a political magnate, but his friends often
spoke of him as "the Old Man" or the "Dictator," while
his opponents described him as an arch-conspirator.

So much about him the public could readily comprehend.   But there was another source of his power, less
well understood.   That was his control of public opinion
through his influence with the press of the State.   From
natural sympathy as well as policy, he was the intimate
friend and adviser of other journals and journalists.   He
was always ready to help them with material for their
columns and aid in their business enterprises.   Every
county in the State had its local Whig journal at the
county seat, whose editor looked to Thurlow Weed as his

political guide and personal friend. His views were echoed and repeated, and when some important problem was under discussion, the *Evening Journal* would reproduce and quote their editorials, to show their practical unanimity, on a page devoted to "The Voice of the Press."

One of the natural results of this *esprit de corps* and friendly intimacy, was his thorough knowledge of editorial plans and projects. Very few changes of proprietorship and very few schemes for new newspaper enterprises were entered upon without previous consultation with him. When in the Presidential election of 1840 it was decided to start a Whig campaign paper called the *Jeffersonian*, Mr. Weed went to New York to look up an editor for it. He found a young man struggling with a not very prosperous literary periodical. Earnest and industrious, of advanced opinions and somewhat eccentric habits, he possessed a philosophical temper and a positive genius for editorial work. This was Horace Greeley, who thenceforth became a frequent visitor to the *Journal* office and a warm friend of Thurlow Weed. The *Jeffersonian* was succeeded by the *Log Cabin*, and after General Harrison's election it developed into the *New York Tribune*, and entered upon its long and enduring career.

Several years later, after I had become an assistant editor of the *Journal*, I was present at a consultation over the feasibility of establishing a new morning journal in New York. Charles A. Dana, then of the *Tribune*, and Henry J. Raymond, then of the *Courier and Inquirer*, had come to Mr. Weed to ask his advice and approval of such an enterprise. All agreed that no new journal could hope to compete with the *Herald* in the business of gathering world-wide news, or with the *Tribune* in advocating measures of progress and reform. But Raymond was confident that there was a field somewhere between the two, for a paper that would suit the taste of a great middle class of New York, conservative in politics, wanting accurate news, rather than reforms or sensations, or gossip and scandals. The outcome of this conference was the starting of the *New York Times*, and the tall tower that stands today in Times Square is a monument to the wise judgment of its founders.

How to get the busy New York public to turn aside from its accustomed papers long enough to buy or read the new newspaper was the next problem. Dana's opinion was that it should follow Weed's method of short, crisp editorial articles, keenly critical and yet humorous. His success, in after years, with the *New York Sun* exemplifies what he had in mind. Raymond believed that the way to win public attention to a new paper would be to make it the special source of information on one great topic at a time, that might then be engrossing the public mind. This line of action he afterward pursued at the time of Kossuth's visit, and again in the investigation and pursuit of the Tweed Ring. The press like the drama must "hold the mirror up to nature," and reflect the temper of the time.

Journalism I found a pursuit quite attractive, and well suited to my tastes and disposition. Political questions and contests had more interest for me than legal ones. To lead and rightly guide public opinion seemed to me the height of any reasonable ambition. I had no hankering for public office. Although only just arrived at the voting age, it seemed as if I had already had a lifetime of observation of the working of the business of office-seeking and office-holding, and I had no desire to engage in that struggle. Public office I had been taught to consider a duty, to be neither sought nor shunned; I heartily agreed with that instruction, and intended to avoid, so far as possible, its lures, its responsibilities, and its inevitable unsatisfactory ending. So I was resolved that whatever public duty I might be called upon to perform should not be of my own seeking.

Editorial Topics. Looking now over the files of the *Evening Journal* of half a century ago, I note how topics have passed away or lost interest. Questions have been settled, opinions changed, things local and temporary have been relegated to oblivion. One can perceive the changes that have taken place in the country's history, as well as in the character of its journalism. If a contrast were to be drawn between the newspaper articles of that day and this, I should say the older ones had more of strenuous earnestness, and the later ones more of the air of judicial impartiality.

My own editorials were numerous, the earlier ones crude enough—some well intended but based on mistaken premises—but some of the later ones containing forecasts since verified.

There was no lack of topics for discussion and comment during the ten years I spent in the *Evening Journal* office. The foreign news, then received by steamer instead of Atlantic cable, brought many events of stirring interest: the revolutionary movements in European capitals; the Hungarian revolution and Kossuth's visit to America; the Crimean War; Louis Napoleon's *coup d'état;* the war in Italy; the liberation of Venice and Rome; the doings of Garibaldi, Victor Emmanuel, and Cavour.

Then there were the political movements in the United States: the Compromise and the Fugitive Slave Law; the Presidential campaign between Pierce and Scott; the gradual disintegration of parties; the "Old Hunkers" and "Barn-burners"; the "Hards" and "Softs"; the "Old Line Whigs"; the rise and fall of the "Know-nothing" or "Native American party"; the collapse of the Whigs; the rise of the Republican party and its progress throughout the Northern States; Douglas's Nebraska Bill and the repeal of the Missouri Compromise; the Presidential campaign between Buchanan and Frémont; the Dred Scott Decision and the claim of the extension of slavery to all States and Territories; the struggle in Kansas between the free-State settlers and the "Border Ruffians"; the appointment of Kansas governors and the application of Kansas for admission to the Union; the national conventions at Charleston, Baltimore, and Chicago; the nomination and election of Lincoln and Hamlin and the advent of the Republicans to political power— altogether an exciting series of critical events both at home and abroad.

Chief among the topics of political discussion during the ten years prior to the Civil War, was the question of the extension of slavery.

1853.

A New Word. One morning my friend, E. Peshine Smith, who was a lover of linguistic and other historical problems, came into the *Evening Journal* office with a new suggestion.

He said: "It is time that we invented a word to take the place of our cumbrous phrase, 'telegraphic despatch' or 'telegraphic message.' Now that we have the telegraph we ought to have some shorter word to take the place of two long ones."

"Well, what word do you suggest?"

"Telegram. That is of Greek origin like 'telegraph' and is a perfectly proper derivative. Telegraph is the machine that writes. Telegram is the thing that it writes. It is analogous to 'epigram,' 'anagram,' and 'monogram.'"

"Well! let us try it in the *Evening Journal* today."

So the new word was put forth. But individuals and

newspapers did not take kindly to it. They thought it looked queer, and was an affectation. Some said "telegraph" was a good enough word to use. One or two newspapers followed the *Journal's* example, but the general public pooh-poohed it, and so the word fell into gradual disuse.

Six months later, E. Peshine Smith came in again, triumphantly waving a copy of the *London Times*.

"See here," said he; "the 'Thunderer' has got our word, and what is more, it applauds it as a very convenient abbreviation."

I asked: "Does it call it an Americanism?"

"No," said he. "Just uses it. Now we will see whether the papers here will take any more kindly to it, when it comes to us with a foreign stamp on it."

And sure enough they did. "Telegram" came soon into general use, and is so still.

I said to Mr. Smith: "It seems that a new word is like a new opera singer. She may have ever so good a voice, but she will not be appreciated, if born in this country, until she has been to London and back again."

A Thanksgiving Relic. Anniversaries and holidays were of course recorded in the *Evening Journal* with suitable editorial comments. Thanksgiving was especially observed, and Mr. Weed, on that day, presented each one of his employees with a turkey for his family dinner.

Thanksgiving, in those days, was a State and not a national festival. The governor of each State designated the day at his pleasure. Perhaps as an assertion of "State rights," these days were often of different dates. But it happened that in 1853 quite a large number chose the same date.

I wrote an editorial article, on this occasion, for the

Journal. Then I heard no more of it for fifty-nine years.

In 1912, I received a letter enclosing a newspaper clipping from my old friend Judge Nott, ex-Chief Justice of the United States Court of Claims. It ran as follows:

"PRINCETON, June 19, 1912.

" I have kept this tribute to Thanksgiving all these years; and send it to you now, because I think that there is no one in the world who will appreciate its beauties so much as you, except me.

"Do you remember it? I stand ready to bet that you have forgotten its existence. It is associated in my mind with two men, Mr. Blatchford and Mr. Weed. Mr. Blatchford read it and said: 'Weed, that is the very best thing of the kind that you ever wrote, or ever will write.'

"Mr. Weed replied: 'Yes, that is very true, except that I did not write it, and Fred Seward did.'

"The explanation of my having found it is that we are leaving Princeton and I have been through my packages of old letters and literary treasures and here is this one. I hope that you will appreciate it half as much as I do and (like me) wonder that you ever wrote anything so good.

"C. C. N."

(From the Albany *Evening Journal*, Nov. 23, 1853.)

"THANKSGIVING DAY

"Twenty-two States are to dine together tomorrow. The invitations have been out for a month. The dinner is given in honour of Connecticut, the oldest invited guest, who sits down to the anniversary feast for the hundred and fifty-fifth time. The table will be three thousand miles long—so there is sure to be room. New Hampshire has agreed to preside, at the upper end, in a huge granite chair. The clergy of the Union will say grace two hours beforehand. Thirty-six thousand church bells have been arranged to chime the music. The viands will be various to suit all tastes—from ice at the upper end, to wines and fruits at the lower. But the majority of the guests will probably make their dinner of roast turkey and pumpkin pie, out of compliment to old Connecticut, the founder of the festival.

"It must be a pleasant sight for her to see the whole family gathered around her table, with Uncle Sam, about halfway down, in the midst of them. The old fellow is pretty well in years now (seventy-eight last July) but still hale and hearty, thanks to an excellent constitution. Virginia, his eldest daughter (a well-meaning person, though with a deal of family pride, and very much given to talking about her son 'George,' for which, however, nobody can blame her), will have a seat at his right hand. Texas, a rough-and-ready sort of backwoodsman, has a place at the other end of the table, and will probably contrive to sit very close to Louisiana, one of the youngest and prettiest of the old gentleman's nieces. New York will be there as long as he can spare time; but business on 'Change will probably call him away by the express train, before dinner is over. Maine and South Carolina were too impatient to wait, and so they have been already accommodated at a side table. California (a stout little fellow, of three years, who, his elder sisters vow, is worth his weight in gold) is too young to come.

"Of course, there have been idle stories in circulation about this family, as there are about all families, which this Gathering will do much to dispel. Some, for instance, have asserted that they were head over ears in debt, and so near bankrupt that they could not afford sugar in their tea. Uncle Sam will chuckle at them well when he pulls

out a surplus of $20,000,000 which he proposes to exhibit.
Others, again, have privately hinted that Mississippi has
applied for a divorce, and that she is going to run away
with a worthless adventurer. But her presence at the
dinner, smiling and contented, will pretty effectually stop
that gossip. Others again, pretend that there is a deadly
quarrel between New York, Virginia, Massachusetts,
and two or three others. But you will see that they will
be shaking hands over the dinner table before sundown.

"The old folks will take great pleasure in talking over
the days when they were young, and all thirteen of them
lived together—down on the seashore. The young ones
will, of course, be full of a thousand visionary schemes by
which they think they are going to make a great noise
in the world by and by. But, at any rate, they will all
be the better for the old tales that will be told, the old
jokes that will be made, and the old songs that will be
sung, until late in the evening, when Hope and Memory
(two old servants of this family who have done more to
keep it together than any amount of compromises could)
will light them all up to bed, and supply them with the
material for their Thanksgiving dreams."

Albany Life. Albany is proverbial for its hospitality
—an inheritance from its old Dutch founders. Its importance as the State capital and a political centre drew
to it, every winter, many persons of public distinction,
and families of culture and refinement. My residence
there was a pleasant one, and when I look back at it now,
there come up memories of acquaintances that ripened
into lifelong friendships, and events that it is a renewed
pleasure to recall.

At an evening party there I met a young lady just
entering society, whose home was near the well-remembered
scenes of "Kane's Walk." Talk of youthful remembrances

and congenial tastes soon led to mutual regard; and a
year later, this resulted in our marriage—a union which
has proved the chief element of my life's happiness—and
which has long transcended the "Silver" and "Golden
Wedding" anniversaries, both of which so many hope
for, and so few attain.

Daily observation and contact with the workings of
the State government doubtless inspired the young men
of Albany with more than ordinary interest in public
affairs. I found my contemporaries alive to questions
of State and national progress, ardent reformers, zealous
for good citizenship; and yet with less of partisan bitterness than is often found in more isolated communities.

My association with them, as well as my daily newspaper work, served to keep me in touch with public opinion, and to increase my faith in the belief that the world
was gradually progressing. They honoured me with
their confidence, choosing me to be their spokesman, or
presiding officer, on occasions of importance, among them
the demonstrations of sympathy with European struggles
for liberty, the welcoming of Kossuth, the founding of
the University and its branches, and the preliminary
steps toward the formation of the Republican party.

An Albany Concert. In those days, concerts and lec-
tures were favourite amusements for Albany society.
The list of lecturers comprised such names as Wendell
Phillips, Henry Ward Beecher, Dr. Bethune, George
William Curtis, George Sumner, Judge William Kent,
John P. Hale, and others well known to fame.

Among the concerts were those of the Hutchinsons,
Dempster, Madame Bishop, Eliza Greenfield (the "Black
Swan"), the Swiss Bellringers, Parodi, Piccolomini, and
other operatic stars.

One of these concerts was a notable one. Strakosch

and his wife, who was Amalia Patti, had brought with them little ten-year-old Adelina Patti, with her wonderful voice. Ole Bull was also of the troupe.

Association Hall was packed with a great audience. All went well until about the middle of the evening when some hitch occurred. There was a long wait. Excited voices were heard from the little greenroom, just off the stage, apparently in dispute and remonstrance.

After a while Ole Bull came out, and intimating there would be some delay, said that if the audience would permit, he would play something of his own, which was not on the program. Of course the audience approved.

Remarking simply that it was a dialogue between a young Venetian husband and his wife, on their way to the Carnival, he raised his violin to his shoulder.

The violin began softly, with the familiar strains of the *Carnival of Venice*, and then, with endless variations on that theme, proceeded to tell the story. We heard the young couple gaily chatting and laughing. The husband hummed a dancing tune, and the wife skipped along as an accompaniment. Then they united in a love song. Presently something was said that gave offence. There was a sharp rebuke. His tones became abrupt and gruff. Hers were shrill and defiant. The quarrel went on louder and louder. He scolded. She mocked and sneered. He stormed and swore. She wept and wailed and sobbed. But now they are at the door of the cathedral. The organ notes come pealing forth. They drop their voices. He softens his tones. She begins to plead and coax. Reconciliation and forgiveness follow. They enter the doorway and join in the *Jubilate* chorus that comes down from the choir above.

Suddenly the music stops. Ole Bull is making a bow and retiring.

We of the audience sit silent. Then presently we awake

7

to a realizing sense that we have been listening to an entirely imaginary scene. There is no quarrel. There is no young couple—no Venice. The witchery of the violin has conjured up the whole scene before our eyes and ears. Now the spell is broken. Next moment we are all laughing at each other, and applauding Ole Bull.

Then Ole Bull caps the climax by leading out the little girl—her eyes red with crying, but smiling through her tears, and ready to sing sweetly the little aria which had been assigned to her.

Next morning, Strakosch came round to the *Journal* office and we congratulated him on the artistic triumph of the night before.

"Yes," he said, "but think of the trouble I was in. That little d—— [he did not say "diva"] refused to sing unless she had a pound of candy. I had provided none. I rushed downstairs and out into the street to look for a confectionery shop. It was after nine o'clock and all were closed. Finally, on a side street I found an old confectioner, who lived over his shop. I persuaded him to come down and sell me a pound. Then I ran back, and found how good Ole Bull had saved the situation."

Kossuth at Albany. Bells are ringing, whistles blowing and cannon booming. Flags are flying over streets and buildings. Among them our national colours predominate but here and there are also the Hungarian tricolour and the Turkish crescent. As we stand on the dock at East Albany and look across the river, the city seems to be in gala attire. His honour, the Mayor, with local dignitaries and leading citizens, are gathered in a group that is awaiting the arrival of the train bringing the great Hungarian. Behind them are the young men of the "Hungarian Liberty Association," of which I am the President,

William Barnes the Treasurer, and Rabbi Wise the Chaplain.

The train rolls in, and is greeted with cheers; Kossuth presents himself, and descends from it. He looks dignified and impressive, with iron grey hair and full beard, as he bows courteously to the crowd. He holds in his hand the broad-brimmed soft hat, which is already the symbol of European revolutionists, and which is to become shortly the fashionable headgear in America, and is known as the "Kossuth hat."

Some of his companions or staff officers wear a feather or a bit of gold braid on it, and in their costume are indications of military rank, but most of them are in ordinary civilian dress.

Interchange of greetings and introductions follow. Then all cross the river in a ferryboat. Landing near the Delavan House, we find an improvised procession waiting to escort him up State Street to the Capitol Hill.

A crowd is gathered there also—too numerous to allow all to enter the building. So Governor Hunt comes out to the top of the broad steps, and gives his address of welcome, which receives suitable response.

The national guest is lodged at Congress Hall, just adjoining the Capitol. After paying my respects to him and his companions, I visit a parlour where the representatives of "the Press" are gathered. There I meet several acquaintances, among them James W. Simonton of the *Times* (and afterward head of the Associated Press). There is a busy rustling of pens and paper as they are preparing their notes of the day's proceedings. Two or three of them tell me that they are accompanying the "Governor," as they call him, in his whole tour through the States. They share in the popular enthusiasm, which they are so busily engaged in creating, and speak of him in terms of warm affection, recounting instances of his tact, address, and fascinating eloquence. He is always affable, yet on the whole his manner is grave and sad, as it well may be, after his experience of the rise and fall of "the Hungarian republic."

Our American people have always been interested and warmly sympathetic with any European nation which they believe to be struggling against despotism; and especially if it announces its desire for republican government. The Greeks, the Poles, the French, the Italians, the Spanish have, in turn, received demonstrations of our sympathy, and some of our more impulsive leaders have urged us to go to war in their behalf.

Of Hungary and the Hungarians we had known but little, until the wave of revolutionary outbreaks began to sweep over the continental nations in 1848. But now the newspapers and speakers are eagerly read or listened to, when they try to familiarize us with hitherto unknown localities and unpronounceable names. They awaken our admiration for military heroes and eloquent orators, who, like ourselves, are advocating "Freedom."

Kossuth's romantic story and his unavailing struggle against the Austrian and Russian Empires appealed strongly to the people of the United States. His imprisonment, escape and exile, the refuge and shelter afforded him by the Turks, his rescue and voyage to us in an American frigate, the popular outburst of welcome that greeted him in New York and other cities, the honours extended to him at Washington and the State capitals, have carried the popular enthusiasm to fever heat, and he is the hero of the hour.

Even after the Hungarian Republic had become a dream of the past, and the Hungarians had divided into varying political groups, finding peace at last under the Iron Crown of the Dual Empire, a permanent impress had been made upon America by Kossuth's visit and his eventful tour and his appeals for "material aid" for Hungary. Hungarian hats, Hungarian wine, Hungarian bands, Hungarian music and dances began to come in vogue. Hungarian history is to be studied. A steady flow of Hungarian immigration has set in, which still continues and is adding to our complex nationality, which absorbs and assimilates so many diverse elements.

In his subsequent visits to Albany, although there is no longer such a rush to see him, yet the desire to hear him is unabated. Halls and churches are crowded when he is to speak. Our society gives him a welcome in the Young Men's Association Rooms. The tickets of admission are little red, white, and green cards, the Hungarian tricolour. All these are sold, and several thousand dollars are raised as a contribution to the fund for "material aid" for the revolutionists.

He is singularly fluent, with hardly a trace of accent, though occasionally a quaint idiom or phrase reminds the hearer of his foreign birth, or his Shakespearian studies. He is ready and effective in illustration. At one meeting he was repelling the charge that he was the arch-agitator and responsible for all these revolutionary outbreaks in Europe. "No," said he, turning toward the great clock that hung on the wall behind him. "No, I am only like yonder clock. I tell the hour; I make not the time."

Since 1848, European affairs had been arresting American attention. Now the news of Louis Napoleon's *coup d'état*, its details, and its probable results are eagerly studied. Kossuth is felt to be a representative of European republicans, and the demonstrations in his honour are expressive, not merely of sympathy for the Hungarians, but of protest against despotism everywhere.

In April, after a trip to the South, he returns to Washington. A letter from my mother to her sister describes his social experiences, and a visit with him to Mount Vernon.

At that period, the neglected grounds and dilapidated buildings and fences there were beginning to call for public attention, but no governmental action had yet been taken for their preservation.

" WASHINGTON, 17th April, 1852.

"The Kossuths have come and gone.   When they left us before, Kossuth was the orator who won our hearts by his genius.   He was surrounded with a large suite of followers, who seemed to regard him as a superior being. He had hope and confidence in the professions of men who had power to assist him.   His rich habiliments attracted the gaze of the multitude.   He was going to make new friends.

"He returns from the South where he has met little favour, to the politicians of Washington whose favour has grown cold, with his hopes diminished, his followers reduced from seventeen to four, his own dress even changed with the change of his prospects.   The Kossuth who has left us today is a gentle, brave man who will toil on for Hungary.

"Monday Evening.

"Mesdames Kossuth and Pulszky came to see us.   They said they had thought a great deal about us while at the South and Madame Pulszky added in a whisper, 'We think you are right about slavery.'

"Thursday evening was our dinner.   We had, as usual, a singular combination of ultra-Southern men, 'Free-Soilers,' and Democratic members of Congress.   Messrs. Mangum and Hale of the Senate, Mr. Fisher, editor of the *Southern Press*, Mr. Morehead, of North Carolina, and New York members.   A very sociable time they had.

"Kossuth sat on my right and Mr. Morehead on my

left. Kossuth did not talk much, and when he did addressed his conversation chiefly to me. Mr. Fisher, who is called a 'disunionist,' said, across the table, 'Governor Kossuth, don't you think that some portion of the human family is decidedly inferior to the others?''

"Kossuth replied with his usual gentle gravity: 'If that is the case, I think it should teach us humility, and make us more strenuous in our endeavours to assist the weaker portion.'

" Mr. Fisher then alluded to the African race.

"Kossuth disclaimed any particular allusion to them, but said he spoke for the oppressed generally.

"It was nearly eleven o'clock when our guests departed, previous to which Henry had arranged that we and Mr. Fisher should accompany the Governor to Mount Vernon the next day.

" So at nine o'clock we all met on the wharf with nearly a hundred other persons going in the same direction. Madame Pulszky, who is a very charming person, was not well enough to go. Madame Kossuth summoned up resolution to go without her interpreter. I was glad to see her once alone. She has learned a little, very little, English, which with the little French I could command enabled us to have some conversation. She looked very pretty with her white muslin bonnet and green veil.

"We soon arrived at Mount Vernon. Mr. Fisher went up to the house to propitiate the proprietor, while we went to the tomb. Kossuth took the arm of his wife and went with her to the door of the vault.

"They were considerably in advance of us, and when we came up, they were both coming away, with tears streaming from their eyes. Madame was more excited than I had ever seen her. She caught me by the arm and hurried me back to the tomb talking French with great earnestness. 'It is *très triste,*' as Madame said. 'It is a shame,' said a rough-looking young man, 'to leave *him* in such a place.'

"They invited our party to one room in the house which is not generally open to visitors. It contains the library of Washington, a plaster bust, and some family pictures. Washington's large Bible was on the table. The books were mixed up with many others of modern date. I could not but remark that most of the old library was the counterpart of our father's.

"It seemed difficult for Kossuth to make up his mind to go, but again the bell summoned us to the boat, and we joined the other passengers.

"Thomas, who had all this time been perambulating the grounds with a basket of provisions which we brought from home, now spread some napkins on some chairs and produced the cold ducks, bread and butter, oranges, and champagne. As there were only plates sufficient for the ladies, Kossuth, Henry, and Mr. Fisher took theirs in their fingers, so we made a picnic. We were joined in this by young Calhoun, son of John C. Calhoun, a very gentlemanly and agreeable person, who was one of the passengers.

"Had not the Kossuth party absorbed us so much, we should have found other interesting company. There was Dr. Bellows of New York, and his sister, and Grace Greenwood. We parted at the wharf intending to go and see Madame Pulszky in the evening.

"We went to the National in the evening. Found Kossuth had gone out with the intention of coming to our house. I took my leave, promising to go to the cars this morning to say 'good-bye.'

"Madame Pulszky was still too ill to travel, I thought, but we found her at the depot this morning looking very ill, but going on, notwithstanding.

"We had only time to take a hurried leave, a kiss from

the ladies and a warm grasp of the hand from the gentlemen, and they were gone. When and where, if ever, shall
we meet again?

"Mrs. Horace Mann, who had walked over to the depot
with her little boys, was the only other person who came
to pay them the compliment of taking leave."

The Fugitive Slave Law. "The Slavery Question is
settled!" Upon this the majority of each of the two
great parties seemed agreed in 1851. Flags were hoisted,
salutes fired, and meetings held in the large cities, where
orators vied with drums and guns in loud congratulations.

That the slavery question, which had threatened to
disturb the national peace, was finally laid at rest many
believed; and many more who did not believe, deemed it
politic and prudent to affect that they did. Engravings
and biographies were published, testifying public gratitude to the great patriotic "men who had saved the
Union." Histories were written detailing how the great
peril of disunion, imminent in 1851, was, in that year, by
Congressional wisdom, happily ended for ever. Some of
these volumes, still extant, were for years used in schools,
teaching the boys lessons that they afterwards unlearned
at the point of the bayonet.

The Fugitive Slave Law was put in force, and announced
to be "a law of the land, to which every good citizen owes
obedience." Hardly was the ink dry with which it had
been signed, when slaveholders on the border who knew
the whereabouts of their former "chattels" began to
invoke its aid for their recapture.

If the statesmen who adopted the Fugitive Slave Law
as a panacea to repress the "agitation of slavery" had
been seeking, instead, for one to inflame that "agitation"
to its highest pitch, they could hardly have found a more
effective instrument. It went through the land like the

flaming war torch of the Highlands, summoning clansmen
to battle. It roused even the apathetic and lukewarm.
They might ignore slavery in distant territories, but here
was a command to personally become slave catchers.

It brought the slavery question home to every Northern
hearthstone. Clergymen and lawyers who counselled
"obedience to the law because it was a law" did not feel
enthusiasm when called upon to take a hand in its enforce-
ment. It was one thing to tacitly acquiesce in slavery as
an inheritance from Biblical times and the mother country,
and quite another to join in the chase with bloodhounds.
It was one thing to stand and declaim about the "Compromises of the Constitution," and quite another to deny
the prayer of the trembling fugitive at the door for food,
shelter, and escape. But the "Great Peace Measure"
was relentless on this point. It commanded "every good
citizen" to assist the deputy marshal in his slave catching
whenever called upon, and imposed fine and imprisonment
on him who refused to obey.

Experience of the working of the Fugitive Slave Law
was the first thing that opened the eyes of many to the
discovery that possibly Governor Seward might be right
in thinking there was some "higher law" to be obeyed
than this brutal statute.

Soon there was a fugitive slave case in New York, in
which the poor man was seized while at work at his trade,
hurried into a back room, tried in haste, delivered to the
agent, handcuffed, and carried off to Baltimore, without
opportunity even to say good-bye to his wife and children.

There was a similar case in Philadelphia, and another
in Indiana.

Then came the spectacle of Henry Long, a captured
fugitive, marched down to Jersey City ferry, under guard
of two hundred policemen, amid a crowd of thousands.

Ten days later it was announced that he had been

"sold at auction in Richmond for $750, to a Georgia trader, to be taken farther South," and that "there was great applause" at the sale.

In another case in Philadelphia, a woman who had been twenty-two years free, and had five children, was arrested as a fugitive slave.

At Columbia, in Pennsylvania, William Smith was seized as a fugitive, and while endeavouring to escape was shot, dying instantly.

A kidnapper seized a free coloured girl in Nottingham and carried her off to a Baltimore slave pen. A coloured man who went on there to testify to her having been born free and to her never having been a slave was found next day hanging dead, on a tree by the roadside.

But of all these cases, none stirred the popular heart more deeply than those in which the national administration took a hand to enforce the obnoxious law. At Boston, Shadrach, a coloured waiter, was seized, taken before the commissioner, and duly remanded to custody, when a crowd of coloured men rescued him, and sent him off to Canada.

Thereupon the President issued a proclamation, commanding all public officers and calling on all citizens to "aid in quelling this and similar combinations," and to "assist in capturing the above-named persons," in which business the Secretaries of War and of the Navy directed the army and navy to help.

Later came the case of Sims, who, though defended by some of the best legal talent in Boston, was surrendered to his master, marched to the Long Wharf, in a hollow square of three hundred armed policemen, while the militia were posted in Faneuil Hall, chains stretched across the front of the State House, and the church bells tolled as for a funeral.

Then there was the romantic story of William and Ellen

Craft, escaped slaves from Georgia. Ellen, whose complexion was light, had dressed herself to personate a young planter, going north for his health, attended by William, who personated a family servant, greatly devoted to his young master. When the slave catchers tracked them to Boston, Rev. Theodore Parker gave them refuge in his house. He said: "For two weeks I wrote my sermons with a sword in the open drawer under my inkstand, and a pistol in the flap of my desk, loaded and ready for defence, until they could be put on board a vessel for England."

There was a case in Chicago, another at Poughkeepsie, another at Westchester, and another at Wilkesbarre, each attended with circumstances that awakened popular detestation of what the newspapers called "Man Hunting on the Border."

At Buffalo, Judge Conkling granted a writ of habeas corpus to an alleged fugitive. His counsel, Talcott and Hawley, moved his discharge for lack of evidence. It was granted, and in a few moments he was on his way to Canada.

At Syracuse, Jerry McHenry was seized and carried before the commissioner, but a crowd surrounded the court-room, broke in the doors, rushed in, overpowered the officers, and rescued the prisoner. Among those who participated in this riot were Gerrit Smith, Rev. Samuel J. May, and other leading citizens. Eighteen of them were indicted, and summoned to appear at Auburn to answer for their offence. They were escorted by a hundred of the prominent people of the place. Being required to give sureties, my father headed the list, which was soon filled with well-known names.

At Christiania, in Pennsylvania, when the officers and slaveowner, with the commissioner's warrant, came to a house where a fugitive was concealed, they fired into it.

The fire was returned, the owner killed, his companions put to flight, and the fugitive escaped.

The news of these seizures and conflicts alarmed all fugitives, some of whom had been residing for years in supposed security in the free States. Canada was the only place of refuge, and they began to pour into it. They crossed at Detroit, and at Niagara, and at Ogdensburg. Of those in New England, some went up through Vermont, some fled to Maine and crossed over into New Brunswick. Settlements sprung up in Canada, composed of negroes escaped from slavery. The one at Chatham was especially well known, and was a favourite point for those who fled from Kentucky, through Ohio and Michigan.

It is to the credit of human nature, that few men were zealous in executing the Fugitive Slave Law, except those who were paid for it. Even those who thought it ought to be obeyed did not hurry themselves to obey it. Many such would give food and shelter to a casual coloured man, and even point out the road leading north, while prudently refraining from asking any questions that might prove embarrassing to both parties. Others devoted time and money to help the fugitives. Free coloured people in the Northern cities were especially active in this work.

The mysterious rapidity with which fugitive slaves were smuggled through the States and "across the line" soon gained for the system the name of "The Underground Railroad." The passengers on that road increased every month; and its managers devised new facilities for travel. A poor wretch, with his little bundle, knowing nothing of his route, save that he must hide by day, and follow the north star by night, would find himself urged and helped forward by friendly hands, until he stood, without knowing how, on British soil.

Sometimes they came in squads of four or five, or even a dozen. Stories almost incredible were told. One man escaped in a hogshead. One woman had come on in a box, and was nearly suffocated when it was piled among the merchandise on a wharf. One had come in the straw of a farm wagon; another by hanging on underneath the cars; several in the holds of coasting vessels. But the majority had fled on foot, looking hourly behind them for the master and his hounds, and before them for the north star and liberty.

As the *Evening Journal* was the chief anti-slavery paper at the capital, we had many visitors and appeals for aid from "the Underground." Stephen Myers was a coloured man of some prominence, having been head waiter at the Executive Mansion, and chief steward on Hudson River steamboats. He was a frequent caller.

One morning he slipped in mysteriously, and asked George Dawson and me to step out into the back passage-way of the office. There we found a dozen or more young coloured men, "lined up" against the wall. "These," said Stephen, pointing to them with pride, "all comes on last night, and all goes on to Canady this morning."

Dawson, with mock seriousness, said: "Oh, boys, now don't you think you'd better all go back?"

The grin of white teeth that flashed down the line showed that their perils had not dulled their sense of humour.

One evening as I sat alone at work, in the editorial room, a tall, ragged black man came softly in, and holding out a dirty scrap of paper said: "Be this for you, Mas'r?"

I took it, and found it pencilled simply with the words: "Help this poor fellow along. He has his ticket." It was not signed, and was addressed merely to "Leonard," which someone reading it to him had mistaken for "Seward," and so had directed him to my office. He was very reluctant to tell anything about his antecedents or his journey, but said "he was from Ole Virginny," where "some men" had put him on a boat, in which he came to New York. There "some more men" put him on another boat, in which he came to Albany. I told him I would show him the railroad station.

"No, 'fore God, Mas'r, don't take me to no railroad here. Dey said dere might be marshalses watching at the station, and that I was to walk sixteen mile, to some place dey called Snackaday. Does yo' know de road to Snackaday, Mas'r?"

I told him I would show him. So we walked up the hill, stopping to get him a bite on the way, and he started off on the Schenectady turnpike, which doubtless led to his destination.

"Stephen," I inquired once of the Underground manager, "where do you get these contributions from? I suppose you go to old Whigs and Republicans. Any Democrats?"

"Why, Mr. Frederick," he answered, "some of the Democrats is my best contributors. They don't ask no questions neither, like Republicans does, about what I does with the money. The Judge says he's willing to help poor folks, but he don't want to hear no details."

"So the Judge contributes, does he? But I suppose you don't go near the Deputy Marshal? It is his business to arrest fugitives."

"That is just what he says to me, sir. He gave me a five dollar bill, and told me to keep out of his sight. Yes, sir, and I'se a-earning that money."

Van Zandt and "Uncle Tom's Cabin." John Van Zandt, who lived not far from Cincinnati, was an old farmer, poor and uneducated, but honest, worthy, and benevolent. He had passed the earlier part of his life in Kentucky; and from what he had seen and heard there, had become a hearty hater of slavery.

The Ohio River was well understood by slaves to be the dividing line between bondage and freedom; and many were led to cross that barrier by opportunity, courage, or despair. When any ragged trembling fugitive knocked at John Van Zandt's door, it was not in John Van Zandt's heart to refuse him food, shelter, and help on his way to Canada.

One night in April, 1842, nine poor wretches risked their lives in an attempt at liberty. Among them were a husband and wife, and three small children. They got across the river and as far as Walnut Hill, two miles beyond. Here they were met by John Van Zandt. He had been to the Cincinnati market, with a wagon load of farm produce, and was returning home. He heard their story, pitied them, told them to get into his now empty wagon, and decided to try to carry them toward Lebanon. At three o'clock in the morning the horses' heads were turned northward. One of the fugitives, who could drive, was intrusted with the reins; and the other eight huddled together in the wagon.

But there was money to be made on the highways, in those days in Ohio, and plenty of enterprising knaves ready to turn slave catchers. Early in the morning a gang of this class met the wagon, about fourteen miles north of Cincinnati. They knew nothing; suspected everything. They were armed, and they at once seized and stopped the horses. Andrew, the driver, had just time to jump and run. The others were obliged to surrender at discretion. Before long they were travelling back to slavery.

A futile attempt was made to punish the slave catchers, by indicting them for kidnapping. But public sentiment was on their side, and they walked out of court with the proud consciousness that they had "upheld the Constitution and laws," and made $450 by it.

Eight slaves had been recovered, but one had escaped. That "pound of flesh" was now to be exacted through the courts of the United States. Andrew's owner, Wharton Jones by name, brought suit against John Van Zandt.

Salmon P. Chase became Van Zandt's counsel. The case was tried before Judge McLean, at Cincinnati, in July, 1842. The jury brought in a verdict against Van Zandt for $1200 damages. A like verdict was rendered against him for $500 more, the penalty for violating the Fugitive Law of 1793.

Motion was made for a new trial and arrest of judgment. The judges of the Circuit Court were divided in opinion upon questions stated in the argument, and the cause was carried to the Supreme Court of the United States.

Van Zandt was poor, and could not meet the cost of the trial. But the case had begun to attract some attention, and a small amount was contributed by friends, though it proved not enough to cover the actual expenses of the case. My father was solicited to take part in conducting it, and cheerfully assented. Both he and Chase gave their services without compensation.

In their arguments before the court, they took the ground that the law of 1793 was in conflict with the Ordinance of 1787 under which Ohio was organized, and which enacted that slavery or involuntary servitude should never exist there. They held that the slave law was, so far as it affected the questions before the court, unconstitutional and void.

With their usual grave deliberation the judges took the case under consideration. But when the decision was finally promulgated, it was against Van Zandt. Judgment for the penalty was entered against him in the court below. Impoverished and embarrassed by the long litigation, he never recovered from its effects. He died a few

8

years later, probably without ever dreaming that the whole system of law under which he suffered would so soon be swept from the statute book.

When the "Compromise Measures" of 1850 were adopted by Congress, both the great parties formally gave them their approval in conventions, and the general public, weary of the long debate, acquiesced in them as being, however distasteful, at least a settlement of the long-standing controversy over slavery. Most of the measures were regarded with apathy if not approval, and with the hope of future peace between North and South.

But there was one of them that speedily dispelled any such illusion. That was the new Fugitive Slave Law. It added new pains and penalties to the law of 1793, already drastic enough; and it practically required every citizen to become a slave catcher, when called upon. Naturally, it raised a storm of indignation among the Northern people. Press and pulpit joined in denouncing it. Meetings were held to express abhorrence. Orators like Wendell Phillips anathematized it, and even the peaceful "Quaker poet" Whittier made it the theme of his impassioned verse.

Dr. Bailey, the editor of the *National Era*, an anti-slavery paper at Washington, of course devoted many columns to the subject. He asked Mrs. Harriet Beecher Stowe, already well-known in literary circles, to write something for the *Era*.

The theme was one that appealed to her sympathies. Her residence in Cincinnati had given her an insight into life in the slave States, in contrast with the free ones. Accordingly she contributed a story about fugitive slaves, basing some of the scenes and incidents upon those of the Van Zandt case, and others upon those of the life of Josiah Henson. In the story she portrayed Van Zandt as "Honest old John Van Trompe" and Uncle Si Henson as "Uncle Tom." The first chapters awakened interest, and created a demand for more. So *Uncle Tom's Cabin* was evolved, running serially in the *Era* for several months of 1851 and 1852.

Then it was published in book form in Boston. Among its earliest readers, of course, were Mr. Chase and my father. The former, as he laid down the volume, said: "That book is Van Zandt's best monument."

The publishers found the demand for the new novel steadily and rapidly growing. Every new phase of the political conflict over slavery added to the number of its readers. Soon it was read and talked of through all the North, and at last it began to be realized by the public that there was a romance destined to have world-wide fame, and to exert an influence upon history.

1857.

A Village of Louis XIV.'s Time. We are lying becalmed in the August sunshine, off the Isle d'Orléans in the river St. Lawrence, which here begins to broaden out to the dimensions of an inland sea. Our craft is the schooner *Emerence*, of Quebec, commanded by Captain Couillard de Beaumont.

Until quite recently she was a fishing schooner, but is now promoted to the dignity of a gentleman's yacht. Under the judicious direction of our friend, Mr. Dunscomb, the Collector of the Port, she has been scrubbed up, repaired, partially painted, and fully equipped, manned, and provisioned for a voyage to Anticosti and Labrador. She is rated at thirty tons—not much, but Columbus discovered a New World in a vessel not much larger.

She flies the British flag and has no other. She possesses a compass, but no sextant or chronometer, her officers not being familiar with scientific navigation, but depending on their native powers of observation to ascertain their position and reckoning.

The crew consists of three, who share the work about equally between them. They are M. le Capitaine, M. Pilot, and *cet homme*. The latter is the one who is always to blame, when anything is lost or goes wrong. As the *Emerence* has no cargo, they occupy the hold for their quarters. With them is John, the cook, who presides at the galley. He is able to fry the fish we catch, and to supplement them with slapjacks.

In the cabin there are three of us, my father, my wife, and myself. The cabin is only twelve feet square, with four berths in it. A table, a lamp, some camp-stools, comprise the rest of the furniture, and there is room for no more. As the cabin has no windows, but gets air and light only from the hatchway, most of our time is spent on deck.

Here we sit, chatting or reading, or studying the shore through the telescope lent us by the collector, with the help of the charts of the British Admiralty.

The shore is a puzzling one. It does not seem to have towns, with stretches of farm lands between, as one might expect, but rather looks like one long line of little white houses, now and then thickening up around each church spire. Our sailors tell us of their names. Here is St. Valier, yonder is St. Michel, farther on is St. Pierre, and largest of all is St. Thomas.

We decide to go ashore to inspect. M. le Capitaine and M. Pilot lower the boat and take the oars. *Cet homme* remains on board to watch the schooner.

Arrived at the wharf, the puzzle begins to unravel itself. There is one long road, or street, or boulevard, running through all the villages. Along this road stand the farmhouses at intervals of perhaps one hundred to two hundred feet.

But these long and narrow farms have a unique advantage. The family in each house enjoy the privileges of living both in the town and in the country at the same time. The owner may step out of his back door and walk a mile or two over his own domain, through his gardens, his fields, and his woods. Or, if he steps out of his front door, he is at once in town, within call of his neighbours, and within easy walking distance of shops, stores, offices, church, and school. His front windows look out upon the boulevard and the river. His back windows command an unbroken landscape, all the way back to the mountains.

Surely it was French ingenuity and taste that devised this simple plan of living at once *en ville* and *à la campagne*!

A quaint, old-fashioned inn, that looks as if it might have been transported bodily from Normandy, is near at hand. In the open doorway sits a comfortable looking dame, engaged in knitting, whose smile of welcome as we approach intimates that she is the hostess.

In reply to our inquiry, she responds in the tongue of the seventeenth century that assuredly we may have dinner, and fortunately it is at present the very hour.

A glance into the spacious apartment, which is at once parlour, dining-room, and kitchen, shows us the *pot-au-feu* simmering in the great stone fireplace, and the table spread in front of it. Few modern hotels have such conveniences for dining, and so close at hand. Under the windows the fruits and vegetables are growing, beyond is the well and the poultry yard, and beyond that is the St. Lawrence, stocked with the finest of fish.

When our repast of rural luxuries is finished, we inquire if any conveyance can be had for a drive. Madame thinks not. But yes, she has a nephew, a farmer living near, who has a horse which is old, but safe, and a cabriolet, which is so, also, and will enable us to view the *voisinage.* He shall be sent for.

This is done, and presently Pierre appears, with the reliable vehicle. He takes us up and down the road, and proves a cheerful and voluble conductor.

It is like one continuous village. Its different portions are named from their respective churches, but apparently there are no dividing lines to show how far each Saint claims jurisdiction. Pierre knows all the houses, and the names of their occupants—some of whom salute us from their vine-clad doorways.

Yes, he and all the rest of them were born here. Is there work for all? Work—plenty of it, that goes without saying. He himself cultivates his terrain. His brother Auguste owns the schooner, which carries the produce and the fish to the market at Quebec. Others have their farms, their shops and offices.

How about amusements? "Oh, at evening, all the world amuses itself after its own fashion. As may be seen, we live near our neighbours. We meet, we eat a little, drink a little. We sing, we dance, we play at games, we talk *politique* and hurrah for Papineau!"

"Doubtless," he adds, "Madame and the Messieurs would like to see the church? It is open all days, and the good Curé will be pleased to show it to them. A fine man—though he grows old, which is a pity."

So we call at his study. The good Curé comes out, hospitably invites us to enter. He shows us the mediæval-looking edifice, its altarpiece, statues, windows, and decorations, and tells us of their history, as well as that of the settlement and its people.

In the time of Louis XIV. and Louis XV., these lands were granted to great Seigneurs, who enjoyed favour at Court. They held them, according to old French custom, as lords and owners of the soil. They brought out from

France peasants and artisans to become their tenants. The land was divided into these long, narrow farms, so as to accommodate as many as possible.

All that is now changed, of course. The land-titles are now under the British common law. The inhabitants have multiplied, and own their homes. Villages have grown up. Manufactures and trade have come in. But the old subdivisions, to a considerable extent, remain, because they are found convenient, and sales are few.

We tell the good Curé that it seems to us an ideal plan for a rural community, and ask if the inhabitants appreciate it.

"Ah, yes, *le bon Dieu* has given them pleasant homes, and they are industrious, peaceable, and thrifty. We who are old know this, and are content to spend our lives here. But the young people! What would you? They must have change. They want to see the world and seek their fortunes. They go to Quebec, and Montreal, perhaps to Boston and New York, possibly to Paris, or to dig gold in California."

And they come back? — "A few of them, but not many."

Pierre then drives us on, past dwellings, shops, and warehouses, and pauses before the doors of the Female Seminary, a modern building with modern improvements, which is under the charge of gentle-voiced, dark-robed Sisters, having their chief house in Montreal.

They show us their airy and scrupulously neat rooms, and call up some of the pupils to display their proficiency. One bright-eyed girl surprises us by her brilliant rendering of *Landing of the Pilgrim Fathers*, accompanying herself at the piano.

When we ask where she is from, she replies, "Boston."

The Sister placidly remarks: "Yes, we have many from

the States, whose parents prefer our quiet ways and
healthful climate, and the kind of training the girls receive
here."

Our last visit is at a stately mansion, the summer residence of Colonel Tacher, a member of the Royal Council,
whom we had previously met. He welcomes us with
courteous hospitality, and gives us further information
as to the origin and history of the province. When he
learns that our destination is "Labrador," he laughingly
remarks that we are more venturesome than most Canadians, in visiting that wild and far-away region, so little
known save for its fish and furs.

Once more on board the *Emerence*, we look back to
the scene of Arcadian simplicity we have just left. One
wonders that nobody has ever thought of adopting such
a plan for some one of the villages we are constantly
building in the United States. Our senior member says
that the explanation is not far to seek. "These were
Frenchmen, and we are Americans. They inherit habits
that are the growth of centuries. We like to change ours
every year or two. Fifty years from now, many of their
characteristic traits will have passed away and they will
be like the rest of the world."

Anticosti. "Anticosti?" said the skipper, who was
our guest, setting down his glass of Jamaica rum and
water, "yes, I know it. Cruise all round it. Bad coast.
Dangerous. Reefs and shallows everywhere."

"Not an easy place to get to, then?"

"It's a devilish sight easier to get to Anticosti, than it
is to get away from it. Squalls and cross currents sometimes get you ashore there before you know it. If
you're out for pleasure, you'd better give Anticosti a
wide berth."

"Anybody living there?"

"Nobody but the people at the wrecking station. They have to stay."

"What is the interior like?"

"Sort of wilderness or desert, I guess. The government leases the island out, though, to folks who want to hunt or fish there in summer. Lots of game there, they say, and shoals of fish."

"Pretty good whaling ground in these waters, isn't it? Two came up close to our bows, one morning, and our lookout yelled, thinking they would stave us in."

The captain of the whaler here joins in the dialogue.

"Why, I struck a fine one a week or so ago out here a way, a big fellow, and then lost him."

"How did that happen?"

"Sea was rough, and he ran away with so much of my line that it looked like he'd pull us under. Had to cut the line and let him go, and then had a two-mile pull back to the ship. I calculate he's floating around dead somewhere, with my harpoon in him."

"Think you killed him?"

"I know I struck him good, and that harpoon's in him yet. Somebody will pick him up."

"Who does he belong to, if he is found?"

"He'll belong to me, if I can get a sight at him, and I'll prove it by my harpoon. If you happen to run across him on your cruise, you'll know him by that."

This conversation takes place in August, 1857, at Mingan in Labrador. A week later, we have bid adieu to Labrador and its navigation and are slowly beating our way, against a head wind, up the St. Lawrence toward Quebec.

Four days elapse with the wind still "dead ahead." Then suddenly it rises to a gale, and our captain decides to put about, and run before it for a harbour.

We are swept back in an afternoon over the miles we

had so tediously gained, until at 7 o'clock in the evening
we see before us a long blue line, which our seamen tell
us is the dreaded coast of Anticosti.

But the wind falls now, almost as suddenly as it arose,
and we are left in a dead calm. We are powerless to
reach an anchorage and have to lie outside all night,
rolling in a heavy ground swell.

In the morning the "head wind" rises again, but this
time very gently and softly. Captain Beaumont thinks
we may be able to get in far enough to find an anchorage, and to replenish our water cask and supply of wood
for the galley.

"Is there any harbour?"

"No good one, but this is Ellis Bay, which I know. It
is where they have the wrecking station. The *Emerence*
is light, with no cargo, and can make it."

So we let the wind blow us where it listeth. Evidently
we are to visit Anticosti, like some other folks, whether
we will or no. The wind carries us smoothly over the
quiet sea. The bay opens before us, broad and spacious and shallow. Skilful handling of helm and sails
take us between reefs and over bars, although the sandy
bottom sometimes seems to come perilously near our
keel.

We are still two miles from shore when Captain Beaumont thinks it prudent to drop anchor.

The scene looks wild and desolate. But there seems
to be another vessel already at anchor in the bay—a
schooner, rather larger than our own.

The bay is semicircular and broad, surrounded by a
sandy beach, interspersed here and there with jagged
rocks. The woods come nearly down to the water's edge.
Behind them rises a range of low hills.

We conclude to row over to the other schooner, and to
ask for some fresh cod, mackerel, or the like. On getting

alongside, we accost the prominent person on board, and ask him what his schooner is engaged in.

"I am a Jack-of-all-trades, sir," he answers, "confined to no one thing."

"Are you an American?"

"No, I belong to the island."

"Fishing for mackerel now, I suppose?"

"No, I am the lessee of the island. I set out last week for Quebec, but on the way I fell in with a pretty large whale, and he being too heavy for my boat to manage, I towed him in here into shoal water, and am now cutting him up and getting out the oil."

Sure enough, we can see a great, greyish mass lying close to the water's edge, and can discern figures of men moving actively over it and hacking at it. A strong, almost sickening greasy smell comes off from it, and the smoke is rising from several fires along the beach.

As we row back, the lady member of our party remarks that this is probably our friend Captain Coffin's lost whale. We dissent but she replies that the proprietor of Anticosti took care to avoid claiming to have killed or even found the whale alive. But what do women know about whaling?

A long pull across the bay brings us to the vicinity of the stranded leviathan. He is sixty-five feet long—ten feet longer than the *Emerence*. The extreme end of the tail is seventeen feet wide. The odour of the oil infects the atmosphere for a mile around it. A dozen persons are cutting the "blubber" into small pieces, from which the oil gushes out, and fills kettles, pots, and barrels. Nothing is heard, seen, touched, or smelt of that is not redolent of the great prize.

We land at a respectful distance from the whale's carcass and endeavour to get "betwixt the wind and his nobility."

There are wooden signs along the shore for the benefit of castaways, which indicate the paths to the place of refuge.   This is not far distant.   It is a neat, substantial, but rough-looking wooden building, unpainted and without any attempt at architectural decoration.   It has a good chimney, but otherwise might pass for a barn or shed.

The keeper, a Canadian Frenchman, is gratified to find that we are not in distress, and need nothing, unless we can get a good "shore dinner."

This he promises us, and says there is a room or two in the station fitted up with simple furniture, which are reserved for the use of hunters or visitors like ourselves.

We promptly avail ourselves of these.   Even such quarters look luxurious after the schooner's cabin.   The bare board walls have been covered by the Frenchman with pages of the London *Illustrated News*, ingeniously pasted on, so that the lodger lying on the bed can see all the leading events of the world's history for the past year or two, spread before him like a panorama.

Then we stroll out to look at the farm.   There are fifty acres—the only land reclaimed from nature on the island of Anticosti.   There is or was a potato crop, but it was blighted by frost on August 18th.

There is a suggestive feature about the door of the house.   It is not near the ground, but high up, and entrance to it is gained by a ladder.   At night this ladder is drawn up, to prevent incursions by bears, wolves, and other midnight marauders.

There are other lodgers in the house besides ourselves. The Frenchman refers to them as "the people upstairs" but does not mention who they are.   Occasionally a lady appears in the balcony, or descends from it with her children, and we soon come to understand that she is a privileged person.

At length tea-time comes.   The lady from upstairs is

introduced to us by the lessee of Anticosti as his wife, and here the patroon and his family spend the summer. He is a Scotchman, of pleasing address and well-informed. His wife is agreeable and ladylike.

The conversation, of course, turns on the great prize. We cautiously tell him how Captain Coffin of Gaspé had called on us, at Mingan, to enquire about a whale that he had killed and lost, and we laughingly remark that some of us were simple enough to imagine that this might possibly be Captain Coffin's whale.

He inquires the date of Captain Coffin's report, about the harpoon, etc., and very frankly and magnanimously says: "Beyond a doubt this is the very whale that he killed. We found it dead and horribly mangled by sharks."

He has found nothing so far to show how it came to its death, but perhaps he may yet find the harpoon.

In the course of the afternoon, the Frenchman informs us that he is going lobster fishing and asks if we would like to accompany him.

"Where are we to go?"

He points to a series of huge boulders in the water near the opposite shore, about two miles off.

"Very well. How do we get there? Do we walk round on the beach?"

"Oh, no,—ride."

"Do we row out?"

"Oh, no, we ride in a cart."

"Which road?"

"Right across through the water."

See us then, we two travellers, our host, and a driver, embarked on the bay in a common cart, drawn by a strong, square-built black horse. On he walks, splash—splash— and we after him. He understands French well, and obeys all such commands as *Allez donc*, and *Marchez*, but pays no regard to English.

At length we reach the fishing ground. Two great seals are mounted on the rocks, like sentinels guarding the entrance to the port. The Frenchman takes his stick, to which is attached a codfish hook, and proceeds to ferret out the lobsters in their retreats under the rocks. He finds one or two under every rock. They cling to the stones, or whatever else offers, so tenaciously that often their claws break off. The horse wades from rock to rock with patience, and in less than an hour we fill our basket with two dozen.

Returning, we share our catch with the patroon's family, and in return they supply us with mustard, oil, and vinegar for lobster salad, in which our ship stores are deficient.

We spend the evening pleasantly with Mr. Corbet and his wife. He informs us further as to the tenure of his "Seigneury." In Canada, successive provincial legislation, with the sanction of the Crown, has modified these "Seigneuries," so that, in that region, they have now little more than a nominal existence.

But the "Seigneuries" of Labrador and Anticosti still remain. Those regions, not only being in a state of nature, but there being no desire anywhere to colonize them, because they are so inhospitable and barren, the "Seigneury" is at present valuable only for the chase and the fisheries; and it might be made so for mines, forests, and minerals.

The "Seigneurs" (successors to the old grantees) are understood to live at Quebec. They rent or assign all their privileges to assignees for terms of years, at fixed rates. The Hudson's Bay Company is the assignee of Labrador. Mr. Corbet is the assignee of Anticosti. He pays five hundred dollars a year for the whole enjoyment of that domain one hundred and twenty miles long by twenty broad, and he reimburses himself out of the fisheries, chiefly salmon and seal, and the chase, principally of

bears, sables, martens, foxes, etc. There is no government
there; but for political purposes the territory is subject
to the laws of Canada.

Mrs. Corbet inquires if we do not find the odour of
the whale almost unbearable, as she does.

But Mr. Corbet holds up his hands and smiles.   He
says: "We are making money, my dear, making money."

And so he undoubtedly is, this time.

Another day, and at last the wind has "hauled round"
to the south-east. We bid adieu to Anticosti and its
kindly inhabitants, and in the evening set sail once more for
Quebec. It is a soft, balmy, starlit night, with a gentle
breeze wafting us on even keel over a calm sea. Our
easterly wind next brings us its usual accessories of mist
and fog. Three days elapse, in which the fog seems to
grow denser. We seem to be moving in a magic circle
of sea, perhaps two hundred feet in diameter. Above
and below and all around is the fog, apparently moving
with us. Nothing else is visible.

Our whereabouts becomes a matter of guesswork.
There are no landmarks. There is no opportunity for an
"observation," even if we had the instruments to make
one. We know by the compass that we are heading for
Quebec, and we know we are still on the open sea, for we
are out of soundings.

Our captain and pilot do not seem worried over the
situation. They are not apprehending collisions, for
they say the steamers cannot run in this fog, and that
the sailing craft, if moving at all, are going in the same
direction as ourselves.

But this easy confidence receives a shock. At half-
past two in the morning, while we are still in the impenetrable fog and going as rapidly as before, there is a crash,
and the helmsman cries out in wild consternation for
"All hands on deck."

There is hurrying backward and forward, shouting and unintelligible orders about sails, some French profanity and an unmistakable volley of British oaths coming down from somewhere above us, in the darkness; which presently drifts away and grows fainter in the distance.

Our ship's lanterns are brought into active requisition to find out what has happened. The schooner proves to be all safe and sound, except that a piece about two feet long has been broken off the end of our bowsprit. It looks very much as if we have run into some ship lying at anchor, with happily no worse results.

Warned by this experience, we proceed now under shortened sail, and at a slower rate. Is it the same day, or the next one, when, toward noon, we are suddenly startled by the loud report of a cannon, seemingly close at hand! The pilot's face is at once beaming with smiles. He says:

"It is Bic!"

So he knows where we are. We ask where and what is Bic. We learn that it is an island where the government has a lighthouse and a fogbell, and, at intervals of a few minutes, fire a cannon, as a warning to mariners. We have not seen the light, nor heard the fogbell, but we could not help hearing the cannon. So we drop anchor at once.

When the fog lifts, as after a while it does, with the swiftness of raising a curtain, we find we are in a spacious harbour, surrounded by a whole fleet of vessels, steamers and sailing craft, which, like ourselves, have sought shelter under the protecting care of Bic. We are out of the Gulf and well up the river, and have come in the fog nearly two hundred miles from Anticosti.

Napoleon III and Eugènie at Compiègne. My father's visit to Europe in 1859 has been described in the published extracts from his letters. But the story of one of the most interesting days of that journey is not told there. A subsequent conversation of his with M. Drouyn de l'Huys gives the narration here.

"Then you were in France before you were Secretary of State, were you not, Mr. Seward?"

"Yes," he replied, "being in the Senate and a member of the Committee on Foreign Relations, I came to Europe in 1859, to study the strength and disposition of the nations with whom we had important questions, and in a possible contingency, might have critical ones."

"Whom did you see in Paris?"

"I met and saw much of Count Walewski and other members of the Imperial Government."

"Walewski had charge of foreign affairs at that time, did he not?"

"Yes, I first saw him on his day for giving audiences to the ambassadors of foreign Powers. We were shown into a fine hall embellished with pictures and statuary peculiar to the Empire. Over the mantel was a very large picture commemorating the Treaty of Paris, which closed the Russian War. I recognized at once in this the British Minister, Lord Clarendon. The most important figure was, however, that of the French Secretary of State.

"I saw at once that it was the likeness of the first Napoleon softened and made agreeable. When I asked who that was, I was surprised by the answer that it was Count Walewski. I remarked the strange resemblance to the Napoleon head. The answer was that Walewski was the son of a Polish lady, with no acknowledged father, and that he was usually believed to be the natural son of Napoleon I. He was a very intelligent and engaging man. He conversed freely, and I learned the imperial dynasty at that time had no special fear of England's

9

policy. It was feeling very strong. I was introduced there to Lord Cowley and all the foreign ministers, and found the state of Europe was the subject of much anxiety. Lord Cowley spoke of his sister, Lady Bulwer, whom we had known in Washington when Sir Henry Bulwer was the British Minister there."

"When was it that you saw the Emperor?"

"Some time afterward he invited me to visit him at Compiègne, and I spent a day there."

"Pray tell us of that visit."

"I arrived at the palace about ten o'clock, and was ushered into the antechamber, filled with clerks, writing and recording orders for the special departments of Paris. Presently an officer came to say that the Emperor would receive me in his private room.

"It was a chilly morning, and he was warming himself before an open fire. He sat down immediately, after shaking hands with me, and expressed himself glad to see me in France. He asked some questions in regard to my travelling experiences, which led me to give a humorous turn to some incident which had befallen me. After a laugh together over this, he suddenly asked me what the people of the United States thought of his administration. I replied: 'Your Majesty may well imagine that the people of the United States think better of your administration than they expected to when it began!'

"Then we talked on. He was not merely courteous but genial. We talked on political subjects everywhere but in France. We talked fast and freely. It seemed difficult to find a subject on which we could differ, or which he did not discuss wisely. He asked my opinion of the European statesmen whom I had met, and inquired who had impressed me most.

"I told him Count Cavour in Italy, the Emperor Francis Joseph in Austria, and Gladstone in England. Recalling the incident of our having met once before, in 1837, at the house of Chancellor Kent in New York, the Emperor expressed a high admiration for the United States, and said that owing to the extreme illness of his mother he was obliged to return to Europe without having seen Washington, which he much regretted.

"A door opened, and a lady, graceful and pensively beautiful, entered. The Emperor arose and said: 'The Empress.' She glided lightly toward the table, gave me her hand, and sat down. She asked me a courteous question about my arrival; and the Emperor told her that I had a good story about one of my adventures, and insisted that I should tell it to her. Whereupon we laughed ourselves into a perfect agreement. The Empress asked me: 'Which party do you belong to? Mr. Mason, the American Minister here, is on the Southern side. Do you agree with him?'

"I answered: 'That is the government side at home, but I must avow, in frankness to your Majesty, that my political position is so boldly defined there that I am called an Abolitionist.'

" 'I like you for that. I dislike slavery so much.'

"After speaking these impulsive words her countenance showed embarrassment, and on turning to the Emperor I saw that she had received from him, by a look, an admonition against imprudence.

" 'Never mind, Madame,' said I, 'there is no harm done. While I thank you for your ingenuousness, what you have said shall not be repeated.

" 'And perhaps I must ask a great favour from your Majesties. John Brown has just been captured and imprisoned at Harpers Ferry, charged with high treason against Virginia. Although I had no knowledge whatever of the transaction, the Democratic party charge me with complicity in the crime, and the *New York Herald* announces that the Emperor will be required to surrender me as a fugitive from justice, and so I may be obliged to ask your Majesties not to give me up.'

"Both the Emperor and Empress laughingly assured me of their protection.

After breakfast a large company gathered in a salon. Of course the imperial infant, son and heir, was brought in, and received compliments and caresses all around.

" 'Mr. Seward, you must see my little boy,' said the Empress. She put his little hand in mine, and he repeated after her: 'How do you do, Mr. Seward?'

"Shortly after, the Emperor brought the child to me and said: 'I desire to show you my son.'

"The same salutation having passed again, I took the beautiful boy in my arms and said: 'It will do the Prince no harm to receive a kiss from an old man, although he is a republican.' The Emperor smiled and cordially approved.

"The Emperor went to the chase with a party of gentlemen, and I joined the Empress's party in a drive through the magnificent forests.

"When, later, the guests had retired before dinner, and I was waiting for my train, the Emperor remained conversing with me in the salon, giving me the plan and full particulars of the changes he was making in Paris, and pointing out various localities on a map of Louis XVI.'s time. In the midst of this conversation, he stopped to inquire of me about Niagara, and asked if it could be true that Blondin proposed to walk on a wire across the river. I told him that I had just learned from an American newspaper that the feat had been accomplished.

"I brought away from Compiègne very pleasant memories of the kindly expressions and greetings received there.

And I learned then that the chief, the ruling, thought of the Imperial Government was, how to frame a policy which should render the Napoleonic dynasty safe and perpetuate it."

PART II

During the War

The Baltimore Plot. In February, 1861, Mr. Lincoln
was on his way to Washington. Leaving Illinois on the
11th, he and his friends were making a journey necessarily
protracted by the receptions and ovations which the
people were eager to tender to the newly elected President.
Newspapers chronicled the incidents of his trip, the public
greetings at Indianapolis, Columbus, and Pittsburgh,
and the preparations for his welcome at New York,
Philadelphia, and Baltimore.

About noon on Thursday, the 21st, I was in the gallery
of the Senate Chamber when one of the pages touched my
arm, and told me that Senator Seward wished to see me
immediately. Going down I met him in the lobby.
He said that he had received a note from General Scott
and Colonel Stone, communicating information that
seemed of grave import and requiring immediate attention. He handed me a letter which he had just written
to Mr. Lincoln, enclosing the note from General Scott.
He said:

"Whether this story is well founded or not, Mr. Lincoln
ought to know of it at once. But I know of no reason
to doubt it. General Scott is impressed with the belief
that the danger is real. Colonel Stone has facilities for

knowing, and is not apt to exaggerate. I want you to go by the first train. Find Mr. Lincoln wherever he is.

"Let no one else know your errand. I have written him that I think he should change his arrangements, and pass through Baltimore at a different hour. I know it may occasion some embarrassment, and perhaps some ill-natured talk. Nevertheless, I would strongly advise him to do it."

The train, a tedious one, brought me into Philadelphia about ten o'clock at night. I had learned from the newspapers, and the conversation of my fellow-passengers, that the party of the President-elect would spend the night at the Continental Hotel, where he would be serenaded.

Arriving at the hotel, I found Chestnut Street crowded with people, gay with lights, and echoing with music and cheering. Within, the halls and stairways were packed, and the brilliantly lighted parlours were filled with ladies and gentlemen who had come to "pay their respects." A burst of animated conversation pervaded the throng, and in its centre presentations to the President-elect appeared to be going on. Clearly, this was no time for the delivery of a confidential message. I turned into a room near the head of the stairway, which had been pointed out as that of Mr. Robert Lincoln. He was surrounded by a group of young friends. On my introducing myself, he met and greeted me with courteous warmth, and then called to Colonel Ward H. Lamon, who was passing, and introduced us to each other. Colonel Lamon, taking me by the arm, proposed at once to go back into the parlour to present me to Mr. Lincoln. On my telling him that I wanted my interview to be as private and to attract as little attention as possible, the Colonel laughed and said:

"Then I think I had better take you to his bedroom. If you don't mind waiting there, you'll be sure to meet him, for he has got to go there sometime tonight, and it is the only place I know of where he will be likely to be alone."

This was the very opportunity I desired. Thanking the Colonel, I sat and waited for an hour or more in the quiet room that was in such contrast to the bustle outside. Presently Colonel Lamon called me, and we met Mr. Lincoln, who was coming down the hall. I had never before seen him; but the campaign portraits had made his face quite familiar. I could not but notice how accurately they had copied his features, and how totally they had omitted his careworn look, and his pleasant, kindly smile.

After a few words of friendly greeting, with inquiries about my father and matters in Washington, he sat down by the table under the gas light to peruse the letter I had brought. Although its contents were of a somewhat startling nature he made no exclamation, and I saw no sign of surprise in his face. After reading it carefully through, he again held it to the light, and deliberately read it through a second time. Then, after musing a moment, he looked up and asked:

"Did you hear anything about the way this information was obtained? Do you know anything about how they got it?"

No, I had known nothing in regard to it, till that morning when called down by my father from the Senate gallery.

"Your father and General Scott do not say who they think are concerned in it. Do you think they know?"

On that point, too, I could give no additional information further than my impression that my father's knowledge was limited to what had been communicated to him by Colonel Stone, in whose statements he had implicit confidence.

"Did you hear any names mentioned? Did you, for instance, ever hear anything said about such a name as Pinkerton?"

No, I had heard no such name in connection with the matter,—no name at all, in fact, except those of General Scott and Colonel Stone.

He thought a moment, and then said:

"I may as well tell you why I ask. There were stories or rumours some time ago, before I left home, about people who were intending to do me a mischief. I never attached much importance to them—never wanted to believe any such thing. So I never would do anything about them, in the way of taking precautions and the like. Some of my friends, though, thought differently—Judd and others—and without my knowledge they employed a detective to look into the matter. It seems he has occasionally reported what he found, and only today, since we arrived at this house, he brought this story, or something similar to it, about an attempt on my life in the confusion and hurly-burly of the reception at Baltimore."

"Surely, Mr. Lincoln," said I, "that is a strong corroboration of the news I bring you."

He smiled and shook his head.

"That is exactly why I was asking you about names. If different persons, not knowing of each other's work, have been pursuing separate clues that led to the same result, why then it shows there may be something in it. But if this is only the same story, filtered through two channels, and reaching me in two ways, then that don't make it any stronger. Don't you see?"

The logic was unanswerable. But I asserted my strong belief that the two investigations had been conducted independently of each other, and urged that there was enough of probability to make it prudent to adopt the suggestion, and make the slight change in hour and train which would avoid all risk.

After a little further discussion of the subject, Mr. Lincoln rose and said:

"Well, we haven't got to decide it tonight, anyway, and I see it's getting late."

Then, noticing that I looked disappointed at his reluctance to regard the warning, he said kindly:

"You need not think I will not consider it well. I shall think it over carefully, and try to decide it right; and I will let you know in the morning."

At the breakfast table the next day I found the morning papers announced that Mr. Lincoln had risen early, in order to go over to Independence Hall to attend the flag raising there on Washington's Birthday. They gave also a report of his remarks there. One sentence in these had a deeper meaning than his audience guessed. Adverting to the principle embodied in the Declaration of Independence, he said: "If this country cannot be saved without giving up that principle, I was about to say, I would rather be assassinated on this spot than surrender it."

Shortly after breakfast, Colonel Lamon met me in the hall, and, taking me aside, said that Mr. Lincoln had concluded to do as he had been advised. He would change his plan so as to pass through Baltimore at a different hour from that announced. I hastened to the telegraph office, and sent to my father a word previously agreed upon; on receiving which he would understand that his advice had been taken.

Accordingly, he was at the railroad station in Washington on Saturday morning, with E. B. Washburne of Illinois, when Mr. Lincoln and Colonel Lamon, very much to the surprise of the bystanders, got out of the night train from Philadelphia.

After breakfast, my father introduced him to the President and Cabinet, and then went with him to call on General Scott. Rooms had been taken for the President-elect at Willard's Hotel, and most of the afternoon was passed in receiving visits from his friends, the members of Congress, and of the Peace Conference. Mingled with the expressions of gratification at meeting him, was an undertone of regret that it should have been deemed necessary or wise to make the hasty night trip through Baltimore. This was natural enough. The time had not yet come when Americans in general could realize that a crime at once so nefarious and so foolish as the assassination of the Chief Magistrate was possible.

Mr. Lincoln himself, conversing with his friend Leonard Swett, intimated that, while he had been impressed by the Pinkerton warning, yet he had about made up his mind not to be influenced by it, unsupported as it was by any other evidence. When, later in the evening, I arrived with the letters from my father, General Scott, and Colonel Stone, resulting from a different investigation, it became manifest to him that at least the matter had too much importance to be disregarded.

So he made his quiet entry into the national capital by the night train—thus defeating the plans of the conspirators to attack him in the tumult expected to follow the arrival of his train in Baltimore at noon.

The Old State Department. "Your nomination was confirmed in the Senate today. So you are now the Assistant Secretary of State," said Senator Sumner, looking in, with a smile on his usually grave face. "No objection was made, and you will be able to enter upon your duties tomorrow."

Accordingly I walked over to the historic old building in the morning, took the oath of office, and began my work.

In Major L'Enfant's original plan of Washington there were four buildings, all just alike, at the four corners of the square devoted to the grounds and groves surrounding the Executive Mansion. They were for the four departments, of State, Treasury, War, and Navy. They were substantial modest brick edifices, without architectural ornament, except a lofty portico, with white columns, on the north side of each, covering its principal entrance.

The revenues and expenditures of the new Republic soon began to exceed all expectations; and the Treasury Department was torn down to give place to a much more spacious and pretentious structure, having a long colonnade on 15th Street. The War and Navy establishments also outgrew their quarters, but their buildings were still standing, and were supplemented by additional ones rented on the adjoining streets, for bureaus and clerks. Only the State Department retained its original dimensions; for the whole number of its officials in Washington hardly amounted to a hundred men. It had a certain stately dignity, enhanced by the remembrance of what had transpired within its grey walls in the course of seventy years.

Here the foreign relations of the United States were conducted for the greater part of the first century of the nation. Here were kept the archives and the correspondence with all foreign governments, and here were prepared the instructions, replies, and treaties, which were to determine the nation's foreign policy.

From here Oliver Ellsworth and his colleagues were sent out to make the treaty with Talleyrand which averted a threatened war with France. From here Jefferson sent the first written President's Message to Congress. Here Madison prepared the instructions to Robert R. Livingston as Minister at Paris, to guide him in negotiating the purchase of the great Louisiana territory.

Here Decatur and Preble were instructed to break up the piracy of the Barbary powers, to release the captives, and make an end of the tribute. From here Monroe and Pinckney set out to try to stop the impressment of American seamen and the seizure of American ships by the British navy. From here emanated Jefferson's proclamation, ordering all British men-of-war out of American waters. Here Secretary Monroe gave the British Minister his passports, and President Madison proclaimed the war with England. Here, soon after, came the Russian envoy to offer friendly mediation in the conflict, and from here, soon after that, Henry Clay and his colleagues went out to effect the restoration of peace by the Treaty of Ghent. From here was promulgated the celebrated "Monroe Doctrine," that this continent was to be thenceforward free from European dictation. Here John Quincy Adams concluded the treaty with Spain for the acquisition of Florida. From here went out the recognition of the independence of Mexico and the South American republics. Here Lafayette was welcomed; and from here Harrison bore greetings to Bolivar. Here was penned General Jackson's message denouncing nullification by South Carolina. Here Webster concluded his treaty with Lord Ashburton settling all boundary and extradition disputes with Great Britain. And here he made his famous declaration that "Every merchant vessel on the high seas is rightfully considered part of the territory to which it belongs." From here Secretary Calhoun, on the night before President Tyler's retirement from office, sent out a messenger offering annexation to Texas. Here Secretary Buchanan drafted the treaty of peace with Mexico, and from here went out Polk's proclamation of the new treaty of Guadelupe-Hidalgo and the acquisition of California and, New Mexico. Here Clayton heard the knell of his political hopes, when the bell over his head began to toll for the death of General Taylor. From here went forth the invitation to Kossuth, then exiled in Turkey, to come to the United States on board an American frigate. Here were framed the instructions and treaty through which Commodore Perry was to open Japan to American commerce. Here Marcy penned his celebrated dispatch in the Koszta case, maintaining the rights of American citizenship. And here President and Queen exchanged congratulations, in the first messages that ever went over the Atlantic cable.

Now, in the beginning of 1861, the State Department was in a condition of suspended animation. The Secretary of State, General Cass, had resigned, on account of a difference of opinion with President Buchanan. The Assistant Secretary of State, Mr. Trescott, had gone home to South Carolina, to take part in her secession from the Union. The Attorney-General, Mr. Black, was in nominal charge of the office but exercising few of its functions. The actual head of affairs departmental was Mr. William Hunter, the Chief Clerk.

Fortunately he was admirably equipped for that work. Appointed in his youth to a clerkship in the Department by John Quincy Adams, he had passed the greater part of his life within its walls, under different secretaries, through successive administrations, and rising by successive promotions from the lowest to the highest rank. He took no part in partisan conflicts. His loyalty to the Union was undoubted. His allegiance and fidelity were to the Government. So every secretary trusted him and depended on him. He was a walking encyclopædia of the decisions and precedents and questions arising out of our foreign relations. Of course he was familiarly acquainted with the personnel of the Department and of the diplomatic corps, past and present. Conversing fluently in French and Spanish, he was an excellent medium for intercourse with the foreign representatives,—most of whom liked to have a private unofficial interview with Mr. Hunter, when they were not sure whether their carefully studied English would correspond with the customary American idioms. His functions had gradually come to be very like those of the permanent Under Secretary in the British Foreign Office, a post held for years by Sir Julian Pauncefote and by other eminent diplomatists.

The stern dislike of our forefathers toward monarchy and titles of nobility found expression in our Constitution and laws. The President was to be simply "The President," not "His Majesty" nor "His Highness" nor even "His Excellency." No titles of nobility or decorations were to be granted. We were to have no ambassadors, or field marshals, or lord high admirals. We were to be represented abroad by ministers and chargés. In the departments, those high dignitaries known at European courts as lord high chancellors, lord high treasurers, and other lordships and excellencies were shorn of such distinctions, and even the keeper of the seal and clerk of the rolls and such important officers were described in the statute books as "1st, 2d, 3d, and 4th class clerks." So the officials of the State Department, many of whom had occupied responsible diplomatic positions and discharged important functions, were relegated to that democratic level.

Ever since General Jackson's time there had been usually almost a clean sweep of department officials after each Presidential election, on the ground that "to the victors belong the spoils." Active partisans received the offices as their rewards. But it was soon learned that the Department of State must be made an exception to that rule, unless we were ready to sacrifice all the tact and experience gained by long service in diplomacy, of which we needed as much as any European Power. So many officers of the Department represented successive administrations, and some had a record of ten, twenty, or thirty years' service.

On the morning after his appointment to be Secretary of State, my father sent for Mr. Hunter, and requested that a complete list of all the officers, clerks, and employees should be brought to him. Then inquiry was made as to which ones were trustworthy and loyal to the Union and which were disaffected or openly disloyal. It was not difficult to select them, for Washington had so long been a Southern city and so many of its officials were in sympathy with the Secessionists, that outspoken disunion sentiments were freely avowed. In fact all the departments contained many whom it was believed only remained in order to use their positions to give aid or information to the opponents of the Government.

The new Secretary of State promptly dismissed all except those whose fidelity to the Union was undoubted. Then he informed Mr. Hunter he should make no further inquiry or discrimination in regard to past party affiliations, but should expect all who remained to act with him in zealously maintaining and upholding the Federal Union.

The good results of this policy were immediately apparent, and continued throughout the period of the Civil War. Faithful and zealous service was rendered by all. No duty was neglected, no state secrets betrayed, and no removal ever found necessary. In fact most of the State Department clerks remained at their desks during the time of Presidents Lincoln, Johnson, Grant, and Hayes, several being promoted to higher diplomatic or departmental work.

A year or two after the close of the Civil War, it was decreed that the old department building should be pulled down to give place to more spacious and imposing edifices. While the demolition was going on, and we were occupying temporary quarters on 14th Street, Mr. Cox of the Disbursing Office called to present a mahogany cane to the Secretary of State.

"This cane, Mr. Secretary," said he, "has been in the hands of every President of the United States since Washington, of every Vice-President, of every Minister sent abroad and every foreign representative sent here by any foreign Power, of every cabinet officer in every administration, as well as in the hands of every Senator and member of Congress who has been at all prominent in government affairs."

"Your tale rather taxes one's credulity, Mr. Cox. What is this remarkable cane that you offer me?"

"It is one, Mr. Secretary, that has been carved out of the handrail of the stairway in the old Department of State, which all visitors have used on their way to the Secretary's room."

The cane is now preserved at Auburn.

The Month of Suspense. When Mr. Lincoln had been peaceably inaugurated, it seemed to many both at the North and the South that the worst was now over. There had been no riot or tumult. All was decorous and orderly. True, there were several States that declared themselves "seceded"; but State after State during the winter had "gone out," and nothing had happened. They had made no hostile demonstration, and none had been made towards them. There was a popular feeling that the "seceded" States would simply hold aloof from participating in public affairs, maintain an attitude of sullen defiance, coupled with preparations for military defence, and so would await or make overtures of readjustment.

The people of the North were incredulous of Southern

threats. That any one should actually make war upon the general government was to them hardly imaginable. Besides there was no immediate reason or provocation. The Republican party had declared that it had no intention of interfering with slavery in the States, and there was now no Territorial issue. The Republican President had been elected and inaugurated, but he was powerless to act while Congress was opposed to him. Furthermore it was known that there were many differences of opinion among the Northern people. Numerous public men and bodies had declared that it was "unconstitutional" for the Federal Government to "coerce a sovereign State." Many of the Northern Democrats were believed to be in sympathy with the South and with slavery; while it was well known that there were many stanch Union men in the Southern States.

There were three points on which public interest was centred, Fort Sumter, Fort Pickens, and the State of Viriginia.

Fort Sumter, in Charleston harbour, was claimed by South Carolinians as legitimately belonging to the State, although held by a small Federal garrison. They announced that they would allow it to be neither reinforced nor supplied, and they were diligently erecting batteries and throwing up earthworks around it, to prevent any succour from reaching it. They confidently hoped that the little garrison would soon be starved out or surrender.

Fort Pickens, on the coast of Florida, had also a small garrison, which the Secessionists hoped to capture by the simple expedient of taking the men, one by one, on a writ of *habeas corpus* before a neighbouring judge, by whom, on one pretext or another, they were promptly discharged from the United States military service. So the garrison was slowly but effectively reduced.

Meanwhile the State of Virignia was holding a convention at which the disunionists were hoping to pass an ordinance of secession. The Union men, however, claimed a majority. If Virginia refused to pass the ordinance and remained in the Union, the revolution would be shorn of its proportions, whereas if she sided with the rebellion, Maryland would follow, and all the slave States would be united. This, it was held, would convince the North of the utter hopelessness of subjugating so vast a territory, covering nearly half of the Union.

All the energies of the disunionists were put forth therefore to acquire Virginia. It was confidently believed, however, at the North, that the disunion leaders were in a minority, though a very active and persevering one. The disunionists themselves insisted that their policy meant peace, not war, for all the free States, even if united, could not hope to conquer all the slaveholding ones. While the debates in the Virginian convention thus dragged along, the leaders cast about for means to "fire the Southern heart," and so secure a "united South."

On his way home from St. John's Church, the first Sunday after his arrival in Washington, Mr. Lincoln had said to my father: "Governor Seward, there is one part of my work that I shall have to leave largely to you. I shall have to depend upon you for taking care of these matters of foreign affairs, of which I know so little, and with which I reckon you are familiar."

President Lincoln now had set about his laborious duties in good faith, and the first shape in which they presented themselves to him was in the swarm of office-seekers that beleaguered the White House, filling all the halls, corridors, and offices from morning till night. The patient good humour and the democratic habits of the new President led him to give audience to everybody, at all hours. Even the members of his Cabinet, sometimes, had to force their way through the crowd, and get the private ear of the President in the corner of a roomful of visitors, before they could impart to him grave matters of state.

My father was a daily and frequent visitor at the White House during this month of crowds and confusion. I found myself often a bearer of messages from one to the other, about matters too important for longer delay. At first, when I would take up to the President a paper for his signature, he would spread it out and carefully read the whole of it. But this usage was speedily abandoned, and he would hastily say, "Your father says this is all right, does he? Well, I guess he knows. Where do I put my name?"

While President and people were resting in the confident belief that, if the offices could only be satisfactorily disposed of, and the Southern trouble somehow staved off, all might yet go well, a new and unlooked-for danger was not only threatened, but actually close at hand from Europe.

My father had now been in the State Department long enough to discover that the three great Powers of western Europe were actively engaged in helping the plots to break up the United States. This was their opportunity. Public attention in the United States had been so absorbed in affairs at home that none had been given to affairs abroad. But these three great Powers had been closely watching our troubles, and preparing to take advantage of them. If the great American Republic was going to pieces, it meant to them that the republican form of government, everywhere, was doomed to like destruction.

Spain, England, and France were monarchical governments, having little faith in republics. Now, the progress of events in the United States seemed to show that the old order of things was coming back, and they could resume the building of their empires on monarchical lines.

The "Monroe Doctrine" could safely be ignored, and the interference of America need not be feared.

Spain had already openly seized the government of San Domingo, toppled down the Dominican republic, and again planted the banner of Castile on the island where it first waved four hundred years before.

England, through Lord Lyons, had formally notified the American Secretary of State that any "paper blockade" of Southern ports would be disregarded by her Majesty's government, and that none would be regarded unless "rendered effective by ample naval force." He significantly added that the American navy was by no means such a force.

France was evasive as to her designs in Mexico, and certainly would not regard any "paper blockade" of the "seceded States," but instead she might recognize those States themselves.

The whole fabric of American republics threatened to fall like a house of cards. To European statesmen, this result seemed to be exactly what they had so long predicted.

On Sunday afternoon, the 1st of April, my father wrote out a series of suggestions for Mr. Lincoln, to aid him in thinking over topics which would come up at succeeding interviews. This paper was headed, "Some thoughts for the President's consideration." It was not to be filed, or to pass into the hands of any clerk. As my father's handwriting was almost illegible, I copied it myself, and dispatched it by private hand.

In this paper were briefly outlined suggestions in regard to the crowd of office-seekers, the relief of the two forts, the navy and the blockade, the suspension of the *habeas corpus* at Key West, the issues of slavery and the Union or disunion, and the foreign policy to be pursued with reference to the various European Powers.

Mr. Lincoln acknowledged its reception in a kind and dignified note, in which he said that if these things were to be done, then he must do them. So the "Thoughts" became, as intended, the basis of subsequent interviews between the President and the Secretary of State. They also proved useful hints for Cabinet discussions. My father found the President ready and willing to sanction and co-operate in most of the points and suggestions. Accordingly, on the very next day, Spain was called upon, through her Minister, Mr. Tassara, for "explanations" in regard to her acts in San Domingo. The secret expedition for the relief of Fort Pickens was approved, fitted out, and dispatched without attracting public attention until it reached its destination and accomplished its purpose. It carried the executive order for the suspension of the writ of *habeas corpus* at Key West. On succeeding days, the "explanations" from France, Great Britain, Russia, and Spain were called for with more or less satisfactory results.

And now the month of suspense drew to its inevitable ending. The events dreaded at the North, and hoped for at the South, actually took place. As Fort Sumter was to be either evacuated or reinforced, the Administration decided to supply and reinforce it. South Carolina decided to bombard and capture it.

Virginia thereupon promptly passed the Ordinance of Secession. And so, amid general Southern exultation, the dream of the Secessionists for a " united South " was at last realized—to be followed by an awakening to four years of bloody war—and the final restoration of the Union.

The Call to Arms. It was on Friday, the 12th of April, that news came that the Secessionists were about to attack Fort Sumter, and would endeavour to carry it by assault before the relief expedition could reach there.

It was while the batteries in Charleston were opening fire on the national flag that my father was penning his instructions to Burlingame.   In them he remarked: "We are just now entering on a fearful trial, not only unknown but even deemed impossible.   Ambitious and discontented partisans have raised the standard of insurrection, and organized a revolutionary government. Their agents have gone abroad to seek, under the name of 'recognition,' aid and assistance.   A premature declaration of recognition by any foreign state would be direct intervention, and the state which should lend it must be prepared to assume the relations of an ally of the projected Confederacy.   Both the justice and the wisdom of the war must be settled, as all questions which concern the American people must be determined, not by arms but by suffrage.   When, at last, the ballot is to be employed, after the sword, then in addition to the questions indicated, two further ones will arise, requiring to be answered, namely, which party began the conflict, and which maintained in that conflict the cause of freedom and humanity."

Saturday morning came the news of the bombardment, and the gallant defence of their flag by the handful of men in the garrison, against the overwhelming odds of batteries erected all round the harbour and manned by besiegers, who were to the besieged more than a hundred to one.   Occasional telegraphic dispatches, sent out during the day and evening by the assailants, chronicled the progress of the unequal struggle.

Sunday morning it was known in Washington that the defenders, having faithfully performed their duty so long as their guns and ammunition held out, would haul down their flag at noon, and evacuate the fort.

President and Cabinet passed most of the day in consultation over the grave, though not unexpected, event,

and its far-reaching consequences. As to their own immediate duty there was no difference of opinion. The time
had manifestly arrived to call for troops. It was no
longer a question of "coercing States" but of defending
the existence of the nation. Nor was there any delusive
hope that a small force would suffice. Each of the Cabinet
members realized that the contest would be gigantic.

The point for anxious consultation was, not how many
soldiers would quell the rebellion, but how many it would
be wise to call for at the very outset. The lowest figure
suggested was fifty thousand; the highest one hundred
thousand. My father advocated the largest number.
It was finally deemed prudent to fix the limit at seventy-
five thousand. By this an effective force of fifty thousand
men might be counted on at once from the Northern
States. In the border States there would be lukewarm-
ness and delay, perhaps refusal.

The next question was as to calling Congress. The
executive branch of the Government could not levy armies,
and expend public money, without Congressional sanction.
Congress would be loyal, but it would be a deliberative
body, and to wait for "many men of many minds" to shape
a war policy would be to invite disaster. So it was concluded to call Congress to meet on the 4th of July, and
to trust to their patriotism to sanction the war measures
taken prior to that time by the Executive.

President Lincoln drafted the substance of his proposed
Proclamation. The Secretary of War undertook to arrange the respective quotas of the several States. The
Secretary of State brought the document to his Department, and, calling together his clerks, had it duly per-
fected in form and engrossed. The President's signature
and his own were appended, the great seal affixed that
evening, and copies were given to the press that it might
appear in the newspapers of Monday morning.

The response to the Proclamation at the North was all or more than could be anticipated. Every Governor of a free State promptly promised that his quota should be forthcoming. An enthusiastic outburst of patriotic feeling—an "uprising of the North" in town and country —was reported by telegraph. Dispatches poured in announcing the readiness not only of individuals, but of whole organizations, to volunteer. Party lines seemed to be swept away. Disunion sympathizers were silenced. Whole communities were vigorously at work mustering troops and sending them forward for the defence of the national capital. The newspapers were filled with vivid pictures of the scenes of popular enthusiasm in New York, Boston, and Philadelphia, where regiments were forming amid the waving of flags, the roaring of cannon, and the shouts of assembled thousands.

From the South, the echo to the Proclamation was more sullen, but equally significant. Troops for the Confederacy already organized were hurrying forward. Veteran soldiers were marshalling recruits. Popular feeling in the seceding States was declared to be unanimous. "Union" utterances were silenced and the South was said to be "bitterly in earnest in fighting for independence."

From the border States came indications that, while there was still division of opinion, the outbreak of hostilities was paralysing the Union men and lending new energy to the Secessionists. To the call upon them for militia, defiant answers were returned. "You can get no troops from North Carolina," telegraphed the Governor of that State; "I regard the levy of troops made by the Administration for the purpose of subjugating the States of the South, as a violation of the Constitution, and a usurpation of power." The Governor of Tennessee replied: "Tennessee will not furnish a single man for coercion, but fifty thousand if necessary for the defence of our rights and those of our brethren." The Governor of Kentucky answered: "Kentucky will furnish no troops for the wicked purpose of subduing her sister Southern States." The Governor of Missouri said: "Not one man will the State of Missouri furnish to carry on so unholy a crusade." The Governor of Delaware answered more mildly: "The laws of this State do not confer upon the Executive any authority allowing him to comply with such a requisition." From Maryland came no immediate response. From Virginia came ominous news that the convention had hastily and secretly reversed its previous decision, had adopted an Ordinance of Secession, and had joined the Confederacy.

The President of the Confederate Government, at Montgomery, issued a proclamation, offering "letters of marque and reprisal" to armed privateers of any nation. Active measures were begun for organizing troops to attack Washington.

Of the regiments called for, New York was to furnish seventeen, Pennsylvania sixteen, and Ohio thirteen; while the quotas from the other States ranged from one to six.

The day after the Proclamation was issued, the Massachusetts Sixth Regiment mustered on Boston Common, and on the following evening, armed and equipped, was on its way to Washington. Acclamations greeted it along the roads, and the march down Broadway in New York roused the popular enthusiasm to the highest point. The evening of Thursday the 18th found it at Philadelphia.

The same evening witnessed the arrival in Washington of three or four hundred Pennsylvanians, to be armed, equipped, and placed in regimental organization after reaching the capital. These were the first comers of the new levy.

A day later the telegraph announced that the New York

Seventh was also en route through Philadelphia and that others would speedily follow.

Amid a general outburst of patriotism nothing was more significant than the promptness with which many influential Northern Democrats announced their determination to "stand by the Government." Chief among them was Stephen A. Douglas, Lincoln's chief competitor in the election, who now, on the day the Proclamation was signed, visited the President to assure him of hearty sympathy and co-operation.

Washington Beleaguered. Washington had supposed itself to be the capital of the United States; but now it was suddenly transformed into an isolated city, in an enemies' country, threatened with attack from the hostile communities all around it.

On the 19th came the news that Virginia, having suddenly become a hostile power, had sent troops to seize Harpers Ferry. The lieutenant in charge had escaped with his little garrison, after setting fire to some of the buildings; but the rebels had thus gained an important post, with valuable machinery and a large amount of arms.

Later in the day came the startling intelligence that the mob had attacked the Massachusetts and Pennsylvania troops as they were coming through Baltimore. The telegraph and evening papers soon brought confirmation showing that the rioters had practical control of Baltimore, and of the railways north, thus cutting off all communication between the North and the capital.

A day later came the news that the navy yard at Norfolk would probably share the fate of the armory at Harpers Ferry. Protected only by a few marines, it was exposed to easy capture. The vessels, arms, supplies, machinery, buildings, and docks had cost the United States Government many millions, and their value to insurgents at the very outset of a rebellion was incalculable. Possession of armory and navy yard would place in the hands of the rebels, for instant use, more of the material of war than the Government would have at hand.

Commodore Paulding was sent down with the *Pawnee* to rescue and bring such of the ships and supplies as might be found practicable. He found on arrival that the ships had already been scuttled, and, after a hasty conference of the officers of the expedition, it was determined that since the property could not be saved, it was best to burn and destroy as much as possible, to keep it out of the hands of the rebels.

Dangers were thickening around the Federal city in all directions. With Virginia in active hostility on one side, Maryland was taking steps to prevent all help on the other. The Secessionists were holding meetings, mustering troops, stopping trains, burning railway bridges. By Saturday it was known that railway communication with the North was cut off. By Sunday night the telegraph had ceased to work, and it was realized that Washington was beleaguered by its enemies on every side.

Washington was still a slaveholding city. Southern sympathies pervaded its social circles and, as yet, were in its official circles. When it began to look as if the city were cut off from all Northern help and would soon be captured by troops advancing from the South, the exultation of secession sympathizers was neither concealed nor repressed. The Confederate flag was flying at Alexandria, in full view from the Capitol and the White House. Confederate scouts were reported to be posted at the end of the bridge connecting the city with Virginia.

In the streets and hotels the wildest rumours gained credence. A mob was reported to be coming over from Baltimore, to burn the public buildings and sack the town.

Confederate vessels were declared to be coming up from Norfolk to bombard it. Confederate troops were asserted to be marching up from Richmond, and down from Harpers Ferry, to take possession. Forty thousand "Virginia volunteers armed with bowie knives," it was said, were coming over the Long Bridge. Business was at a standstill. The railway station was silent, the wharves deserted. Groups of people gathered at street corners exchanging, in low tones, their forebodings of disaster, or their hopes of relief.

Government clerks cherishing disloyal sentiments made haste to vacate their places, and Southern army and navy officers to resign their commissions, so as to be ready to join the ranks of the coming conquerors.

The newspapers, cut off from their usual telegraphic facilities, gave such intelligence as they could get, but their columns would hardly hold a tithe of the startling stories that were flying about the streets. It was announced that the Confederate Secretary of War at Montgomery predicted that the "Confederate flag would float over the Capitol at Washington before the 1st of May."

The War Begun. Half a dozen companies of the regular army had been gathered by General Scott, and distributed where most needed about the city. The batteries of light artillery were posted to guard the bridges. The Capitol was barricaded, and the Massachusetts Sixth, which had fought its way through Baltimore, was quartered in the Senate Chamber. The Pennsylvanians had been armed and assigned to similar duty. The marines were charged with the defence of the wharves and the navy yard.

The District militia, which the General had organized for the inauguration, now proved a valuable arm of defence. It mustered fifteen companies. They were distributed to guard the avenues and public buildings. Sentries were posted, ammunition distributed, and a system of signals arranged, so as to ensure rapid concentration at any point attacked.

Muskets were distributed to clerks in the various government offices, and many private residences were armed for defence. Two companies were hastily formed by visitors at the hotels and others, under the leadership of Cassius M. Clay and James H. Lane, which patrolled the streets and performed guard duty.

About two o'clock in the morning, I was aroused by loud knocking at the front door, and descending the stairs to ascertain the cause, I found, outside, one of these night patrols. They informed me that they had caught a suspicious prisoner, evidently a Virginian, whom they thought might be a spy. He had avowed his purpose of going to Secretary Seward's house, so they had brought him around for identification. He was hastily taken up, under guard, to my father.

Rousing himself, my father said: "George, is that you?" He turned out to be a young man from Virginia, who had been sent over by his mother, a loyal Union woman, to tell us that trains were running on the Orange & Alexandria Railroad at frequent intervals, all night, loaded with armed men who it was presumed were going to attend some Confederate rendezvous at Manassas or elsewhere.

George was released by the patrol, as he had proved to be no spy, but a friend, and the information he brought confirmed the news that the Confederates were mustering somewhere in formidable numbers.

Our military force, though small, was believed to be sufficient to preclude danger of a surprise.

A few days later came the welcome intelligence that the New York Seventh and the Massachusetts Eighth and the Seventy-first of New York had arrived at Annapolis.

The rails of the branch railroad had been torn up, and the engines disabled, for a distance of nine miles to the Washington junction. But "Yankee" soldiers were not to be checkmated thereby. General Butler drew up his forces, in parade order, at the Annapolis navy yard, and requested that any one familiar with track laying, or engine repairing, should step to the front. Twenty or more skilled mechanics promptly responded to the call. So the relieving army made its way to the capital, laying down the rails, and putting the trains in order, to keep up its communication. Of course they were received at the national capital with shouts of joy by the Union men.

Now troops came pouring in for the defence of the capital. Every day came the welcome sound of drum and fife, and the cheering gleam of bayonets. The long lines of newcomers marched up Pennsylvania Avenue, passing the State Department and the White House, and pausing at the portal of the War Department "to report for duty," and to be assigned to their respective camps.

These were at first in the vacant squares of the city, but as time went on, and the army continued to grow, they were pushed out into the suburbs, and on the adjoining heights. Many of these, under the direction of the engineers, soon became fortified camps and forts. In the course of a few months, every hill around Washington was crowned with an earthwork, and the city was ultimately surrounded by a cordon of fortifications, sixty miles in circumference.

The President and Cabinet found it necessary and desirable to have personal representatives in New York, empowered to act with promptness in the emergencies now daily arising. Orders were therefore given for the purchase, charter, and arming of steamships in New York, Boston, and Philadelphia, and extraordinary powers, in behalf of the War and Navy Departments, were bestowed upon Governor Morgan, George D. Morgan, William M. Evarts, R. M. Blatchford, and Moses H. Grinnell, to whom officers should report for instruction and advice in forwarding troops and supplies.

Similar powers to act for the Treasury Department in expending the public money were conferred upon John A. Dix, George Opdyke, and R. M. Blatchford. These gentlemen were to give no security, and to act without compensation, reporting their proceedings when communications should be re-established.

How faithfully the great trust was discharged, President Lincoln himself, at a later day, bore testimony.

He said: "The several Departments of the Government, at that time, contained so large a number of disloyal persons, that it would have been impossible to provide safely, through official agents only, for the performance of the duties thus confided to citizens favourably known for their ability, loyalty, and patriotism. The several orders issued upon these occurrences were transmitted by private messengers, who pursued a circuitous way to the seaboard cities, inland across the States of Pennsylvania and Ohio and the Northern Lakes. I believe that by these and similar measures taken in that crisis, some of which were without any authority of law, the Government was saved from overthrow. I am not aware that a dollar of the public funds, thus confided without authority of law to unofficial persons, was either lost or wasted."

The Proclamation of Blockade was issued on the morning of the 19th of April. Upon the Secretary of State of course devolved the duty of preparing and perfecting its details. My father had bestowed upon these much care and forethought, in view of the many warnings already received from abroad that advantage would be taken by foreign Powers of any opportunity to evade and nullify it.

The Confederates themselves, at the outset, had little apprehension that they would find it any serious trouble or annoyance. They knew that our navy was entirely inadequate to make such a blockade "effective," and they had plenty of assurances from England and France that anything in the nature of a "paper blockade" would be disregarded. "Cotton is King," was the exultant cry, "Europe must have it for its factories"; and the South had almost a monopoly of the staple itself, with twenty or more seaports to ship it from, and millions of slaves to cultivate, convey, and ship it.

Having possession of "King Cotton," they confidently believed that that potentate would ensure them the aid and comfort of all others. It would give them continued trade and assure them of ample resources for carrying on the war.

These expectations were doomed to disappointment, for by the activity of the Government at Washington, and that of its vicegerents in New York, the army and navy were increasing with magic rapidity. Whole fleets of transports and gunboats were called into existence, and dispatched to the scene of hostilities.

A College Classmate. In the freshman class at Union College in 1845, Daniel Butterfield and I were the youngest members. We were friends all through our college days, and graduated together in 1849. Then we drifted apart, he to Utica and New York, I to Albany and Washington. Then for ten years we saw no more of each other.

In April, 1861, after the fall of Fort Sumter, and the first call for seventy-five thousand volunteers, Washington

11

was in an excitement bordering on panic. The Secessionists had cut the telegraph wires, and torn up the railroad tracks and bridges, cutting off communication with the North. They were erecting batteries on the Potomac, and the city seemed practically beleaguered. It was still a Southern town, and predictions were freely made that within a fortnight it would be captured by the Confederates. The small detachments of regular troops and the companies of district militia organized for the inauguration were able to guard the public buildings and supplies, but there was no force to repel such an invading attack as we might any day expect. Excited crowds thronged the streets and buzzed in the Departments.

My room at the State Department was filled with visitors, officials on business, members of Congress with their protégés, who wanted offices, consulates, clerkships, claims, or commissions, reporters who came to get news, or to bring it, and loungers and rumour-mongers who appear at such times like birds of ill omen. I noticed in the crowd the face of my old college friend, Butterfield. Taking him by the hand, I said:

"Why Dan, where did you come from? And what are you doing here."

"I am going back home, tired and disappointed," he said. "I thought I might be of some service, but find I am not wanted. I have been all day at the War Department, and can't get a hearing. The halls and rooms are crowded. The doorkeepers say they are not allowed to take any more names, or cards, to the Secretary of War. The officials are all too busy to listen, or, if they listen, have no power to act."

"What was it you wanted at the War Department?" I asked.

"Only permission to bring my regiment on here, to defend the capital. I supposed troops were wanted."

"So they are, and urgently and immediately. There must be some misapprehension. Come with me, and I will go back with you and get you an audience with Secretary Cameron."

We hastened over to the War Department and found things as he had described. Of course I was known to messengers and doorkeepers, and my official name gave me immediate access to the Secretary's room. He was sitting at his desk, which was surrounded by an eager crowd, the foremost of whom seemed to be haranguing him on the merits of something he wanted to sell to the Government.

"Mr. Secretary," said I, "here is my friend, Colonel Butterfield, who has something to say to you that I think you will be glad to hear."

"What is it, Mr. Seward?"

"He has a regiment to offer to the Government."

"Why, Colonel, that is just what we want. What is your regiment?"

"The Twelfth New York State Militia, sir, of which I am commander."

"But are they armed or equipped or clothed?"

"Yes, sir, and tolerably well drilled. We foresaw some time ago that there might be trouble, and so we got in readiness to respond to any call."

"And how soon could you get them here?"

"Within twenty-four hours after receiving orders to start."

"But how can you get through? You know communications with New York are cut off."

"We will march through Baltimore, sir. Or we can come round by sea, and up Chesapeake Bay and the Potomac. I have made a provisional arrangement with the steamer *Coatzacoalco*, which is all ready to bring us on."

"Are you sure, Colonel, that the Government can rely on these statements of yours?"

"I believe the Secretary of State will vouch for me, sir."

When this assurance was confirmed, the Secretary of War looked much relieved.

"Well, Colonel, your regiment will be very welcome. You shall have your orders, at once."

Butterfield hurried off. When, soon after, the Twelfth New York came marching up Pennsylvania Avenue, it received an ovation of cheers, accompanied by the waving of flags, hats, and handkerchiefs, like all other early comers "to the front."

The Twelfth was assigned to Franklin Square for its camp ground. Its white tents and neatly kept camps in the heart of the city, its well drilled companies in their parades and tactical exercises, drew continued throngs of visitors and made it a fashionable resort. Colonel Butterfield's prompt address and soldierly bearing made him a favourite at the War Department, and the Twelfth was one of the first to be sent out on active service.

In May, when additional regiments were to be raised for the regular army, Secretary Cameron notified my father of officers needed for New York's quota and asked for names for new commissions. My father suggested that of Butterfield for a Major's place. Secretary Cameron heartily assented, and Butterfield was appointed.

Before the year was over, he was promoted to be a Brigadier-General. Then, for bravery in battle, he was again promoted to be Major-General, and in 1862 had become Chief of Staff in the Army of the Potomac.

His subsequent career is a part of the history of the war. After its close, he resigned and went into business in New York—where, a few years later, he became Assistant Treasurer of the United States.

.   .   .   .   .   .

Somewhere toward the close of the century, I was attending a banquet of the Alumni of Union College. Butterfield, as President, had on his right hand General Miles, then the Commander-in-Chief of the army, while I sat on his left. Introducing us to each other, he said: "General, it was my friend Fred Seward here who put me into the army."

"Have you ever thought, Butterfield," said I, "where you would be now, if you had stayed in it?"

"No," said he, "but, by George, I believe I would have been at the head of it,—for I was Miles's senior in service!"

General Scott. General Scott's services to the Union, at the outset of the Civil War, have never been fully appreciated. His military experience and unswerving loyalty greatly helped to save Washington during the interregnum between the Presidential election and the inauguration.

He was born in Virginia, like Lee, but if his ideas of fidelity to the Government had been like those of his subordinate, Washington might have been in the hands of the Confederates before Lincoln was inaugurated.

"Old Fuss and Feathers," as they called him when they tried to drive him out of his responsible trust, was inflexible in his devotion to the Union. It was not easy to protect the capital from its enemies plotting in its midst. So strong was President Buchanan's desire to avoid a clash of arms during his time, and so widely had the notion spread that the Federal Government "could not coerce a State," that General Scott was hardly allowed to order to Washington a slender guard for the inauguration ceremonies. As for reinforcing the Southern forts, that was effectively blocked by the Secessionists, until too late even for provisioning them.

After the disunion members of the Cabinet left in January, and Dix, Stanton, Holt, and King were among the President's trusted advisers, it became possible for the General to summon small detachments of regular troops and post them where they could be of service. With the help of Colonel Stone, he also organized an effective force out of loyal companies of the District militia. So that danger was tided over.

The General favoured every form of conciliation that would avert war. When war proved inevitable, he set vigorously to work, in spite of his seventy-five years and infirmities, to maintain and defend the Union, organize and equip its armies, and plan its campaigns.

After the fall of Fort Sumter, and the first call for troops by President Lincoln, the Confederates seized railroads and telegraphs, cutting off Washington from communication with the North. It became like a beleaguered city. While hoping for and expecting its defenders, there was no assurance that they were on their way. The General took up his post, by night as well as by day, at the War Department. In the middle of one night, I was roused up by one of the several scouts we had sent out for news.

He brought the welcome intelligence that the Eighth Massachusetts, the Seventh New York, and Seventy-first New York regiments had landed at Annapolis and were in possession of the navy yard. The railroad having been torn up by the enemy, they would march across country to the capital. I took the bearer of the good news over to the War Department, and found General Scott wrapped in a military cloak and stretched on a settee. He rose with difficulty, but was at once alert and ready for business. He summoned his staff, and before daybreak he was issuing orders about routes and rations, and advising how obstacles and surprises were to be avoided. Thenceforward every incoming regiment marched up Pennsylvania Avenue to salute the President and the Commanding General, and receive their orders as to their location and their duties.

By the end of April, ten or twelve thousand troops had arrived and others were on their way. It was my father's custom, at this period, after the Department closed for the day, to take an afternoon drive to visit the camps of the different regiments. Frequently the drive was terminated by a call upon General Scott, at his office or his lodgings. In either place, his surroundings were those of active military service, the sentry pacing before his door, the orderly sitting in the hall, the aides-de-camp at their respective desks, and the General's table covered with maps, dispatches, and calculations.

One day, while exchanging news and comparing views, my father remarked: "We are gathering a large army. What I do not yet foresee is how it is to be led? What are we to do for generals?"

"That is a subject, Mr. Secretary," said the old commander, "that I have thought much about. If I could only mount a horse, I—" then checking himself, with a shake of his head, he added, "but I am past that. I can only serve my country as I am doing here now, in my chair."

"Even if you had your youth and strength again, General, it might not be worth as much to us as your experience. In any case, you would need commanders of military training to carry out your orders."

"There are few who have had command in the field, even of a brigade," said the General. "But," he added reflectively, "there is excellent material in the army to make generals of. There are good officers. Unfortunately for us, the South has taken most of those holding the higher grades. We have captains and lieutenants that, with time and experience, will develop, and will do good service."

Proceeding to name over several officers, or West Point graduates, in whom he evidently felt interest and pride, he mentioned McClellan, Franklin, Hancock, Hooker, Mansfield, Sherman, Sumner, Halleck, and others actually or recently in the army.

"There is one officer who would make an excellent general," he continued, "but I do not know whether we can rely on him. He lives not far away, and I have sent over to see. I had expected to hear from him today. If he comes in tomorrow, I shall know."

"I will not ask his name until you hear from him, then, General, though I think I can guess whom you mean."

A day or two later, reverting to their conversation on the subject, my father remarked:

"You were expecting to hear from some officer you thought well of. Did you?"

"Yes," said the General, "it was too late. He had decided to go 'with his State,' as the phrase is now. I am sorry, both on our account and on his own."

That was the turning point in the life of Robert E. Lee.

At the beginning of the conflict we had a rapidly growing army, and capable officers to organize and drill it. But there was no one except General Scott to devise a general plan of campaign. The Administration had no member who had ever "set a squadron on the field," and our military commanders had not yet become versed in the problems of "great strategy."

Scott therefore was the authority to whom all turned. His "plan of campaign" was submitted to the Cabinet. It was simple and yet comprehensive. Briefly it was, to fortify Washington, and mass a great army in and around it; this army, at the outset, to be held and used, not as an aggressive, but a defensive one, and as a base for expeditions elsewhere. Meantime, to begin aggressive operations by marching another army down the Mississippi, clearing the river, fortifying it, and opening it to commerce. This would cut the Confederacy in two, and weaken it, both in men and resources, for the final struggle, which would doubtless take place at the East.

The plan was approved and pursued. In the coming months and years, there were frequent departures from it, due to impatience or miscalculation, and nearly all ending in disaster. But, reverted to again, it was, on the whole, the line of policy which led to ultimate success, by opening the way for the final "great strategy" of Grant and Sherman.

May, 1861.

General Scott's Stories. General Scott's massive military figure and dignified demeanour were rather awe-inspiring to strangers. In social life, his conversation was always entertaining and his anecdotes often amusing. One of his stories, when the subject of dreams was under discussion, was of an incident of the battle of Chippewa, in 1814.

On the eve of the engagement, for which both Americans and British were preparing, he was sitting in his headquarters, issuing orders and arranging for the disposition of his forces. Unexpectedly, there appeared in the doorway the familiar form of a friend engaged in mercantile pursuits in Philadelphia.

"Why my dear fellow," said he, "what in the world brings you here? Always glad to see you,—you know—but really I haven't time to talk to you. It is a very inopportune time for a visit. We are just on the eve of a battle, probably tomorrow morning. You will have to leave me now, and come again later."

"Yes," his friend replied, "I understood you might be having some fighting about now. In fact, that was what brought me up here."

"How can that be? You are a civilian, and are running into unnecessary danger, where you can be of no use."

"Don't let me interrupt you, General. Go on with your work. I think I'll stop over here tomorrow. I can get an army blanket, and lie down for the night anywhere out of the way."

"But what possible object can you have in such a proceeding?"

"Well, General, I have been a good deal disturbed by a dream I had lately."

"A dream? What has that to do with it?"

"Why, I dreamed I was in a battle. And while the battle was going on, I ran away. Then I woke up, and wondered whether I really was such a coward. It has worried me ever since. So I came up here to see."

The General laughed. "Why, my dear friend," said he, "that's nothing. Everybody runs away in their dreams. We are swayed by momentary impulses in our dreams—not by reason or judgment. That doesn't prove you a coward."

"Perhaps so," his visitor said, doubtfully, "but I'd like to find out."

All the General's arguments could not move him from his purpose. Finally he said: "Well, if you insist on staying, there is certainly work to be done, even by civilians. You can serve as a volunteer aide, and I'll promise you that you'll get under fire."

"Just what I want," said the visitor.

Sure enough the battle came on, hot and heavy. All the General's aides were soon dashing across the field, on various errands. Only the volunteer was left.

"Do you think you could carry an order to Colonel so and so, whose regiment is posted on yonder hill?"

"Try me."

In another moment, he was on his way—regardless of the hail of bullets. Back to report, he asked for another order and another. So he fought gallantly all day, till the victory was won.

Scott congratulated him. "Now you have found your true vocation. You are a soldier. I am sending my dispatches to the War Department, and shall ask a commission for you, on my staff."

"Oh, thank you, General, but I am not looking for military glory. I have found out that I am not a coward. That was all I came for. I shall go back to Philadelphia now to my business perfectly contented and satisfied."

And that was just what he did.

Saint Cyr Cadets. Once, when in France, the General went to make a visit to the military school of St. Cyr. He found a group of young cadets gathered around an old soldier, and listening eagerly to his stories of Napoleon's campaigns. He was a sergeant of the "Old Guard." He was telling them of the charge up the hill at the battle of Austerlitz. Even the "Old Guard" was twice repulsed with fearful slaughter, losing more than one third of its whole number. Then, said François, "I heard the order of the officer reforming our lines, and saying, '*En avant, mes braves*, that battery must be taken.'"

"Oh, François," interrupted one of the young cadets, "how did you feel when you heard that dreadful order?"

"Feel," said François, "feel—why, I felt to the left, to be sure, how else should a soldier feel?" (French soldiers kept in touch with their comrades with the left elbow.)

The Circular Dispatch on the Military Situation. "Wars and rumours of wars," is but a mild expression for the mass of wild conflicting rumours and reports, mistakes and misstatements, misrepresentations and falsehoods, that pass under the name of "news" in time of war.

So manifestly contradictory and unreliable was the news sent out from Washington during April and May, 1861, that my father decided to prepare once a week a circular dispatch to each and all of our diplomatic representatives abroad, a concise and reliable statement of the news received by the Government, from its army and navy. This was entitled "The Circular Dispatch on the Military Situation." It was usually prepared by his own hand, so that it might be free from all exaggeration. It was continued throughout the war.

Our ministers abroad found themselves much aided in their work by this weekly circular. Not only was it useful to them in contradicting unfounded reports, but foreign governments themselves soon learned that if they wished to keep themselves posted on the events of the war, they could rely on the advices received by each American minister for accurate facts, instead of trusting to the chaotic utterances of the press, or even the dispatches, necessarily based on imperfect information, of their own legations at Washington.

Of course, these circulars amounted in the course of four years to a considerable volume. Mr. Baker, in his fifth volume of *Seward's Works*, has gathered them all together, under the title of *Diary or Notes on the War*. Now, after the lapse of half a century, I find they offer a convenient compend of the history of the war. Events and dates are there set down in exactly the order in which news of them was received each week by the Government at Washington.

Under Fire from a French Frigate.   In the early part
of President Lincoln's Administration, a French frigate
(I think the *Gassendi*) came up the Potomac on a visit
of observation, and lay for a time at anchor just off the
Washington navy yard, which was then under command
of Captain (afterwards Admiral) Dahlgren.   The usual
courtesies were exchanged between ship and shore.

One day the French Minister, M. Mercier, brought
her captain to present him to the Secretary of State.   He
said they would esteem it a special favour, if the President
would visit the *Gassendi* and receive from her a national
salute.   It was a graceful suggestion, and would tend to
promote international friendship.   Our relations with
the French Government had already been somewhat
strained, and threatened to become more so.

So the Secretary thought it would be good policy to
accept the invitation.   Mr. Lincoln expressed his willingness to go, and remarked that, as yet, he was not very
familiar with war-vessels, and would like to see how the
French frigate looked.

A day was appointed, and I drove down with him to
the navy yard.   Neither of his private secretaries accompanied him, but there were two other young men.
Received with due honours at the navy yard, he was escorted to the barge of the commandant, manned by half
a dozen sailors.   Captain Dahlgren himself took the tiller
ropes, and we were pulled rapidly out toward the ship.

She lay with her bows pointing out into the stream, so
we approached under her stern.   She was gay with bunting in honour of her distinguished guest.   Her crew were
beat to quarters, and her commander and officers in full
uniform were at the gangway to welcome him.   Presentations followed, drums rolled and bugles sounded, while
the Stars and Stripes were unfurled at the top of the
mainmast.

Champagne and a brief conversation in the captain's cabin came next; then a walk up and down her decks to look at her armament and equipment. Though the surroundings were all new to Mr. Lincoln, he bore himself with his usual quiet, homely, unpretentious dignity on such occasions, and chatted affably with some of the officers who spoke English. The visit over, we were escorted to the side ladder, and re-embarked in our barge.

As Mr. Lincoln took his seat in the stern he said: "Suppose we row around her bows. I should like to look at her build and rig from that direction." Captain Dahlgren of course shifted his helm accordingly. The French officers doubtless had not heard or understood the President's remark, and supposed we were pulling off astern in the ordinary way.

We had hardly reached her bow, when, on looking up, I saw the officer of the deck pacing the bridge, watch in hand and counting off the seconds, "*Un, deux, trois,*" and then immediately followed the flash and deafening roar of a cannon, apparently just over our heads. Another followed, then another and another in rapid succession. We were enveloped in smoke and literally "under fire" from the frigate's broadside. Captain Dahlgren sprang to his feet, his face aflame with indignation, as he shouted: "Pull like the devil, boys! Pull like hell!"

They obeyed with a will, and a few sturdy strokes took us out of danger. After he had resumed his seat and calmed down, I said in a low voice: "Of course those guns were not shotted, and we were below their range?"

He answered, gritting his teeth, "Yes, but to think of exposing the President to the danger of having his head taken off by a wad!"

I did not know, until he explained, that the wadding blown to pieces by the explosion sometimes commences dropping fragments soon after leaving the gun. Whether

Mr. Lincoln realized the danger or not, I never knew.   He sat impassively through it, and made no reference to it afterwards.

August, 1861.

Why Maryland did not Secede.   On a bright summer day in 1861, callers at the White House in Washington were informed that the President had gone out for a drive, and that he was accompanied by the Secretary and Assistant Secretary of State.   When more curious observers noted the course of the carriage, they saw that it stopped at the door of the headquarters of the Army of the Potomac. Presently, General McClellan came out and joined the party, taking the vacant seat.   The carriage was then rapidly driven over toward Georgetown Heights.   It was a natural and reasonable conclusion, that the official party had gone up to inspect the camps and fortifications now beginning to cover the hills in the direction of Tennallytown.   So the event was duly chronicled in the press, and the statement was deemed satisfactory by the public.

But, on reaching the Heights, there was no stop for inspection, and only cursory glances were bestowed on camps and troops.   The occupants of the carriage had been generally silent while passing through the city, but once outside of the military lines they began to converse.

"General Banks will be expecting us, I reckon," observed the President.

"Yes, sir," replied General McClellan.   "I have telegraphed him.   He will meet us at his headquarters, at Rockville, and will provide a quiet place for conference."

"I suppose," queried General McClellan, in turn, "that General Dix has his instructions also."

"Yes," said Mr. Lincoln.   "Governor Seward went over to Baltimore a day or two ago, and spent some hours with him at Fort McHenry.   So he is fully informed."

"Then he will take care of the members in that part of the State?"

The Secretary of State smiled: "General Dix's views on the subject of hauling down the American flag are pretty well known. He can be depended upon."

The carriage whirled on, as fast as the rather rutty and broken roads would permit, until, some hours later, it drew up at the door of a tavern in the little village of Rockville, which for the time was in use by General Banks as his headquarters. He was in command of a district of rather uncertain size, with a limited force, posted to the best advantage to watch the river crossings. His aides and a squad or two of soldiers were with him.

He greeted his visitors courteously, and soon after led the way to a small grove near by, which had shady seats and no obstructing bushes. Here they could converse freely, without being overheard, or even seen, unless they themselves noticed their observers.

The purpose of the conference was then unfolded and discussed. It was in regard to a measure that it was thought wise not to trust to paper or to subordinates.

The Secessionists had by no means given up the hope of dragging Maryland into the Confederacy. The Legislature was to meet at Frederick City on the 17th of September. There was believed to be a disunion majority, and they expected and intended to pass an ordinance of secession. This would be regarded as a call to active revolt by many who were now submitting to Federal rule. In Baltimore and throughout Maryland the bloody experiences of Virginia and Missouri would probably be repeated. Governor Hicks was a loyal Union man, but would be unable to control the Legislature. The Union members were understood to be divided in opinion as to the expediency of going to Frederick to fight the proposed ordinance, or staying away, in the hope of blocking a quorum.

The Administration, therefore, had decided to take a bold step that would assuredly prevent the adoption of any such ordinance. To forcibly prevent a legislative body from exercising its functions, of course, savours of despotism, and is generally so regarded. But when, departing from its legitimate functions, it invites the public enemy to plunge the State into anarchy, its dissolution becomes commendable. So the Administration reasoned and decided.

As few persons as possible would be informed beforehand. General Dix and General Banks, commanding respectively the eastern and western portions of the State, were instructed to carefully watch the movements of members of the Legislature who were expected to respond to the summons to Frederick. Loyal Union members would not be interfered with. They would be free to come and go, perform their legislative duties, or stay away, just as they pleased. But disunion members starting to go there would be quietly turned back toward their homes, and would not reach Frederick City at all. The views of each disunion member were pretty well known, and generally rather loudly proclaimed. So there would be little difficulty, as Mr. Lincoln remarked, in "separating the sheep from the goats."

It was late in the evening when the carriage party returned to Washington. Sentries had been posted for the night, but the commanding General had the countersign, and all reached their homes quietly without observation.

The public anxiously awaited the coming of the eventful day which was to determine whether Maryland would sever her connection with the Union. When the time arrived which had been appointed for the assembling of the Legislature, it was found that not only was no secession ordinance likely to be adopted, but that there seemed to be no Secessionists to present one. The two generals had carried out their instructions faithfully, and with tact and discretion. The Union members returned to their homes rejoicing. No ordinance was adopted, Baltimore remained quiet, and Maryland stayed in the Union.

Of course the Administration were prepared for the storm of invective that was hurled at them through the press. Their "high-handed usurpation" was said to be paralleled only by "the acts of Cromwell and Napoleon." But even the denouncers were somewhat mystified as to the way in which things had happened. Cromwell and Napoleon were more spectacular, but Dix and Banks were equally effective.

There are still some who unconsciously lament these events in the history of "My Maryland" to the melodious strains of *Lauriger Horatius*. But Union men and disunion men alike had good reason, during the next three years, to thank God that Maryland had been spared the misery and desolation that overtook her sister Virginia.

France and England vs. the United States. Early in the war, we learned through the Legation at St. Petersburg that an understanding had been effected between the governments of Great Britain and France that they should take one and the same course on the subject of the American war, including the possible recognition of the rebels. Later, this understanding was distinctly avowed by M. Thouvenel to Mr. Sanford at Paris.

This alliance for joint action might dictate its own terms. From a joint announcement of neutrality, it would be but a step to joint mediation or intervention; and it was hardly to be anticipated that the Washington Government, struggling with an insurrection which had rent the country asunder, would be willing to face also the combined power of the two great empires of Western Europe. To the mind of the French and English statesmen the project was even praiseworthy. It would stop the effusion of blood and increase the supply of cotton. It would leave the American Union permanently divided; but that was a consummation that European statesmen in general would not grieve over.

On the morning of the 15th of June, a scene occurred at the State Department, which, though it has elicited but cursory attention from the historian, has had more influence on the affairs of the nation than a pitched battle.

My father was sitting at his table, writing dispatches, when the messenger announced:

"The British Minister is here to see you, sir, and the French Minister also."

"Which came first?"

"Lord Lyons, sir, but they say they both want to see you together."

He instinctively guessed the motive for so unusual a diplomatic proceeding. He paused a moment, and then said:

"Show them both into the Assistant Secretary's room, and I will come in presently."

I was at my writing table when the two ministers entered. We exchanged the usual salutations, though I fancied I perceived there was an air of rather more than usual constraint and reserve in their manner. They sat down together on the sofa.

A few minutes later, as they were sitting there side by side, the door opened and my father entered. Smiling and shaking his head, he said:

"No, no, no. This will never do. I cannot see you in that way."

The ministers rose to greet him. "True," said one

of them, "it is unusual, but we are obeying our instructions."

"And at least," said the other, "you will allow us to state the object of our visit?"

"No," said my father. "We must start right about it, whatever it is. M. Mercier, will you do me the favour of coming to dine with me this evening? Then we can talk over your business at leisure. And if Lord Lyons will step into my room with me now, we will discuss what he has to say to me."

"If you refuse to see us together——" began the French envoy, with a courteous smile and shrug.

"Certainly I do refuse to see you together, though I will see either of you separately with pleasure, here or elsewhere."

So the interviews were held severally, not conjointly, and the papers which they had been instructed to jointly present and formally read to him were left for his informal inspection. A brief examination of them only was necessary to enable him to say, courteously, but with decision, that he declined to hear them read, or to receive official notice of them.

His next dispatches to our ministers at London and Paris informed them of the event. To Mr. Dayton he said:

"The concert thus avowed has been carried out. The ministers came to me together; the instructions they proposed to read to me differ in form, but are counterpart in effect. This is conclusive in determining this Government not to allow the instruction to be read to it."

To Mr. Adams he added:

"We should insist, in this case, as in all others, on dealing with each of these Powers alone. This Government is sensible of the importance of the step it takes in declining to receive the communication."

July, 1861.

After Bull Run. From the window of the State Department we looked down upon a motley crowd of demoralized soldiers and curious civilians which thronged the streets for a day or two after the battle of Bull Run. Our chief subject of anxiety was not so much the possibility of retrieving the disaster, as the certain effect that the event would have upon opinion in Europe.

Meanwhile my father sat at his desk penning these words for his "circular dispatch on the military situation."

"You will receive the account of a deplorable reverse of our arms at Manassas. For a week or two that event will elate the friends of the insurgents in Europe, as it confounded and bewildered the friends of the Union here for two or three days. The shock, however, has passed away, producing no other results than a resolution stronger and deeper than ever, to maintain the Union, and a prompt and effective augmentation of the forces for that end. The heart of the country is sound. Its temper is now more favourable to the counsels of deliberation and wisdom. The lesson that war cannot be waged successfully without wisdom as well as patriotism has been received at a severe cost, but perhaps it was necessary."

The French Princes. The Emperor of the French was a student, as well as a sovereign. And he had convinced himself that the best and most enduring form of government was the imperial one. The lives of Cæsar and of Napoleon were the models that he set up for his own imitation. There were other opinions in France, but it was realized very early in our war that he regarded the Republic, for which we were battling, as doomed to defeat. Unfriendly action by him might therefore be looked for, and intervention, if a pretext for it could be found.

Among those who dissented from this opinion, it was rumoured that his cousin Prince Napoleon Jerome was an outspoken friend of the Federal Union. How far his views would influence the action of the Government was, of course, unknown.

In August, 1861, it was announced that Prince Napoleon was coming to visit the United States. Arrived off the Battery, in his steam yacht the *Catinat*, accompanied by the Princess Clotilde, his wife, and his suite, he spent a day or two in New York harbour. I was sent to welcome him and invite him, on behalf of the President and Secretary of State, to visit Washington.

He met me at the gangway, gave me a courteous greeting, and, in excellent English, said it would give him great pleasure to accept the invitation. Then, taking me aft, he presented me to the Princess, who was in the cabin.

Reaching Washington a few days later, my father received him, and presented him to the President. A state dinner was given in his honour. Another at the French Legation was followed by one at the Secretary of State's residence, and that by an evening reception at which the diplomatic corps, cabinet officers, and military commanders were present. As he stood on the hearth rug, wearing a white vest with red ribbon and decorations, and with his hands behind his back, his features, hair, and attitude showed a startling resemblance to the pictures of the first Napoleon,—a resemblance that he was said to cultivate, although he was a trifle taller than his uncle.

At the President's dinner, the marine band was stationed in the vestibule. The bandmaster was desirous of giving airs appropriately French, but being a German was not versed in Parisian politics. So, instead of the imperial air *Partant pour la Syrie*, he struck up, in one of the solemn pauses incident to every state dinner, the

Marseillaise. As that revolutionary lyric was tabooed in Paris during the Empire, a smile appeared on the faces of the guests, as they looked toward the Prince. He took it very good humouredly, saying: "*Mais, oui, je suis Républicain—en Amérique.*"

Republican he certainly was, as regarded the war. His belief in the Union, and his cheerful talk of its coming triumph, were all in strong contrast to the undertone of despondency in the conversation of those around him. He was much interested in army matters, and drove out with my father to visit several of the camps, and study the character of this novel organization of citizen soldiers.

The French Minister, M. Mercier, who still kept up his acquaintances with leading Confederates, now came to know whether there would be any objection to allowing the Prince to pass "through the lines," in response to an invitation which the Confederate generals had sent him. There was none, and so, accompanied by the French Minister, he visited the Confederate headquarters, both armies allowing him to pass through their lines.

When he returned he said he had been treated with courtesy and hospitality. He of course refrained from speaking of what he had seen or heard. But it was manifest from his general conversation that his opinions on the outcome of the war had undergone no change.

In another month, three princes of the royal house of Orleans arrived in Washington, the Prince de Joinville, son of King Louis Philippe, and his two nephews, the Comte de Paris and the Duc de Chartres. The Comte de Paris was the lineal heir of the throne of France. Sharing in the traditional friendship of their house, they had come to proffer their services, and peril their lives for the Union.

Of course they were welcomed by my father, who arranged the preliminaries for the entrance of the young princes into the army. They were assigned to positions on General McClellan's staff.

How well and faithfully their duties were performed has been told by General McClellan, who wrote that:

"Far from evincing any desire to avoid irksome, fatiguing, or dangerous duty they always sought it, and were never so happy as when some such work devolved upon them, and never failed to display the high qualities of a race of soldiers."

While the army remained at Washington, they occupied a house on I Street. They were frequent visitors at our house. One day at lunch, my father remarked: "I should think your names and titles might occasion some embarrassment. What do your brother officers call you?"

"Oh!" said the Duc de Chartres, laughing, "that is all arranged. My brother is Captain Paris, and I am Captain Charters, and we are excellent friends with all our comrades."

Still another member of the family came over to enter the service. This was the Prince de Joinville's young son, the Duc de Penthièvre. He was placed at the Naval School, which, during the war, was moved to Newport. He subsequently entered the navy, serving with credit and gaining promotion.

As the French Legation represented the imperial government, the members of the exiled royal family never entered it, and had no intercourse with its officials. At the Brazilian Legation, on the other hand, they were honoured and welcomed guests, the Prince de Joinville having married a sister of the reigning Emperor of Brazil.

Invited on one occasion to the Brazilian Legation I found the dinner was a family celebration in honour of "Peter." Peter had come over on a cruise across the Atlantic, and had been intrusted with the navigation of a ship. He was the "navigating officer."

"So," I said, "I perceive human ambition goes in circles. When you are once a royal prince, the next grade that you can aspire to is to be a sailing master."

"Prince," asked my father of the Prince de Joinville, one day at lunch, "how long do you think this Empire will last in France?"

The Prince smiled, and, taking up his plate and turning it round, he said: "Governments in France come round, *so*, in succession. I should give the Emperor ten or twelve years at the most."

The Empire fell in 1871.

Mount Vernon in War Time. There used to be a good old custom on the Potomac River the observance of which was always impressive. When a naval vessel or a passenger steamer came abreast of Mount Vernon, the flag was lowered in salute, the engine stopped, and the bell tolled as the steamer drifted slowly past the home and grave of George Washington. Even during the hurry and strife of the Civil War, the custom was not entirely forgotten.

While the Civil War was raging, the banks of the Potomac were the scenes of many bloody conflicts. Armed vessels patrolled the river. Fortifications were erected on its heights. Armies encamped along its shores. The sound of cannon or musketry daily echoed over its waters. Homes and fields were abandoned by their owners, for none felt safe against the raids of the scouting or foraging parties of the Union or Confederate troops.

But there was one exception. Both sides respected Mount Vernon. Neither army sought to occupy or fortify it. No foraging or plundering took place within its precincts. The old furniture stood peacefully in the old rooms. The old trees stood unharmed in the old groves. It was the one bit of neutral ground in that long and bloody war. Reverence for Washington's home and memory hardly needed to be inculcated by the commanders, for it was implanted in the heart of every soldier, whether he was a Northern man or a Southern one.

There was a story current in those days—I do not know how far it was true—that the old mansion was left in charge of two persons, a man and his sister. He was a Union man. She was a sympathizer with the Confederacy. When the visitors approached from the river side, they were presumably from the Union gunboats, and he went out to meet them. When they approached from the landward side, they were presumably from the Confederate camps, and she went out to greet them. But it made little difference. Whichever they were, they all came as friends, and were received as such.

When Prince Jerome Napoleon, with his suite, visited Washington during the war, he inquired about Mount Vernon. "Is it in your hands, or held by the enemy?"

"Neither, Prince," was the reply. "It is sacred, and treated as neutral ground."

One of the French visitors remarked: "*À présent vous avez la guerre, mais pour lui, c'est toujours la paix.*"

It was an augury of the coming time when we should find that there were some things we could not divide. We had found we could not divide the glory of George Washington. In due time we were to find that we could not divide the Union he had founded, nor the Flag he had unfurled over it.

1861–1862.

The Trent Case. With the intelligence of military success came another piece of news, which was hailed with similar public rejoicing. This was the taking of Mason and Slidell from the British steamer *Trent*, and their incarceration at Fort Warren in Boston harbour. The Northern people applauded the act. Eminent publicists wrote in justification of it. Official approval was warmly expressed at the Navy Department, and in Congress. The idea that they might be reclaimed was hardly mentioned. Any thought of their release was scouted.

But a few days more, and the foreign mails brought the news of the outburst of anger in England over the *Trent* affair, and the preparations for war with America. The intelligence that it was regarded as not only an insult, but an intentional one, was received with surprise. The popular exultation had been over the discomfiture and capture of the rebel envoys. The incidental question as to what Great Britain would think of it had excited little attention.

Doubts began to be felt, and to find expression in the press, as to what might be the outcome. A fall in stocks, and a sudden rise of the premium on gold, reflected the popular apprehensions.

But as yet no one was prepared to relinquish the prisoners. Frequent inquiries were made at the State Department about the line of action to be adopted, but my father declined to talk of the case until the expected communication from the British Government should be received. Lord Lyons was equally reticent, and the newspapers contented themselves with speculations on the probabilities of war, and descriptions of the captives' life at Fort Warren, usually winding up by asserting, "Of course they can never be given up. The country would never forgive any man who should propose such a surrender."

On the 20th of December Lord Lyons came to the Department of State. He had received from the Foreign Office the demand of the British Government for the liberation of Mason and Slidell. Before presenting it, he would leave with the Secretary of State a copy for his informal examination and perusal. This was quietly done, and the Secretary of State commenced the draft of his answer before the arrival of the dispatch was generally known in Washington. Closing his door against all visitors, he devoted one entire day to the preparation of the reply.

It was long and carefully considered. It recited not only the story of the case, but made an elaborate analysis and review of the principles of international law which seemed to bear upon it. Arriving at length at a point which was the gist of the whole controversy, he said: "I have not been unaware that in examining this question, I have fallen into an argument for what seems to be the British side of it, against my own country. But I am relieved from all embarrassment on that subject. I had hardly fallen into this line of argument when I discovered that I was really defending and maintaining not an exclusively British interest, but an old, honoured, and cherished American cause, resting not upon British authorities, but upon principles that constitute a larger portion of the distinctive policy of the United States. These principles were laid down for us in 1804, by James Madison, when Secretary of State in the Administration of Thomas Jefferson, in instructions given to James Monroe, our Minister to England. The ground he assumed then was the same I now occupy, and the arguments by which he sustained himself upon it have been an inspiration to me in preparing this reply."

He remarked therefore: "If I decide this case in favour of my own Government, I must disavow its most cherished principles, and reverse and for ever abandon its essential policy. The country cannot afford the sacrifice. If I maintain those principles, and adhere to that policy, I must surrender the case itself. It will be seen, therefore, that the Government could not deny the justice of the claim presented to us, upon its merits. We are asked to do to the British nation just what we have always insisted that all nations ought to do to us."

Adverting then to the effect of this decision upon the future relations of the two countries, he said: "Cases might be found in history where Great Britain refused to yield to other nations, and even to ourselves, claims like that which is now before us. She could in no other way so effectually disavow any such injury as we think she does by assuming now, as her own, the ground upon which we then stood."

He concluded with an expression of satisfaction that "by the adjustment of the present case, upon principles confessedly American, and yet, as we trust, mutually satisfactory to both the nations concerned, a question is finally and rightly settled between them, which for more than half a century alienated the two countries from each other."

The Cabinet meeting which considered the question was an anxious and earnest one. The Secretary of State stated the case, and gave the substance of his views in regard to it. Other members, not having studied the subject, naturally shared in the popular feeling. "At least," as one said, "we need not decide at once. Let us settle it that we won't surrender them today. We can meet again, and consider about it tomorrow." So the matter went over.

After the other gentlemen had retired, the President said: "Governor Seward, you will go on, of course, preparing your answer, which, as I understand, will state the reasons why they ought to be given up. Now I have a mind to try my hand at stating the reasons why they ought not to be given up. We will compare the points on each side."

My father heartily assented. The mutual confidence between the two had now grown so great, that each felt the other would ask approval of nothing that was not sound.

On the next day the Cabinet reassembled. The Secretary of State again read his reply. There were some expressions of regret that the step was necessary, but it was adopted without a dissenting voice. The council broke up reassured on the point that war with England was averted, but not without misgivings as to the temper in which the people would receive the decision. The President expressed his approval.

When the others were gone, my father alluded to their conversation of the day before. "You thought you might frame an argument for the other side?" Mr. Lincoln smiled and shook his head. "I found I could not make an argument that would satisfy my own mind," he said, "and that proved to me your ground was the right one."

This was characteristic of Lincoln. Presidents and kings are not apt to see flaws in their own arguments. But fortunately for the Union, it had a President at this time who combined a logical intellect with an unselfish heart.

On the evening of Friday, there were several guests at dinner at our house, among them Mr. and Mrs. Crittenden, and Anthony Trollope, the novelist. Afterward came friends who, hearing rumours of a decision in the *Trent* matter, desired to have them verified, and to thank the Secretary for extricating the country from its dilemma. Coupled with their compliments, however, were many regrets, that the act must inevitably doom him to unpopularity, since the people would resent the loss of their prisoners, and would deem themselves humiliated by their surrender. "It was too bad that he must sacrifice himself."

But now came the evidence of the sterling good sense of the American people. When the decision was announced in the papers, its first visible effects were the relief manifested by all loyal men, and the chagrin which the disloyal could not conceal. Public confidence was restored and renewed. Men meeting each other in the street shook hands over it, and said: "Now we shall pull through."

Down dropped the premium on gold. Up went the prices of United States stocks. Recruiting officers showed that volunteering was briskly renewed. The expected storm of public indignation did not come. Nobody seemed to feel humiliated. Nobody condemned the act but the sympathizers with secession, and they shook their heads over "Seward's infernal cunning."

A day or two later, when the public had time to read the document, and the newspapers had opportunity for comment, it was seen that in returning Mason and Slidell the United States had established beyond peradventure the doctrine for which the War of 1812 was fought, and had committed England to it also. Then the sense of relief gave place to exultation. Thanks and congratulations began to pour in upon the Secretary of State by every mail. Apparently, instead of working his ruin, it was likely to prove one of the most popular acts of his life.

The morning after the Secretary's reply had been formally handed to Lord Lyons, and communicated by him to his Government, Captain Fox, the Assistant Secretary of the Navy, came for a confidential call. He warmly commended the decision and said: "Of course it is wise and right. But now, as to the actual delivery of the prisoners. That will be a somewhat embarrassing duty for any navy officer to perform. No one would like to be chosen for it, and I hardly know what ship or commander to detail for the service."

"Of course," my father said, "it is a duty that naturally belongs to the State Department, which will take charge of it. Lord Lyons agrees with me that it should be done unostentatiously. To avoid any public demonstration at Boston or elsewhere he will send her Majesty's frigate *Rinaldo* to any point that we may designate to receive the prisoners."

Captain Fox replied that he thought Provincetown, on the tip end of Cape Cod, would be a safe and quiet place.

So it was settled that the British frigate should proceed to Provincetown.

I was called into the consultation, and undertook to find a trustworthy officer of the State Department, who would perform the mission with celerity, discretion, and secrecy.

Mr. E. D. Webster, who had before discharged confidential missions for the Secretary, was selected. He proceeded at once to Boston, hired a tug, and went to Fort Warren, without attracting any public attention.

Captain Martin Burke, the commandant of the fort, was glad to be relieved of his prisoners, and helped to put them on board the tug.

Mason apparently was unfeignedly glad to get out of confinement, but Slidell, who was more keen-witted and sagacious, saw that their release would end the possibility of the hoped-for clash between Great Britain and the United States, and would be a blow to the Confederacy. He, at first, flatly refused to be taken from Fort Warren, until a British ship should come there for him. Finding this ground untenable, and being warned that force, if necessary, would be used, he consented at last to go on board the tug.

Webster found the trip across Massachusetts Bay rather rough and stormy, but uneventful, and both the prisoners decidedly reticent. They found the *Rinaldo* at anchor awaiting them, and her captain ready to receive his unusual passengers with every respect and courtesy.

The frigate weighed anchor at once, and proceeded to

England.   So the interrupted journey begun on the *Trent*
was finally completed on the *Rinaldo*.   But it was a
question whether the prisoners who had so warmly resisted capture by Captain Wilkes were not equally
chagrined at their release from the custody of Captain
Martin Burke.

Webster was back in Washington with his report and
engaged in his usual duties before the public had any
wind of his errand to Cape Cod.

February, 1862.

A Series of Victories.   Several months of the war had
now passed.   Begun without any military preparation,
at least as far as the North was concerned, it was not
strange that it opened with disasters.   The work of en-
listing, equipping, and training the soldiers all had to be
done while hostilities were in active progress.   But this
period had now passed.   The work had been accomplished
with spirit and energy, and we had at last an army, with
commanders capable of effective action.

In his "Circular dispatch to ministers abroad" my father
was now able to say:

"Cloudless skies with drying winter winds have at last
succeeded the storm which so long held our fleets in em-
bargo, and our land forces in their camps.   The Burnside
expedition has escaped its perils and is now in activity
on the coast of North Carolina.   The victory of General
Thomas at Mill Spring in Kentucky has been quickly
followed by the capture of Fort Henry on the Tennessee
River, and the interruption of the railroad, by which the
insurgents have kept up their communication between
Bowling Green and Columbus. . .

"The success of the Union army in the West having
brought the whole of Missouri and a large part of Tennessee under the authority of the United States, and having

13

already a passage opened for us into Alabama, Mississippi, and Arkansas, it has been determined today to permit the restoration of trade upon our inland ways and waters, under certain limitations and restrictions.

"You will have noticed our successful advance down the Mississippi and along its banks. Next week we shall ascertain the strength of the obstructions at Memphis. . . . General Butler, with an adequate land force, and Captains Farragut and Porter with a fleet, are already in motion to seize and hold New Orleans."

A month later he continued: "The events of the week have been striking and significant, the capture of Newbern by Burnside, with the consequent evacuation of Beaufort and Fort Macon by the insurgents and the destruction by themselves of their own steamer *Nashville*— the rout of the insurgents on their retreat from Winchester to Strasburg by General Shields—the victory of General Pope at New Madrid and the bombardment of Island No. 10 by Commodore Foote."

A few weeks later, he continued: "The victories of Fort Henry, Fort Donelson, the occupation of Bowling Green, Nashville, Murfreesboro, and Columbus, the capture of the fortified position of Island No. 10 in the Mississippi, with one hundred heavy guns, thirty pieces of field artillery, and six thousand prisoners, are the events of the week. Today the country is assuming that the fate of this unnatural war is determined by the great event of the capture of New Orleans, which was effected by a naval expedition on the 24th."

May, 1862.

A Cruise between Two Armies. The tide of success seems now to be flowing in our direction. General McClellan is marching up the Peninsula toward Richmond, and General McDowell is opening his way downward from

A Cruise between Two Armies 195

Fredericksburg. Our fleets are patrolling the Potomac, controlling the entrances of the Rappahannock, the York, the James, and the Elizabeth rivers, and mustering in force at Hampton Roads.

The Secretary of the Navy deems this a favourable time for an inspection of the fleets, and observation of the progress of the joint operations of army and navy. He has invited his colleagues, the Secretary of State and the Attorney-General, to accompany him. Some of the members of their families and of the official staff of their Departments will be of the party.

Monday.

The river steamboat *City of Baltimore*, which has been fitted up for naval patrol and blockade duty, has been selected as the one for this special cruise. Captain Dahlgren will be in command. She carries, for protection against attack, two field howitzers, with muskets and cutlasses for the crew.

The voyage should be an instructive one as a sort of reconnoissance, enabling us to more fully comprehend the relative position and strength of our own forces and those of the Confederates.

Tuesday.

The Navy Department, of course, will be left in charge of Captain Fox, during the absence of Secretary Welles. Mr. Hunter will take charge of the Department of State.

We go on board this afternoon. Our party consists of Mr. and Mrs. Welles and niece, Mr. Attorney-General Bates, Mr. Faxon, Chief Clerk of the Navy Department, and his son, Dr. and Mrs. Whelan, of the Navy Department, and their son, Mrs. Goldsborough and Miss Goldsborough, wife and daughter of the Commodore, and

Mr. Goldsborough, the Commodore's brother,—all naval people except Mr. Bates and ourselves.

We have two pilots and thirteen sailors, two howitzers and two dozen muskets. We have as stewards Wormley and his cook and waiters, and we carry coal and provisions for a week.

Wednesday morning.

Leaving the Navy Yard yesterday afternoon, we came down the Potomac, passing the evening in looking at Fort Washington, Alexandria, Mount Vernon, White House Point, Shipping Point, Budd's Point, and Martha's Point, famous for their Confederate batteries—all now deserted. We slept peacefully through the voyage during the night down the lower Potomac. This morning we woke up in the York River, between the earthworks of Yorktown on one side and Gloucester on the other.

Wednesday night.

This day has been spent on the York River and the Pamunkey. We passed on up the York River, full of transport and provision ships, and saw the white flags waving from the houses on either shore.

We reached West Point at noon, and found there the gunboats and Franklin's battleground. Then we passed on, up the Pamunkey, a stream as large as the Hudson at Troy, and so winding that you go three miles to advance one. We saw deserted houses, no whites, but many negroes, who bowed and grinned obsequiously when they saw the national flag. At three o'clock we reached Cumberland. There we found a clearing in the woods containing two houses, suddenly transformed into a great city of a hundred thousand people by the advent of McClellan's army and its supporting fleet.

The General and his staff, with the French princes,

Major Palmer, and several other Washington acquaintances, came on board, and then took us ashore, up and down the hills, through the camps, the Secretaries reviewing ten or twelve thousand of Porter's and Franklin's men.

At night, the long lines of lights on the shore, the shipping and bustle in the river, made it almost impossible to believe we were not in the harbour of Philadelphia or New York.

Thursday.

We passed safely down again through the sunken ships with which the Secessionists supposed they had obstructed the river, and woke up again this morning off Yorktown.

Proceeding on our way again in a drizzling rain, we reached Fortress Monroe about noon. Here we found spread out before us a great fleet at anchor in the Roads.

Thursday evening.

On arriving, we ran alongside the flagship *Minnesota*, and took Commodore Goldsborough and his lieutenant, and Mr. Tucker, Assistant Secretary of War, on board.

Then we steamed on, passing the *Vanderbilt*, the *Arago*, the *Ericsson*, the gunboats and the transports which crowded the Roads, and so past Sewall's Point and Craney Island, and the sunken *Merrimac*, up the Elizabeth River to Norfolk.

Wrecks of vessels destroyed by the Secessionists lay in the channel. The hulk of the old frigate *United States* lay moored, ready to be sunk, but not sunk, because they left it in too much haste.

We dined, and then, as the rain had stopped, went to the wharf, and sent for General Viele, the Military Governor, one of my old schoolmates in Albany. He and his staff came on board, and after a little, a crowd gathered on the wharf, sullen and sour and curious.

The General pointed out one or two Union men, who had stood firm through the long night of secession, and they were called up on board to be congratulated. One burst into tears on finding himself once more among loyal men, under the old flag, and all were almost demented with joy.

We went ashore and walked up and down the streets: all the shops shut up, all the doors and windows of private houses closed, all the population idle, a sentry at each corner, a patrol in each street, no woman visible, and no man, except now and then some exultant Unionist, venturing to say a word.

"Do you see me," said one, taking off his hat. "They beat me and robbed me, and drove me from town, six months ago, because I wouldn't hurrah for their cursed flag. I've just come back home today. They hate to see me in their streets as much as they hate to see you. But the sight of the old flag and the sound of *Hail Columbia* here pays me for all I've suffered."

Returning on board, we steamed up to the frigate *Susquehanna* and cast anchor for the night. She manned her yards and fired a salute in compliment to the Secretaries, while Norfolk sank into darkness like a city of the dead, in strong contrast with the magic town sprung from nought where we passed last night.

Friday.

This morning we steamed on up the river to the navy yard. Portsmouth, inhabited mostly by working people, is more loyal than Norfolk, and such as could get a Union flag hung it out from their trees or chimneys. The *Susquehanna's* band was on board, and, not desiring to parade our triumph or gall the people's feelings, they were told to play only airs without significance. But the people who ran along the shore and cheered, called out:

"Oh! play the *Star Spangled Banner!*   Do let us hear the *Star Spangled Banner* once more."

And when they heard it, they shouted and cried, and waved their hats, handkerchiefs, and anything they could get; and seemed to be willing to follow for any distance, to hear it still.   The coloured folks were especially in their glory—such an amount of coloured chuckling and laughing had not transpired in Portsmouth for a year at least.

We landed at what was the navy yard, and is now a mass of smoking ruins.   Long rows of crumbling walls, and roofless, empty, charred brick buildings, piles of still smoking ashes, docks and wharves torn up by gunpowder, wrecks of vessels burned to the water's edge, cover many acres.

A Massachusetts regiment was encamped among the ruins, and one man, with Yankee readiness, had contrived to establish a blacksmith shop out of the fragments, and was driving a successful business, mending guns and shoeing horses.   A huge gun, burst in the middle, was recognized as one which a ball from the *Cumberland* destroyed on board the *Merrimac*, and Captain Dahlgren found it one of his own make.   The soldier who stood guard over it asked me if I remembered, about eighteen months ago, reading in the newspapers of a Boston shoemaker, cruelly beaten and tarred and feathered in Savannah for supposed "abolitionism."   I told him I remembered printing it in the Albany *Journal.*

"I am that shoemaker," said he.   "I enlisted in the first Massachusetts regiment I could find, and I have got so far on my way back to Savannah to see those gentlemen again."

Returning to our boat, we found Captain Hewett, of the British steamer *Rinaldo*, who had come to pay his respects to the Secretary of State.   The *Rinaldo* took

Slidell and Mason when they were released from Fort Warren; and is now returned to Norfolk.

We steamed down the river again, stopping to look at the deserted rebel fortifications on Craney Island and Sewall's Point, and to get a piece of the wreck of the *Merrimac*,—and so on to Fortress Monroe—landed again —were received by General Wool with a salute and all the honours—went on board the *Minnesota*—were received by the Commodore with a salute and all the honours there— examined her armament, her five hundred men, her depths of decks below decks, and machinery below them all— and now we are returned to the wharf of the fort, where we are to sleep tonight.

Saturday.

Saturday Commodore Goldsborough had fixed upon for an expedition up the James River, to attack and destroy the fortifications which the *Monitor* and *Galena* had run by without reducing. At seven in the morning the ships got under way in order of battle—a magnificent sight. A large steam tugboat, under command of Lieutenant Selfridge, with one large gun, led the way, to open the attack, then at about an eighth of a mile behind came the *Dacotah*, an equal distance behind her the *Susquehanna*, with the blue pennant of the Commodore, then behind her the *Wachusett*, and behind her the *Maratanza*. Last of all followed our boat.

We passed on up the river fifteen miles. We found the first battery at Day Point; reconnoitered with the glass; found it deserted and passed on. A few miles farther up, the telescope showed a secession flag still waving over "Fort Huger" on Hardy's Bluff.

We saw the signals hoisted on the flagship, heard the drums beat to quarters, and saw the guns run out, as the whole fleet slowly steamed up in line toward the fort.

Presently a puff of white smoke from the tug, and then the dull report of her gun.   No reply from the fort.   Then the *Dacotah* veered slightly; and a larger puff of smoke from her, followed by a louder report.   A second after, we saw the shell burst over the fort.   Then the *Susquehanna* opened with her hundred pounders, of which we could see the flash as well as the smoke.   Then the *Maratanza*, just before us; and we saw the shells go, tearing up the earth of the fort in a shower.   Still no reply.   The flagship again signalled, the firing ceased, and a small boat, filled with sailors and marines, with cutlasses and muskets, pushed off from each vessel.

They landed, and ran up the bank like mad.   Presently, we saw the flag, staff and all, come down with a crash and a hurrah.   Then it went up again with the Stars and Stripes substituted, and then another cheer.   Then the sailors returned, and the tug came alongside with an officer to report that the enemy had evacuated the battery, leaving all the guns, some shotted and ready for use, their stores, their dinner half eaten, and the flag nailed to the staff.

So the James River was opened.   We started again up the river, but found nothing for some miles.   At last, two steamers carrying the Union flag hove in sight around a point.   They fired a gun when they saw us.   We hailed them, and sent for the commanding officer to come on board.   He came, a young lieutenant, the commander having been wounded in a battle near Richmond.   His boat was the *Port Royal*, the other the *Naugatuck*.   He told us of the repulse at Fort Darling, and then went on down to report to the Commodore, who came on board for a consultation as to what next.

About dusk we started up again, to try to go up as far as Jamestown, to see the ruins of historic interest.   Three of the gunboats went along to convoy us in safety.   But the channel was crooked and shallow, and the pilot new. The *Wachusett* went aground; then the *Port Royal.* We left the *Maratanza* trying to draw her comrades off, and went on alone. The shores were dark and desolate, the river without a craft, and the night still and silent. Presently we went aground, but in a quarter of an hour we were off again.

About eleven o'clock Captain Dahlgren announced that we were off Jamestown, though the river and shore looked as dark and desolate there as anywhere else. To guard against surprise, the lights were all put out, the howitzers loaded, the muskets distributed to the crew, and the steam kept up, ready for a start at a moment's notice. But nobody disturbed us.

Sunday.

At daylight we were up to see Jamestown. The whole of it consists of a ruined brick doorway of the old church where Captain John Smith worshipped. There was one house nearby, and an earthwork for a fort, from which smoke was ascending. We sent a boat ashore. They found the house and fort both empty; two dogs and two "contrabands" were the only living beings. The "contrabands" reported that the people in the house and in the earthwork, alarmed by our boat, had fled in the night. They, the "contrabands," asked to come on board; so the sailors brought them.

Soon after, a large boat was seen pulling down from the direction of the rebel lines. Spy-glasses were brought into requisition. The boat was heading directly for the steamboat, but whether its occupants were armed could not, at first, be ascertained. Presently an officer remarked: "I think they are all black, sir,"—a welcome announcement; for in that case they were all friends.

Sure enough, when it came nearer and drew alongside,

the boat was seen to be filled with thirteen men, one woman, and two children, in shabby clothes, but having neither arms, provisions, nor plunder. Not a word was spoken, as they pulled fearlessly up to the gangway, until the leader stood up and was preparing to climb on board.

"Ahoy, there," called out the officer of the deck. "Who are you? Where are you going?"

The answer was respectful but sententious. "Going along with yous, Mas'r."

"But you don't know where we're going. Don't you see that we are headed toward Richmond? What made you come to us?"

The coloured spokesman grinned and pointed upward.

"Ain't afraid to go nowhar' with you, Mas'r, under dat flag."

So they set their boat adrift, and confided their lives and fortunes to our charge. The woman was as white as Louisa, and the children whiter still. They said they were slaves of Colonel Millroy and Colonel Stratton of the Confederate army; that their masters had carried off the corn to the mountains in North Carolina, and were going to take them there. So they took a boat out of a pond, carried it in the night on their shoulders, launched it on the James River, and met us. One of them said his master "swore up to his waist" when he told them he was going to take them to Carolina.

We turned our steamer down the river again—passed on without incident, except the discovery of plenty of Confederate barracks, sheds, and fortifications—all deserted—rejoined the fleet, stopped at Newport News to pay a visit to General Mansfield, were received with salutes, etc., saw the wrecks of the *Cumberland* and *Congress*, the hole made in General Mansfield's room by a shell from the *Merrimac*, and finally returned to Fortress Monroe at noon. Captain Gautier, of the French frigate *Gassendi*,

came on board to pay us a visit. We landed our "contrabands" to go to work in the navy yard, except the woman
and children, whom we decided to bring to Washington.

Monday.

We left Fortress Monroe last evening, had an uneventful voyage up Chesapeake Bay and the Potomac during
the night, and have arrived here safe and well today.

I cannot close this chronicle of our "Cruise" better
than by quoting my father's comment on it in a letter to
his daughter Fanny:

"Our excursion into Virginia was very interesting and
very instructive. We saw war, not in its holiday garb,
but in its stern and fearful aspect. We saw the desolation that follows, and the terror that precedes its march.
We saw, in the relaxation of African bondage, and the
flight of bondsmen and bondswomen with their children,
how Providence brings relief to some out of the crimes
and sufferings of our common race.

"All the hopes and fears and anxieties of this unhappy
strife renew themselves at this moment, and cluster about
the armies at Richmond and Corinth. The public mind,
accustomed to successes, is little disturbed—but for one
who has such responsibilities as mine, there is nothing but
unwearied watchfulness. I believe that the good cause
will prevail, but I know very well that it must encounter
occasional reverses. I prepare to meet them."

July, 1862.

A Season of Reverses and Depression. When the news
came of the "Seven Days' Battles" on the Peninsula, the
first effect on the popular mind was that of incredulity and
bewilderment. Then succeeded conflicting arguments
over contradictory reports, and then followed general
consternation and alarm. It was claimed that McClellan

had only made a "change of base." But the "change of base" was evidently compulsory. The base might be a better one, but it was one he was forced to take. Every one of the battles was claimed to have ended in a victory, yet the general character of the movement was very like a retreat. The army had behaved with great gallantry and bravery, and the loss of life was fearful. But what had been gained or lost? Perhaps a humorous bit in *Vanity Fair* well enough expressed the state of the public mind. Its war correspondent "MacArone" said: "Yes, my boy, we have had a great victory. And now we want to know who is to blame for it! Believe nothing about the army until you see it in the newspapers. P. S. Believe nothing that you *do* see in the newspapers."

General Heintzelman, afterwards, speaking of the movement, said he had always seen the train of stragglers and camp followers moving behind the army, but this time they went ahead.

There were frequent and anxious meetings of the Cabinet, and a general command over all the land forces of the United States was given to Major-General Halleck, who came from the Western Department to the capital. It was evident that a new appeal to the country for additional troops was necessary. The Secretary of State went to New York to summon a conference of all the loyal governors, and to ascertain from them how many it was safe to call for. He telegraphed the result of this conference and thereupon the President issued his proclamation for three hundred thousand men. The response to this proclamation was more favourable than could have been anticipated. On it was based the celebrated lyric: "We are coming, Father Abraham, three hundred thousand more!"

The "Circular on the military situation" continued its chronicle of events, saying: "General Halleck, upon

taking command of the army, made a careful survey of
the entire military position, and concluded thereupon to
withdraw the Army of the Potomac from the Peninsula,
and to combine all our forces in front of Richmond.   The
measure was a difficult and delicate one."

Three weeks later the "Circular" contained this:

"Military affairs here have taken an unfavourable direction during the last three weeks.   The Army of the
Potomac, which was in command of General McClellan,
having evacuated its position on the James River, reached
the Potomac, near Alexandria, unpursued and in safety.

"The Army of Virginia, under General Pope, which
was advanced to the Rappahannock, was flanked by the
insurgents, in large force, and retired to Manassas.   Here
it became involved in a series of severe engagements.
Meantime the insurgents, executing a long-cherished
design, advanced on the south side of the upper Potomac,
which at this season is fordable at many points, and,
crossing it at and above Edwards Ferry, occupied
Frederick.   When there, menacing equally Washington,
Baltimore, and Harrisburg, they put forth an appeal to
the people of Maryland, to rise and join in the insurrection.   Our troops having recovered from a temporary
disorganization, an army was immediately organized and
dispatched, under General McClellan, to meet the insurgents at Frederick."

June and July, 1862.

Farmers' Boys in Battle.   Those were gloomy days
in Washington, during the latter part of June, in 1862.
High expectations had been suddenly extinguished by
the reverses in the campaign on the Peninsula.   Union
men were disappointed and discouraged.   "Copperheads"
were elated.   Censures and complaints were rife.   Rumours of disaster multiplied.

The Cabinet realized that the situation had become critical. They knew also of dangers that, as yet, the general public were not aware of. Recruiting had fallen off. The army itself was melting away, under the influence of casualties, desertions, discharges, and disease. Large and speedy reinforcements were needed. How could they be obtained? The reports from the recruiting officers showed that popular feeling was even more despondent in the great cities than in the country at large.

There were frequent conferences at the War Department. Stanton was sending forward regiments, rations, and supplies as rapidly as they could be obtained. The President spent many hours there daily, so as to be in immediate touch with the telegraph, bringing good news and bad, and in consultation with the Secretary and the military commanders. The Secretary of State arranged to go north, to try to rouse popular feeling, hoping by coöperation with the loyal governors and public bodies to hasten the progress of enlistments, and, if possible, to convert despondency into renewed enthusiasm.

Before starting for New York, he invited the members of the New York delegation in the House of Representatives to an afternoon conference at his house. Congress was near the end of its session. Its work had been practically done. It had aided the Government with such legislation and appropriations as were practicable.

He suggested that they could now best help the Union cause by hastening homeward, without waiting for the adjournment, and endeavouring to aid in the work of raising and sending forward the new troops so greatly needed.

His suggestion met with hearty response. Such members as could be spared from committee labours agreed to go at once. Several believed they could do effective work in that way. Some even declared they could organize new regiments, and bring them to Washington themselves before the reassembling of Congress. Wheeler, Pomeroy, Van Valkenburg, Diven, and others started home for this patriotic duty.

They accomplished it with speed and zeal, and the regiments they raised were among the first of that great army that soon was chanting, in response to the President's proclamation:

"We're coming, Father Abraham, three hundred thousand more."

Two of the members whose districts adjoined each other, Van Valkenburg and Diven, agreed to combine their efforts, and so hasten the mustering of the first regiment. It was a proud day for them when they marched it along Pennsylvania Avenue, a thousand strong, with the two Congressmen at its head, as Colonel and Lieutenant-Colonel. They gave the President a marching salute, and then were speedily hurried northward to overtake and join the reorganized Army of the Potomac, which was following Lee up into northern Maryland.

They arrived while Lee and McClellan were confronting each other, apparently on the eve of battle in the vicinity of Sharpsburg.

The Colonel presented himself at headquarters to announce their arrival and report for duty. General McClellan received him.

"Your regiment are raw recruits, I believe, Colonel?"

"Yes, General, and the officers are about as raw as the men. Hardly a veteran among them. Many of them farmers' boys who have never handled a musket. But they saw their fathers and older brothers 'go to the front' last year, and they are eager to follow their example."

"Are they armed and equipped?"

"Yes, fully. Secretary Stanton saw to that."

"Have they had any drills, at all?"

"Hardly any. Hastily organized and lacking time and drill-masters."

"What can they do?"

"Why, they are ready and willing to do anything they can, if somebody will show them how."

"Can they support a battery, do you think?"

"I do not believe I quite know what that is myself, General."

"Why, a battery of artillery is posted, say on yonder hill, to throw shot and shell at the enemy. If the enemy see that it is exposed, with no large infantry force to protect it, they will probably send out cavalry to capture it by a dash or break it up. What you would have to do would be to draw your regiment up in line and in rear of the battery, so as to defend it, if attacked, and perhaps discourage attempts to attack it. Can you do that?"

"Oh, yes, General, they can do that. They know how to stand in line, at least."

"Very well, then, your orders will reach you this evening. Don't let your men break, if you can help it, Colonel. If you are attacked—do the best you can."

In the grey of the early morning, a battery of light artillery was occupying the crest of the hill, and the "regiment of farmers' boys" was drawn up in line behind it. The artillery duel began, and was echoed by other artillery duels going on, at right and left, on other similar heights. A broad stretch of country was exposed to view. Moving bodies of troops in the distance with puffs of smoke rolling ever them, followed by roar of cannon or rattle of musketry, made it an exciting and even exhilarating spectacle—though its method or plan was unintelligible to the spectator.

At first there seemed to be little hint of danger to the new soldiers. But presently they began to hear the whis-

14

tling of bullets in the air overhead, or saw them tearing up the ground at their feet. Evidently, the Confederate sharpshooters were "getting the range." Soon a soldier dropped his musket and fell with a groan, a spurt of blood on his uniform showing where he was hit. The Colonel ordered two of his comrades to take him to the improvised hospital in the rear. Before they returned to the ranks, a similar "casualty" occurred at another part of the long line. They were "under fire."

The Colonel and Lieutenant-Colonel strode up and down in front of the line, from end to end, with brief words of encouragement. "Steady, boys, steady." "Stand firm." "Keep to the ranks." "You're doing your duty." "Don't forget you're defending the old flag." "Whatever happens to us, we mustn't let that battery be taken." The men looked at each other and at their officers, as they saw their comrades fall, but said little. One muttered: "I wish the Johnny Rebs would charge, or we could. I'd rather fall fighting than stand here to be shot at."

And now the fire grew hotter and fiercer. Not only hissing bullets, but screaming, bursting, death-dealing shells began to come over from the enemy's lines. Killed and wounded men lay on the grass at their feet. "Hell had broke loose."

An aide-de-camp, carrying orders to some distant regiment, came galloping past, in their rear. Without stopping his gallop, he shouted as he went by:

"You d——d fools, why don't you lie down?"

It was a rough but welcome salutation. They had not supposed they could lie down. Even the Colonel had not known that to be any part of the game.

Availing himself of the implied order to "get under cover," he ordered the regiment to assume a less exposed attitude, telling them to continue to show enough of themselves, or of their caps and bayonets, to let the enemy see that they were still there, and ready to resist attack and "protect the battery." In this recumbent position, the casualties were much less frequent. Bullets whistled over them and fragments of shell passed by them, that would have killed them, if they had remained standing.

The horrible storm continued for hours, but at last it began to show signs of slackening. Word passed from man to man, and from regiment to regiment, that the enemy were falling back, perhaps preparing to retire from the field.

The rumours increased in number and persistence, until at last, as the sun was setting, news came that General McClellan announced a success. The Union army had won a victory, and it would be known in history as the "Battle of Antietam"!

In the evening, brigade and regiment commanders were summoned to headquarters, to report the casualties and experiences of their respective commands. The Colonel found an excited and joyous crowd of officers exchanging congratulations, and explaining the bandages and slings that some of them were wearing. General McClellan seized him by both hands.

"Colonel, your regiment behaved splendidly. Never saw raw troops do better. They held their ground like veterans. How did you manage to keep them so firm and steady?"

The modest Colonel said: "Well, General, perhaps it was partly due to our ignorance of the art of war. We did not know how to run away. We were put there to support the battery, and so we just stayed on doing it."

The General smiled. "Your farmers' boys are good fellows. They will make a fine regiment, and have an honourable record. Give them my congratulations."

February, 1863.

The Military Situation. At the close of the second year of the war, and the beginning of the third, the aspect of the military situation was still indecisive. The victories of Antietam and South Mountain had restored the popular confidence, and recruiting was going on briskly. But the two great armies, face to face with each other across the Rappahannock, seemed inclined neither to advance nor retreat. At the West, Vicksburg still held out against a protracted siege. The Union troops were making active movements with the general result of gaining ground. The Southerners gained no new ground, but stubbornly held their own.

As the winter wore on, there were two favourable and two unfavourable movements. General Burnside, who was now in command of the Army of the Potomac, crossed the river and made an attack upon the Confederates, but was repulsed with heavy loss, and retired to his former position. In like manner, General Sherman made an unsuccessful assault upon Vicksburg, hoping to carry the fortifications by storm. Repulsed, his army retired, and under the command of General Grant resumed the siege. The two victories to offset these defeats were a victory by General Rosecrans at Murfreesboro, and the capture of Arkansas Post with a large amount of military stores by General McClernand.

Meanwhile the Government was continually adding vessels to the navy, and had commenced the construction of ironclads to take part in the blockade. But the South was also active in this direction, chartering and constructing numerous blockade runners, and, having British sympathy on its side, had no difficulty in raising loans, and purchasing arms and supplies. American merchant vessels were exposed to capture by the enemy's privateers or vessels of war, and so the American merchant marine sustained a blow from which it has never recovered.

Our Foreign Relations in the War. As the progress of the war developed new opportunities, redoubled energy and daring were shown in blockade running enterprises, as well as in sending information and supplies to the insurgents through the Union lines.   The Southerners naturally hated the blockade.   The British as naturally shared in that feeling.   The South encouraged communication in every possible way with England, while the North had for its own safety to impose a vexatious system of passports, police surveillance, frontier guards, and blockading squadrons.

Arrests and seizures were of frequent occurrence.   Then the Secessionists would avail themselves of the protection of European governments for those engaged in these enterprises.   Havana, Nassau, and the towns on the Canadian frontier became favourite points of rendezvous.   They could meet, consult, and mature their plans with impunity, and could find there many whom cupidity or love of adventure would lead to join them.

The authorities, both British and Spanish, were jealous of interference by United States officers with any vessels or persons under their jurisdiction.   The vessels and men engaged, if successful, loudly boasted of their connection with the rebels, but when intercepted or captured declared themselves "neutrals" and claimed the protection of foreign governments.

An infinite variety of questions arose, and the shelves of the Department of State to this day groan under the burden of the documents and discussions to which they gave rise.   Many of the cases, arising under novel conditions of modern warfare, were without any precedent to govern their decision.   Yet it was necessary, not only to render exact justice, but to do it in a way that should not offend the roused susceptibilities either of the American or the foreign nation.

Sometimes a single seizure would give rise to half a dozen different questions, while the "Laird rams," the *Florida* and the *Alabama*, came up, in one shape or another, by every foreign mail.

The Queen's proclamation of "belligerent rights" was claimed as a convenient screen for all kinds of daring enterprises. They were further encouraged and stimulated by London insurance companies. Those engaged in them often obtained insurance on their vessels and cargoes at Lloyds and other offices, at fifteen per cent. for running in, and fifteen per cent. for coming out. Insurers were tempted to share in these ventures by the enormous profits, while the shippers and merchants made money if even but half of their vessels got safe into port.

Unusual activity and unwonted industry pervaded the Washington legations of all the maritime Powers. The attachés of the British Legation found themselves as busy as hard-working attorneys' clerks. A dozen communications a day would frequently pass between the Legation and the Department. There were vessels unlawfully detained, on suspicion of running the blockade; vessels lawfully captured in attempting to run it; rebel cruisers receiving aid and comfort in colonial ports; Federal cruisers in the same ports denied ordinary courtesy; rebel ships escaping the vigilance of British authorities; British ships complaining of the surveillance of American ones; prisoners wanting to be released on taking the oath of allegiance; prisoners taking it and breaking it as soon as released; seamen claiming exemption because they were British subjects; claims of shipowners for damages; intercepted dispatches; vessels wrongly seized, or rightly seized but wrongly dealt with; customs regulations not in accordance with treaties; customs decisions not in accordance with facts; duties that ought to be refunded; duties that ought not to be collected; foreign subjects claiming exemption from draft; enlisted soldiers claiming release as foreigners after having spent their bounty money; officers arrested as spies and spies escaping as clergymen; rifles shipped as farming implements, and gunpowder as white lead; rebel munitions of war purporting to be "arms for the Indians"; and treasonable documents pretending to be "Bibles for the heathen."

The French Government, like the British, had no faith that our national Union would ever be restored, and from time to time manifested its impatience at the continuance of what it deemed our hopeless struggle. On at least seven different occasions, the preliminary steps towards intervention were taken, and only checked by diplomatic address on the part of the United States, or by news of success of the Union arms.

First was the project of joint action with Great Britain already described. This was nipped in the bud in 1861.

Then the plan to make common cause with Great Britain in the "Trent Affair." This was thwarted by the diplomatic settlement.

Next the notice given to the United States, that the manufacturing and commercial classes of France were suffering from the depression caused by the blockade, which prevented the export of cotton, and the import of French goods at Southern ports. This was checked by the capture of New Orleans and other ports, and reopening them to trade under the flag of the Union.

Then came the denunciation of the Federal Government for temporarily obstructing Charleston harbour by sinking vessels loaded with stone. This was answered by saying that France herself had done the same thing, under the Treaty of Utrecht, and had not only temporarily but permanently closed a harbour, that remains closed today.

In 1862, the Emperor's address to the Chambers was prepared, and contained an intimation that he was about to take steps for active measures to break the blockade. The secession advocates in Europe were jubilant over the expected announcement, and stock speculators of the London Exchange and Paris Bourse were going to make their fortunes by its effects on the market. At the last moment, the Emperor became convinced that the step was a dangerous one, and the threatening paragraph was stricken out. As the American Minister, Mr. Dayton, wrote: "The Emperor's address came; but it was not what they expected. They said that just before its delivery the 'switch had been turned off,' and forthwith the British ministry, the *London Times*, and other portions of the English press ran off along with it."

In 1863, the Emperor renewed his proposal for joint interference in the American contest, saying that if other Powers refused, he would proceed alone. But, before he was ready to do so, came the fall of Vicksburg and the victory of Gettysburg, and the French Minister at Washington wrote his Imperial master that in view of these great successes of the Union arms he had better wait still longer.

The projected intervention was again and again attempted in some different form, during each succeeding year. At one time, the plan was seriously discussed at Paris of putting forward some small power like Belgium to pick a quarrel with the United States, and then the two great empires, suddenly espousing that side of the controversy, would be able jointly to crush the American Government, thus drawn into a trap.

The latest and most dangerous perhaps of all the French movements was the expedition to set up an empire in

Mexico, overthrowing the republican government there, and menacing it in the United States.   The French Minister of Foreign Affairs, M. Drouyn de l'Huys, in conversing with Mr. Dayton, the American envoy, assured him that France had no thought of conquering Mexico, or establishing a permanent power there.   "In the abandon of a conversation somewhat familiar," added Mr. Dayton, "I took occasion to say, that in quitting Mexico France might leave a puppet behind her. 'No,' replied M. Drouyn de l'Huys, 'no, the string would be too long to work.'"

In this opinion the Minister was sagacious and wise. But ultimately he was overruled by the Emperor, who had determined to try the experiment with Maximilian. It resulted as M. Drouyn de l'Huys had predicted, "the string was too long to work," and the unfortunate Archduke finally lost not only the empire, but his life.

But all foreign governments were not unfriendly during the war.   The Latin-American republics, though they could not give aid, did not withhold their sympathies. Even the threatening cloud of European intervention was relieved here and there by a ray of sunshine.   Sweden and Denmark sent words of sympathy.   Italy expressed the friendship that had been expected from her.   Prussia sent assurances of just and generous feeling.   The President of the only republic in Europe wrote that Switzerland regarded the struggle with the deepest anxiety, adding that "Switzerland passed through a similar crisis fourteen years ago. May God grant that the United States of America may also emerge renewed and strengthened from this crisis."

Mr. Hitz, the Consul-General of Switzerland at Washington, was a frequent visitor to the arriving regiments on Capitol Hill, and relieved their wants as far as he was able.

Russia was a steadfast friend of the United States during the war. In the volumes of diplomatic correspondence, there are very few pages under the head of "Russia," and these contain only messages of amity and good will. Russia had no grounds of complaint for damages, or if she had she never presented them. The plan for an intercontinental telegraph, to connect the United States and Russia by way of Behring Strait, and the survey of the route made under the auspices of the two governments, helped to promote the mutual good feeling.

It was through the legation at St. Petersburg that information was received of the design of France and England to enter upon a scheme of joint action adverse to the United States. Russia was invited to join in their plans for "mediation" and "intervention," but promptly refused unless the United States should ask her.

When the threatened "intervention" seemed, nevertheless, to be impending, two Russian fleets appeared in American waters, and passed summer and winter there. One came up the Potomac to Washington, and subsequently visited New York. The other appeared at San Francisco.

Official announcement of their purposes might be embarrassing, and Prince Gortschakoff was a sagacious diplomatist. He simply sent over the fleets, and instructed the Russian Minister to say that they came for "no unfriendly purpose." The Government and people of the United States intuitively understood that, while their help might never be needed, yet if needed it would be forthcoming. Courtesies and festivities were exchanged on ship and shore, between the naval officers and the authorities at New York and Washington. The Secretary of State gave an official dinner to the higher officers of the fleet, and the Russian Minister responded by another. Congress was invited as a body to visit the

fleet at the navy yard, and a great ball was held in the
Russians' honour at the New York Academy of Music.
The significance of these events was fully appreciated
at London and Paris.

February, 1862.

A Moorish Episode. Quaint, mediæval, and Sara-
cenic, the city of Tangier rises out of the blue sea, toward
the commanding heights of the African shore.   The castle
and fortifications, with their frowning walls, give it a
formidable air, and the glare of its whitish buildings in
the blazing sun give it an aspect of cleanliness, which
is not borne out by closer inspection of its narrow,
unsavoury streets.

A motley population, of all complexions, throng these
streets, shouting at each other in a babel of tongues,
Frankish and Mahometan, Jewish, Italian, Spanish, and
Portuguese.   White turbans and black slaves, red fezzes
and gleaming simitars, dogs, donkeys, and camels, add
to the general picturesqueness, so that it has been aptly
said by a traveller that in Tangier one is never certain
whether he is living in the Old Testament or the Arabian
Nights.

To such a traveller, it seems odd to see the Stars and
Stripes gaily fluttering over one of the antique structures
with calm assertiveness.   Tangier is one of the few places
in the world where the United States Government owns
the home of its diplomatic representative.   The fact that
his flag has waved there undisturbed for more years than
any living man can remember lends to the American Consul-General a prestige and dignity not always accorded to
consuls who lodge in shabby, shifting quarters, over shops.

Trade and intercourse with America are not great,
but "down along the coast of the High Barbaree" there
is a traditional respect for the American flag, handed

down from the days when the navy of the young Republic amazed Europe by sweeping the Barbary pirates out of the Mediterranean waters, where they had prowled and plundered for centuries.

In the year 1862, the occupant of the Consulate was Judge De Long, of Ohio. He was not much versed in Oriental wiles or modern diplomacy, but he was a zealous patriot, an honest lawyer, and an upright official. His blunt, straightforward talk was sometimes displeasing to his European colleagues, but it impressed the Moslem authorities, whose ears found it a novelty after many years of listening to glib phrases uttered in every language, from modern Parisian to ancient Sanskrit.

One February morning news was brought to the Consulate that two well-dressed Americans, with an air of authority, were sauntering through the streets of Tangier, indulging in offensive and insulting remarks about the American flag and its Consul, and expressing views in general that were highly derogatory to the honour of the United States.

Further inquiry easily discovered who they were, for they made no secret of it. One was called Tunstall and said he had been acting as United States Consul at Cadiz, until the previous summer. The other was Myers, formerly in our navy and now lieutenant of the Confederate cruiser *Sumter*, which was lying in the port of Gibraltar, where she had put in for coal.

Greatly scandalized by such proceedings, the Judge remarked: "American citizens may plot treason and rebellion at home, but they shall not do so where I am, if I have the power to prevent it." Thereupon, he promptly dispatched a messenger to Sidi Mohammed Bargash, the Minister of State, with whom he held intercourse and requested that a file of soldiers should be sent to aid him in dealing with some traitorous fellow-countrymen.

Treason and rebellion are not uncommon offences in Morocco, where the constituted rulers regard them as cardinal sins, and the usual penalty for them is decapitation.

When Sidi Mohammed Bargash inquired what the Consul-General wished to have done with his malefactors, he was relieved to learn that the Judge did not ask to have their heads cut off, nor to have them thrown into the dungeons of the castle, but only to have them delivered under guard at the door of the American Consulate.

The soldiers were sent. They overtook the offenders, who were leisurely proceeding toward the French steamer on which they were about to re-embark. The Moorish soldiers arrested them and marched them up to the American Consulate.

Now some explanations from them were in order. They began to expostulate. Their arrest, they declared, was absurd, an egregious blunder. They were peaceable travellers in a foreign land. True, they were at war with the United States, but Morocco was neutral soil, and nobody had a right to stop them there. They pointed out that international law, and the rules of neutrality, entitled them to immunity from arrest. In fact, according to law, the Consul could not arrest them.

The Judge's reply was succinct and to the point. He said he not only could arrest them, but that he had.

They declared they would appeal for protection to the European Powers, all of whom would demand their release.

The Judge intimated that they might appeal to all the governments in Christendom, if they chose; but that it would take considerable time. Meanwhile, they were under the jurisdiction of a Mahometan one, which was friendly to him and to the United States.

Finding him deaf to persuasion and argument, they

dispatched a communication to the French Consul, stating their case. They had come over for a pleasure trip across the Straits, on the French steamer *Ville de Malaga*, intending to re-embark on her in the evening. They had been arrested and locked up, under a guard of four Moorish soldiers, without any warrant or justification. They asked his interposition to end this absurd state of affairs.

The reply of the French Consul was courteous but diplomatic. He regretted their detention. But they were not French subjects, and when they left the French steamer and landed on Moorish territory, he had no right to protect them, nor to interfere in any way whatever.

A similar application to the British Minister, Mr. Drummond Hay, met with similar unsatisfactory results. Firstly, the Minister said, he had no power to interfere, and secondly, Her Majesty's Government had given positive instructions to her ministers and consuls to observe strict neutrality in this unhappy American contest.

The prisoners were not disheartened. Like their captor, they were quick-witted, resolute Americans, so they cast about for other help. Surely, there must be plenty of sympathizers with the Southern cause here in Tangier. They had found them at Gibraltar, at Cadiz, in fact, everywhere that the *Sumter* had touched. It seemed ridiculous that they should be left to lie here in a Moorish prison.

They had heard that Moorish guards sometimes were open to bribery. They mustered up a hundred dollars in gold coins and a gold watch, and with them opened negotiations.

Unluckily the Judge got wind of it, and promptly stopped the bargain. Then he sent to Sidi Mohammed Bargash for more guards, and ordered the prisoners put in irons. Someone lent them a case knife, with which

Myers cut the rivets. He then jumped out of the window. But he only landed in the consular courtyard, where he was immediately caught and brought back to confinement.

But other instrumentalities were at work in their behalf. Now appeared upon the scene no less a personage than the Military Secretary of the Governor of Gibraltar.

He was the bearer of a letter to the Moorish Minister of Foreign Affairs, from the commander of the Confederate States steamer *Sumter*. It demanded the immediate release of the prisoners,—implying that terrible things would occur if the demand were not complied with. It was a trifle arrogant in tone, considering that the *Sumter* was out of coal, and was under close watch by the United States warship *Tuscarora*, which was cruising off Algeciras. But it had weight with Sidi Mohammed Bargash. He immediately sat down to write a polite note to Judge De Long, saying:

"We have received a letter from the captain of the steamer *Sumter*, from the Confederate States, in which they inform us that the two men you have seized are of the best of men, and they are guiltless,—except that they are from the separated Confederate States. We have no doubt that when you receive this letter, you will put them free."

This was couched in the politest of Arabic. The answer to it was in vigorous American.

The Judge informed his Excellency: first, that there was no government known or recognized as the "Confederate States," either by the United States or the Empire of Morocco, and that the captain and crew of the *Sumter*, as well as the men in custody, were all citizens of the United States resisting its authority; furthermore, that the *Sumter* was a Federal vessel, seized by rebels, and engaged in capturing, plundering, burning, and sinking peaceable American merchant vessels. He concluded by asking, "Shall seventy-six years of uninterrupted friendship between your government and the United States be brought to an end for the sake of pirates?"

By this time the sympathizers with the Southern cause were actively stirring up the motley nationalities in Tangier to disorder. They perceived that instead of waiting for the slow action of the Moorish and European governments they might as well deliver the prisoners themselves, by means of inflammatory speeches, indignation meetings, and a mob.

The movement was started in the market-place, where they had a table set out, with pen, ink, and paper, in the middle of the street, and began signing and pledging themselves in solemn form to force the release of the prisoners at all hazards. The mob, when gathered, would march to the Consulate, groan, howl, curse and swear, break in windows and doors, and, in the height of the tumult, would free the men in spite of their guards.

Word of the threatening state of affairs in the market-place was hastily brought to the Palace, where the Viceroy, Prince Muley el Abbas, was enjoying a quiet smoke.

The Prince listened, and, calmly removing the nargileh from his lips, remarked, "Allah is great. But what the devil have these Christians to do with the American Consul's prisoners?" He signified that it was the province of the lieutenant-governor to take troops, and disperse these riotous Christians.

And now comes another new and unexpected actor in the drama. Off the harbour appears the United States warship *Ino*, flying the American flag. She heads for the anchorage and prepares to exchange the customary salute of twenty-one guns with the Moorish forts. Her captain and officers come ashore in uniform and proceed to the Consulate and the Palace, to make the usual calls of ceremony. The Consul-General joins them.

The Prince and his ministers receive them with courtesy.

Their requests are presented and are acceded to as entirely reasonable. They are, that the *Ino* shall be allowed to land thirty armed marines, who shall march the prisoners from the Consulate down to the ship. The Moorish troops will quell the mob and accompany the prisoners to the beach.

All this is speedily done, within an hour or two. The mob resolves itself into a gaping crowd of three thousand spectators, who stand gazing at the departing warship, carrying away those troublesome Americans.

Then comes to the Consulate a scroll fastened with red cord, of which the substance is this:

"Praise to the One God!

"To the Clever and Wise Gentleman, Consul-General for the American Nation.

"We continue to make inquiries for your welfare. We are deeply penetrated with the expressions of gratitude made use of at your interview with us for the assistance we rendered you in removing the insults offered to you by the Christian subjects, who surrounded the consular residence, thus offering indignity to the American flag.

"We request you to express to your government our sentiments of good will, and to assure them that the friendship between us not only exists and continues, but on our part has become confirmed and consolidated by time; and that we heartily wish them the victory (victorious as they always are) over those who have rebelled against them and peace.

"EL ABBAS,

"Son of the Prince of the Believers.

"May he rest in Glory."

Out of the maze of official documents and personal statements, the story is gathered as here presented.

15

Finally it fell to me, as acting Secretary of State, to "end the diplomatic incident," and close the correspondence, by a formal dispatch to the Consul-General, expressing our appreciation and reciprocation of Morocco's friendship, and adding:

"Good relations between the two countries have existed too long, to be in danger of disturbance from light causes; and serious ones are not likely to spring up between governments whose interest and whose desire it is that they should cherish toward each other good will, and practise frankness and justice.

"You will communicate these sentiments to the Prince; and at the same time assure him, that his wishes for our success over those who are waging an unholy war against the government they had sworn to support are honourable alike to his judgment and his feelings; and that they have given much satisfaction to the President and people of the United States.

"F. W. SEWARD,
"Acting Secretary of State."

After his release from Fort Warren, in Boston harbour, which occurred some months later, Tunstall came to see me at the State Department. He agreed that there was a spice of grim humour in the predicament which unexpectedly overtook him and his friend at Tangier. He said he should not have much minded being captured as a prisoner of war, but that he was not quite prepared to forgive "that Ohio Judge" for putting him in irons.

January 1, 1863.

Signing the Emancipation Proclamation. New Year's Day is always a busy one at the Executive Mansion. The Diplomatic Corps, in official uniform, are presented to the President by the Secretary of State. Civil, military, and naval officers are then received in due succession. Meanwhile the porch, carriage ways, and sidewalk are gradually filling with a gathering throng, awaiting the hour of two o'clock, when the doors are thrown open to the general public.

Thursday, January 1, 1863, was marked by an event that will always be memorable in history. Slaves, in all the regions remaining in rebellion, were to be on that day declared entitled to freedom. The Emancipation Proclamation had been duly prepared at the State Department, and was ready for President Lincoln's signature.

At noon, accompanying my father, I carried the broad parchment in a large portfolio under my arm. We, threading our way through the throng in the vicinity of the White House, went upstairs to the President's room, where Mr. Lincoln speedily joined us. The broad sheet was spread open before him on the Cabinet table. Mr. Lincoln dipped his pen in the ink, and then, holding it a moment above the sheet, seemed to hesitate. Looking around, he said:

"I never in my life felt more certain that I was doing right, than I do in signing this paper. But I have been receiving calls and shaking hands since nine o'clock this morning, till my arm is stiff and numb. Now this signature is one that will be closely examined, and if they find my hand trembled they will say 'he had some compunctions.' But anyway, it is going to be done."

So saying, he slowly and carefully wrote his name at the bottom of the proclamation. The signature proved to be unusually clear, bold, and firm, even for him, and a laugh followed at his apprehension. My father, after appending his own name, and causing the great seal to be affixed, had the important document placed among the archives. Copies were at once given to the press.

May, 1863.

A Visit to the Army of the Potomac.   A year ago this month we made our "Cruise between Two Armies" in a naval vessel.   This year we are to make a visit to the Army of the Potomac, and to traverse part of the same region, besides visiting other points not then occupied.

During the year, both our own army and that of the enemy have been increased and reinforced.   Both have extended and strengthened their fortifications.   General McClellan was then endeavouring to reach Richmond by way of the Peninsula.   Now, General Hooker is seeking to reach it by way of Fredericksburg and the Rappahannock.

Our present expedition is, in some respects, a diplomatic one.   The Secretary of State goes down to visit the troops, and to confer with commanders.   Some of the members of the Diplomatic Corps have been invited to accompany him, in order that they may better understand the situation, and report to their respective governments concerning the condition of the army and the magnitude of its operations.

Our party comprises eleven—Baron Gerolt, the Prussian Minister, Baron Grabow, the Secretary of Legation, Mr. Schleiden, the Minister from the Hanseatic Cities, Count Piper, the Swedish Minister, Judge Goodrich, Secretary of Legation at Brussels, Mr. and Mrs. Titian R. Peale, and ourselves.   The baggage, consisting of carpet bags, shawls and overcoats, spy-glasses and maps, was packed with us into three carriages, and we proceeded to the Arsenal wharf over a mile of very rough and muddy road.

At the Arsenal, the guard received us, and Colonel Ramsey, the commandant, was waiting to escort us to the boat.

Sunday evening.

Our boat is the *Carrie Martin*, a pretty little steamer that used formerly to run between New York and Shrewsbury, and is now used as a government dispatch boat, carrying General Halleck, General Hooker, or the President, when business calls them, to or from Washington and the army.

We have passed down the river, inspecting the fleets of steamers and schooners, with which the Potomac is filled nowadays. Alexandria and Fort Washington look now all peaceable and quiet, as well as Mount Vernon, where the bell tolls a passing salute according to the old river custom.

Acquia Creek then came into view. Here was a busy scene—a fleet of transports at anchor—tugs and steamers whistling and puffing about—long rows of new unpainted wooden buildings, offices and storehouses on shore, with piles of boxes, bales, and barrels, containing ammunition, provisions, muskets, clothing, shot and shell, and all the supplies of a great army.

Crowds of soldiers and labourers thronged the wharf, sick men going to the hospital, well men discharged or furloughed or returning to duty, officers superintending the shipment of supplies; and all shades and sizes of "contrabands" in all manner of cast-off clothes of everybody else, some at work, some basking in the sun.

The Quartermaster, Captain Hall, had a train waiting to take us to Falmouth. The railroad is a military one, and has only freight cars and locomotives. Our train consisted of one of the latter, and one of the former with some wooden benches in it. Upon these we seated ourselves and were whirled rapidly out of Acquia, through cuttings and over embankments and bridges at the rate of forty-five miles an hour.

The country presented a strange sight. Not a house,

not a fence, not a field, not a bush, nor hardly a tree. Everywhere the bare ground, everywhere on the hills, valleys, and plains, one vast encampment.   Roads crossing and recrossing each other in every direction.   Groups of tents, stockades, and earthworks.   On every side, bodies of troops on the march or at drill.   Squads of cavalry galloping to and fro, long lines of army wagons, droves of mules and horses, sentinels pacing before camp-fires, and soldiers scattered and rambling about every-where.   This was the scene for fifteen miles, which we made in twenty minutes.   Then came another collection of new wooden storehouses.   This was Falmouth Station.

We descended from the train, and got into a couple of large ambulances, which took us another half-mile through camps extending apparently without limit, up to General Hooker's headquarters,—a large tent, with a small one behind it.   The General and his Chief of Staff, General Butterfield, received us very cordially, and made us im-mediately at home, by assigning us a couple of tents near his for our night's quarters.   Mr. Peale had brought his camera, and while we were talking, photographed the scene.

Then we made an excursion down to the river bank, to look across at Fredericksburg.   It lay in the shadow, under the hill,—looking very quiet, peaceable, and near. It made a fine picture for Mr. Peale,—the narrow river in front, then the houses and steeples, with the background of lofty heights rising in the rear, covered with the rebel tents and earthworks.   On the river bank just below us paced the Union sentries; and on the other side, just opposite, we could see with distinctness the rebel sentries, also pacing their rounds.   The two were near enough to call to each other across the stream.   There is a sort of tacit understanding that the pickets shall not fire at each other, so they did not molest us, although the carriages and the squadron of lancers which accompanied the

General as an escort must have attracted attention, for we saw groups of curious observers, like ourselves, gather on the wharves of Fredericksburg to look at us, and heard them calling, one to another, though we could not distinguish the words.

Back to the camp again, through what is left of Falmouth,—two houses only, the Lacy house and the Phillips house. There were two or three more, which have been destroyed. We supped with the General in his tent, sat and talked till the drum beat for "taps," and then betook ourselves to our tents.

The three ladies had one; the seven gentlemen of the party had the other. The beds were plank floor, the pillows carpet-bags, the bedclothes army blankets. The night was clear and warm, and we slept soundly.

Monday.

At five o'clock this morning, the drums and bugles wake us with the reveille. Toilets are soon made in camp. Then we strolled through the encampment and back to breakfast, some with the General, and others with officers of his staff.

At ten o'clock, the General had ordered a review of General Sickles's corps, and columns of infantry, cavalry, and artillery were already assembling. We rode on the field at that hour, and found a magnificent spectacle. The long lines of troops, with flags waving and arms glistening in the sun, stretched more than a mile. A cavalcade of officers accompanied the General, and, as they galloped down the line, were received with drums beating, colours saluting, and thousands of troops cheering. It was an inspiring sight.

After the review of the troops, there came a review of a wilderness of army wagons and ambulances, covering the plain in long rows, as far as the eye could reach.

On our way back we asked the General how much space the Army of the Potomac occupied in its encampments. He said that the distance around it was one hundred miles, the distance through it from one side to the other at least thirty. Beside the army corps which we had seen pass in review, there were three others of equal magnitude that today were marching toward the Rappahannock to make the crossing.

After the review, the general officers of the corps were assembled at Headquarters for presentation and conference. And then we took our leave.

The train landed us again at Acquia Creek. We re-embarked on the *Carrie Martin*, and proceeded down the river. The night was bright moonlight, and we spent a good deal of it on deck.

Tuesday.

This morning we found ourselves in the York River, and at ten o'clock reached Yorktown. Here General Keyes and General Rufus King came on board to welcome us, and took us on shore with them.

After a salute of fifteen guns, they took us round the fortifications and earthworks—the labours of two great armies. They are vast in extent and look impregnable. Then we went to see the great gun fired. The roar was deafening, and we saw the shell thrown from it burst three miles away toward the Chesapeake.

Then we went through the town, which consists of but few houses, and no inhabitants except troops and "contrabands." The houses are old and quaint. The bricks for some of them were brought from England. Lord Cornwallis's headquarters, General Washington's headquarters, and the Governor's house were pointed out. One was occupied by General Keyes and one by General King. Mrs. Keyes had two or three ladies staying with her—officers' wives and sisters. The General gave us lunch.

Then we went down to the river, and across to Gloucester Point,—rode around, and saw the earthworks and a review of the garrison.

Then back again, and found at the wharf a gunboat of the York River squadron. Captain Gilliss, her commander, took us on board, gave us a salute of fifteen guns, and then a cruise up the river five or six miles, beyond the lines of the army. Here he experimented with his one hundred pounder, throwing shot and shell at distant points on the shore. Returning we fell in with a fleet of oyster boats, and got two or three barrels of the famous York River oysters, one of which we agreed to take to the President.

We took leave of Yorktown at five o'clock, and steamed on down the bay. Dinner was over, and it was quite late in the evening when we reached Fortress Monroe. Here General Dix and some of his staff came on board, among them a Prussian officer who had been a protégé of Baron Gerolt. We slept on board, under the guns of the fort.

Wednesday.

This morning General Dix took the Secretary of State with him on an excursion to visit the beleaguered post of Suffolk. The rest of us went on shore with Colonel Ludlow and Dr. Gilbert, the Medical Director, to visit the hospitals and the ruins of the village of Hampton. The hospitals are very like those of Washington.

Hampton was, before the war, a pretty village, but it was burnt by the rebel General Magruder in 1861. It presents an odd appearance now. The "contrabands," who number several thousands, have encamped upon its site. They have cleared away the rubbish, and then, going out into the adjacent swamps, have cut down cypress trees, which, after their fashion, they have split into boards and shingles. With these they have built shanties to live in. Of course, when the old houses were burned, the chimneys were left standing. Each of the shanties is ingeniously built around one of these chimneys, and the appearance of a town of such diminutive houses, with such majestic chimneys towering over them, is funny enough.

The "contrabands" were all neatly dressed, cheerful, and comfortable. They are employed by the Government, and receive pay and rations. The most striking ruin is that of the old English church, built before the Revolution, and surrounded by the graves of British officers.

Returning on board, we went over to Norfolk, which we found in much the same condition as last year, only much neater, thanks to military supervision, and with a little more business stirring. There is still a strong secession feeling there, which was evinced by sour looks and suppressed remarks, as we walked through the streets. We called on General Vielé, the Military Governor, but did not find him at home.

Then we went over the ruins of the Gosport Navy Yard, on the opposite side of the Elizabeth River, and then back to Fortress Monroe. A thunder-storm came up in the evening, but was soon over; and we slept quietly again under the guns of the fort.

Thursday.

This morning we went ashore, and paid a visit to the fortress. It is a strong and imposing fortification, mounting hundreds of guns, and embracing seventy acres within its massive stone walls. It is the largest single work in this country.

Inside, the trees, the green grass, gravel walks, and neat

houses gave it the appearance of a summer resort rather than a fort. We were received with the salute of the usual fifteen guns, then visited General Dix's headquarters; then returned to the *Carrie Martin*, and went over to the Rip Raps.

This is a stone fortification constructed on a small island, and covering the whole of it. The walls are several feet thick, and the whole affair, island, fort, and all, looks as if it was carved in stone. There is no room for a blade of grass to grow. It is unfinished, and the workmen are still engaged on it. The ship channel runs between it and Fortress Monroe; so that whatever passes will be exposed to the fire of both.

Then we next steamed five or six miles up the James River, to visit Admiral Lee's fleet, lying above Newport News Point. The Admiral received us on board his flagship, the *Minnesota*, with the usual salute. After passing through her decks and looking through her heavy armament, we went on board the *Lehigh*, one of the new "monitors" in the squadron, and viewed her turret, her little pilot-house, her monster gun, her compact cabins under water, and so on. The ingenuity and strength these vessels display seem even more striking when seen so closely. The *Sangamon*, the *Galena*, and the *Ossipee* are also in the squadron. We did not go on board of them, but exchanged salutes by dipping ensigns and waving hats as we passed them.

Then we ran into Norfolk to take in a supply of coal, thence back to the fort; and so ended another day.

Friday.

At sunrise this morning, we started on our way home. It was a clear cloudless day: the bay as calm as a lake, and the air like summer. We devoted the entire day to the cruise up the Chesapeake and the Potomac, through hundreds of vessels.

Once we passed through a fleet of forty schooners, all moving in the same direction, and near together, the white sails glistening in the moonlight; and shortly after, through another fleet of fifty more, riding, black and silent, at anchor. The clock struck ten as we debarked once more at the Arsenal wharf.

An Excursion with the Diplomatic Corps. The members of the Diplomatic Corps were frequently asked by their governments as to whether the war, so long protracted, was not beginning to exhaust the energies of the combatants.

The Secretary of State had often told them that they could learn little of the true state of the country by spending their summer vacations at Newport, Cape May, Saratoga, and other places of fashionable resort, and had often advised them to leave the seaboard and the great cities, and visit the rural regions of the interior. He saw how difficult it was for them to realize that the country was not becoming exhausted, or that the causes which led to the draft riots in New York might not be at work in every town.

When he invited them to accompany him on a visit to his home, in Central New York, "the heart of the North," several of them signified that they would go with willingness and pleasure.

Some of the diplomatic gentlemen started with him in a special car from Washington, others joined the party at New York. Its number varied at different stages of the journey, but Lord Lyons, the British Minister, M. Mercier, the French Minister, Señor Tassara, the Spanish Minister, Commander Bertinatti, the Italian Envoy, Mr. Schleiden, the Minister from the Hanseatic Cities, Mr. Stoeckl, the diplomatic representative of Russia, Count Piper, the Swedish Minister, and Mr. Molina, the Central American representative, continued through nearly the whole journey.

They visited New York and its vicinity, they went up the Hudson, then through the Valley of the Mohawk, then over the hills into Otsego County. They saw Albany, Schenectady, and Little Falls, visited Sharon Springs and Trenton Falls; they spent a night at Cooperstown and sailed on Otsego Lake. They went to Utica, Rome, and Syracuse. They stopped at Auburn, visited Seneca Falls and Geneva, traversed Cayuga and Seneca Lakes, saw the mills and factories of Rochester, and the harbour of Buffalo swarming with lake craft, and having its elevators in full operation.

Hospitalities were showered upon them, more than they could accept. Serenades greeted them in the evening, with kindly invitations for the morrow. But every day's ride was a volume of instruction. Hundreds of factories with whirring wheels, thousands of acres of golden harvest fields, miles of railway trains laden with freight, busy fleets on rivers, lakes, and canals, all showed a period of unexampled commercial activity and prosperity.

Then the flag flying everywhere, the drum heard everywhere, the recruiting offices open and busy; the churches, the hospitals, the commissions, and the benevolent associations, all labouring for the soldiers' care and comfort; all attested the resources of an Empire, and the self-reliant patriotism of a great Republic.

One of the ministers, writing to his government, said, "The resources of the Northern States, instead of being exhausted, seem practically inexhaustible."

A photograph of the party on the rocks at Trenton Falls hangs in my library, and another at Auburn.

Changing the Commanding General.　Military men all
know that success or defeat in battle is a part of "the
fortune of war."　The best of generals may sometimes
encounter a reverse, and sometimes a defeated commander
may, by experience and opportunity, retrieve his ill fortune by subsequent victory.

But, in our Civil War, events were influenced largely
by Congress, the press, and public opinion.　A lost battle
was immediately followed by a clamour for a change
of commanders.　As Postmaster-General Blair once remarked in Cabinet meeting, "Success in battle may not
be the best of tests of a general's capacity, but it is the
one the public knows of and has the power to apply.　So
it is the one usually adopted."

After Fredericksburg, Burnside was the first to ask to
be relieved of his command of the Army of the Potomac,
and after Chancellorsville Hooker followed his example.

There were several anxious consultations in Cabinet, as
to who the next commander should be.　It was believed
that one of the corps commanders would be the best
and most expedient appointment.　But which one?
All had now proved themselves tried, capable, and experienced soldiers, and all, so far as public opinion in and out
of the army indicated, seemed to be regarded as having the necessary qualifications for commander-in-chief.
Burnside, Hooker, Hancock, Howard, Reynolds, Meade,
Sickles, Couch, Heintzelman, all had warm friends and
admirers.　Among the members of the Cabinet there were
differing views, perhaps each somewhat influenced by
personal friendship.

"But what do you say, Mr. Secretary of War?" said
one of his colleagues.　"You best know them all, and
your judgment should be the controlling one."

Mr. Stanton paused before replying; "Well, I think on
the whole I should prefer Meade."

"Meade?" was the reply. "Have we seen or heard much of him here in Washington? Who are his sponsors? Seems to me we know less of him than of any of the others."

Stanton looked sharply at the speaker through his spectacles, and then, with a laugh, said, "Perhaps that is the reason I like him. No, he has no backers, and nobody is urging him for the place. He does not come to Washington to ask for transfers or assignments or special privileges. He has his own record. He sticks to his work, does it, and does it well."

"Don't you suppose he has aspirations like the rest?"

"I rather think," said Stanton, "he expects to see Reynolds chosen, and would prefer him first, and any one else afterwards."

Ultimately, the President and all the members present agreed that Stanton's judgment should be accepted, and that Meade should be at once notified.

There was reason for haste, for battles were imminent. Lee's army was marching northward with evident purpose of invading Maryland or Pennsylvania. The Army of the Potomac was marching in a parallel direction with it, but on an "interior line," thereby protecting Washington and Baltimore, and keeping in readiness to repel the threatened invasion, wherever and in whatever form it should be made.

General Hardie of the War Department was dispatched to inform Meade. The Secretary of War supplied him with orders and instructions, and ordered a special engine and car to take him as far as possible. Then he was to find such conveyance as he could for the rest of the way. Railroads and all other roads are more or less demoralized and broken in war time.

Hardie had various delays, which prevented him from reaching Frederick till long after dark. He had donned civilian's dress, to avoid observation, but this very fact added to his trouble in getting through parties of obstreperous soldiery. When at last he found a horse and buggy to drive to Meade's headquarters, which were some miles outside of Frederick, it was after midnight. The guards had been set for the night, and they were not ready to admit a suspicious stranger, even when he claimed to be an official with a message to the General. However, at last he was ushered into General Meade's tent, and found the General half dressed, lying on his camp bed asleep.

"Is that you, Hardie?"

"Yes, General, just come from Washington."

"Something important up?"

"Yes, General, bad news for you. Better get up and hear it."

General Meade arose and commenced putting on the rest of his fatigue uniform.

"Bad news, you say? What is it?"

"You are going to lose the command of your army corps, General."

The General was silent a few moments, as he was putting on his coat. Then, turning around, he said:

"Do you know, Hardie, I am not very much surprised. When I saw so many heads around me coming off, I rather wondered whether mine might not go next. Who do they put in my place?"

"Don't know yet. Probably your ranking division commander."

"And what do they do with me?"

"You—you are to take command of the Army of the Potomac!"

"What?" exclaimed the astounded General. "Are you joking? Are you in earnest?"

When the General was convinced that the news was

true, he was by no means elated.   He had no desire for the
heavy responsibility thus devolving upon him.   He said
he was too ignorant of the positions and dispositions of
the different army corps.   He had thought that if Hooker
should be relieved, Reynolds would take his place.   Hardie
was able to assure him that Secretary Stanton had fore-
seen his reluctance, and therefore his orders had been
so explicit and almost peremptory.   The change was to be
made and made at once, without postponement or delay.

Meade said half-seriously, half-jokingly, "Well, I've
been tried and condemned without a hearing, so I suppose
I must submit."

He insisted, however, that he must reserve his acceptance till he had had a conference with the other corps
commanders.   It was essential to success in the campaign
that there should be harmony and co-operation between
them all.   Discord would be fatal.   His own desire was
not to assume dictatorial powers, but to have full and
frequent consultation with the others, over the army's
movements.

The conferences were held.   The other generals,
according to Hardie's report, were less surprised than
Meade had been.   While some of them evidently were of
opinion that the appointment might as well have come to
them as to him, yet, on the whole, they were better
satisfied with his selection than they might have been with
some other.   Of course, they all agreed to give him their
best counsel and hearty co-operation in the management
of the campaign,—a pledge that was faithfully carried
out, and which resulted in the master stroke of the campaign that has made the name of Gettysburg immortal.

The story of Hardie's night ride and interview is the
one that was told in Washington official circles.   Very
probably, it is incorrect in several details, but its general
tenor is now accepted as history.

16

1863 and 1864.

Altered Aspect of the War. The great victories at
Gettysburg and Vicksburg and Port Hudson mark the
beginning of a new phase of the war.   Public sentiment
in regard to it is changed and confident.   The Mississippi
is now opened to trade throughout its whole length.
There is no longer any probability of an attempted
invasion of the free States.   The Confederacy is now
confined within definite limits, which will contract and
not expand.   So there is a reasonable hope that the war
will be ended and the Union restored within the space
of a year or two.   On the other hand, the public has now
no illusions in regard to a speedy termination of hostilities.
The Confederacy is still a power, composed of men of our
own race, who are as tenacious of their opinions, as we are
of ours.   So we have settled down to consider the war as a
lasting one.

We have become inured to war and its experiences.
We regard its chances and casualties as deplorable, but
inevitable.   We have grown accustomed to the long
list of the killed and wounded in the battles.   Not that
this implies any callousness to this great amount of human
suffering.   Every conceivable expedient is eagerly seized
upon to relieve the dangers and hardships of the soldiers
and sailors.   Hospitals are multiplied, nurses are eager
to volunteer.   Commissions are organized to furnish
the soldiers and sailors not only with comforts but with
luxuries.   Fairs and festivals are held in all the cities, for
the benefit of all who are fighting for the Flag.   Everyone
sends his gift or contribution.   Private families are
busily engaged in the manufacture of garments.   Knitting
of socks is going on in every loyal household throughout
the North.

And all this laudable work is attended with prosperity.
Business is thriving.   Commerce is showing unexampled

activity. Every trade and occupation is finding employment. The Government is spending a million of dollars a day and "greenbacks" are plentiful.

The military telegraph has now been extended to every army in the field. Its wires centre in the War Department, now the focus of interest. Here sits the master spirit of the contest, Edwin M. Stanton. Day by day, and hour by hour, he is on the watch for news from the front, and for opportunities to send forward reinforcements, arms, and supplies wherever they are needed. Stern and inflexible in discharge of his duty, he rarely leaves the Department. Impatient of visitors who come to seek personal ends, he is always ready to respond to the calls of "the service" or the country.

His Cabinet colleagues are his frequent callers, and the President spends hours in listening to the intelligence or demands ticked off from the wires. Here, they learn how Gilmore is shelling the fortifications of Charleston with long range artillery five miles away, how Burnside is capturing Knoxville, how Rosecrans is before Chattanooga, how Franklin is advancing towards Sabine Pass, how Banks has encountered a check in his march through Louisiana, but has retrieved it, and is marching on Shreveport, how varying conflicts are resulting in Florida, Mississippi, and Alabama, and how Admiral Farragut is preparing for active operations in the Gulf of Mexico.

1864.

Washington during Early's Raid. It was in July, 1864, that a Confederate movement in the Shenandoah Valley was developed. A column reported as thirty or forty thousand strong, under Breckenridge, passed the Potomac fords above Harpers Ferry, crossed the South Mountain, and entered Frederick in Maryland on Saturday the 9th.

It was evident that the Confederates, hard pressed by General Grant's campaign in "the Wilderness," had taken the bold step of making an attack on Washington from the rear, where the fortifications were weakest.

Washington, in its fancied security, had sent forward nearly all its available troops to aid General Grant. If the attacking column could reach there before reinforcements could be sent back by General Grant, it might result in a surprise, and even a capture of the capital. General Early was reported to be in command of the movement.

Major-General Wallace with about seven thousand men hastily drawn from Baltimore met the whole or a considerable portion of the enemy's force at the bridge at Monocacy, which opened a way equally to Washington or Baltimore. A deadly conflict was maintained from nine in the morning till five in the afternoon. The Union forces, overpowered by double their number, gave way and retreated to Ellicott's Mills.

My younger brother William H. was now in command of the Ninth New York Artillery. His regiment was a part of the force sent out to check the Confederate invasion.

Early, the Confederate commander, had moved with rapidity and secrecy. General Wallace, the Union commander, found himself confronted with this overwhelming force. He could not drive the enemy back, but every hour he could delay their advance was important, since it gave time to put Washington into a condition for defence.

My brother's regiment fought bravely nearly all day, but, overpowered at last, was forced to retreat, while its Colonel, wounded, narrowly escaped capture. His horse was shot under him and fell upon him. Lieutenant-Colonel Taft, who stood near by, at the same moment lost his leg by the explosion of a shell. When the final order was given to retire, Colonel Seward had little more than a colour guard left. Crippled and surrounded by the enemy, he escaped with great difficulty.

With the help of one of his men, he reached a piece of woods. Mounting a stray mule, and using his pocket handkerchief for a bridle, he succeeded after a painful ride of many miles, during the night, in rejoining the forces which had then made a stand at Ellicott's Mills.

It was now evident that the rebel movement was no mere raid, but a skilfully arranged strategic advance, to suddenly attack the Federal city on its weakest side.

When the news spread about in Washington that a rebel army was within a few miles of the city, and that there was no longer any Federal force to oppose its advance, there was general alarm. Farmers living in the path of the coming enemy fled to the city for refuge. By every northern road their wagons were coming in, loaded with their household goods, accompanied by cattle hastily gathered and driven before them.

Soon clouds of smoke in the northern sky showed that the abandoned dwellings and barns had been fired by the rebel scouting or marauding parties.

Presently came intelligence that "Silver Spring," Francis P. Blair's beautiful country seat, had been made the headquarters of the rebel Generals Early and Breckenridge. Then that the house of his son Montgomery Blair, the Postmaster-General, had been fired and burnt to the ground.

Meanwhile the military authorities were making every possible preparation for defence. The forts were manned by invalid soldiers and militia volunteers. Rifle pits between different fortifications were hastily made. The slender force at the disposal of the Government was distributed to the best advantage.

Railway and telegraphic communication with the

north was again cut off, and it seemed as if the experiences of 1861 were to be repeated. But this time the popular feeling was very different. There was no gloom nor consternation. Three years of war had inured even the noncombatants to military vicissitudes. The citizens could even appreciate the grim humour of their predicament, in being thus suddenly attacked from the north, after having sent their available troops to the south. Succour was known to be coming from the Army of the Potomac in war steamers and transports. But would it arrive before the rebels were in the streets? It was not believed that the rebel troops could long hold the city, if they should take it. But they might inflict irreparable damage by burning public buildings, destroying records and military stores, capturing valuable prisoners, and seriously damaging the prestige of the national cause by even a day's occupation of the capital.

One of the family letters, written at the time, graphically describes the events in Washington:

"During Saturday evening, we had been hearing successive reports of the battle, the disaster, and the retreat of General Wallace from Monocacy. The Secretary had just returned from the War Department at midnight, when Mr. Stanton himself came over and called him up, to tell him of the dispatch saying that William was wounded and a prisoner.

"None of us slept much the rest of the night, and it was arranged that Augustus should go over in the first train to Baltimore to make inquiries.

"All the morning the city was filled with panic rumours of the advances of the rebels in every direction, and troops were organized and posted to meet the anticipated attack. The teamsters and other employees of the Quartermaster's Department were armed, equipped, and mustered into regiments, volunteers were accepted, horses impressed, and the streets were full of bustle with the marching of different bodies of troops.

"Meanwhile visitors were constantly coming in to make inquiry, or to bring reports said to have come from the field. At three o'clock a telegram from Augustus assured us that though wounded William was not a prisoner. By that time the citizens began to get reassured, and matters to look more cheerful, as the enemy had not pursued Wallace, had not attacked the railroad, and had not presented themselves anywhere in force.

"On coming home we learned that a battalion of the Ninth Artillery, just arrived from Petersburg, had marched up the avenue to the fortifications. We followed them in the carriage, and on the Tennallytown road began to overtake the stragglers in the rear of the column. We took in two of them, and presently overtook the main body, who had halted to rest before taking their positions in the forts. They were dusty and tired, but brown and hearty—all glad to see us, and to get back to their old camping ground.

"Their first inquiry was about their Colonel, of whose reported capture they had heard. They lavished praises on him for his bravery and his conduct with them before Petersburg, and were delighted to find that it was not true that he had been taken.

"Major Snyder was in command of the battalion. We found him and all our other acquaintances, and indeed found none who were not. We stayed half an hour while they made their coffee, and fought their battles over again, and left them in excellent spirits.

"On reaching home at eight o'clock, we found General Wallace's dispatch about William. We think he will be here today or tomorrow. The whole regiment has now been ordered here to garrison the forts, as they are trained artillerists. Two battalions went to Baltimore, and so were in the battle, but they will now come here.

"With the preparations now made, and the strength we are hourly gaining, the military authorities are confident not only of resisting, but perhaps of overpowering the rebel force and capturing it. The country round is full of the raiding and scouting parties of their cavalry."

Washington was well fortified. A triple girdle of earthworks now surrounded it. The open space between the fortifications and the region of streets, shops, and dwellings was thickly dotted with hospitals, mostly substantial wooden or canvas structures, with all modern appliances for ventilation and comfort. An army of maimed or convalescent soldiers on a sunny day could be seen resting or lounging on the turf around their doors.

In the afternoon of the day when the enemy's advance guard was expected, my father and I drove out with President Lincoln to Fort Stevens, near the junction of the roads running from Seventh and Fourteenth Streets. As this was an exposed point, it would probably be the first attacked.

A barricade had been thrown across the turnpike. General McCook was in command. A crowd of officers gathered round the carriage, to welcome and salute the President. He alighted, went up into the fort, and was standing on the parapet looking over the long stretch of comparatively level country, when a soldier touched his arm and begged him to descend, "for the bullets of the rebel sharpshooters may begin to come in any minute from the woods yonder."

The caution was timely, for in a few moments the prediction was verified, and a bullet or two whistling over the sentry's head showed that the riflemen "were getting the range."

A portion of the Sixth Corps and two divisions of the

Nineteenth, which General Grant had sent up for the relief of Washington, were now arriving and debarking at the wharves. Detachments were hastily formed and marched up to the aid of the threatened forts. One arrived at Fort Stevens while the President was there.

Thrown out as skirmishers, the men soon came in sight of the rebel scouts, who, recognizing the well-known cross, which was the badge of the Sixth Corps, informed their commanders that the Federal reinforcements had arrived.

On Monday and Tuesday, the space between the fortifications and the attacking force was a scene of uninterrupted skirmishes between the cavalry and sharpshooters of the respective parties.

A force of two thousand men sent out from Fort Stevens on Tuesday evening assaulted the enemy with spirit and decision. In this engagement each party lost about three hundred killed and wounded.

That night the enemy's sharpshooters were replaced by cavalry pickets, and on Wednesday morning their cavalry disappeared. At the same time the rebels withdrew from the vicinity of Baltimore. A column of considerable strength was dispatched on the 13th to pursue the enemy across the Potomac.

December, 1864.

The Year's Record. We are at the end of another year of the war. This is New Year's Eve. A crowd of holiday merrymakers has just gone by, singing the plaintive strains of the latest war song,—"When this cruel war is over." When will it be over? Will it last another year, or more? Looking back over the events of the year just closed, they seem of great, even of amazing importance:

The appointment of Lieutenant-General Grant to the chief command of the armies; his coming to Washington and reorganizing the Army of the Potomac; his order for a general advance, in April, of all the armies; his taking the field and driving Lee's troops from their intrenchments and pursuing them into the "Wilderness"; the long and bloody campaign in the "Wilderness"; the sanguinary battles of Spottsylvania and Cold Harbour; the junction with the forces of General Butler at Bermuda Hundred; and the preparations for a long siege of Petersburg and of Richmond, at which points the insurgent forces are now concentrated. Then the advance of General Sherman, pursuing Johnston's army to the Chattahoochee; the flanking of the enemy on Kenesaw Mountain; the battle near Atlanta where McPherson lost his life; the fall of Atlanta; and the historic march of Sherman through Georgia, and the capture of Savannah.

Then the exploits of the navy: the sinking of the *Alabama* by the *Kearsarge*, under Captain Winslow; the great naval engagement and victory by Farragut in Mobile Bay. Then the cavalry successes of Sheridan, Averill, and Kilpatrick,—Sheridan's famous ride, and his victory at Cedar Creek. Then the failure of Early's Raid, and the clearing of the Shenandoah Valley,—all point to an early termination of the war.

Not less significant is the result of the Presidential campaign,—the nomination and re-election of Abraham Lincoln, showing that the country stands behind him, determined to prosecute the war to the end.

My father and I, in walking to the State Department, every morning find that the headquarters of General Augur, the District commander, has a crowd of forty or fifty persons in front of it. On inquiry, we learn that some of these are prisoners, but the majority are deserters from the Confederate ranks, who have come in, given up their arms, taken the oath of allegiance, and are to be forwarded by the Government during the day to Philadelphia, where they will find peaceful employment.

My father remarks, "That means a company a day,— a regiment a week,—a brigade a fortnight.   How long can any army stand such a drain upon its resources, when there are no new recruits or conscripts to replenish it?"

April, 1865.

The End of the War.   When my father was disabled by his serious carriage accident, his official functions were devolved upon me.   As Acting Secretary, I wrote the following, as the closing "Circular on the military situation":

"The past week has been characterized by a rapid and uninterrupted series of military successes, more momentous in their results than any that have preceded them during the war.   Richmond and Petersburg, with all their communications and vast quantities of supplies and material of war, have been captured by our armies. The insurrection has no longer a seat of its pretended Government.   Its so-called officials are fugitives.   Its chief army, after being reduced by repeated defeats and demoralization to less than one third of its former numbers, has been retreating, closely pursued and hemmed in by the victorious forces of the Union, and encountering fresh losses at every step of its flight, until the triumph of the national armies finally culminated in the surrender of General Lee and the whole insurgent Army of Northern Virginia to Lieutenant-General Grant yesterday afternoon, at half-past four o'clock.

"Henceforth it is evident that the war, if protracted, can never resume its former character.   Organized operations of campaign or siege, carried on by disciplined and effective armies, are no longer possible for the insurgents. Depredations by marauding gangs, and defence of remote and isolated inland fastnesses, may, perhaps, still be continued, but even these can endure but for a time.

"Not the least significant feature of these triumphs is the reception extended by the inhabitants to the advancing armies of the Union, their entire acquiescence, and, in many instances, their apparently sincere rejoicings at the return of its protecting authority over the insurgent district.

"The insurrection has now no port or access to the sea; no fixed seat of its pretended Government; no coherent civil administration; no army that is not, in consequence of repeated defeats, rapidly dissolving into fragments; and the only ships that assume to carry its flag are those foreign-built vessels, which, from the day their keels were laid on neutral soil, have never ventured to approach within hundreds of miles of the scene of the insurrection; and have only derived their ability to rob and plunder from the concession to them of belligerent privileges, by powers which have repeatedly assured us of their disposition to be neutral in the strife."

Next, was the preparation of two proclamations for the President's signature, giving notice of the changed aspect of affairs as regarded foreign nations. One of these announced that, as the Southern ports had been recaptured, their blockade was no longer necessary. The other gave notice to the foreign governments who had refused to vessels of war of the United States the privileges to which they were entitled by treaty, public law, and international comity, that henceforth their own vessels would be treated in precisely the same way by the United States, until the obnoxious restrictions were withdrawn.

So the end had come at last. Joyous and enthusiastic crowds were going about the streets exchanging congratulations. Flags were floating, and music re-echoing the glad tidings,—"The cruel war was over."

April, 1865.

Last Meeting of Lincoln and Seward. Soon after the capture of Richmond, President Lincoln went down there to visit the army and the city. While there he heard of the carriage accident by which my father had been badly injured on the 5th of April.

Returning to Washington, he found that news of the great Union successes had spread abroad. Improvised meetings and processions were hourly occurring, and all Washington seemed to be pervaded with excitement.

He hastened to visit my father in his sick chamber. It was in the evening, the gaslights were turned down low, and the house was still, everyone moving softly and speaking in whispers. The injured Secretary was helpless and swathed in bandages, on his bed in the centre of the room. The extreme sensitiveness of the wounded arm made even the touch of the bed clothing intolerable. To keep it free from their contact he was lying on the edge of the bed farthest from the door. Mr. Lincoln, entering with kindly expressions of sympathy, sat down on the bed by the invalid's side.

"You are back from Richmond?" whispered Seward, who was hardly able to articulate.

"Yes," said Lincoln, "and I think we are near the end at last."

Then, leaning his tall form across the bed and resting on his elbow, so as to bring his face near that of the injured man, he gave him an account of his experience "at the front," Seward listening with interest, but unable to utter a word without pain. They were left together for half an hour or more.

Then the door opened softly, and Mr. Lincoln came out gently, intimating by a silent look and gesture that Seward had fallen into a feverish slumber and must not be disturbed.

It was their last meeting.

Lincoln's Last Cabinet Meeting. On the 14th of April, 1861, the Civil War had opened with the fall of Fort Sumter. Four years of battle had followed. Now, the return of that anniversary was accompanied with the advent of Peace. It was deemed a proper day to again raise the Union flag on the fort, with appropriate ceremonies. This year it happened that the 14th was also Good Friday.

Early that morning, a messenger from the White House brought me a note in President Lincoln's well-known handwriting. It ran:

"Acting Secretary of State:
"Please call a Cabinet meeting at eleven o'clock today. General Grant will be with us.

"A. Lincoln."

As my father was confined to his bed by the injuries received in his recent carriage accident, I was acting in his stead. I sent out the notices, and at the appointed hour came Secretaries McCulloch and Welles, Postmaster-General Dennison and Attorney-General Speed soon arrived, and I appeared as representative of the State Department. Mr. Lincoln, with an expression of visible relief and content upon his face, sat in his study chair, by the south window, chatting with us over "the great news." Some curiosity was expressed as to what had become of the heads of the rebel government—whether they would escape from the country, or would remain to be captured and tried; and if tried, what penalty would be visited upon them?

All those present thought that, for the sake of general amity and good will, it was desirable to have as few judicial proceedings as possible. Yet would it be wise to let the leaders in treason go entirely unpunished?

Mr. Speed remarked that it would be a difficult problem if it should occur.

"I suppose, Mr. President," said Governor Dennison, "you would not be sorry to have them escape out of the country?"

"Well," said Mr. Lincoln slowly, "I should not be sorry to have them out of the country; but I should be for following them up pretty close, to make sure of their going."

The conversation turning upon the subject of sleep, Mr. Lincoln remarked that a peculiar dream of the previous night was one that had occurred several times in his life,—a vague sense of floating—floating away on some vast and indistinct expanse, toward an unknown shore. The dream itself was not so strange as the coincidence that each of its previous recurrences had been followed by some important event or disaster, which he mentioned.

The usual comments were made by his auditors. One thought it was merely a matter of coincidences.

Another laughingly remarked, "At any rate it cannot presage a victory nor a defeat this time, for the war is over."

I suggested, "Perhaps at each of these periods there were possibilities of great change or disaster, and the vague feeling of uncertainty may have led to the dim vision in sleep."

"Perhaps," said Mr. Lincoln, thoughtfully, "perhaps that is the explanation."

Mr. Stanton was the last to arrive. He brought with him a large roll of paper, upon which he had been at work.

General Grant entered, in accordance with the President's invitation, and was received with cordial welcomes and congratulations. He briefly and modestly narrated the incidents of the surrender. Mr. Lincoln's face glowed with approval when, in reply to his inquiry, "What terms did you make for the common soldiers?" General Grant said, "I told them to go back to their homes and families, and they would not be molested, if they did nothing more."

Kindly feeling toward the vanquished, and hearty desire to restore peace and safety at the South, with as little harm as possible to the feelings or the property of the inhabitants, pervaded the whole discussion.

At such a meeting, in such a time, there could be but one question,—the restoration or re-establishment of the seceded States in their former relations as members of the Federal Union.

The conference was long and earnest, with little diversity of opinion, except as to details. One of the difficulties of the problem was, who should be recognized as State authorities? There was a loyal governor in Virginia. There were military governors in some of the other States. But the Southern legislatures were for the most part avowedly treasonable. Whether they should be allowed to continue until they committed some new overt act of hostility; whether the governors should be requested to order new elections; whether such elections should be ordered by the General Government—all these were questions raised.

Among many similar expressions of the President, was the remark: "We can't undertake to run State governments in all these Southern States. Their people must do that,—though I reckon that at first some of them may do it badly."

The Secretary of War then unrolled his sheets of paper, on which he had drafted the outlines of reconstruction, embodying the President's views, and, as it was understood, those of the other members of the Cabinet. In substance it was, that the Treasury Department should take possession of the custom houses, and proceed to collect the revenues; that the War Department should garrison or destroy the forts; that the Navy Department should, in like manner, occupy the harbours, take possession of navy yards, ships, and ordnance; that the Interior Department should send out its surveyors, land, pension, and Indian agents and set them at work; that the Postmaster-General should reopen his post-offices and reestablish his mail routes; that the Attorney-General should look after the re-establishment of the Federal courts, with their judges, marshals, and attorneys: in short, that the machinery of the United States Government should be set in motion; that its laws should be faithfully observed and enforced; that anything like domestic violence or insurrection should be repressed; but that public authorities and private citizens should remain unmolested, if not found in actual hostility to the Government of the Union.

It must have been about two o'clock when the Cabinet meeting ended. At its close, the President remarked that he had been urged to visit the theatre that evening, and asked General Grant if he would join the party. The General excused himself, as he had a previous engagement. He took his leave, and some of the others followed him.

Then I said, "Mr. President, we have a new British Minister, Sir Frederick Bruce. He has arrived in Washington, and is awaiting presentation. At what time will it be convenient for you to receive him?"

He paused a moment in thought, and replied:

"Tomorrow at two o'clock."

"In the Blue Room, I suppose?"

"Yes, in the Blue Room," and then added with a smile,

"Don't forget to send up the speeches beforehand. I would like to look them over."

I promised to do so, and then took my leave.—I never saw him afterwards.

17

Assassination Night. It was the ninth day since the carriage accident in which my father had been injured, and he still lay helpless and suffering. His symptoms alternately inspired hope of his recovery or grave apprehensions that he could not survive. The physicians held frequent consultations. The family took turns in watching at his bedside, and two invalid soldiers were sent to assist in his care. Aggravated pain and inflammation brought on occasional delirium, but every day, although unable to talk, he would intimate his desire to be informed of current events.

He essayed to make a suggestion or two in reference to a Thanksgiving proclamation, and in regard to the relations with Great Britain, but after enunciating a few words with difficulty could not continue. He listened with a look of pleasure to the narrative of the events of the Cabinet meeting.

Night came, and about ten o'clock Dr. Norris, the last of the physicians who called during the evening, had taken his leave. The gaslights were turned low, and all was quiet. In the sick-room of my father were his daughter Fanny and the invalid soldier nurse George T. Robinson. The other members of the family had gone to their respective rooms to rest, before their term of watching.

There seemed nothing unusual in the occurrence, when a tall, well dressed, but unknown man presented himself below and, informing the servant he had brought a message from the doctor, was allowed to come up the stairs.

Hearing the noise of footsteps in the hall, I came out and met him. When he told me that he came with a message from the doctor that was to be delivered to Mr. Seward personally, I told him that the Secretary was sleeping, and must not be disturbed, and that he could give me the message.

He repeated two or three times that he must see Mr. Seward personally. As he seemed to have nothing else to say, he gave me the impression that he was rather dull or stupid.

Finally, I said, "Well, if you will not give me the message, go back and tell the doctor I refused to let you see Mr. Seward."

As he stood apparently irresolute, I said, "I am his son, and the Assistant Secretary of State. Go back and tell the doctor that I refused to let you go into the sick-room, because Mr. Seward was sleeping."

He replied, "Very well, sir, I will go," and, turning away, took two or three steps down the stairs.

Suddenly turning again, he sprang up and forward, having drawn a Navy revolver, which he levelled, with a muttered oath, at my head, and pulled the trigger.

And now, in swift succession, like the scenes of some hideous dream, came the bloody incidents of the night,—of the pistol missing fire,—of the struggle in the dimly lighted hall, between the armed man and the unarmed one,—of the blows which broke the pistol of the one, and fractured the skull of the other,—of the bursting in of the door,—of the mad rush of the assassin to the bedside, and his savage slashing, with a bowie knife, at the face and throat of the helpless Secretary, instantly reddening the white bandages with streams of blood,—of the screams of the daughter for help,—of the attempt of the invalid soldier nurse to drag the assailant from his victim, receiving sharp wounds himself in return,—of the noise made by the awaking household, inspiring the assassin with hasty impulse to escape, leaving his work done or undone, of his frantic rush down the stairs, cutting and slashing at all whom he found in his way, wounding one in the face, and stabbing another in the back,—of his escape through the open doorway,—and his flight on horseback down the avenue.

Five minutes later, the aroused household were gazing horrified at the bleeding faces and figures in their midst, were lifting the insensible form of the Secretary from a pool of blood,—and sending for surgical help. Meanwhile a panic-stricken crowd were surging in from the street to the hall and rooms below, vainly inquiring or wildly conjecturing what had happened. For these, the horrors of the night seemed to culminate when later comers rushed in, with the intelligence that the President had also been attacked, at the same hour,—had been shot at Ford's Theatre,—had been carried to a house in Tenth Street,—and was lying there unconscious and dying.

On the following morning Secretary Stanton telegraphed to General Sherman:

"WASHINGTON, April 15, 1865, 12 M.

"President Lincoln was murdered about ten o'clock last night, in his private box at Ford's Theatre, in this city, by an assassin, who shot him through the head with a pistol ball. The assassin leaped from the box, brandishing a dagger, exclaiming 'Sic semper tyrannis,' and that Virginia was avenged. Mr. Lincoln fell senseless from his seat, and continued in that state until twenty-two minutes after seven o'clock, at which time he breathed his last. General Grant was published to be at the theatre, but did not go.

"About the same time, Mr. Seward's house was entered by another assassin, who stabbed the Secretary in several places. It is thought he may possibly recover, but his son Frederick will probably die of wounds received from the assassin.

"Vice-President Johnson now becomes President, and will take the oath of office and assume duties today.

"I have no time to add more than to say that I find evidence that an assassin is also on your track, and I beseech you to be more heedful than Mr. Lincoln was of such knowledge.

"EDWIN M. STANTON,
"Secretary of War."

The country was plunged in grief. Indeed the whole civilized world was startled by the news of the bloody crimes at Washington. The cities were draped in mourning for the murdered President. Hourly bulletins of the condition of the Secretary of State gave little hope that he could survive his wounds.

The number and the purposes of the conspirators were as yet unknown, and this uncertainty added to the general feeling of uneasy apprehension. Energetic efforts to ascertain the identity of the assassins and to arrest them were at once begun by the military authorities. Sentinels paced the sidewalk in front of Seward's house, to guard against another attack. Anxious inquirers thronged at the door. Letters and telegrams of condolence and sympathy poured in upon the afflicted family.

For several days my father lay in a critical state. His physicians had feared the injuries from the carriage accident might prove fatal, and now to these were added the frightful wounds inflicted by the assassin's knife. At intervals he was partly conscious, and then would lapse for hours into a condition of apparent stupor.

Of the scenes passing outside he had no knowledge, except as they were told him by his attendants. The funeral of President Lincoln, the inauguration of Vice-President Johnson in his stead, the surrender of Johnston, the capture of Davis, the arrest of the assassins, all took place while he was still unable to move.

He used at a subsequent period to tell of his vague and

dreamy memory of being propped up with pillows, and drawn to the window, to witness the passing funeral pageant of the President. The great black catafalque, with its nodding sable plumes, caught his eye, but he was physically too weak to grasp its full significance.

After the Assassination. I who write, and you who read these things, have to remind ourselves that they occurred fifty years ago. Needless then to dwell upon the horror-stricken household, the gruesome details of surgical relief, the physical pain and suffering, the slow return to consciousness, the tedious weeks of convalescence, the unavailing grief for the loved ones who succumbed to the shock, and the sorrow for the dead President.
All these things belong to the irrevocable past.

Let us rather recall with pleasant remembrance the loving care for the sufferers, the consummate medical skill displayed, and above all the outburst of world-wide sympathy throughout all civilized lands, evincing, as no other event in our time has done, the Brotherhood of Man.

PART III

After the War

Washington, Dec. 29, 1865.

Our West Indian Cruise.   This is the 29th of December. Congress has adjourned for the holiday recess.   The flags are lowered.   The Capitol ceases to swarm and buzz.   Even the throng of visitors at the White House is thinned out.   Public business slackens.   The Diplomatic Corps are more occupied with the festivities of the season than with notes and despatches, and the Department of State has a breathing spell.   The time seems auspicious for the Secretary to take that brief respite from official cares which his physician has warned him that his health requires, and which seems essential, if he is ever to recover from the effects of his injuries.   He has accordingly decided to take a run down into the genial air of the tropics for a month or so.   In so doing, he will accomplish a double purpose.   Besides regaining his strength, he will have an opportunity, long desired, of observing the West Indian islands, noting their political, social, and commercial condition, and studying the problems arising out of their proximity to the United States—problems that increase in number and difficulty every year, as our relations with them grow more intimate.

The Secretary of the Navy has kindly placed at his disposal the *De Soto* a fine steamer of one thousand six

263

hundred tons, belonging to the West Indian squadron, which, without departing from her own field of duty, can take him to visit the islands speedily and comfortably. This will bring him back to work again before Congress shall have advanced more than a fortnight in its session, so that he will be in time to receive his share of that fire of resolutions of inquiry which seem to be the indispensable preliminary to all legislation and "reconstruction."

Washington, Dec. 30, 1865.

Today we are sending our supplies down to the steamer. Our party will consist of six. There will be two ladies (my wife and her sister); two gentlemen, the Secretary of State and myself; and two servants (John Butler, who has served us so long and faithfully, and Joseph Smallwood, whose marine experience will render him useful on the voyage).

Our latest advices from the navy yard are that the steamer has taken in her coal and is "in the stream,"and that we are expected on board tonight.

On Board U. S. Steamer *De Soto*,
Off Giesboro, Dec. 31, 1865.

Under a bright, clear, moonlit sky we embarked last night at the navy yard, on a tug which we found lying at the wharf, ready to take us to the *De Soto*. Half an hour brought us alongside of the great black hull, towering up above even the smoke pipe of our little craft. A voice from above hailed "Tug ahoy!" and inquired our errand; and in response to our reply came, "Ay, ay, sir.   Please to come this way to the gangway."   In five minutes more we had shaken hands with the Attorney-General, the Colonel, and the squire, had climbed the ladder, were welcomed by the captain, and were on board, "outward bound."

Descending to the cabin, we were shortly followed there by confused piles of trunks, bedding, crockery, etc., giving the party the appearance of a large family just going to housekeeping in a small house. A couple of hours were devoted to the business of getting things "shipshape," and at half-past ten we "turned in," with the comfortable assurance that when we awoke we should find ourselves steaming down the Potomac below Fort Washington and Mount Vernon, and "going out with the tide" to sea.

Early this morning drum and fife sounded the reveille, and daylight (though rather a dim and dubious specimen of the article) began to stream down through the skylight. But the ship was ominously tranquil, and there was neither clank of engine nor jar of timbers. Presently the bell struck thrice. Just so, we said; there is "three bells"—signifying, when translated into the dialect of land-lubbers, half-past five o'clock. Presently it struck three bells again. Then it struck three bells a third time. Then it kept on striking three bells every five minutes. We began to doubt our familiarity with marine horology. "What o'clock is that?" The reply was brief and succinct: "Fog, sir."

Fog it was. And fog it is yet. We are off Giesboro, just where we were last night, and though we are already out of sight of land, we are not more than half a mile from the old cavalry barracks, nor out of hearing of the crows that there do congregate. The fog is impenetrable. It has congealed on the masts, the rigging, the guns, and the decks, covering the latter with a glare of ice, admirable for skating purposes, but not well adapted to walking. So we sit below in the cabin around the breakfast table, reading yesterday's morning papers, wondering what they are doing at home, and when anybody will be able to do anything here. On the latter point we consult successively the barometer, the thermometer, the compass, and the captain. But, so far, they all decide the question in the negative. The tide has come and gone, but we haven't.

Off Piney Point,
Monday, Jan. 1, 1866.

We are steaming down the Potomac at eleven knots an hour, and rapidly approaching the Chesapeake. Since this time yesterday, it has rained, it has snowed, it has frozen, it has thawed, it has grown clear, it has grown foggy; and through these changes we have gradually and cautiously felt our way down the river. We have passed Alexandria, whose wharves look deserted and desolate in these "piping times of peace," though so busy and bustling during war. We have passed Fort Foote with its frowning four-hundred-pounders, and Fort Washington with imposing parapets. We have tolled the bell and lowered the ensign as we passed the grave of Washington, at Mount Vernon. We have passed the Occoquan and Acquia Creek, Belle Plain and Indian Head. We have seen the deserted ruins of the rebel batteries that once blockaded the Potomac from Freestone to Matthias' Point. We have noted the spot, marked by a tall, blackened chimney, where Ward was killed in trying to carry one of them; and have traced the line where Booth crossed, in making his escape toward Richmond. We have met and passed perhaps a dozen schooners, loaded with hay and oysters, where we saw so recently fleets, navies, and argosies of warlike ships and transports, appearing as if evoked by charm, and now disappearing as if by magic. And with them has gone the last of the four memorable years of civil war in America.

This is New Year's Day. Officers and men are exchang-

ing, this morning, the salutations of the season. But
we have no New Year callers, except a party of seven white
seagulls, who came early this morning and still follow the
vessel, occasionally screaming a "Happy New Year" to
us, and evidently not unwilling to be invited to partake of
refreshments suited to the occasion.

As the *De Soto* threads her way through the devious
channel, her decks present an animated picture. On the
paddle-box stands the pilot, encased in india-rubber coat
and hat, and peering over the top of a screen of sail-cloth
erected before him to keep off the driving rain and sleet.
On the other paddle-box stands the lieutenant-commander,
speaking-trumpet in hand, to give the necessary orders to
the deck. Behind each paddle-box are two sailors
heaving the lead, and at intervals chanting, "By the
deep, five," etc. At the wheel stand four seamen, under
the eye of a burly quartermaster, who echoes the word of
command, "Sou'east, half east, sir," "Ay, ay, sir,"
"Hard-a-port it is." On the quarter-deck the officers
pace monotonously up and down on their appointed round.
Away off forward, in the vicinity of the forecastle, groups
of sailors are standing joking, chatting, scuffling, until the
boatswain's shrill whistle summons them to some duty.

For our own part, we keep below today while the rain
lasts, except an occasional turn on deck to see how we are
getting on. Our accommodations are ample, and, for the
sea, spacious. The captain's cabin is our parlour and
dining-room and library; it is nearly the size of our "yellow parlour" at home. On each side of this is a stateroom,
and a third sleeping apartment has been ingeniously
added by a partition slicing off a piece of the ward-
room. Just behind the staterooms there is, on one side, a
steward's pantry, and on the other a bathroom. A short
circular stair leads from the cabin to the quarter-deck
protected by a tarpaulin from the weather. Light is

supplied sufficiently by skylights and portholes, and heat is (or ought to be) furnished by a sheet-iron coal-stove, which yesterday chose not to burn, and so let the thermometer down to forty degrees. But, accidentally, the bottom of it fell out last night, and then it worked admirably, the temperature rising to eighty degrees, and all the rooms becoming warm and comfortable. But we hope soon to dispense with stoves and overcoats. We have come one degree of latitude to the southward, and the thermometer on deck has risen from twenty-five degrees yesterday to thirty-six degrees today. The shores of the river are still white with snow, but the ice is disappearing from the rigging and the decks.

January 1, 1866.—Evening.

New Year's Day has brought us to pleasant acquaintance with our ship and its officers. The captain is our old friend, William M. Walker, who has now been thirty-eight years in the service. At the opening of the war he was a commander. When doubts were expressed about the naval officers from "Border States," he settled the question as far as he was concerned, by asking to be "counted in" in the expedition to relieve Sumter. He has been zealous and active; in the early part of the struggle going out to England on a confidential mission, to examine the construction of ships, arms, etc.; receiving his captain's commission in 1862, and latterly doing good service in the Gulf and the North Atlantic blockading squadron. His junior officers are fine-looking, active, gentlemanly young men, and have all achieved creditable reputations in the war. Three of them are graduates of the Naval Academy. Mr. Howell, who is from our own State, and received his promotion last year to be lieutenant-commander, is the executive officer. Lieutenant Sumner is from Kentucky. To him is assigned the responsible and laborious duty of "navigating" the ship. Lieutenant Read is of New Jersey; has been seven years in the service, and nearly five of them afloat. Dr. Kidder, the surgeon, is a Massachusetts man, and came into the service at the beginning of the war. So did the paymaster, Mr. Cochran, of Philadelphia. Mr. Brice, Mr. Locke, and Mr. Roberts are volunteer officers of more recent appointment. Then there are the engineer officers, under the direction of the chief engineer, Mr. Hebard, of New York, who at noon every day reports in writing exactly how many pounds of coal have been used during the voyage, and how many remain in the bunkers.

The vessel herself is evidently a favourite with the officers, as she deserves to be. Built originally for a New Orleans packet, she was early seen to be a craft that had both speed and strength enough to make her useful in our improvised navy. Her spacious cabins were turned into wardrooms, officers' quarters, and magazines; eight one-hundred-pound Parrott guns mounted on her deck; and for the last two or three years she has been cruising up and down the Atlantic and Gulf coasts of the Southern States, capturing blockade-runners with a success that has been much more beneficial to the Government and to her officers and men than to the English insurers of those ill-fated craft.

The *De Soto* began her naval career in 1862 by pouncing upon unlucky schooners that were creeping out of the Louisiana bayous with loads of cotton, or in with loads of powder, etc. The next year she flew at larger game in the Gulf and on the Atlantic, and brought in such prizes as the steamers *Alice Vivian*, *Montgomery*, and *James Battle*, besides various sloops and schooners.

In 1864, she rounded off her record with the capture of the steamer *Cumberland*. Afterward she was ordered down to the West Indies, and was at Cape Haytien at the time of the "Bulldog affair," which led to the diplomatic difficulty between England and the Haytian Republic. The *De Soto*, as Captain Walker describes the scene, took no part in the hostilities, though she did help to rescue some of the combatants who were menaced with the triple danger of bombardment, burning, and drowning.

To this last narrative, Mr. Seward listens attentively though imperturbably, as he sits and smokes his cigar, occasionally asking some pertinent question. He has had already two official versions of this same story from eye-witnesses, one through the American consulate and the other through the British legation. And now here is a third which differs from both in some material points. Nothing is so hard to get at as the exact truth about a fight, even when the narrator aims to be perfectly truthful and disinterested. Each one's story necessarily centres in his own circle of vision, and his sympathies colour the tale unconsciously to himself. Mr. S. does not give his opinion at present on this mass of conflicting evidence about the "Bull-dog," but will look into the case more fully hereafter.

January 1, 1866.—Evening.

We have had our New Year's dinner, and have passed on down the Chesapeake toward the Capes. The pilot has taken leave of us, and has gone off in a small boat to the light-ship near Old Point Comfort. And now we have passed the Capes and are at sea. We have just been on deck to take our last look at the United States. All that we see of them are the two bright lights behind us that mark Cape Henry and Cape Charles.

January 2, 1866.—At Sea.

Heavy gale! Just imagine it!

January 3, 1866.—At Sea.

Gale somewhat abated. Seasickness ditto. One by one we have crawled up on deck. We sit on chairs and a lounge which the officers have placed near the middle of the ship. We have breakfasted, after a fashion, on chicken broth, and are sitting under an awning that keeps off the rain, and comparing notes on the general appearance of the sea.

Yesterday, it seems, was passed pretty much in traversing the Gulf Stream. The thermometer rose from forty-two degrees to seventy degrees, and, when plunged into a bucket of sea-water, rose to seventy-seven degrees. Sailing on the Gulf Stream, according to my brief observation of it yesterday, looks not unlike cruising on a vast kettle of boiling water—the water whitened, troubled, and tossing; the air hot, damp, and steaming, and clouds of vapour rolling and scudding in various directions. Perhaps this resemblance does not hold, however, on a less tempestuous day and with a less seasick observer.

Today we are emerging from the Gulf Stream. The thermometer has fallen to sixty-eight degrees. The sailors have just drawn a bucketful of water and announce the temperature of it to be seventy-one degrees. This operation is repeated hourly, as is that of heaving the log, by which we learn we are making nine knots an hour. About noon the sun came out for a few minutes, and the captain succeeded in getting an observation. We are in latitude 33 degrees 24 minutes; in longitude 71 degrees 43 minutes. So we are below Hatteras, and between it and Bermuda. Shakespeare was right in calling it "still-vexed Bermoothes," when he made it the scene of his *Tempest*. It has been the scene of a great many others since, and has a right to be vexed about it. (How did Shakespeare, with the light of only such geography as existed three hundred years ago, acquire so correct an idea of it? Perhaps from Sir Walter Raleigh, who was one of his contemporaries, and whose voyagings to Carolina and back must have made him familiar with the weather about Hatteras and adjacent waters.)

And now we have come six hundred miles from the Capes, and nearly eight hundred from Washington. We are nearly halfway on our voyage to Santa Cruz, distant from us about one thousand miles more.

The rain circumscribes our view, which is drearily monotonous. This afternoon two "Mother Carey's chickens" have made their appearance, flitting rapidly over the waves a short distance from the ship. Two "sails" are also seen—one a large ship labouring heavily against the wind, a few miles off on our port side, and the other, too distant to be readily made out, on our starboard quarter.

At two bells (five o'clock) the crew is "beat to quarters." This, on a man-of-war, corresponds to "evening parade" in camp. Two boys with drum and fife beat the signal. The marines are drawn up in line on the quarter-deck, under their sergeant. The sailors are grouped around their respective guns and wherever else their station is to be in time of action. The officers move about from place to place inspecting each group. The drum and fife play a national air. The colours are lowered for the night, and the men disperse.

At Sea, January 4, 1866.

The weather continues stormy. There is a south-west gale, with rain at frequent intervals. Today we are all together on deck for the first time. We breakfast and dine there, after a desultory and irregular fashion, not venturing in the cabin more than is necessary. John, who has kept up, fortunately, while the rest were seasick, is today *hors du combat* himself.

At twelve o'clock there is a cry of "Sail ho!" Soon we see her, a large ship bearing down directly toward us from the southward. She has a good deal of sail set, and the wind, which is so unfavourable for us, is favourable for her. As she passes us she seems to be labouring and plunging through the waves, and they occasionally break over her bows. The two vessels are not more than half a mile apart. They salute each other by raising and lowering the national ensign. So she is an American like ourselves, but she is not near enough to hail, and we shall know no more of her than this.

A glimpse of the sun is improved to take an observation. Latitude 31 degrees, longitude 70 degrees 31 minutes. We are south-west of Bermuda, and nearly on the same parallel as New Orleans and St. Augustine. We are farther south than the Mediterranean, and are nearly on a line with Cairo in Egypt.

The wind toward nightfall changes more to the northward, and we go below in the hope of better weather tomorrow. This afternoon we have made but six knots an hour. Our seats on deck have to be lashed fast.

Our little group of passengers sit huddled on the deck back of the "house," under a short awning spread to keep off the rain. Mr. Seward, wrapped up in overcoat and shawls, sits in a great chair, whose back is braced against the captain's stateroom, and which is lashed fast to keep it from slipping about the deck. The ladies occupy, one a lounge and the other a chair, both of which are lashed fast, and for still greater security the ladies are lashed fast in them. Time is divided between the dreary and monotonous view of the sea and such books and papers as we have brought along to read.

Today Smallwood comes out brilliantly, and proves that he has not been fourteen years at sea for nothing. There is a heavy sea on, and it is a sight to see him come

18

gliding down from the galley, the whole length of the deck, with that swift indescribable gait, compounded of a shuffle and a slide, dexterously balancing a plate of hot soup on the fingers of each hand, and never spilling a drop of it.   He sways and balances as if he was part of the ship itself; and the soup, in his hands, looks so quiescent that it seems natural enough to take the plates into our own hands.   But if we do, presto change!—it jumps about until it is all deposited on our clothes or on the deck. I soon find that the only way is to divide the labour with Smallwood, he holding the plate and I eating the soup.

Later we betake ourselves to our snug quarters below, and gather round the cabin lamp.   Mr. Seward is reading history and voyages, the ladies reading the January magazines, and I writing up the journal of the day.

At Sea, January 5th.

High times in the cabin last night!   About midnight the plates and dishes began to rattle vivaciously in the pantry.   Cups, saucers, and bottles precipitated themselves headlong, with a frantic desire to smash upon the floor.   The sugar-bowl took a flying leap across the cabin, wildly dashing itself against the opposite door, and leaving a white trail across the carpet to mark its flight.   Trunks rose up and rushed to mortal combat with chairs and tables.   The stove, hard pressed by blows from all sides, held its ground manfully.   The sofa executed a double somersault in the highest style of acrobatic art, only unfortunately breaking its neck in the process, and suddenly depositing John, its occupant, under the table.   The furniture seemed possessed with a desire for spiritual manifestations and emulous of the Davenport brothers.

Going on deck today, we find a clearer sky and a fresh north-west wind, which rolls us about, but hastens us on our course. We have our sails set to aid our engine, and are making eleven knots an hour, against six yesterday. We are now in latitude 28 degrees, longitude 69 degrees, and not more than six hundred miles from our destination.

Last night, for the first time since leaving Washington we have seen the moon and a star or two. This morning for the first time the deck is dry. The carpenter has been called in to restrain the insane freaks of our unruly furniture, and all is made "snug" and securely lashed.

At Sea, January 6th.

We are bowling along at eleven and a half knots an hour, and are in latitude 24 degrees. Today we cross the Tropic of Cancer, and tonight shall sleep within the torrid zone. We have entered upon that region of the trade wind "which is nature's highway" of western commerce. We have crossed the track of Columbus's first voyage of discovery; and San Salvador, where he first landed, lies just to the west of us.

It will be a week today that we have been on board; and during all that time we have not seen five minutes' sunshine; although we were coming farther and farther, as we had supposed, into what is the sun's peculiar domain.

But though we do not see him, we are steadily gaining on him. We have stolen half an hour's march on him already, as my watch declares. That, now, says half-past eleven o'clock, which is your time in Washington while here the ship's bell is striking noon.

Every day's stay on board brings new illustrations of the admirable method and order which characterize a man-of-war. A ship-of-war is the locality where that often-quoted maxim is followed which, everywhere else, is preached but not practised: "A place for everything and everything in its place." Every rope is coiled in its own particular spot. Every bucket hangs on its own particular peg. Every spike and tool and hatchet, every gun and cutlass, every inch of bunting, every grain of powder, every ounce of coal is in the place where it can be most conveniently reached and is most commodiously stowed. It is a standing remark, how so much can be put away in so small a space, and yet every article be at hand at a moment's notice. The rule applies equally to officers and men. The daily form of "beating to quarters" is gone through with, so that a roll of the drum may, at any time, summon every man to the post which he is to occupy in action, and impress upon him a perfect understanding of what he is to do there when that time comes. Thus the ship may be put into perfect fighting condition in less time than it takes a land pugilist to roll up his sleeves.

Sometimes the form of "beating to quarters" varies. One day all are summoned to the guns; another, all are summoned to the pumps. Neither a battle, a fire, nor a leak can find the ship unprepared.

Our cabin, however, is at present an exception. Here the usages of civil life have temporarily superseded naval system, and here there is chaos enough sometimes.

Up to the present date we have had no day when we (the inkstand will not stand steady on the table, so I write with pencil) could sit at table. We have lived literally from hand to mouth. Today we made an attempt to lunch in the cabin, but it resulted in total failure. The plates became endowed with vitality, the herrings turned into flying-fish, the apples went off as if to fulfil some engagement to play at tenpins, and, as the nursery song says, "the dish ran away with the spoon." So, on the whole, we concluded to dine on deck again, while the *De Soto*, like the world, "rolls on."

It is the inflexible law on a ship-of-war that, although the vessel is well lighted from stem to stern, there must be no light not contained in a lantern, and there must be

absolutely no matches.   Our exemption from this law we
concluded to put an end to, last night, on seeing a candle
jump from its candlestick into the bedclothes; and especially on learning that our cabin was placed just over the
magazine!

Part of the same orderly system of neatness is the continual cleaning up that is going on.   There is every day somebody scrubbing up the brass of the guns, somebody going
round with a pot of black paint, to touch up the boats,
the capstan, and the rail.   This scrupulous neatness of
the decks reminds one of the floors of those models of
cleanliness, the Shakers at Niskayuna.

It seems that the reason of all the bad weather we are
having is because there are ladies on board.   An old sailor
recalls the fact that on the frigate where he sailed the
weather never cleared up until the captain's wife was put
ashore.   We are debating, therefore, whether we are
to be resigned to storms as long as we shall have the
ladies on board, or whether we shall throw them overboard at once.

At Sea, January 7, 1866.

A pleasant Sunday morning.   A rainbow gives token
that the rain is over, the wind and sea have abated, and
the thermometer has risen to seventy-seven degrees.   We
breakfast for the first time in the cabin—our first breakfast
this year.   The repast only varies from ordinary ones in
the amount of vigilance required to keep the dishes on the
table, and the calisthenic postures adopted to keep our
own seats.

This morning we have our first sign of land.   Two white
birds are hovering round the ship, and one has perched,
for a moment, on the masthead.   It was somewhere in this
vicinity that Columbus saw the same indication of his
nearness to the undiscovered land he sought.

At nine o'clock the drum beats to quarters for Sunday inspection. The men are neatly dressed, and all in precise order. Everything is carefully scrutinized, from stem to stern. Then work is suspended for the day, except so much as may be necessary for the navigation of the ship. The men are gathered here and there in decorous and cheerful groups. The officers are sitting reading under the awning; quiet reigns throughout the ship. The whole scene presents a Sabbath tranquillity that would do no discredit to a Sunday in a country village of New England. Usually there is divine service on Sunday morning, the captain officiating. Today as the weather and the motion of the ship are not propitious, it is passed over.

As the evening draws on, the stars come out, and we sit chatting on deck till late at night, without shawls or overcoats, and hardly able to realize that it is not summer.

Off Porto Rico, Jan. 8, 1866.

At four this morning the captain notified us, according to promise, that we could now see the Southern Cross. We were soon on the moonlit deck, and found a calmer sea and cloudless sky. Away off in the south were the four bright stars forming the brilliant constellation that the United States never look upon. Below it, in the dim distance, was an obscure dark line, to which the captain pointed: "That is Porto Rico."

January 8th, 12 M.

Decidedly we are in the tropics. To-day we realize it. Blue waves, bright skies, and scorching sun. The mercury touches eighty-seven degrees. The wind has sunk into a soft summer breeze. Thin clothes are in demand. The captain dons his straw hat, and the doctor his white pantaloons. In the evening there are flashes of heat-lightning near the distant horizon. On our starboard side the zodiacal light streams up into the sky, of a pale reddish tint somewhat resembling a mild aurora borealis. Ice-water becomes a staple luxury. Meats have lost their relish, and at table we dwell upon pleasing anticipations of oranges and bananas. Conversing of some recent event at Washington, it was referred to as having occurred "last winter" before we remembered that this winter is not over yet, and that this is not July.

Our monotonous sea view was relieved this morning by the appearance at the east of us of the rocky little isle of Derecho, uninhabited save by gannets and sea-gulls. We have entered the Mona Passage, and are now coasting along the shores of Porto Rico. We can only see that they are uneven in height and barren toward the crest, but luxuriant in vegetation at the foot, and that blue mountains rise behind them. We have scanned them with telescope, but can see no cities, villages, or houses, either because we are too distant or because there are none there to see. To the west of us the dim outline of the island of Mona, lying in the centre of the Mona Passage, and beyond that is, though invisible to us, the coast of San Domingo.

So the scene of our adventures changes. We are no longer on the open Atlantic Ocean. Under the lee of Porto Rico, we are cruising in the Caribbean Sea, that favourite scene of the fearful tales of the once famous buccaneers, the Caribs, and the pirates of the Spanish Main.

Under the lee of Porto Rico the wind is shut off, and the sea is calm, like one of our lakes. Peering down into its blue depths this morning, a look-out shouted that he saw bottom. The bell instantly sounded the signal to stop the engine, and for a moment there was excited and hasty movement. When the paddle-wheels ceased motion, one looking over the side of the ship down through the clear water could easily see the irregular whitened patches of sand and coral. We felt our way cautiously by the lead for a while, and presently the chant of "By the mark, five!" "By the mark, seven!" "By the deep, ten!" "By the deep, twelve!" relieved us from our apprehensions.

Latitude, today, 18 degrees. We are below Cuba and the greater part of Mexico. We are farther south than the great African desert, and about in the latitude of Timbuctoo.

January 8th. Evening.

All this bright summer afternoon we have been running along the shore of Porto Rico. The ship hardly makes more than a ripple in the quiet sea, and we sit on deck under the awning, fanned by the gentlest of breezes, watching the varying outline of the coast, reading and chatting about its character and eventful history. As we draw nearer to the shore we can observe that the mountain ranges run from east to west, and that the broad, level country between their base and the sea is covered with luxuriant growth of sugar-cane, palms, and coffee-trees.

Porto Rico is a fertile and productive island, with good harbours but few great towns. It has a great deal of trade in sugar, coffee, and tobacco, principally with the United States. Columbus discovered it in the same year that he discovered Cuba. But it has always occupied a secondary place in public estimation and in the march of historical events. And yet, if the statistics of the Porto Riquenos themselves are reliable, it may challenge comparison. Its soil is claimed to produce much more to the acre than Cuba. Its climate is asserted to be much more salubrious. As regards snakes, it is a rival of "Ould Erin," for there is said to be no poisonous reptile in its borders. Even in the matter of fidelity, it beats the "ever faithful isle," for it has been three centuries and a half under the flag of Castile, and never strayed away to the embrace of invader or revolutionist. The English made a lodgment on it once, but the mortality among the troops was so great that they were withdrawn, which would seem to prove that the climate, so salubrious for Spaniards, does not agree equally well with Englishmen. Then there was an attempted revolution in 1820, but it languished and died without ever coming to power.

But the romantic period in the history of Porto Rico was in the days of Ponce de Leon; for this was his island. As we look off toward the distant mountains over which the golden sunshine is streaming with such mellow tints, we recall his golden visions. How he and his followers went there from Santo Domingo to seek the precious metal, perhaps to find the "El Dorado." How they fortified themselves against the deadly poisoned arrows, which the Indians were said to dip in the juice of the manchineel, so that they caused the instant death of whomsoever they wounded. How the poor savages, when they saw the gallant and glittering Spanish warriors, forgot or forbore to use their poisoned arrows, superstitiously believing that the white men were invincible and immortal, and if killed would come to life again—a belief in which they were strengthened by seeing that as fast as the Spaniards perished, fresh ones came down to join them from heaven, or from Santo Domingo, which was the same thing as far as they were concerned. How the docile islanders, submitting, were made slaves, and compelled to dig for gold, until their cruel taskmasters had done to death half a million of them. How Ponce de Leon ransacked the golden sands of the rivers, and explored the mountain rocks until he had gold to his heart's content, sacks and bags full. How he was seized, then, with the popular delusion of his time, of seeking the "Fountain of

Youth," whose waters insure perpetual life and strength and beauty. How he interrogated the simple Indians, who were ready to acknowledge anything he demanded of them, and they told him the fountain was on an island away off to the north and west. How he fitted out an expedition, and went off to the north and west, cruising through the Bahamas and Bermudas, going from island to island, and tasting spring after spring, but everyday getting older and older instead of younger and younger. How, when he was almost despairing, there rose out of the sea on Easter morning a radiant vision of an "island" of enchanting beauty, covered with such majestic trees, carpeted with such rare verdure, and gemmed with such charming flowers as never mortal man beheld before. How he landed on it and took possession of it, and called it "Florida"—the name we call it by to this day. How he celebrated high mass, and thanked Our Lady and Santiago and all the saints and angels for having brought him, at last, to the land of the "Fountain of Youth." How months afterward he sailed into the harbour at Porto Rico, and his friends rushed down to greet him and ask how his errand had prospered; and how, when he stepped ashore, sad and dejected, they drew back and dared not ask him, for his grey beard and wrinkled cheeks showed that the question would be a bitter mockery. True, he had discovered the boundless resources of the American continent; but what is the American continent to a man who wants the Fountain of Youth?

And then, how his gracious Majesty, the King, who had not had very great expectations about the fountain, but was delighted to hear of any addition to his dominions, thanked him and congratulated him on the discovery of Florida, and sent him out a commission to be its governor and viceroy. How Ponce de Leon loaded up his treasures on two ships, and sailed back to Florida, where, like a wise and humane governor, he commenced his reign by exterminating his subjects. How they, being disloyally inclined to live, resisted him and fought him, and, unlike the Porto Riqueno Indians, did not hesitate to pour a shower of arrows into the Spanish ranks, one of which hit and mortally wounded Ponce de Leon. And then, at last, how the poor old man was dragged down to his boat and carried off to Havana, to give up that life which neither his gold nor his governorship nor his Fountain of Youth could save any longer.

Eight bells, is it? Then it is time to turn in. And so here ends the journal of our first West Indian day.

St. Thomas, Jan. 9, 1866.

St. Thomas. At six this morning we were summoned on deck by the welcome news that we were approaching St. Thomas. Looking from the bow of the steamer, a beautiful panorama gradually opened before and around us. The sky was clear, the sea blue and tranquil, and islands rising from it on every hand, of varying size and contour, some seeming mere isolated rocks, some resembling green hillocks, some like the faint outlines of distant mountains. Largest of all, near us and directly before us, was St. Thomas, with its high, steep hills covered with verdure on the top, but here and there terminating at the base, on the sea, in abrupt, craggy cliffs and reefs.

As we came nearer, the sunshine lightened up two fantastic shapes. One was a white rock looking like a ship under full sail. ("Sail Rock," they call it.) The other was a high, rocky wall of variegated tints—red, yellow, and purple.

Presently the hills before us grew more distinct, houses began to appear here and there, and gradually the harbour opened to view—a deep hollow almost encircled by the steep hills, crowned here and there by a fort, a signal station, or a picturesque-looking villa; while the town itself, with its regular architecture, its rows of square yellow houses with square red roofs, and its circular-headed trees, presented an appearance somewhat resembling that of a German toy village. It stands on three hills of about equal height, making three triangular-shaped groups of buildings. Sailing vessels, large and small, under various flags, and here and there a large ocean steamer, were riding at anchor. Altogether, it was a picture so vivid in colouring and so suddenly spread before us that it was like the drop scene of a theatre.

And now there comes dancing off toward us a little white boat bearing a red flag with a white cross, and rowed by men with white clothes and black faces. In it is the pilot. He climbs the ladder and gives us the latest papers from New York, of the 29th of December, which are not so late as our own, and those from Southampton, which are later. We enter the harbour, drop the anchor, and are presently surrounded by boats whose occupants are of every possible shade of complexion; the men airy in straw hats and white and brown linen, the women gorgeous in Madras handkerchiefs of bright-flowered patterns. These are voluble and earnest in their proffers to do our washing or to furnish us with tropical fruits of every variety.

Presently come various visitors: West Indian gentlemen with swarthy Spanish features; American merchants and sea captains; soon after the United States Consul, and under his guidance we row ashore, leaving the jurisdiction of the Navy Department for the more accustomed one of the Department of State.

Everything on shore looks quaint, bizarre, and odd to our American eyes. It is a medley of all nations, races, and languages. Narrow, crooked streets, of hard, dry earth, run between rows of Spanish- or Moorish-looking

houses, with thick, strong walls, arched doorways and
windows. They are rarely more than one or two stories
high. No carriages and no waggons; but here and there
a horse or a donkey, loaded with sugar-canes projecting
all around him like the quills of a porcupine. Crowds of
negroes, of mulattoes, and of people of all shades of colour
are traversing the streets in all directions, all vociferating,
gesticulating, laughing, talking, shouting, at once. Some
of the women are carrying burdens on their heads. Most
of the men are lounging lazily. None seem to have any
especial aim or purpose; but they pass and repass, go and
come, and perpetually reappear, now in one group, now in
another, now on the sidewalk, now on the street, but always
shouting, talking, and laughing at the longest possible
range and on the highest possible key.

Some are standing in the sun munching bananas,
some sitting down in the shade and sucking long sticks
of sugar-cane. Their language is generally English, but
with Spanish accent and negro intonation that make
it impossible for a newcomer to understand. Many of
them are traders. A man requires no other capital than
a tub at the street corner, half filled with bananas, cane,
oranges, cocoanuts, sapodillas, and other fruits, plucked
from trees that grow wild on the hillsides. A woman
generally carries her stock on a board placed on her head.
This she balances with the utmost ease and precision,
almost unconsciously, walking with an erect, queenly
gait, but without restraint, pausing now and then to drop
a courtesy, or exchange a remark, or make a bargain
with perfect self-possession, and spilling nothing, however
great the crowd or haste may be.

We stopped at the hotel to rest a moment, and then
climbed the hill toward the residence of the consul, which
stands on a fine airy plateau overlooking the bay.

The houses at St. Thomas are well built, and are peculiarly adapted to the climate. One, or sometimes two stories high, most of them have windows and doors on every side, to catch every breath of air and give every facility for ventilation. For the same reason, the rooms on a floor are so arranged as to be practically thrown into one, and this one is opened up to the rafters of the roof. It has a strange look to Northern eyes, especially as there is no fireplace, no chimney, no place even for a stovepipe. Generally the cellar walls are of solid masonry, and a substantial flight of stone or brick steps leads to the upper door. Thus, in earthquakes and hurricanes, the family has only to retire to this basement stronghold to feel secure, and the superstructure may topple down or blow away, if it chooses. But such events are very rare. The houses, for the most part, have apparently stood for forty or fifty years without being destroyed by any elemental convulsion.

Within, all arrangements wear the same tropical aspect. No carpets, except a rug under the centre table. No curtains to obstruct the windows, but cool easy-chairs and lounges, fans, blinds, shades, and whatever else may conduce to keeping cool.

The dooryard and garden are as novel as the house. There is a profusion of shrubs and flowers and trees, hardly one of which can be recognized as having been seen at home. It is January, yet the flowers are abundant. It is winter, and yet everything is green. It is not the season of fruits; yet fruits hang everywhere, tempting the touch and the eye. There is the cocoanut, the palm, the banana, the orange, the lemon, the shaddock, the forbidden fruit, the soursop, the lime, the sapodilla, the plantain, the coffee tree, the cotton tree, the India-rubber tree, the agave, the guava, and a hundred others, to us new and unknown.

Luxuriant vines and creepers trail up and down the walls,

among them roses and jessamines, the only two familiar acquaintances we meet. The walks are bordered with large conch shells, here worth only a few cents a hundred, though with us so rare and valuable. The cacti in varied profusion climb up the angles of the house and wall, of dimensions that make those of our conservatories look dwarf-like.

Leaving the Consulate, we descended the hill to call at the house of Mr. Phillips, an American merchant, who kindly offered to place it at our disposition during our stay. Here was a pretty children's party going on, in celebration of the ninth birthday of his little daughter. Some twenty or thirty boys and girls composed the guests. Music and dancing, and sweets of all classes, graced the entertainment.

Thence we take a walk through the streets, looking at the shops and the churches. Of the latter there are many, for the town is composed of all religions, as of all nationalities.

The Episcopal, the Catholic, the Lutheran, the Methodist, the Baptist, the Jew, are all represented in the church edifices; and looking down the line of wharves, one sees the Spanish flag, the English, the American, the French, the Russian, the Italian, the Swedish, the Hamburg, the Bremen, the Dutch, the Chilian, the Peruvian, the Colombian, the Brazilian, the Mexican, the Haytian, and I know not how many more, waving over the offices of their respective consuls.

On returning to our ship we found all these consuls, who had come on board in a body with the Danish governor of the island. The latter, with his aides, on reaching the deck, was duly honoured with a salute, to which the fort —a picturesque, old-fashioned work—responded through the mouths of old-fashioned guns, cast long before the days of Parrott and Dahlgren.

Other visitors followed—the officers of ships, the merchants, the citizens, the officials, travellers, etc. After that, another row to the town, and a glance at the fish market—as curious in its products as the garden. Fish of form and colour unknown in Washington Market, some brilliant crimson, some bright green, blue, white, and yellow, reminding one of those enchanted fish described in the *Arabian Nights'* tale of *The Fisherman and the Genie.* We had some fried for dinner, and found them good eating, though, unlike their celebrated counterparts, they did not turn into princes and princesses.

St. Thomas, January 10th.

The night has been enlivened by the coaling of the steamer. Like everything else at St. Thomas, this commonplace business here takes on a picturesque aspect. The labourers are men with barrows and women with baskets, which they carry on their heads, and they march on board in procession by moonlight, to the sound of the fife and violin, empty their coal into the bunkers, and march off again. For a night's work they receive a dollar and a half apiece.

Today is raining and showery and windy. Instead of the usual trade wind from the eastward, we have a northwester blowing down from the hills. To us it seems pleasantly cool after the heat of yesterday. To the West Indians it seems chilly and uncomfortable. We are amused at every step by the difference in our respective notions of temperature. One gentleman gravely informs us that he has experienced a cold uncomfortable night, the basis of his complaint being that he was obliged to cover himself with a single blanket and spread.

Another warns us against the bad effects of a draught of cold air, and proceeds to close doors and windows against what seems to us the faintest and most desirable of zephyrs. When we propose to take a walk, they tell us it will occupy twenty minutes, and, to our surprise, it occupies but five at our usual rate of progression. Invalids though we are, we walk distances up and down the hills through the misty air, which our St. Thomas friends sitting sheltered under verandas and awnings think extraordinary and fatiguing.

To visit a rural seat which a patriotic American has rented and christened "Bunker Hill," we take a two-horse carriage, one of the two vehicles of that sort that St. Thomas boasts. At the foot of the acclivity, however, our horses stop and positively refuse to go one step farther, apparently thinking this eminence as difficult to be gained as its historical prototype was.

So we ascend on foot, and are amply repaid for our trouble by the magnificent view of the harbour, the islands, the shipping, and the town which lies at our feet. Behind and around us are hills, once cultivated, but now neglected and desolate, covered with rank grasses, wild herbs, and cactuses of every kind, some erect and stiff, some recumbent, trailing or climbing, many in flower, and a few bearing their ripened, prickly fruit.

On two of the heights near the town are a couple of ancient-looking castellated edifices which were originally built as strongholds by the buccaneers. One is called "Blackbeard's Castle," and is popularly assumed to have belonged to the renowned pirate of that name. The other has a still more doubtful legend which describes it as the veritable mansion of that terrible Bluebeard of nursery fame; and the dungeon of the poor lady who tried one key too many is pointed out, as well as the tower from which "Sister Ann" descried the approaching cloud of dust that heralded the coming rescue.

From the fictitious chieftain we go to visit a real one. In a pleasant, airy residence, overlooking the bay, we find

the Mexican ex-President, General Santa Anna, who had
sent congratulations and kind wishes to the Secretary of
State on his arrival.   He rises from his table, covered
with papers and manuscripts, to bid us welcome with
Castilian courtesy, and then sits down to chat awhile on
the past, present, and future of Mexico.   He is a large,
tall, fine-looking man, of Spanish features and complexion,
dark keen eyes and dark hair, and showing no sign of
bodily infirmity save a slight limp.   One would pronounce
him between fifty and sixty, instead of being, as he really
is, nearly seventy.   Briefly recapitulating his position in
reference to Mexican national politics, he says he is, and
always has been, a Republican and a Conservative; that
his people have failed thus far in maintaining their independence because they lacked organization and a head;
that partisan dissensions between them opened the way to
the French invasion, but that the French domination is
repugnant to them; that Jaurez is an uneducated Indian,
once an hostler, incapable of grasping the high responsibilities of his present position, or of uniting the Mexican
people in his support; that, on the other hand, the Empire
of Maximilian is a delusion and a failure, that it loses
strength instead of gaining it, and is a drain instead of a
source of revenue to the French exchequer; that the day
is approaching, perhaps not far remote, when the Mexicans
will reunite for nationality and liberty; that when they do
so unite, they cannot but succeed; that he, for himself, is
impatient for the accomplishment of that patriotic purpose; that once he sacrificed one leg in fighting for his
country, and is now ready, if need be, to sacrifice the other
in the same manner; that he hopes in this coming contest
for American sympathy and American aid.   Finally, he
places in our hands a copy of his recent Proclamation, in
which his views and his purposes are even more fully set
forth.

From Santa Anna's we descend the hill to Mr. Phillips's, and thence to the wharf. While waiting for the boat, to return on board, we are amused by the scene of street life passing before us. A shower comes up, and then a sudden gathering of incongruous characters for shelter under the awning of the opposite store. A crowd of women, all turbaned with Madras handkerchiefs, bearing all sorts of burdens on their heads, are standing conversing, or rather loudly jabbering at each other, in that negro dialect which is the principal sound heard at St. Thomas. None of them seem to be in the least incommoded by the heavy weights they carry, and walk about, gesticulate, and laugh and talk, without even taking the trouble to set their burdens down on the ground while they are waiting there. A caballero, well dressed, but swarthy, unceremoniously rides his horse right in amongst them on the sidewalk, under the awning, and stands there, his coming evidently being accepted as a matter of course. Two drunken negroes get up a vociferous quarrel, whose threatening tones and gestures would seem to imply immediate resort to blows; but neither contemplates any such result, and they content themselves with noisy demonstrations toward each other at a distance of fifty feet. Then there comes a lady in the height of extravagant fashion, dressed in delicate light fabrics, a head-dress of Parisian elegance, a train of court dimensions, picking her way through the mud in satin shoes. She is a mulatto; as is a gentleman in a high shirt-collar, white coat, and pantaloons, and with a dignified step and businesslike air, who is pointed out to us as one of the richest men of the island.

We row back to the ship, and find that in the gale she has had a narrow escape from serious trouble. She had dragged her anchor and drifted nearly into collision with the English steamer, and subsequently was in danger of getting ashore. The captain had by vigorous efforts rescued her, and she was now securely anchored again at a little distance from her former ground.

At five this afternoon we returned to the town to dine with the Governor. He had kindly sent his carriage, which was in waiting for us at the wharf. A salute of fifteen guns from the fort welcomed the Secretary of State. The road led us up a winding but not steep ascent, along the hillside and through the woods, to his house, which has a commanding position on the very top, and overlooks the whole city. We found his family agreeable, refined, hospitable, warm in their Danish patriotism, as well as fully observant and sympathetic in our American contest. His two daughters had just returned to the island, having finished their education in Copenhagen. The dinner party consisted only of his family and official aides, ourselves, and the captain of our ship. The dinner was like a dinner in Washington, except that (like ourselves) the host and hostess undervalued the productions of their own region, and set before their guests foreign delicacies artificially preserved. It closed with the pleasant Danish custom, the words "Well bekommen," and handshaking with each guest.

We returned by what looked like a perilous breakneck ride, the night being pitch dark, and the road winding by abrupt turns around the hillside and along the edge of the cliff. Had we been endeavouring to find the way ourselves, we should have infallibly driven over the precipice. But the Governor's two white horses (the only things visible to us) knew the way perfectly and followed it, bringing us safely back to the wharf.

January 10th, 1866.

Yonder, on the heights overlooking the town, stand the ruins of the two ancient stone structures built and occu-

pied, two centuries ago by the buccaneers. While the
sunshine lights up the jagged outline of their grey battlements, we sit in the shade of this hospitable veranda,
enjoying a delicious breeze, and still more delicious tropical
fruits, while we chat with our companions over what is
known here about the towers and the piratical rovers
who built them.

Traditions and legends of the buccaneers still abound
in the West Indies, but materials for authentic history of
them are scanty, for they were not much given to records
and statistics.

When they began their piratical career they were
few in numbers and poor in resources. A becalmed merchant vessel would have its first warning of them by seeing a small boat stealthily and rapidly approaching,
with no human being visible above its sides, and presenting only its sharp bows toward the ship, so as to baffle the
skill of her gunners. Once alongside, up would spring
fifty or a hundred horrible-looking villains, armed to the
teeth with sabres, guns, and pistols, who, climbing like
cats over the bulwarks, would pour down upon the
deck and commence a bloody massacre of all they found
there. Desperadoes by profession, they would recklessly
attack even superior numbers, trusting to the suddenness
of the surprise to achieve success. Sometimes their
captain would scuttle his boat as he approached the ship,
leaving his men only the alternative of drowning or of
boarding and overpowering the crew. Sometimes he
would be ready, with lighted match, to fire the magazine,
in case the fight should go against him, and so send both
the buccaneers and their victims to swift destruction.
When the crew surrendered, if they did so without resistance, and without concealment of whatever valuables
might be on board, they were sometimes spared and set
ashore; but even this was a matter of caprice with the

pirates, who, for the most part, seem to have preferred to butcher or throw them overboard at once. All sorts of wild and some very improbable stories are told of the atrocities of Morgan, Montbar, De Basco, Lolonois, Lawrence, and other pirate captains who have come to special renown, and who still figure with incredible vices and impossible virtues in the pages of popular fiction.

As a general thing, outward-bound European vessels were not molested by them, for these had but little spoil to invite attack. Their favourite prizes were the treasure-laden galleons from the Spanish Main, whose stores of metals and precious stones were at once their most profitable and most portable harvest.

At first they used to rendezvous at the little island of Tortuga, off the north shore of Hayti, where they fortified themselves. But very soon their captures supplied them with vessels, arms, and wealth, which enabled them to enlarge their operations and establish themselves at different points on various islands, where they could divide their booty, carouse, riot, and squander it, and then plan new schemes for getting more. Other reckless characters from the islands and from Europe flocked in to join them, and before long they became masters of the Caribbean. Emboldened by their success on the sea, they next turned their attention to the land, and fitted out expeditions to attack and ravage the Spanish and Dutch settlements. Maracaibo, Porto Bello, Carthagena, Campeachy, and Vera Cruz were successively plundered; and, crossing the Isthmus, they took Panama, and inaugurated a new series of piratical operations up and down the Pacific coast. It is a striking illustration of the feebleness of European naval strength and the remoteness of the West Indies at that date, that Spain and Holland, two chief maritime powers in Europe, were unable to arrest, or even check, the exploits of these bands of piratical adventurers.

Their career culminated at last, however, as many a better one has, by their "killing the goose that laid the golden eggs." When they had captured or sunk the vessels engaged in carrying treasure, and robbed and burned the towns where it was stored, the very impunity with which they had done it discouraged the renewal of the commercial ventures so entirely at the mercy of such unscrupulous marauders. "Trade diminished, ships decreased in number, and towns were no longer built and supplied to be sacked." The buccaneers gradually found themselves without business. They scattered in various directions; and those that escaped the hangman, or violent death in drunken brawls, were reduced to honest industry for a living. So ended that bloody page of West Indian history; and so the two old towers at St. Thomas fell into dilapidation and decay, as we see them today.

In the garden they point out to us the coffee-tree with its leaves of glossy green, like our laurel. When the fruit is ripening it looks not unlike a cherry, red, sweet, and palatable. The preparation of the coffee for market is simple. The fruit is gathered, dried, passed between rollers which remove the skin and pulp from the kernel, then passed through a fanning-mill to separate the chaff, and it is ready for use. But the longer it is kept the better it becomes, for age improves coffee as it does wine. It is claimed here that the superiority of the Mocha coffee is due to this cause, the fruit being no better except that it is preserved longer before being shipped.

The coffee-tree of Arabia is the parent of all the others. The Dutch carried it from there to Batavia, and afterward from Batavia to the West Indies. They presented two trees to the King of France, which were kept as curiosities in the royal garden. When a failure of crops in Martinique threatened that island with disaster unless some new cultivation was resorted to, the French Government sent out a messenger bearing two shoots from the royal coffee-trees. The voyage was long and tedious, the vessel's supply of water was scanty, and the King's messenger only saved his coffee-trees by dividing with them his daily allowance of it. He did save them, and they were the original stock of all the coffee-trees in Martinique and San Domingo.

The coffee-tree likes the same tropical climate as the sugar-cane, but the sugar-cane prefers the lowland, and the coffee-tree the upland. In many islands the two crops, on hill and dale, stand side by side, presaging the neighbourly position of coffee-pot and sugar-bowl on our breakfast-tables.

Pausing before a market woman surrounded by piles of tropical fruit, Mr. Seward inquired the price of her bananas.

"Got no bananas today, mas'r."

"Are not these yours, then?" said he, pointing with his cane to a hugh pile of the red fruit so abundant, in its season, in New York fruit stands.

"Bress your soul, mas'r, dose not bananas; dose is plantains."

So we learned that what we eat in New York as the banana is, in fact, the plantain, here considered not fit to be eaten at all until it is cooked, while the delicate yellow fruit resembling it is the real banana; but as that is smaller, and the American purchaser likes to get a good deal for his money, he is furnished with the coarser and cheaper plantain.

The banana and its kindred fruit, the plantain, are food of universal consumption in the West Indies. Everybody eats them. You find them on the tables of the rich, in the hovels of the poor, in the hands of the children, and among the rations of the soldier. Their growth is exceedingly rapid. Planted from cuttings, the tree attains its full

size in a single year, and commences bearing its heavy
bunches of fruit.

St. Thomas, January 11, 1866.

The little steamer which runs between St. Thomas and
Santa Cruz last night brought over Mr. Moore, our vice-
consul at Frederikstedt, who, with Mr. Walker, our consul
here, came on board to breakfast with us.   He reported a
rough night of it, the voyage occupying ten hours.   It is
usually made in two.

Early hours are among the good habits of the people of
St. Thomas.   The town was apparently all asleep between
nine and ten o'clock last night, and was all up and doing
at seven this morning.

The morning was occupied in visiting the shore, com-
pleting our purchases, dispatching visits of ceremony, and
taking leave of our friends.   We carry away from St.
Thomas coffee and tropical fruits, to which collection of
West Indian products Dr. Brody has added two green
parrots, some curious minerals and tortoise-shells, a carved
calabash, and some concentrated oil of bay leaves, sufficient to make bay rum enough to last a lifetime.

Between two and three o'clock we took our departure.
The trip was singularly beautiful, passing surrounding
islands of all sizes and distances; Santa Cruz before us,
St. John's and Tortola on the left, and various little rocky
islets on the right.

St. Thomas has been not inaptly described as a place
which is on the way to every other place in the West Indies.
To go anywhere, from anywhere else, you go first to St.
Thomas.   This is not merely on account of its central
position, but because of its commercial character.   It
is a free port, and therefore a favourite place for both
buyers and sellers who want a market.   This brings
shipping and travel, and makes it the point for steam

lines and mail communications, both with New York and
Southampton.

The island, before the emancipation era, is said to have
been agricultural.   Now it is commercial, merely.   All
its population, and all its activity, is concentrated in the
town and in trade.   The hills and savannas, once occupied
by plantations of cane, etc., are now deserted, and left to
wild fruits and trees and grasses.   No fences, fields, or
habitations.

Of the population of eleven thousand, nearly seven-
eighths are coloured people of all shades.   They are labourers and traders, as opportunity offers, in the town, but
few, if any, cultivators of the rural soil.   Of the whites,
there is a sprinkling of every nationality, each speaking
their own language; but the one prevailing tongue for
business and social purposes is English.   The Danish
element is an inconsiderable fraction in numbers, though
it is the ruling one, having all the civil officials and the
garrison of the forts.

The story of St. Thomas is briefly this: Just about two
hundred years ago, the Danes, finding that the other
maritime nations of Europe were taking possession of the
islands in the Caribbean Sea, thought they might as well
take one themselves.   They pitched upon St. Thomas, not
because it had special attractions, but simply because it
was the only one they could get, being remote and uninhabited.   The English raised some objection to their
going even there, but did not insist upon it.   So   the
Danes took the rocky little island and planted some colonists on it, who tried to raise a few hogsheads of sugar.
There was a capacious harbour on the southern side, but
nobody attached much importance to that, for in those
days harbours were plenty and ships were few.   The
Danes left the port open to everybody without commercial
restriction, for the poor colonists were only too happy if

anybody would come into that unfrequented, out-of-the-way region to trade with them.

It was about this time that the "buccaneers" were ravaging and plundering on the Caribbean Sea and along the Spanish Main, capturing the gold-laden galleons, hanging their captains at the yardarm, and throwing their crews overboard. But pirates, like other men, when they have gotten a prize, need a port to take it into. The buccaneers dared not take captured vessels to the Spanish settlements. They could not take them to the French and English settlements, for those were on the Windward Islands, and they would have to beat all the way against the trade wind blowing "dead ahead."

But here was the snug, quiet harbour of St. Thomas, out of the way of Spanish frigates, without any custom-houses to molest, or any courts to make afraid, and so placed that their craft would have a favourable breeze, both going in and coming out. Very soon, therefore, St. Thomas became the favourite rendezvous of the buccaneers with their prizes. Very soon, too, traders from afar off snuffed up the scent of their ill-gotten gains. As soon as it became generally known that there were people at St. Thomas with pockets full of gold which they were eager to squander, merchants flocked in with everything that such folks would like to buy. Then there were others who found it equally convenient—smugglers who wanted a place from which to run contraband cargoes to Porto Rico and Santa Cruz; vessels in distress that wanted a port to repair and refit; merchant vessels, in time of war (which was nearly all the time), seeking a neutral port for refuge from the enemy's cruisers. To all these St. Thomas offered a safe anchorage of easy access, without restrictions, and a good market. It grew and throve, and prospered beyond the anticipation of its founders. It was the one free port of the West Indies, and soon became a centre of trade. "Free traders" (which in those days included freebooters) brought it business and life and consequence.

In later years, when the pirates were dead and the smugglers suppressed, and "free trade" came to mean only freedom from duties and imposts, it continued to grow. The settlers named the city after the Danish Queen, Charlotte Amalia; and the Danish Government wisely abstained from collecting revenue, preferring to let natural laws continue to build them up a great commercial entrepôt there. When steamers began to take the place of sailing packets, they naturally followed the same channels of trade, and so St. Thomas has come to be a place where steam lines converge. Furthermore, it happens to be so centrally placed that lines drawn from England to Central America, from Spain to Cuba and Mexico, from the United States to Brazil, from the Windward Islands to the Leeward ones, all meet and cross each other there; and you will see, riding at anchor in its harbour, steamers from Southampton, from New York, from Bordeaux, from Cadiz, from Bremen, besides sailing craft wearing the flags of every nation that "goes down to the sea in ships." In a word, St. Thomas is the result of three advantages it has over other West Indian islands—a fine harbour, a central position, and freedom of trade.

There are in the world a few isolated points whose possession enables the power that holds them to control trade, and to direct naval and military operations with especial advantage. Gibraltar and Aden, the Dardanelles, Sebastopol, Panama and Havana, Quebec and Key West are such places. Great Britain especially has always had a keen eye for such points. They have enabled her to domineer over remote regions, very unexpectedly to their inhabitants. She finds such an one in a sterile rock, a worthless sand-bar, or narrow strait; and presently it

bristles with her guns and forts, and surrounding nations
find she has made a succcessful move in that great game of
chess, of which the world is the board and we are all castles
and pawns.

St. Thomas is a point of this sort. Happily, it early fell
into possession of Denmark, an enterprising power, strong
enough to keep it, but not aggressive enough to use it as a
base of warfare. It has as peculiar advantages for a naval
station as it has for commercial support. Dangerous
reefs and breakers surround it, so that it would be difficult
to land troops to attack it, and it would be easy to repel
such attack by fortifications on its commanding heights.
The harbour is a great basin, capacious enough for a small
navy; and its entrance, though safe and easy, is through
a narrow strait, which even the diminutive forts and
antiquated ordnance of the Danes are able to defend. Its
history demonstrates that it is the place of places to coal,
repair, refit, and take refuge from enemies or storms. It
would have been of infinite value to us had we owned it
during our late war, and of great value to the Confederates
had they owned it. It was fortunate for us that it was
in the possession of a power not only just, but friendly
to the United States. Our vessels, however unfairly
treated at British and French ports, found always a welcome at St. Thomas, a place for repairs and supplies, and
one that gave no aid or comfort to the rebels.

The early Portuguese and Spanish discoverers were good
Catholics. When they came to a new locality they generally named it out of the Church calendar in honour, sometimes, of their own patron saint, sometimes of the patron
saint of their country, sometimes of the saint on whose
day the discovery was made. So nearly every apostle,
evangelist, and martyr came to have his seaport, his
island, cape, or mountain.

Columbus gave to the first land he discovered the title

of the "Island of the Holy Saviour" (San Salvador).
Cuba he did not name, having some doubts whether it was
not the Asiatic Cipango. So it has retained its aboriginal
name to this day. Hayti, the island he prized highest
of all he had found, he affectionately and patriotically
called "La Isla Española" (The Spanish Isle). Upon its
ports he bestowed saintships freely. When he came to
this group of what seemed to be a myriad of little islets,
he named them the "Virgin Islands," in honour of St.
Ursula and her eleven thousand virgin martyrs, whose
bones are still exhibited to incredulous eyes at Cologne.
Later, when irreverent Dutch, English, and Spanish
navigators got among them, some of the virgins were
rechristened, in detail, with odd enough names, based
usually on some fanciful resemblance seen from the ship's
deck. Thus, one is "The Hat" (sombrero), another "The
Thatch," while others are "The Turtle," "The Crab,"
"The Snake," "The Prickly Pear," "The Fat Girl,"
"Beef Island," and "Jost Van Dykes," with an occasional
sprinkling of saints—"St. Peter," "St. Thomas," "St.
John," and "Santa Cruz."

We steamed over to Santa Cruz before dusk, in time to
have a fine view of the island, and of the harbour of
Frederikstedt. But the wind had raised an unusual
surf, and the landing after dark was found difficult, and
so reluctantly abandoned till morning. The harbour is
rather an open roadstead; and, though the customary
trade wind does not reach or disturb it, it is exposed
to high winds from another quarter.

January 12, 1866.

Santa Cruz. Early this morning we debarked at the
wharf at Frederikstedt. Mr. Moore, the Acting Consul,
had carriages in readiness, and in them we traversed the
island from one end to the other.

It was a drive of about twenty miles over a road of easy grade and curves, and throughout its whole extent almost as smooth as a floor. On each side of it was a continuous row of cocoanut and mountain cabbage palms. Similar avenues diverged from it and crossed it at various points.

The fields by the roadside and as far as visible were planted with sugar-cane and tropical fruits. There were no fences or hedges, and the general aspect of the landscape was that of a great garden, luxuriant vegetation covering every hill and dale, with here and there a group of white buildings amid the trees.

These were the mansions of the owners of the sugar estates, each surrounded by its mills and labourers' cottages. The labourers themselves were of all shades of colour, all busy, and for the most part tidy, intelligent, and thrifty-looking.

Remembering our single harvest of hay in the course of a year, it occurred to me to ask how many such harvests there were during the year in this island. Mr. Moore could not say, but, stopping the carriage, inquired of an old negress who was cutting the grass around her cottage with a sickle, "Auntie, how often do you cut the grass here, in the course of a year?"

"Law, sir, I dunno, I 'spect we cuts it every time it rains."

That explained why there were no haystacks. The hay-harvest, it seems, is perpetual.

This reminded one of the gentlemen who accompanied us of an experience that a New Englander had, who brought a hive of bees here from the States, thinking they would make honey for him all the year round. But the bees, after the first year's experience, discovered that, where there was no winter, there was no need of laying up stores of honey, so they abandoned the habit of making any, except for daily use.

A noticeable feature of the drive was the frequent appearance of schoolhouses, at almost every junction of crossroads. They compared very favourably with country schoolhouses in New York and New England.

It was about noon when we arrived at Christianstedt. This is a seat of government, whose offices are in a substantial and stately edifice.

The Governor received his guests with military honours and a collation. Here we met some Americans who were spending the winter in the genial climate of Santa Cruz. Among them was our old friend Mr. Wells of express fame, and the founder of Wells College at Aurora.

After an hour or two spent in looking at the government buildings and walking through the streets of the quaint, substantial little capital, we returned to Frederikstedt, the Governor and his staff accompanying us. On the way we stopped at one or two of the larger sugar estates, to see their methods of making sugar and to look at the view from them of the Caribbean Sea.

My father was much interested in the conversation of these intelligent and well-informed Danes. He inquired particularly into the laws and general polity which had prevailed in the government of these islands. Besides the little islets, there are but three of any considerable magnitude,—St. Thomas, St. John, and Santa Cruz. One of these is the garden spot, and another the favourite harbour of the West Indies. Using them with judgment, and treating their inhabitants with paternal kindness, the Danes have governed these islands wisely and well, and have led their people gradually into the paths of industry, morality, and competence. Denmark, alone of all the European Powers having West Indian possessions, has solved successfully the problems presented by Emancipation.

"As you know, sir," remarked one of the officers, "emancipation in the other islands reduced many of the whites to poverty, drove others to Europe, decreased population, ruined trade, left towns to decay and fields to run to waste. But here careful forethought and strict administration have maintained prosperity."

I observed that everybody I saw was at work. There were no loungers.

"There are none. Every proprietor cultivates his land, because it is his interest to do so. Every labourer works under a contract regulated by law for his advantage. He has, besides his wages, a piece of land allotted to him, where he can raise vegetables for his family or for market. He is given a half or a whole day, in each week, to cultivate it, and is expected to do so. Every landowner has to keep the road good which passes his property, and to keep up its rows of palm trees, by replacing any that die or are destroyed. Every child has a schoolhouse within walking distance and is required to attend it, unless sick.

"You are about to experience the effects of Emancipation in your Southern States, Mr. Seward. Would not some stringent laws like these avert the danger of their falling into disorder or decay?"

"Possibly. But our system of government, you will remember, is very different from European ones. It is one of our doctrines that the best government governs least. We try to guard the rights of person and property, but trust greatly to individual enterprise. Our people are impatient of too close a supervision of their business affairs, and think they can manage them better than any government can."

"It must be conceded that they have done so thus far."

It was just dusk when we parted from our hospitable friends, who accompanied us to the wharf. In another hour we were taking our last look from the *De Soto's* deck at the

Isle of the Holy Cross,
Gem of the Carib Sea.

At Sea, Jan. 13, 1866.

San Domingo. Let us take an inventory this morning of
the tropical curiosities and products which have accumulated in our cabin during our three days of West Indian
island visiting.   First, there are two green parrots; one
with a yellow head, staid and taciturn, one with a red head,
voluble and conceited.   Next we have two barrels of
tropical fruits, limes, lemons, oranges, cocoanuts, bananas,
etc., upon which we live luxuriously three times a day.
Then there are two bags of coffee from San Domingo.
Then there is a quaintly carved calabash from Venezuela,
some rich mineral specimens, and some tortoise-shells from
the same locality.   Then there are two bottles of the quin-
tessence of perfumery, viz., the essential oil of bay leaves,
one drop of which is warranted to prepare a quart bottle of
bay rum.   Then there are canes of the lime and orange
trees that grow at Santa Cruz.

Santa Cruz and Jamaica are both celebrated for their
rum.   It is hardly necessary to say that it is age which
gives it its chief superiority.   The cane doubtless grows as
well in other islands, but the rum distilled from it either is
not as well made or as long kept as in these two.   Even
in these, new rum is hardly distinguishable from that of
other localities, and the old is not to be had except by
taking some time and pains to find it.   Evaporation
gradually diminishes its quantity, and when it has attained
the ripe age of twenty-four years it has shrunken to
one quarter of its original bulk, has lost all sharp, fiery
taste, and is smooth, oily, and strong.

This morning we are steaming past Porto Rico, and are
just coming in sight of the distant mountains of San
Domingo.   The sea is almost unruffled; and, as the

steamer ploughs it up, flocks of little white birds seem to rise from it, scud above it a few hundred yards, and then plunge into it again. These are flying-fish. They are graceful little creatures, some of whom we could gladly welcome on board: but they are proof against the ordinary seductions of net, hook, or line.

San Domingo, Jan. 14.

Sunday morning finds us at anchor in the roadstead off the city of San Domingo, the oldest city of the Western Hemisphere, dating back to the days of Columbus, of whom it was the creation, the prison, and the tomb.

Seen from the steamer, it looks like an ancient Spanish or Moorish stronghold. A wall of masonry runs completely round it, flanked by bastions and a fort which commands the entrance to the river Ozama, on which it stands. Even from here it can be seen that many of the buildings are large and were once imposing, but now dilapidated and nearly in ruins.

The *De Soto* rocks and rolls at her anchors a mile and a half off from shore. There are but ten feet of water on the bar at the mouth of the river, and she cannot cross it. Why was this harbour chosen by Columbus for his colony, when he had already found so many better ones? Simply because the Ozama was just the right size for the caravels of his day, and he did not foresee the great steamers and clipper-ships of the future. Modern vessels have grown too large for San Domingo, and so its trade has fallen off and its buildings gone to decay. Only schooners and light-draught ships can pass into it.

We sat down to breakfast, and wondered the captain did not join us. Finally, just at the close of the meal, he descended the cabin stairs.

"Captain," said Mr. Seward, "you are late this morning."

"Yes, sir," replied the captain, a smile lurking about the corners of his mouth. "I was less pleasantly employed. I was fishing an American Consul out of the Caribbean Sea."

"Out of the sea! What happened to him?"

"Why, he came off from town with the lieutenant, and, as you may notice, there is a pretty high sea running this morning. The time to step up out of the boat to the side ladder is (as you are aware, sir) when the wave is lifting the boat toward it. Unfortunately the Consul hesitated too long, and stepped out just as the boat was dropping away from the ladder, and, of course, he stepped into the sea."

"But he was rescued?"

"Yes, one of the crew succeeded in catching his coat collar with a boat-hook and brought him up. We even rescued his hat, which had fallen off in the *mêlée*."

"Where is he? Won't you bring him down into the cabin, wrap him up in warm blankets, and give him something restorative?"

"I proposed that, but he declines, with thanks. He says he is not exactly in fit condition to be presented to the Secretary of State. He will sit awhile on the quarter-deck, where this hot sun will dry him quicker than anything else would, and he will then pay you his respects."

Sure enough, when we went on deck we found the Consul sitting there quite dry, and not looking at all like a man who, Aphrodite-like, had just emerged from the ocean. He was an intelligent gentleman, a Southern man, loyal to the Union; and gave us his observations on the Dominican Republic during the brief time he had resided here.

After a short interview with the Consul and his friends, we proceed to the shore, having first exchanged the compliment of a salute with the fortress. We row under the guns of the latter, and find it has been once a work of great strength; but that the sea dashing against its base, and the winds and waves of three hundred years beating against its walls, have shorn it of much of its former grandeur. The masonry is of a thickness of several feet, which has conduced much to its preservation so long. Its general aspect is rugged and picturesque in the extreme.

A walk up from the wharf through the streets seems like a visit to another century, so antiquated does everything appear, so different from anything we have seen elsewhere. The streets are long, narrow, unpaved for the most part, though hard and dry. The houses on each side are of the Spanish style of architecture of three hundred years ago. On the main street, where most of them are used for shops, repairs keep them in tolerable condition. In many other quarters they have become mere ruins, or are turned into hovels for the poor.

The inhabitants are of all shades of complexion, save that few are entirely white, and few are entirely black. They are mulattoes, quadroons, mustees, etc., nearly all having a Spanish cast of features. Some of the ladies, going with their children to church, are exceedingly well dressed in the Spanish fashion, with mantillas or veils, and would easily pass muster in Madrid. There is some infusion of Indian blood, perhaps, but its characteristics are not distinctly marked. Their language is, almost without exception, Spanish, with a peculiar local accent.

We stop a moment at the office of Mr. Cazneau, an American merchant here, and then go to the National Palace to visit President Baez.

The palace is well preserved, handsome, and well furnished. A broad flight of stairs, guarded by coloured soldiers in the Dominican uniform, leads to the reception room; and there we find the President and his Cabinet, all swarthy, Spanish, and apparently well-bred gentlemen. President Baez is himself a man of medium size and prepossessing appearance.　He seats himself with the Secretary of State of the United States on the sofa at the top of the room, while the others occupy chairs arranged in two rows, leading up to it like an aisle.

The interview is an important one for Dominica; for, though unofficial, it involves the question of the recognition by the United States of her present government. President Baez, speaking through an interpreter, briefly recapitulates the revolutionary events that have preceded his advent to power, and points to his ministers, who comprise among them General Cabral, General Pimentel, General Serrano, each the chief of a revolutionary party, now all united in one administration, to give peace and permanence to the country.　He closes by frankly admitting that his government still needs one thing to assure it; but, with that, will be strong and firm—that is, a recognition by the Government of the United States.

Mr. Seward's remarks, in reply, briefly recapitulate the past history of the United States, in regard to questions of recognition of American republics, and especially that of republican governments founded by the race represented here.　They refer to the future relations and the unity of interest existing between the republics of this hemisphere, and especially the relations and the duties of the United States in regard to them.　Finally, they give what is equivalent to an unofficial but reliable assurance that the recognition of the present government of the Dominican Republic by the United States will not be long deferred.

He adds: "We have built up in the northern part of the American continent a republic.　We have laid for it a broad foundation.　It has grown upon our hands to be an imposing, possibly a majestic empire.　Like every other structure of large proportions, it requires outward buttresses.　Those buttresses will arise in the development of civilization in this hemisphere. They will consist of republics founded like our own, in adjacent countries and islands, upon the principles of the equal rights of men. To us it matters not of what race or lineage these republics shall be. They are necessary for our security against external forces, and perhaps for the security of our internal peace. We desire those buttresses to be multiplied and strengthened, as fast as it can be done, without the exercise of fraud or force on our part. You are quick to perceive the use of the main edifice in protecting the buttress you have established here; and thus it happens the republics around us only impart to us the strength which we, in turn, extend to them. We have therefore no choice but to recognize the Republic of Dominica as soon as it shall afford the necessary guarantee of its own stability. We have only been waiting at Washington for the report of our Consul here, giving us satisfactory evidences of this stability and permanence." So the interview terminates very satisfactorily.

Thence to the Cathedral—a fine old structure of massive masonry, and in heavy mediæval architecture. It is in good repair, and its altars and shrines are profusely, not to say gaudily, ornamented.

Numerous pictures, mostly of the Saints, adorn it. Under a slab in the central pavement was pointed out to us the place where the remains of Columbus were interred, up to the time of their removal to Havana during the present century. In one of the chapels is an interesting historical relic, the wooden cross which Columbus planted on his first landing on the island. Then we went to the ruins of the Convent of Santa Clara. In its time, it must have been a magnificent structure. The heavy walls, with arched cells and cloisters, the deep wells, the flat tiled roofs, are in some places in tolerable preservation, in others in decay and ruin. The convent garden is all weeds and thickets. In various parts of the edifice were families of poor people, who had evidently been glad of so eligible an opportunity to find house room, rent free, subject only to the trifling inconvenience of having the windows and doors gone, and the roofs and walls considerably dilapidated. But in this climate perhaps these are not important considerations.

Difference of climate brings differences of taste. In one of the shop-windows today we saw a pair of very ordinary looking American quails, in a handsome cage, for sale at twenty dollars; while parrots were to be had for a few shillings. Quails being rare here are kept for household pets, while parrots, being plenty, sometimes get stewed for soup.

Looking down on the harbour just below us, we see a pelican describing slow and stately circles, ending with a sudden plunge into the water, out of which the bird emerges with a fish in his mouth. Then, flapping his wings, he betakes himself to some more secluded spot to devour his prey or divide it among his family. Nobody seems to molest these pelicans while they are making their solemn gyrations just above the roofs of the houses and the masts of the ships.

There is a picturesque drive outside the walls of the city. Two diminutive Spanish horses and an antiquated looking chaise soon take us there. Passing through an ancient gate, with walls and guard-house of solid masonry, around which sentries are pacing and soldiers off guard are lounging and chatting, we find ourselves on a level and tolerably good road, evidently once a handsome highway. It winds, following the course of the coast, though it is at some distance from the sea. On both sides of it are plantations and country seats of the hidalgos of olden time. Their buildings are old, dilapidated, and neglected. Some are in ruins; some partly repaired and occupied by the landowners; others have become mere hovels for labourers. Rich, luxuriant, tropical vegetation has grown up in tangled thickets, half hiding the houses, overrunning walls and fences, choking up roads and paths.

We meet no carriages or wagons, but occasionally men, women, and children, mounted on donkeys, whose loads of cocoanuts, bananas, and sugar-cane so cover them up that hardly more than the head and ears of the animal are visible.

We descend to look at one of the villas, and, passing over a fallen gate, and through paths overgrown with weeds, go up to the mansion, once stately, now dilapidated, surrounded by ruined offices and outbuildings. Its broken windows open on a spacious veranda, commanding a magnificent view of the ocean. Here we rest, while the driver attempts what seems the impossible feat of bringing down some cocoanuts from a palm tree in the grove nearby. Its forty feet of straight, smooth trunk look inaccessible enough. But, with the skill of an expert, he takes a long rope, makes a slip-knot in it, fastens one end to the trunk and contrives to throw the other over a branch, and, mounting this improvised ladder with cat-like agility, presently comes sliding down with a dozen fresh cocoanuts, full of sweet, watery fluid, in such state as we never see them in the United States. The drink is palatable, but warm, and, to our Northern tastes, seems as if it would be vastly improved by a little ice.

Returning to the city, Mr. Cazneau, who is engaged in mining, told us he imported his labourers from New York. On our expressing surprise, especially as the streets seem just now to be full of unemployed idlers, he said he found it impossible to rely upon them. They were unwilling to work for more than a few hours at a time, and not that unless for some special purpose. He said that he used to go among them offering two or three or four dollars per day. Their reply would be, "No, mas'r, don't want to work."

"But you are in rags. Don't you want to earn something to buy clothes?"

"No, mas'r, don't want much clothes. Too hot for clothes."

"But how can you live, if you are idle? You must want to earn enough to buy food for your family?"

"Oh, no, mas'r! Plenty banana—plenty banana!"

So he had to give it up in despair.

We visited other ruins and other streets, glancing at the shops, priced a few articles, including flamingos and monkeys, and then went down to the wharf. On the way we passed and visited the ruined palace, built by Columbus's son Diego, who was at one time governor. We clambered up its ruined steps and walked through the dilapidated chambers and terraces, finding the same architectural features as in the other buildings visited. The only wonder is, that a town built so long ago, and devastated by hurricanes and earthquakes, by sieges and captures, by the British, the Haytians, and the Spanish, and by the lapse of so much time, should have any walls left standing.

As we entered the boat, the ruins of the prison where Columbus was confined were shown us. They stand on the bluff on the opposite bank of the river.

The Dominican soldiers, not uniformed and not very well clad or equipped, were to be seen in considerable numbers at the barracks and on guard duty. A few at the palace were an exception to this rule, appearing neat and well armed. They are all coloured men, mostly of the darker hues.

We took a parting look at the city from the steamer, and at the adjacent forest of truly tropical luxuriance, the trees of immense size, and the underbrush, thick, wild, and varied.

So we leave this curious antiquated town and the Spanish part of the island of San Domingo. Next we visit its western portion, once French, now independent, where the African race, with less mixture, holds complete sway.

Bay of Gonaïves,
Off Port-au-Prince, Jan. 16.

Hayti. This morning, on looking out of the port-hole, we find the Southern Cross shining brilliantly on that side of the ship which we have been accustomed to consider north. The sun, too, rises today over our bow instead of over the stern. It seems we have changed our course during the night, and, instead of westward, are proceeding almost due east. This is in consequence of the peculiar configuration of the island.

To reach Port-au-Prince from San Domingo, it is necessary to make a complete circuit around the long strip of land which lies on the southern side of the Bay of Gonaïves.

The day has been spent in steaming up the bay. It is one hundred and twenty miles long and gradually narrows as we go up toward the city. High mountains are visible on either side. The picturesque island of Gonave, and the numerous islets and coral reefs, render the general appearance of the landscape not unlike that of some parts of the St. Lawrence and the Hudson. Our approach to the capital brings into view indications of its commerce. We have passed several brigs and schooners during the day, and an English steamer is just coming behind us. Numerous little coasters, deeply laden with sacks of coffee and logwood, are running into the harbour before the wind.

The harbour itself offers a fine prospect. Lofty hills around the farther extremity rise like an amphitheatre, and midway in the scene, at their foot, is the city of Port-au-Prince, rising from the water on a gentle eminence, crowned with what seems a commanding fortification. We come to anchor just after sunset, about a quarter of a mile from the shore. The wharves seem to be tolerably filled with shipping, and three ocean steamers are at anchor near us. Two are Haytian men-of-war, one of which is the *Galatea*, lately purchased from our Government, and which is manned by a crew of "contrabands" and coloured men from New York. Discipline seems to be well preserved, and naval customs all complied with on her decks, except that there is an unusual amount of noise, both in the execution of orders and in the singing with which the sailors relieve the monotony of their existence.

The United States Commercial Agent, Mr. Conard, came on board to make us a visit, and was soon followed by Mr. Peck, the Commissioner and Consul-General. As it was too late to go ashore tonight, we have sat on deck together and had a long conversation in regard to the political, commerical, and social condition of the Haytian people, and have arranged to start at an early hour tomorrow morning to see the capital of this peculiar republic.

Port-au-Prince, Jan. 17.

At sunrise, this morning, the *De Soto* saluted the Haytian flag, and a few minutes after came an answering salute from the water battery. We pulled ashore, and landed at the wharf near the American Consulate.

The first thing that strikes the eye of the visitor is, that everybody on shore is decidedly African, in complexion and feature. White men are as few and exceptional here as black men are in one of our Northern towns, and, at first glance, it looks oddly enough to find black men not only the labourers, but officers in uniform, well-dressed gentlemen, men of business, and men of authority. All are talking French; all are busily employed, with a briskness and a polite and easy air, that but for the prevailing sable hue, would lead one to imagine himself on the quays of a city in France.

Through piles of logwood and heaps of coffee sacks we find our way to the Consulate, where we breakfast, and then sally forth to take a drive about the town.

The streets are bad enough. They have once been paved, and since neglected, and are now more rough and uneven than if they had never been paved at all. The drainage is bad, and the sewerage insufficient, so that the streets rival some that are noted for such deficiences in New York and Washington; but, though dirty, they are dry at present, and hence tolerable.

The style of architecture is peculiar. The best buildings, on the principal streets, are of wooden framework filled in with brick between the timbers. The poorer class of houses are of wood throughout, and slate roofs are almost universal. Almost all buildings are of but one or two stories in height. The earthquakes have determined the character of the architecture. There are no brick or stone buildings of several stories, as with us, as the earthquakes would infallibly shake them down on the heads of the occupants. The wooden frame may not only shake, but even rock to and fro considerably, without serious damage. The safest material for all houses in such a climate is wood. Residents told me they remembered no case in which a wooden house was destroyed by earthquake, even when brick ones were tottering and tumbling into fragments. But, on the other hand, there is the danger of fire, which is not less frequent, and is even more destructive. Hence, the compromise of wooden frame with brick filling.

A large part of the city is just recovering from a calamity of this sort. An extensive fire, about ten months since, swept off a considerable portion of the business quarter of the town—a conflagration similar in extent to that which occurred about the same time in Richmond. But it is rapidly being rebuilt. Piles of lumber are strewn about; workmen are busy; and edifices in all stages of completion are rapidly progressing.

The sidewalks of Port-au-Prince are private, not public property. Each house has a paved gallery or veranda on a level with the street, recessed under its second story, and open at front and ends. The owner sits here, ties his horse here, places his merchandise here, keeps his dogs and his parrots here, and may, if he chooses, fence it in and keep it entirely for his family use; and sometimes does so. But the general custom is to leave it open for the use of the foot passengers, who thus step from one house to another on a dry, well paved walk, sheltered from both sun and rain. Politeness and custom require, however, that one shall in passing touch his hat to the ladies, if he finds them on the gallery, when thus encroaching on their rights. So it is no unusual sight to see a gentleman regularly touching his hat at every house, as he walks along.

Emerging from the burnt district, we come upon the market-place. It is a busy scene, filled with country people surrounded by the heaps of rural productions they have brought for sale, and the little donkeys that have brought them—a less vociferous scene than we have met at other similar places; the traffic appearing to go on with less flourish, but more rapidly and effectively. John, who has been sent ashore to do our marketing, comes back with astonishing tales of the magnitude of prices and of transactions. For two pairs of chickens he has paid $64—that is, $16 for each fowl! He has expended similarly for vegetables, and the whole cost of our purchases in one day's marketing is $100.   It is a mitigating circumstance, however, that this is in Haytian paper currency, which is rather depreciated.   He exchanged at the Consulate six gold dollars for $100 of the Haytian paper, and this is what he has laid out.

The principal conveyance, for business or pleasure, to be found in Port-au-Prince is the donkey.   There are wagons and carts, and some good carriages and fine horses, but these are for city use merely.   The roads up the hillsides into the country are not passable for vehicles, though we were told that two hours of pleasant riding on horseback would bring us to the heights, where we should have magnificent prospects, and a temperate instead of a tropical climate.   Up there the pine thrives, and apples, peaches, and other Northern products are easily raised.

From the market we went to the cathedral, a large substantial wooden structure, handsomely decorated and furnished within.   The pictures are numerous, and some of them very fine.   They are generally the productions of French art, some old, but the majority of them of recent date.   A mass for the dead was being celebrated when we entered.   There were not many worshippers— few besides the priests and relatives of the deceased, who was probably of some wealthy family.   When they came out, they seemed, in dress, manners, and carriage— in all respects save in complexion—just such persons as one might expect to meet coming out of a church in Fifth Avenue.

There is one noticeable peculiarity in the style of dress seen in the streets of Port-au-Prince.   The proverbial African taste for bright colours and gorgeous flowers and patterns seems here to have been entirely laid aside.   Instead of brilliant colours, modest, neutral tints and tones seem to be in vogue.   In our drive through the streets we did not see one man in any exaggerated style of costume.

though many dressed like quiet, respectable gentlemen. We
did not see even one woman with the bright Madras handkerchief around her head, elsewhere so common. Black,
white, grey, purple, and the intermediate tints in delicate
material, either plain, or in small checks and modest
patterns, were almost universal. The same thing was
noticeable in the goods displayed in the shop windows.
Altogether, the taste displayed in these points was in
strong contrast to many things to be seen on Broadway or
Pennsylvania Avenue. Whether it is due to French
example and education, or whether the African puts
aside barbaric tastes on coming from slavery into the
higher condition of civilized, free citizenship, may be a
question.

There is an exception, however. The military and
official uniforms are brilliant in contrasts of colour, and
replete with gold lace and ornaments. Yet, perhaps, even
these are only imitations of the style that prevailed in
Europe and in our own country fifty years ago, now
moderated and toned down.

Around the environs of the city, the hills seemed covered with rich vegetation to the very summit. My companion deprecatingly remarked that, at this season, the
leaves were much more off the trees than at any other;
and consequently the landscape was less attractive than
usual. I told him there was even now, in midwinter,
foliage more luxuriant than we have in summer. The
hillsides are in forest—on the lower portion the mahogany,
the satinwood, lignum-vitæ, and other less valuable tropical trees are found; above are oaks and Northern pines.

While we were at breakfast, two aides-de-camp of
President Geffrard were announced. They were handsome young men of light complexion, and attired in a
brilliant uniform of sky-blue coat and crimson pantaloons,
with an abundance of gold lace. They were evidently

well-bred gentlemen, of French education, though speaking English fluently. They came to invite us to the President's palace, and to tender his carriage to convey us there. The carriage was a barouche, attended by servants in green and gold livery, and followed by a guard of dragoons.

Arriving at the gate of the President's palace, we found the troops drawn up in line to give the military salute. There were several regiments, all in gay and brilliant uniforms, all neat and soldier-like. Some of their costumes were like those of the French chasseurs and tirailleurs; others resembled those of our regular troops, though more elaborate and costly. The military bands struck up airs of welcome, among them the *Star Spangled Banner*, and we were ushered through a veranda to the drawing-room.

Here was President Geffrard, a fine-looking, erect, very dark complexioned man, with grey hair, courteous address, and pleasing expression. He was dressed in a uniform somewhat resembling that of our Generals, though more richly ornamented. He received the Secretary of State with warm and gracefully expressed compliments, and conversed in French very fully and fluently upon the condition of affairs in Hayti and in the United States.

The President was attended by several of his Ministers and Secretaries. Mr. Elie, the Minister of Foreign Affairs, a very intelligent, well-informed gentleman, and apparently a statesman of enlarged views, had come to call at the Consulate with General Roumain, whom we had known as Chargé d' Affaires at Washington, and they accompanied us to the President's. Both were in civilian's dress, and both were of such light complexion that they might pass easily for white men. The Ministers of War and the Navy, on the other hand, were entirely African in hue, and were both in uniform. In manner and conversation they were just such polished, educated, and experienced public men as one would expect to find in like positions in any European Court.

Madame Geffrard and her two daughters now entered the room, and received and entertained their guests. They are ladies of refinement and education,—the mother is very nearly white, the daughters a shade or two darker. All were dressed in accordance with the Parisian taste and fashion, and all spoke French only.

The drawing-room was quite as richly and tastefully furnished as the Blue Room at Washington, though of less architectural pretensions. All the decorations of the house were rich and costly, but in good taste. Among the pictures was one of Mr. Lincoln; among the busts one of Washington and another of John Brown.

After a kind and hospitable reception we took our departure, receiving the same military honours as on entering.

On our return, we stopped to look at the two Houses— that of the Senate and that of the Representatives. Neither House is at present in session. The rooms are not large, as the two bodies themselves are not, but resemble the legislative chambers of one of our States. Here were portraits of several of the Presidents of Hayti, one or two historical and allegorical paintings by French artists, and another likeness of John Brown, and one of Wilberforce.

They pointed out to us the portraits of Presidents Boyer, Petion, Rivière, and others.

"But there is one portrait that I do not see which I should have expected to find most prominent of all!"

"Whose is that?" said our companion.

"Toussaint L'Ouverture."

"Toussaint L'Ouverture! There is no portrait of him, here. He was a brave man, but we do not consider him a Republican."

A fresh illustration that "A prophet is not without honour, save in his own country"!

When we arrived at the Consulate we found there the foreign diplomatic and consular representatives at the Haytian capital, among them the British, French, and Spanish. Several American merchants and their families also called.

Our friends accompanied us to the wharf, taking leave of us with many expressions of kindness, and sending on board for us various choice specimens of Haytian productions. Arrived on board, we found the *Galatea* just preparing to fire a salute of fifteen guns, in honour of the American Secretary.

Hayti, so far as we have seen it, is neither the great success in solving the African problem which philanthropists would willingly believe it, nor on the other hand is it the failure in that respect which it is so often represented.

Its people do not achieve those agricultural results which might be expected on a soil of such unsurpassed fertility; and in manufactures they achieve almost nothing. The sugar mills erected by the French are fast going to ruin, and the inhabitants do not seem inclined to erect new ones, nor to use them. So in many other branches of industry for which the island seems peculiarly adapted.

On the other hand, it cannot be said that emancipation and self-government have rendered them idle or degraded. Everything about Port-au-Prince wears an air of activity. The people are busy, steady, enterprising. Everybody appears to have his work, and to be at it. Nobody appears to be lounging or lazy. There is nothing of that noisy talking, laughing, and shouting which characterize the unemployed negro in so many other places; but the sound of the hammer and the saw, the noise of busy workmen and businesslike men.

It is true, that the general impression made upon a

stranger is that of poverty. It is partly so, because the buildings are low and cheap and the streets neglected. It is partly so, because the idea of black people anywhere is habitually associated in our minds with the idea of poverty. It is partly so—principally so—because these people, though free and industrious, lack capital, lack organized labor or enterprise, lack education and experience, and lack that confidence in the stability, peace, and permanence of their own government which is essential to the prosperity of any country.

But the true test by which to measure the Haytians is not to compare their present condition with that of their former white masters, or with that of white nations older and more advantageously situated—but to compare their own condition now, with what it was when they were slaves. There can be no doubt that a vast stride in advance has been made by them, when viewed in that light. It is reasonable to suppose that this progress will continue, especially when aided by the free schools they are now establishing, and when strengthened by permanent and tranquil government, instead of revolutionary plots and outbreaks—if that time shall ever arrive.

There is a natural, perhaps a necessary, dread of a recurrence of the white domination, which has inflicted such calamities on their country and their race. But among its effects are the exclusion of capital, invention, and skill, which might develop resources now neglected. Captain Cutts, an American merchant, who has lived fourteen years in the island, is now endeavouring to make an experiment in sugar manufacture, which hitherto has always resulted in failure. White men are not permitted to own land; and when, heretofore, they have occupied it by lease or mortgage, and engaged in sugar making, the neighbours have, by violence, compelled them to desist, and sometimes destroyed their property.

There is a similar, though less bitter, prejudice against mulattoes, and against the neighbouring Republic of Dominica, which is supposed to be altogether too near white not to share in white avarice, cupidity, or ambition.

As our vessel was just getting under way, a coloured man, in a small boat, rowed by a boy, approached the stern; and the man climbed up a rope ladder suspended there. He had a pitiful story to tell. He was formerly from Auburn, and was induced to emigrate to Hayti, as the land of promise for his race; found himself unsuccessful in his farming enterprise, and unable to employ his abilities with profit in anything else, the inhabitants treating him as a foreigner, who could not speak their language, and looking suspiciously upon him as an American. Now, his family was sick, and his funds exhausted, and he wanted to go home. Meanwhile the boy who had brought him, becoming alarmed lest his boat should be drawn under the paddle-wheels, was lustily pulling away for the shore, and deaf to all calls to come back. The American emigrant took this very philosophically, however, perhaps with a lurking hope of a free passage to the United States, in consequence of his inability to go ashore. Fortunately, however, another boat from the town was not far distant, and on being hailed, came alongside to take him off to the land of his adoption, though no longer the land of his choice.

Bay of Gonaïves, Jan. 18.

We have been steaming, with a clear sky and tranquil sea, down the Bay of Gonaïves, again admiring its picturesque mountain scenery, and now we have entered the Windward Passage, and descry in the distance the dim outline of the shores of Cuba. We passed Cape Maysi at four o'clock, and are heading for the channel between Cuba and the Bahamas.

We are leaving behind us an island whose magnificent natural advantages are not surpassed in the world, yet left to imperfect and neglected cultivation, its fields not half improved, its cities belonging to the past rather than the present.

President Geffrard is wisely seeking to encourage immigration. It has been imagined that Hayti, with its fertile soil, healthful climate, and cheap lands, so easily accessible, inhabited and controlled by the African race, would be the chosen spot for the regeneration of that race, and the development of its capacity for high civilization and self-government—that it would be sought by Africans, coming from all lands where they have been oppressed and degraded, to the one country where they are entitled to all rights and privileges, where all the avenues to wealth and public employment are open to them, and closed against everyone else.

Yet the fact undeniably is, that the "coming African" does not come, but prefers to remain with the whites, in the land of his birth.

The two republics, on the same island, with the same soil, and similar productions, with similar advantages for agriculture, mining, manufactures, and trade, are, nevertheless, in strong contrast with each other. The one speaks French; the other Spanish. The one derives its fashions and ideas from Paris; the other from Madrid. The one copies the codes of French republics and empires; the other models its laws and constitution after those of the United States. The one will have none but a black executive; the other prefers a white. The one jealously excludes white men from office, voting, or ownership of real estate; the other encourages their immigration and citizenship. The one adopts our rule that whoever has any African blood is a black man; the other takes the converse rule that whoever has any European blood is a "blanco." In one, you see hundreds who appear of unmixed African parentage; in the other, you find every shade except pure black. One has the ambition to maintain the right and demonstrate the capability of the African race to govern themselves, without interference. The other aims to be a white republic, and is becoming one. It is not strange, perhaps, that the two should be almost continually in hostilities, especially as they have an unsettled boundary line between them, and each has a sort of traditional claim to ownership of the island.

In this island of San Domingo, with two of the finest harbours in the world, they use instead two of the inferior ones. At the Dominican end the principal port is the mouth of the Ozama, whose bar keeps out all but small vessels. At the Haytian end, Port-au-Prince is at the bottom of a long cul-de-sac, safe enough, but difficult to fortify; easy to blockade and impossible to escape from.

On the other hand, the Dominicans have, and do not use, at Samana, a safe and commodious harbour for whole navies, easy of defence, advantageously situated in the line of mercantile traffic, commanding the Mona Passage— a harbour so well situated that the French used it as their base when they came to reconquer the island in 1802, and the United States themselves long ago saw in it a valuable point for naval operations. General McClellan and Admiral Porter have both been sent out to examine it with a view to its purchase, and at one time treaty negotiations for it through Mr. Cazneau were nearly accomplished. Our supposed desire for it was one of the reasons, or pretexts, for the recent Spanish seizure and occupation of San Domingo.

The Haytians, again, have at St. Nicholas Mole a port hardly inferior, which could be made impregnable, and which, with Cape Maysi, overlooks another important line of mercantile transit.

What is there that this island will not produce? Its dense forests furnish mahogany, logwood, fustic, satinwood, lignum-vitæ, pine, oak, and various other woods used in the arts. Its fields yield, with easy cultivation, corn, millet, and every kind of grain, besides the tropical staples of sugar, cotton, indigo, coffee, cacao, rice, and tobacco. On its hills you can raise the plums, peaches, pears, melons, and grapes of the north, while on the lower levels, fruits and vegetables, enough to feed its entire population, seem to grow almost spontaneously—oranges, lemons, limes, pineapples, aguacates, sapodillas, cherimoyas, guavas, bananas, plantains, yams, batatas, and a host of others.

Animal life is abundant. Not only wild game, but the cattle, hogs, and waterfowl, which we raise with such cost and care, here increase and multiply and roam wild, without any care at all. Fish, turtles, lobsters, crabs, caymans, and alligators abound in its waters. Insects swarm in myriads.

Equally rich in minerals, it has gold, silver, platinum, quicksilver, copper, iron, tin, manganese, sulphur, antimony, marble, jasper and various precious stones, rock salt, and mineral springs.

Its wealth has been its curse, for it has attracted adventurers to devastate and impoverish it; and yet they have but half succeeded, though it has suffered nearly four hundred years of war, and hardly had a dozen of peace.

Havana, Jan. 20, 1866.

At Havana. The coast of Cuba this morning is clear and well defined. As we go on towards Havana, we gradually draw nearer to the shore, so that we see the palm trees, the cane fields, the fishing hamlets and boats, and occasionally, here and there, an inhabitant standing on the beach and gazing towards our steamer.

At noon we are in sight of the harbour of Havana, a beautiful picture, as it gradually opens before us around the projecting bluff on which stands the Morro Castle. Grey, rough, and picturesque, its stone walls frown down upon the channel, which runs just below them. Along the crest of the hill, additional fortifications bristle, giving the town the look of impregnability, on that side, at least.

We stop a few minutes off the Morro Castle to take a pilot; and then steam slowly up the harbour to our place of anchorage.

The harbour is a busy scene—ships at the wharves, ships at anchor under flags of all nations, among them several fine Spanish men-of-war, with the red and yellow ensign flying, steamers passing in and out, and ferryboats crossing to and fro among them—the whole much resembling Philadelphia, as the entrance to the harbour is hardly wider than the Delaware. The town itself has a thoroughly Spanish air, and few of the edifices are new, yet its general aspect, by contrast with our recent view of the antique Spanish town of San Domingo, seems fresh, new, and cheerful. The large open windows and doors, the verandas and balconies, the light tints of buff, green, blue, and white, which everywhere prevail, give Havana a far more attractive look from the sea than any of our northern cities have. Near the wharf we see an American flag welcoming us from the American Consulate.

We come to anchor near the Spanish men-of-war, and exchange the customary salute with the fort. Presently the American Consul-General, Mr. Minor, pulls alongside and comes aboard, bringing with him the acceptable gift of letters from home, and New York papers of the 13th, a fortnight later than any we had before.

All well at home. So, much relieved in heart, we take a hasty dinner; and, with the aid of the Consul-General, plan our disembarkation and sojourn in Havana.

Under his advice we are soon ashore, and comfortably installed in the Hotel de Almy, which is much frequented by loyal Americans. It is a large, quaint, old-fashioned building, which was, in its early days, a Spanish government palace. It is of heavy masonry, with antique ornamentation. Stone balconies project from its windows and a courtyard occupies the centre, into which the hall and dining-room open, by arcades, without the intervention of either door or window.

Mrs. Almy, the proprietress, assigns us our rooms; and we sally out to improve what is left of daylight by a drive through the town.

Near the tavern is the old church of San Domingo, blackened and dilapidated by time and war, and now used as the Custom House. Proceeding up the streets, the first impression they make upon our unaccustomed eyes is that they are extremely narrow. The side walks are only wide enough to accommodate a single foot passenger. The carriageway is just wide enough for two vehicles to pass, and nothing more. In consequence, carriages are allowed to proceed only in one direction. Each alternate street is set apart, either for going up, or for going down; and a vehicle desiring to go to a spot only a few paces distant through the street is frequently obliged to go around the entire block in order to reach it. To warn drivers, there is painted on nearly every corner a black hand pointing in the allowable direction, with the word *subida* (up), or *bajada* (down). Consequently there is no confusion. The streets are well paved with smooth, square stones, and are kept tolerably clean. They are dry, and, from their narrowness, are almost always shady; so that one can comfortably walk anywhere, without being restricted to the sidewalk.

Spanish architecture is massive and imposing. The walls are thick, the ceilings high. The windows of an ordinary dwelling are as large as those of one of our churches; and the doorway is like the massive portal of one of our public edifices. A single story, or at most two, is the prevailing custom.

As we go up the town, we pass the Custom House, the Palace, the Cathedral, and other fine edifices, with two or three small but neatly kept open plazas, ornamented with plants and fountains, and sometimes with statuary. A broad archway like a tunnel leads through the wall which encircles what was once the city of Havana, but is now a small portion of it.

Emerging from this, we find ourselves in broader streets and more open places, among them the Plaza de Armas, near the Tacon Theatre; and farther on we come to the "Paseo," which is the fashionable drive. It is a long, straight avenue, admirably paved and lighted, broad and attractive. We drive as far up as the gateway of the Captain-General's country house.

They are lighting the lamps as we return; and now Havana is in its glory. Everybody seems to have no other object than amusement, out doors and in, on this charming tropical evening. The houses are all lighted; the parlour windows, wide open, extend down to the ground, with which the floor is on a level; and the groups of ladies and gentlemen, children, and servants within, are fully exposed to view, as if out in the street. Some are chatting and laughing, rocking to and fro in the comfortable American chairs, of which every room has several; some are fanning, some smoking, some are playing musical instruments, some dancing; nearly all are dressed for receiving or making visits. An iron grating is interposed to keep off intruders, giving somewhat the aspect of cages of pretty birds.

Any such one group in New York would attract a crowd of curious gazers. Here, one sees such groups in every house; and no one seems to care to look. Crowds of well-dressed people saunter up and down the streets, the ladies fanning and the gentlemen smoking, and the carriageway is full of showy equipages, well-mounted caballeros, and the funny-looking Spanish volantes, in which the horse and driver seem to be an affair entirely independent of the ladies, who are sitting at ease in the distant two-wheeled open vehicle. One can readily understand, when witnessing this scene, how it is that Cubans who visit New York find even Fifth Avenue gloomy and sombre.

The shops, though not large, show to the best advantage and make more display than is practicable in establishments ten times larger. Ours are deep and narrow, while these are broad and open, brilliantly illuminated; everything in them is exposed to full view. Over the doorway is a sign containing the name which is the peculiar designation of the shop—for each shop here has a name, sometimes appropriate, sometimes fanciful. Thus we find "La Flora," "La Perla," "La Diana," "La Honrodez," "El Telescopio," etc., which, for the customers, is sometimes more convenient of remembrance than our system of numbers and names of firms. Numbers are difficult to recollect, and firms are perpetually changing, but the names here may endure for a century.

Returning home, we find various visitors. Our house is an especial American resort. We meet several who are engaged in business in Havana, and some travellers who have come by the last steamer.

Havana, Jan. 21st.

This morning, after breakfast, the Captain-General, with his secretary and aides-de-camp, came to call upon the Secretary of State, to offer him many kind hospitalities and to proffer a country-seat for his use during his stay. General Dulce is a small, spare man, with pleasing face and features expressive of energetic character. He speaks only Spanish, but Havana is polyglot, and there is no lack of interpreters.

Shopping was the next enterprise, and various curiosities of tropical production, use or wear, were the purchases.

Our next visit was to the Cathedral, a majestic edifice, singularly free from the tawdry ornamentation, architectural or ceremonial, which so often disfigures buildings of this character. Its vaulted ceilings are adorned with frescoes, and its several chapels with fine paintings. The remains of Columbus are buried here under the sacristy, and are surmounted by a marble bust and tablet. The Cathedral will hold several thousand worshippers.

In the afternoon we took a drive through the suburbs. The country residences are numerous, and are of the same general style of architecture as the city houses, except for the addition of broad paved verandas. Well-kept gardens, luxuriant in tropical plants and flowers, and ornamented with vases and statuary, are attached to many of them.

Past the suburbs, we find cultivated fields, in various stages, for in this favouring climate one sees fields just planted side by side with others ready for the harvest. Vegetables and fruits for the city markets occupy many of them. Farther on we come upon cane and tobacco fields, with a plentiful sprinkling of palms and cocoanut trees, giving the landscape much the same general air as that we had seen at Santa Cruz.

Everybody, at this season, is eating sugar. The children are sucking bits of the cane. The grown people are feasting on its various forms at table. The soldiers are served with rations of sugar-cane, chopped off into suitable length and served out by the commissary. The donkey rider carries a long cane in his hand and sucks one end while he whips the donkey with the other. The cattle and horses fatten on the refuse of the sugar house, and the dogs lick up the syrup that is trickling plentifully on the ground. There is one exception to the general rule, however. The planter's family, who have become too familiar with the processes of sugar-making, do not care to eat it until it comes back, next year, white and refined, from New York.

Here and there, among the labourers in the cane-fields, we notice the unmistakable faces of Chinese coolies. Their short, spare, lithe, active figures are usually in motion; and they seem not to have the fondness for lounging in the sun which the African has. Some of the landowners whom we have met say that they prefer them, as being more industrious and requiring less watching. They are brought here across the Pacific and the Isthmus. How far their emigration is voluntary is, in most cases, a matter of doubt. The landed proprietor here makes his bargain with the agent of a company which undertakes to deliver so many Chinamen to him as apprentices for a certain number of years (usually eight). They are to be fed, clothed, and to receive so many dollars per month; and then to be discharged at the close of their term of apprenticeship. Usually, they are willing and docile, though comprehending but little of the language of their employers.

Some certainly are voluntary emigrants from Canton who know the nature of the apprenticeship before them. But it often happens that others, when they have picked up some knowledge of the language, tell of the knavish pretences or threats by which they were induced to leave their homes and go on board a vessel bound they knew not whither. Sometimes one of the poor creatures, in utter despair, commits suicide. We were told of one planter who, one morning, found seven of his newly indentured apprentices hanging on the trees of his orchard. There are provisions of law to prevent and remedy these wrongs, but it is difficult to enforce them; especially when the injured party cannot explain his grievance, or when the employer is a man who, so long as he gets labourers, does not trouble himself to inquire how fairly or unfairly they may have been dealt with.

It is said, and there seems no good reason to doubt the statement, that such cases of cruelty and injustice are rare in the islands where labour is free; and that they are most frequent in the slaveholding islands, where popular sensibilities on the subject of justice to Asiatics are naturally somewhat blunted by what they see meted out to Africans.

Here, as elsewhere, the Chinese immigrant comes to make money, in the hope of some day returning to his own country to spend it. But there are some who, at the end of their apprenticeship, seem to prefer to remain. Such a one, who has deliberately taken up his residence for life, is a changed being. He is Europeanized. He has dropped his Chinese tunic, wears the dress of Europeans, and has lost his pigtail. He talks Spanish or English. He has been baptized, and is no longer a "heathen Chinee." His walk, manners, and gestures all seem to have been "translated."

An expression of keen astuteness has crept into his face, instead of the vacuous, childish smile that once reigned there. His very eyes seem to have lost their almond shape; and he smokes, chews, drinks, and swears "like a Christian." But though he may sometimes acquire Christian vices, he fortunately does not lose his heathen virtues. It is said there is no case where he becomes idle, improvident, or a pauper. He is frugal, industrious, thrifty, and if he keeps his health, and lives long enough, is sure to end by being rich. Some highly respectable and well-to-do merchants of this class have been pointed out to us.

Even so near as this to Havana there is some unculti-vated land. Cuba, though of unsurpassed fertility, has never yet fully developed her agricultural resources.

Our ride took us as far as Marinao, a fishing hamlet on the seashore, about ten miles from the city; and we returned in time to witness again the gay scene presented in the Havana streets by gaslight.

After dinner, the American residents at Havana, and with them many of their Cuban acquaintances, called to pay their respects to the Secretary of State, with many gratifying expressions of cordiality and friendship. Each was introduced and shook hands, leaving his card in remembrance of his visit.

Havana, Jan. 22d.

Another walk before breakfast this morning, in which we neither lost our way nor failed to expend our money, quite encouraged us in the belief that we were becoming familiar with the localities, the language, and the coins of Havana.

We are told there is a "norther" blowing outside. It must be a very mild one; for it seems to us that there is no more air than is at least desirable on a warm day. Yet our friends here, as in other West Indian Islands, speak of the night as chilly, the thermometer having gone down to seventy-two degrees; and refer to overcoats, blankets, etc., as if such things were positive discomforts.

On our walk we were twice stopped by men with their hands full of printed and numbered sheets of paper, which they proposed to sell to us, as *muy bonitos* and *muy buenos*. These were lottery tickets. Everybody prob-ably does not buy lottery tickets in Havana, but from the talk one hears of them, it seems as if everybody did.

The lotteries are under the authority of the government, to which they yield a handsome revenue. The numbers of the tickets that draw prizes are conspicuously chalked up on a blackboard at the "Intendencia," and the papers which contain them are always sought for by an eager crowd. For five dollars you get a very slim chance of drawing two hundred thousand dollars, and the hope that this very slim chance or some smaller one may be realized induces many to invest in it every five dollars they can get.

After breakfast we went to see a manufactory of cigarettes—a marvel of ingenuity and enterprise which would do credit to Yankee invention. Everything that science or art has devised applicable to such a purpose seemed to be found in Susini's establishment. He had a machine to make the paper, a machine to cut it, machines to grind the tobacco, and to press it, others to make the boxes, to make the barrels, to print the labels, to engrave the pictures, and to number the packages; besides many various modern inventions that incidentally help the work —fire annihilators, electric lights, electrotypes, copying apparatus, steam elevators, printing-presses, etc. Only the work of rolling up the cigarettes is done by hand, and this is done by Chinese coolies, who do it with great dexterity and rapidity. We were told that they work so industriously that many of them, after doing their daily tasks, work in the evening on their own account, and make twenty, thirty, or even forty dollars a month. The coolies are fed and lodged by the establishment, and they fare in both respects better than either our soldiers or our sailors.

The superintendent called up a short, swarthy, intelligent-looking Chinaman, to show us an illustration of the thrifty economy of his race. He has been eight years in Cuba, on the meagre pittance of eight dollars a month for working ten hours a day. Yet, by working extra

22

hours, and saving up and judiciously investing his wages, he has become worth five thousand dollars and is going back to China next month with that fortune—in that country an ample one. He appreciated the wealth he had gained, and shook his head, smiling, when asked if he would not consent to stay eight years more to get another five thousand dollars.

Then another Chinaman was called up, equally remarkable, though in a different way. He had so carefully combed and nurtured his pigtail that, when uncoiled, it reached to his feet, and touched the floor as he walked. He grinned with becoming pride at the compliments lavished on this personal ornament.

"What will you sell it for, John?" inquired one of the bystanders. "I will give you five dollars."

John grinned, and shook his head.

"Twenty dollars? A hundred dollars?"

John still returned a scornful negative.

"See here, John, you don't think your tail is worth as much as the fortune this other man has saved up, do you? Will you take five thousand dollars for it?"

John, gathering up his highly prized ornament into a knot and carefully readjusting it at the back of his head, laconically replied, "Me no takee," and walked off with it out of the tempter's reach.

Many ingenious devices in the advertising way are resorted to to give the cigarettes a reputation. Some are put up in packages which give the purchaser a handsome coloured lithographic picture; others in packages of which one in twenty will have a lottery ticket enclosed; others are made in imitation of cigars; others put up in mimic champagne bottles, wheels of fortune, etc. A newspaper devoted to their description is published monthly.

Next we went to the palace of the Captain-General to return his visit. The Spanish soldiers on guard at the

entrance were neatly dressed in white, appropriately to
the climate. The Captain-General received us hospitably,
proffered us the invariable Havana welcome of a cigar, and
arranged for a dinner and a visit to the theatre with him
in the evening.

Thence to the Hotel de Angleterra, facing on the Plaza.
Here were cigars, a lunch, wines, and "dulces." Here
we found General Andrew Porter, formerly Provost
Marshal-General at Washington, who is spending the
winter with his family in Havana.

Then we went to an extensive cigar manufactory, that
of Partagas & Son, and saw the process of preparing the
tobacco, cutting and rolling it up into cigars. Three
hundred workmen were busily engaged here, turning
out cigars with marvellous rapidity. They sit in long rows
at each end of a long table, each with two piles of tobacco
leaves before him, one for the filling, the other for the
wrappers. One noticeable feature was a man sitting
in an elevated seat at one side, and reading in a loud
voice from a Spanish novel. This is to amuse the workmen, or, rather, to keep them from talking with each
other and so losing time at their work. Conversation
would distract their attention, but reading, while it di-
verts them, does not interfere with the mechanical labour.
We were taken through vast storerooms, in which bales
of tobacco and boxes of cigars were piled, and cigars in
various packages were very lavishly and hospitably presented to us on leaving.

In the evening we went to dinner at the Captain-General's Palace. It was a brilliant assemblage of about
fifty guests, many of them officers of the government, the
army, or the navy. The dinner was like other state
dinners, with profuse and elaborate dishes and decorations; and all its details went off like clockwork and
with more rapidity than is common in Washington.

A band discoursed music in the anteroom during the dinner. The Captain-General had the Secretary of State on his right hand and Mr. Kennedy on his left. Most of the company were either officers of the Cuban government, representatives of foreign governments, or prominent Cubans.

Toward the close of the dinner, the Captain-General rose to propose the health of the President of the United States, and that of the Secretary of State and his family, with appropriate complimentary remarks, which were responded to by Mr. Seward. The Vice-Admiral then rose to propose the health of the other American guests, and of the American navy, which was responded to by Mr. Kennedy (ex-Secretary of the Navy) and Captain Walker.

After dinner, coffee and cigars; and then the Captain-General took us in his carriage to the Tacon Theatre. Military guards surrounded the carriage, but were hardly able to keep back the crowd collected both at the door of the Palace and that of the theatre, eager to see. In the theatre, we found the ladies in the Captain-General's box. The building is a very fine one, of magnificent proportions, yet very simple in design and in quiet good taste, without the gaudy decoration that is so common in theatrical edifices.

The parterre was occupied solely by gentlemen and fitted up with armchairs; the boxes, of which there were three tiers, were filled with elegantly dressed people, occasionally visiting and receiving each other in their respective *palcos*. Above, there was the gallery, devoted to the general public; and above that another for coloured people. The whole edifice was brilliantly lighted. The Ravels were performing a pantomime.

We returned to the hotel at about eleven, accompanied by the Captain-General and his staff, who took leave of us, but not before saying that his Artillery Band would give us a serenade before retiring.

Meanwhile the halls and passages began to fill up with well-dressed young men. They proved to be the students of the University, who had come to pay their respects in a body to the Secretary of State. They were introduced one by one, each leaving his card. Many of them expressed some sentiment of warm admiration, either for him personally or for the principles and policy of the United States Government—expressions marked with deep feeling and earnestness. Those who could not speak English would often write them on their cards.

With the students came also some of the professors and other residents of the city, American or Spanish.

The Artillery Band, consisting of some sixty performers, was meanwhile drawn up in a hollow square in front of the hotel, with their lights and music stands; and we proceeded to the balconies to hear the serenade. It lasted for an hour or more, and we then retired for our last night in Cuba.

Now that the serenade is over, one of our Havana friends tells us an amusing bit of gossip about its history—which *si non e vero e ben trovato*.

The story goes that the students, being nearly all native Cubans, are most of them ardent republicans, if not revolutionists. They thought they saw in Mr. Seward's visit a long-coveted opportunity for a republican demonstration and speeches such as the Spanish government rigorously and vigilantly represses. They said to one another: "The government cannot refuse us permission to show hospitable courtesy toward Mr. Seward, the Secretary of State of the United States; and having once the right to open our mouths we can talk of liberty and republicanism, naturally suggested, as such topics are, by his whole history." So they sent a committee to the

Captain-General, to ask the needed permission to give a serenade to Mr. Seward. General Dulce received and heard them very courteously, and replied:

"Certainly, gentleman, by all means. You have my permission, of course. Mr. Seward is worthy of all the attention we can show him; and I am glad you are disposed to unite in doing honour to the great statesman."

The committee, delighted with the unexpected success of their mission, were bowing their thanks and taking their leave when the Captain-General called them back.

"You should have a good band, gentlemen, for such an occasion. And now I think of it, there is no band in Havana that is equal to my Brigade Band. I approve your project so highly that I will join in it myself. I will send my band to play for you."

The discomfited committeemen looked at each other, but of course could not object to this generous offer. The result was that the Brigade Band, a magnificent one of sixty or seventy musicians, came, spread itself in a hollow square all over the street in front of the hotel, and played away, air after air, without intermission until one o'clock.

The students, who had gathered on the hotel steps in hope of an opportunity for their demonstration, found no place nor time for speaking. They lingered till towards midnight, and then, dropping off one by one, gave it up in despair, and left the scene deserted. Mr. Seward, taking mercy on the tired musicians, sent to the leader, with his thanks and compliments, a request that they would not fatigue themselves longer. So ended the meeting and the serenade.

On the morning of the 23d, the head of the *De Soto* was again turned towards the sea, and she was steaming slowly out past Morro Castle, homeward bound. Flags were waving from the Consulate and ships, and a crowd

FREDERICK W. SEWARD

As he looked in 1866, while Assistant Secretary of State

of friends, Spanish and American, were gathered on the wharf, to wave hats and handkerchiefs and shout their last adieus.

A steamboat chartered by the students pushed off and accompanied the *De Soto* down the harbour, with farewell salutations. At the Castle they gave three parting cheers. The crew of the *De Soto* responded, as she passed out of the harbour and was again on the ocean.

The homeward voyage was in pleasant contrast with our outward one. Sunny weather and quiet seas attended us all along the Florida coast, and even Hatteras offered no objection to our passing it. Wind, steam, and current all helped the *De Soto* as she made her sixteen knots to the hour, on even keel.

But after the second day, the air around was no longer tropical. Overcoats and wraps were in demand on deck, and fires were started in the cabin stove. The mercury dropped to forty degrees, and in the distance the coast looked white. The midsummer poetry of the trip was gone, and now came stern winter reality. But the *De Soto* successfully avoided all gales on the Chesapeake, and the floating ice in the Potomac.

At noon on the 28th the dome of the Capitol at Washington was in sight, and before nightfall we were on land again, and driving back through Pennsylvania Avenue to our home.

A Year's Interval. A year has passed since the foregoing journal of our West Indian cruise was written. The country has entered upon a new phase of its history. We are now at peace with all other nations, but at the beginning of high political strife among ourselves, over the problem of "reconstruction."

In that strife, my father takes no part. He is assiduously endeavouring to build up the country's safety, commerce, and prosperity, by the establishment of naval outposts in the Caribbean Sea and elsewhere.

The naval officers who have had experience give him hearty co-operation. But Congress is absorbed in its debates and the public is inattentive. Hence, it happens that I have now to write another chronicle of another West Indian voyage. This is devoted to official work. So it is entitled "A Diplomatic Visit to San Domingo."

A Diplomatic Visit to San Domingo. The flags that were floating over the north and south wings of the Capitol at Washington in the winter of 1866–'67 might have been called storm signals, for they indicated a tempest going on below. Hot debates were raging in the Senate and the House. There was a Republican majority in Congress. Its members and President Andrew Johnson had both been chosen at the same election as representatives of the same party; but they had drifted widely apart upon the "reconstruction policy" to be applied to the Southern States. Encouraged by indications of popular approval at the polls and in the press, that majority now found itself strong enough to defy his power, and pass measures over his veto. A resolution for his impeachment was passed, and a committee appointed to take the preparatory steps; but upon their report of "no sufficient grounds," the project remained in abeyance. Various measures were introduced and passed for the avowed purpose of limiting his powers. The President, not at all intimidated by this formidable opposition, was as tenacious of his opinions as they were of theirs. He refused to sign bill after bill, returning it with his objections. His veto, for the most part, was temperately expressed, but doomed to certain defeat. The Congress usually disposed of it summarily by a two thirds vote, without caring to listen to his reasons.

The Secretary of State had been censured by many former friends for remaining in "Andy Johnson's Cabinet." But he deemed it wise to stay at his post, and do what he could toward quelling the storm, and managing the foreign relations of the country to its best advantage. As the questions with which he had to deal were diplomatic ones, in the interest of the whole country and not of any section or party, he was measurably out of the angry debate. His personal friendships, in both the Administration and the Opposition, remained unchanged.

One morning there was a buzz of excitement in the reporters' gallery and on the floor of the House of Representatives, occasioned by the sudden appearance of Secretary Seward, who calmly walked down the main aisle to the seat of Thaddeus Stevens, greeted him, and sat down for a chat. As Stevens was the especial leader of the opponents of the President, the evident cordiality between him and Seward was an enigma to both sides of the House. It grew more puzzling when Stevens went to dine and spend the evening with Seward. A day or two afterward he rose to propose an extra appropriation "for special service," to be expended under the direction of the Secretary of State. So strong and so implicitly trusted by his followers was Stevens that he had little difficulty in inducing them to vote for it, "though much they wondered why." The only information he vouchsafed to them was that it was for a secret diplomatic mission, of which they would be informed as soon as compatible with the public interests.

Many years before Seward and Stevens had sat together as delegates in a National Convention. Though they had rarely met since that time, the whirl of politics had not estranged them. When Seward over his dinner table now unfolded his project, Stevens, putting aside all

346 . A Diplomatic Visit to San Domingo

partisan feeling, heartily agreed to co-operate in a measure "with no politics in it," and manifestly for the public
good. The project was to acquire a harbour somewhere
in the West Indies, where we had none. The need of one,
for a naval and coaling station, had been sharply demonstrated by the events of the Civil War.

Seward had already opened negotiations for the harbour and island of St. Thomas. But it was yet uncertain
whether Denmark would be willing to part with that
possession, and whether the Senate would sanction a
treaty for it. Meanwhile intimations had been received
from San Domingo that an equally desirable harbour
might be obtained by leasing or purchasing the bay of
Samana. Cash payment would be welcome to the island
republic, but if that was inconvenient, part payment
might be made in arms, ships, and munitions of war,
of which we then had a great surplus, after the close of
our Civil War, that would otherwise be sold at auction.

The next question was, who to send to make the treaty?
The Dominican Republic had no minister at Washington,
and we had none at San Domingo. Two officials already
in the public service might be sent off in a naval vessel
for a winter cruise without exciting as much attention
and curiosity as would inevitably attend the creation of
a new diplomatic post and the appointment of a minister.
Accordingly I, being then Assistant Secretary of State,
was duly commissioned as a plenipotentiary, to make
a treaty, if one should be found desirable. My colleague
was the very man for such a mission, David D. Porter, who
was experienced in all naval matters, having served in all
kinds of vessels, sailed in all seas, won fame and promotion
in all wars, and was now Vice-Admiral of the navy. His
keen observation and sound judgment would be invaluable
in deciding upon all points of site, depth of water, facility
of access, and capabilities for defence. The Navy Depart-

ment had small vessels in plenty.   Admiral Porter selected
the *Gettysburg*, a converted blockade runner, low, sharp,
and swift, and she was duly equipped, manned, and
provisioned for the voyage.   Accompanied by Mrs.
Seward and my secretary, I went over to the Annapolis
Naval Academy, where the Admiral had his quarters.
We sent our luggage on board, and on a bright moonlight
evening started on our voyage.

At the very outset ill luck befell us.   Through some
variation of the tide, or some carelessness of the pilot,
the *Gettysburg* ran aground before she was fairly out into
Chesapeake Bay.   Worst of all, she was so firmly stuck on
an oyster bed that she could not be gotten off.   "She will
float at high tide," we said.   But she did not, and when
we returned to Annapolis, three or four tugs were vainly
puffing around her and trying to move her.

The Admiral telegraphed for another ship.   The Navy
Department replied that he might "take the *Don*."   The
Don was smaller than the *Gettysburg*, but was believed
to be staunch and seaworthy.   She was fitted with twin
screw propellers, and had a great 100-pound Parrott gun
mounted amidships on her deck.   We transferred our
provisions and belongings to the *Don*, where we were
welcomed by Captain Chandler.   Then we set off
again.

All went well down the bay and out through the Capes,
and until a day later.   Then a south-east gale caught us
off Cape Hatteras.   They called it a gale, but it seemed of
the dimensions of a hurricane.   At any rate, it was too
much for the *Don*.   She tried going through it, and
running before it, and "lying to," and neither suited.   At
midnight she was labouring in a heavy sea, with broken
rudder, damaged boats and rigging, and miscellaneous
wreckage on her deck.   Finally the thing happened which
Victor Hugo so vividly describes in his *Ninety-Three*.   The

great gun broke loose, and, rolling about the deck with every movement of the vessel, seemed disposed to deal death and destruction to all on board. Sailors jumped for their lives to get out of the monster's way. It rammed the masts, smashed the long boat and deckhouse, and finally stove a hole in the bulwarks and went overboard. That was a great relief. But more disaster was to come. As the vessel fell into the trough of the sea, the foremast snapped short off and fell on the deck. Captain Chandler's men sprang with axes to clear away the wreckage, but had difficulty in keeping their feet. In the cabin, trunks, tables chairs, stove, crockery, and lamps were thrown from side to side with appalling rapidity, and the only safety was in a berth. An officer came down to report to the Admiral about the useless rudder, the boats swept away, and the men with broken arms and legs. He added in a lower tone, "We only keep her head to the sea by using the twin engines. The engineer works them alternately as the officer on deck calls down to him. If one of them gives out, she cannot live till morning." "Well," cheerfully responded the Admiral, "perhaps they won't give out. Anyhow, we'll do the best we can."

They did not give out; and toward morning the gale began to lessen and the sea to subside. The *Don* was headed northward toward Hampton Roads. On arriving there she presented a sorry appearance; dismasted, without boats or gun, with bulwarks knocked to pieces,—but fortunately not leaking. As we sat at our improvised breakfast on a locker, the Admiral said that during the night, while lying on the cabin floor with his clothes on, he heard a knocking and swishing about below, and thought he felt the floor move. He said to himself, "Now she has sprung a leak." Then he was relieved to see a trapdoor cautiously lifted and the heads of the black cook and another servant peering out. Having been asleep in the hold, they had been roused by the racket and were coming up to see what was the matter.

"What did you think, Mrs. Seward, last night when you heard the ship was going to be wrecked?"

"I thought perhaps we would get ashore in boats," she answered.

"Ah," replied he, "the boats were all washed away long before that."

"Well, Admiral," said I, "what did you expect?"

"Oh, I thought I should get ashore somehow, but I was not at all sure any of you would. Well," he added, "I don't believe any of us expected to be sitting here and laughing and chatting over a breakfast this morning."

Landing at Fortress Monroe, the Admiral reported our experiences to the Navy Department, and asked for another vessel. He received the laconic reply that we "seemed to be using up ships pretty fast," but that we might again take the *Gettysburg*, which by this time had gotten off the oyster bed without serious damage.

The next day she arrived at Hampton Roads. We transferred ourselves to her, and were welcomed on board again by Captain Rowland and his officers. We started for the third time on our voyage, and this time all went smoothly. We passed out through the Capes, traversed the Gulf Stream, found fair weather and favouring winds between Hatteras and the "still vexed Bermoothes." A day or two later we entered the tropics, and enjoyed sea travel in its most comfortable form, with blue skies, bright sun, gentle and steady trade winds, ship on even keel, everybody on deck, and everybody donning summer clothes in place of winter wraps. We read and conversed and watched the flying-fish skipping from wave to wave. We found the Admiral the most genial and entertaining of shipmates, and had occasionally a song from some of the younger officers, or a "yarn" from one of the older ones.

We scanned the charts to see if we were on the track of Columbus, but did not discover San Salvador as he did, as our course was too far east of it.   We passed the great bay and peninsula of Samana, the object of our mission, but deferred closer examination of them until our business should be transacted.   In the dusk of the evening we were steaming through the Mona Passage, and early next morning were entering the Ozama River, to cast anchor under the frowning walls of San Domingo.   The Ozama made a harbour large enough for the caravels of Columbus, and also for the *Gettysburg;* but the greater vessels of modern times have to lie outside in the open roadstead.

Standing on a lofty plateau, high above the river, the old city had a mediæval aspect.   Stone towers and an encircling wall, with bastions, gave it the air of a fortified Spanish stronghold, as in old days it was.   But the weather-stained and crumbling walls, and here and there heaps of ruins, showed the ravages of time.   We exchanged salutes with the fort, received official visits from the health and customs officers and the American Consul, Mr. Somers Smith, and then disembarked and climbed the steep, narrow streets.   We took quarters in the hotel, and, through the Consul, presented our credentials to Señor Don José Garcia, the Secretary of State.   He was not unprepared for our visit, and speedily arranged for our presentation to General Cabral, the President of the Dominican Republic.

The President, a tall, swarthy, fine-looking gentleman, in civilian attire, received us courteously, and introduced us to the members of his Cabinet and the principal civil and military officers.   Then we opened the subject of our mission.   The Minister of Finance, Don Pablo Pujol, was appointed to act as plenipotentiary on behalf of San Domingo in the negotiations with us.   They occupied some days, but it is needless to detail them here.   As to the bay of Samana itself, we had already been well informed by the reports of the United States military and naval officers.

In the evening we drove out through the streets of the old town and the adjoining country roads.   The Cathedral and the National Palace were massive and well preserved edifices.   All the buildings were of the Spanish type of architecture, but few were new.   Those occupied as residences or shops were in fair condition.   Of the others, some were roofless, and some almost in ruins.   But this did not prevent their being occupied by the poorer class of tenants.   In that genial climate, shelter and clothing can hardly be considered as necessaries, food is abundant, labour not urgent, and life is easy, for those who are content with little.

Out in the country were broad driveways constructed centuries ago, with stately villas in various stages of dilapidation, and surrounded by a tangled wilderness of tropical vegetation.   We strolled through some of the deserted mansions and gardens, and tasted the fruits that hung abundantly on every side, oranges, cocoanuts, bananas, sapodillas, guayavas, and pomegranates, growing without care or cultivation.   Here and there some wealthy citizen or foreigner had purchased one of these old villas and fitted it up for residence—its neatly trimmed lawns and hedges and newly painted buildings contrasting oddly with the general desolation around.   Far in the distance were the mountain summits and the various plateaus, where every kind of climate and vegetation may be found —altitude taking the place of latitude—so that one may pass in a day from the torrid to the temperate and almost to the frigid zone, without leaving the island.

Nowhere is the memory of Columbus more warmly cherished than in San Domingo.   It was his favourite island, on which he bestowed the loving appellation of

"Hispaniola," or "Little Spain"—now fallen into disuse. They pointed out to us the ruins of the palace of his son, Diego Columbus, surrounded by deserted grounds. Fragments of the flag he planted on taking possession of the island are still preserved. The Cathedral was begun under his auspices, and the lordly title of "Primate of the Indies" was conferred upon the archbishop. Across the Ozama River is shown the overgrown ruin where once the great discoverer was imprisoned; and in the Cathedral is the slab that covers the vault where his remains were interred, until they were taken up and carried to Havana.

One morning at breakfast we were informed that there were no eggs, no milk, and no fresh fruits. On inquiring why, we were told that the city gates were closed against all comers, as it was reported that there was a "revolution" going on outside. Never having met a Spanish-American revolution, we went out to see what it looked like. We found the gates closed and guarded by squads of soldiers, sentinels patrolling the walls, all traffic stopped, and groups of excited citizens talking in every street. Then we went up on the flat roof of the hotel and looked off upon the surrounding country. All appeared peaceful enough, except that there was a straggling line of men, with guns and without uniforms, walking briskly up one hill and down another, away from the city. We counted eighteen, but there may have been more hidden by the dense foliage. These, we were told, were the government forces going out in pursuit of the "revolutionists." No firing was heard, and nothing further seen. At nightfall we went out for our evening drive. The streets had resumed their usual aspect, the gates were open and unguarded. The army had returned and the revolution was over. What it was all about we never heard.

Meanwhile our negotiations were proceeding satisfactorily. The Dominican Government furnished all the information in its power, and its terms for letting us have the use of the Bay of Samana were not unreasonable.   But now an obstacle presented itself, threatening long delay. On careful examination it had become evident the bay, which was always considered defensible in the days of short-range artillery, would now be within range of modern siege guns, if planted on the neighbouring heights.   Therefore we should need much more than we had come prepared to ask for.   We should need to own and fortify those heights.   But the Dominican Constitution forbade the alienation of any territory of the Republic, and no amendment or change could be made without the consent of the Senate.   President Cabral invited us to meet with his Cabinet and confer over this point.   The Senate was not in session, but would be in a few weeks; and they were confident that its consent could then be obtained to the cession.   Meanwhile they would give us a lease of the bay and its islands for a stipulated sum.   It was clear to Admiral Porter that we did not want the bay if we could not have the heights commanding it.   It was equally clear to me that neither the Administration nor Congress would accept the doubtful tenure of a lease, even temporarily.   We must have the "fee simple" or nothing.   Nor could we wait for the convening of the Senate.   So we decided to return to Washington and report progress, the Dominicans assuring us that Don Pablo would soon follow us there, with the Senate's consent and full powers to conclude the treaty.   So we took our leave, with cordial expressions of regard and friendship on both sides.   On the following morning we went on board the *Gettysburg*, weighed anchor, and started for the north.

On our return voyage we touched at Port Royal, Jamaica, and were hospitably received by the British naval and military authorities there.   Commodore McClintock, of Arctic exploration fame, was then in command of the naval station, and General O'Connor was exercising the functions of Governor. Then we were off again through the Windward Passage and the Old Bahama Channel. As our coal supply was running short, we put into Nassau to replenish. There was some doubt whether the *Gettysburg* could get over the bar and through the narrow entrance to the harbour. Captain Rowland signalled for a pilot, and a black one came on board. When asked as to the depth of water, he chuckled and said: "Oh, that's all right. I know this ship. She's the old *Margaret and Jessie*. I've taken her over the bar many a time when she was a blockade runner."

A day or two were spent at the Victoria Hotel, where we met some officers of the United States Army and Navy, the American Consul, Thomas Kirkpatrick, and many American invalids who had come to seek health in a warmer clime. Then, the *Gettysburg* having been duly coaled and provisioned, we started for home. Bright skies and balmy temperature greeted us as we cruised through the Bahamas, and along the shores of Florida, Georgia, and the Carolinas.

It had been remarked by our officers that the *Gettysburg* was not as speedy as a blockade runner might have been expected to be. On our down voyage we had been burning anthracite coal. At Nassau we of course had taken in the soft British coal, for which the engines and furnaces of the *Margaret and Jessie* had been constructed. Feeling the change, like a horse after a fresh "feed of oats," she started off with an accelerated speed of two or three more knots to the hour.

"Off yonder," said the Admiral one morning, "lies Hatteras," pointing westward over the quiet sea.

I inquired what Cape Hatteras looked like when seen near at hand—whether it was a bluff, or a sandspit, or what?

The Admiral said that often as he had passed it in his voyages he could not recall its appearance. The captain and other officers proved to be also unacquainted with it, their service having been chiefly in the Pacific.

"Ask the quartermaster there at the wheel. He'll know."

"Thomson, what does Hatteras look like? Sandy beach, steep bluff, or how?"

The grizzled and weatherbeaten old sailor raised his hand to his cap in respectful salute. "Don't know, sir. Always give it a wide berth."

Up the Carolina and Virginia coasts, through the Capes and Chesapeake Bay, and up the Potomac, we finished our homeward journey.

Arrived at Washington, we were called to President Johnson's Cabinet council, to report what we had learned at President Cabral's. We "reported progress."

Some months later, according to promise, Señor Pujol arrived, with full power to conclude the treaty, and with the Dominican Senate's consent to the cession. Within a week or two his negotiations with the Secretary of State resulted in a treaty, which was duly signed, sealed, and sent by President Johnson to the United States Senate for approval.

But the Senate was in no mood to approve measures submitted to it by President Johnson. Nor was it eager to extend the national domain southwards. The treaty, if even read, was not debated nor seriously considered. It was shelved and disregarded.

When, a year or two later, President Grant came into office, he became satisfied that the acquisition of a West Indian harbour would be an advantage to the United States. He reopened the question, and found the government of San Domingo ready not only to cede a harbour, but willing to have their whole island republic annexed to the United States. But the Senate again would not consent, and the House and newspaper press rang with denunciations of what was called "jobbery," "oppression of weak republics," and so forth.

"Nemo omnibus horis sapit,"

saith the Latin sage. Certainly the American Congress was not at that hour wise enough to accept island and naval stations as a gift, though in later years it was ready to risk thousand of lives and expend millions of dollars in fighting for them.

More than forty years have elapsed, and we now have West Indian harbours and naval stations as a fruit of our war with Spain in behalf of Cuba. It is perhaps useless to speculate on "what might have been." But it is an interesting question whether, if we had accepted San Domingo's offers, we should ever have needed to go to war with Spain at all. With that island commanding the whole Antilles, and with naval stations outflanking those of Cuba, we would have been able to suggest to Spain that she might gracefully submit to the inevitable and retire from Cuba, instead of engaging in a hopeless contest to keep it. As it was, she felt that she was bound in honour to defend it against an enemy whose naval advantages were apparently not greater than her own. Our experiences with San Domingo furnish a fresh illustration of the old historic truth, that nations often solve their problems in the hardest way, because they have blindly refused to adopt any easier one.

1740 to 1867.

The Story of Alaska. Peter the Great naturally desired to know the extent of the gigantic empire of which he found himself the head. On the European side its boundaries were tolerably well defined. But on the Asiatic side, they were vague and uncertain. Explorations and expeditions had traversed the vast wild regions of Siberia, and had reached Kamchatka, which seemed to be the end.

The Kamchatkans looked off over a broad sea to their east. But they had traditions and rumours of "a great land" beyond that sea, inhabited by people much like themselves. There, it was said, the shores were greener, the trees taller, the nuts bigger, the *baidarkas* larger, and the fur-bearing animals more plentiful, the mountains higher, and the climate milder, the islands everywhere, and the fish innumerable.

To find this region, if it existed, and to ascertain whether the continents of Asia and America were joined by land or separated by water, he ordered two expeditions to be fitted out. Before they were ready to start, he died.

His widow, the Empress Catherine, and her daughter Elizabeth took up the work, and carried out his wishes.

Both problems were solved by the expeditions under command of Captain Vitus Bering. He found that the shores of Asia and America converged rapidly as they trended northward, and finally were separated only by a broad strait. He found that the farther shore was a land much as the Kamchatkan natives had described it to be. As no civilized power had yet claimed it, it would thenceforth be known as "Russian America."

The survivors of the expedition, who brought this intelligence, had also a pitiful tale to tell of their own dangers, disasters, and hardships. Shipwreck, disease, and death had lessened their numbers; and among the victims was their commander. He had died of exposure and fever, and was buried on a desolate island in the sea. Thenceforward the sea, the strait, and the island would all bear his name.

The returned mariners had also marvellous tales to tell of the newly discovered coast, of its sables, its martens, its foxes, and its sea otters. Already Siberia and Kamchatka had been ransacked for these costly furs, and now here was a new field, overflowing with opportunities for wealth.

Traders and trappers from Siberia, merchants and adventurers from Moscow and St. Petersburg hastened there by hundreds and even thousands. They had to improvise their own means of conveyance. The first ones hewed canoes out of trees, built boats of planks lashed together with strips of rawhide or sealskin.

Later, wealthy merchants built ships and regularly engaged in the fur trade. One man brought back, the first summer, five thousand skins, and so achieved a fortune. Every such story brought a rush of fresh seekers for wealth.

It was a wild and lawless region for a time. There was no governmental authority to check the sway of drunkenness and robbery, fraud and force. The white men sometimes killed each other, but the chief sufferers were the poor natives. However, this came to an end when the imperial government slowly extended its long arm of power, and grappled with its unruly colonists. Military and naval and civil officers were sent out. Forts were built and garrisoned. Landing places and trading settlements were established, and a governor appointed to supervise the whole.

Of the successive Russian governors some traditions are still extant, especially of the benevolent Shelikoff, who built churches and schools, opened courts, heard and redressed grievances, and sought to supersede savage customs by the usages of civilization. Also, of the rough, rugged, hospitable Baranoff, who built his castle on the rock at Sitka, and from there ruled his subjects with a rod of iron, though in the main with sagacity and rude justice.

Adventurers and traders from other lands began to find their way to Russian America, in such numbers as to threaten the ultimate extermination of the fur-bearing animals. The Russians wanted to keep the fur trade in their own hands. They were ready to sell furs to all comers, but preferred to control the hunting and trapping themselves. The Americans wanted to share in the profitable traffic. The British wanted to push their Hudson Bay Company's stations across the continent to the Pacific.

So arose questions of boundary and of commercial and national rights. It soon became necessary to make treaties to define them. Negotiations were begun, and lasted several years, in which participated such eminent diplomatists as Nesselrode and Poletica, on the part of Russia; John Quincy Adams, Richard Rush, and Henry Middleton, of the United States; and Sir Charles Bagot, Stratford Canning, and the Duke of Wellington, for Great Britain. Finally all was duly and peaceably settled. Russia conceded maritime rights and privileges, in accordance with international law, but held tenaciously to her sovereignty over the forests and broad plains at the north, and the long and narrow *lisière* at the south, between the mountains and the sea. Thus matters remained for forty years.

It was during this period that my father, then a Senator of the United States, in a speech at St. Paul, Minnesota, made his memorable prediction:

"Standing here and looking far off into the Northwest, I see the Russian, as he busily occupies himself in establishing seaports and towns and fortifications on the verge of this continent, as the outposts of St. Petersburg; and I can say: 'Go on, and build up your outposts all along the coast, up even to the Arctic Ocean; they will yet become the outposts of my own country,—monuments of the civilization of the United States in the Northwest.'"

1867.

The Story of Alaska—The Treaty of Purchase.   Soon
after this came our great Civil War.   During its continuance my father, as Secretary of State, had found the
Government labouring under great disadvantages for the
lack of advanced naval outposts in the West Indies and
in the North Pacific.   So, at the close of hostilities, he
commenced his endeavours to obtain such a foothold in
each quarter.

Even as early as during the Oregon Debate in 1846–7,
the suggestion had been made that by insisting on the
boundary line of 54 degrees 40 minutes, and obtaining a
cession from the Emperor Nicholas, the United States
might own the whole Pacific coast up to the Arctic Circle.
But the slave-holding interest, then dominant in the Federal councils, wanted Southern, not Northern extension.
The project was scouted as impracticable, and the line of
54 degrees 40 minutes was given up.

Renewing the subject now through Mr. Stoeckl, the
Russian Minister, my father found the Government of the
Czar not unwilling to discuss it.

Russia would in no case allow her American possessions
to pass into the hands of any European power.   But the
United States always had been and probably always would
be a friend.   Russian America was a remote province of
the Empire, not easily defensible, and not likely to be soon
developed.   Under American control it would develop
more rapidly and be more easily defended.   To Russia,
instead of a source of danger, it might become a safeguard.
To the United States, it would give a foothold for commercial and naval operations accessible from the Pacific States.

Seward and Gortschakoff were not long in arriving
at an agreement upon a subject which, instead of embarrassing with conflicting interests, presented some mutual
advantages.

SIGNING THE TREATY FOR THE PURCHASE OF ALASKA

From the painting by Leutze

After the graver question of national ownership came the minor one of pecuniary cost. The measure of the value of land to an individual owner is the amount of yearly income it can be made to produce. But national domain gives prestige, power, and safety to the state, and so is not easily to be measured by dollars and cents. Millions cannot purchase these nor compensate for their loss.

However, it was necessary to fix upon a definite sum to be named in the treaty,—not so small as to belittle the transaction in the public eye, nor so large as to deprive it of its real character, as an act of friendship on the part of Russia toward the United States. Neither side was especially tenacious about the amount. The previous treaties for the acquisition of territory from France, Spain, and Mexico seemed to afford an index for valuation. The Russians thought $10,000,000 would be a reasonable amount. Seward proposed $5,000,000. Dividing the difference made it $7,500,000. Then, at Seward's suggestion, the half million was thrown off. But the territory was still subject to some franchises and privileges of the Russian Fur Company. Seward insisted that these should be extinguished by the Russian Government before the transfer, and was willing that $200,000 should be added, on that account, to the $7,000,000.

At this valuation of $7,200,000, the bargain could be deemed satisfactory, even from the standpoint of an individual fisherman, miner, or woodcutter, for the timber, mines, furs, and fisheries would easily yield the annual interest on that sum.

On the evening of Friday, March 29th, Seward was playing whist in his parlour with some of his family, when the Russian Minister was announced.

"I have a dispatch, Mr. Seward, from my government, by cable. The Emperor gives his consent to the cession.'

Tomorrow, if you like, I will come to the Department, and we can enter upon the treaty."

Seward, with a smile of satisfaction, pushed away the whist-table, saying,

"Why wait till tomorrow, Mr. Stoeckl? Let us make the treaty tonight!"

"But your Department is closed. You have no clerks, and my secretaries are scattered about the town."

"Never mind that," responded Seward. "If you can muster your legation together, before midnight you will find me awaiting you at the Department, which will be open and ready for business."

In less than two hours afterward, light was streaming out of the windows of the Department of State, and apparently business was going on as at mid-day. By four o'clock on Saturday morning, the treaty was engrossed, signed, sealed, and ready for transmission by the President to the Senate. There was need of this haste, in order to have it acted upon before the end of the session, now near at hand.

I was then the Assistant Secretary of State. To me had been assigned the duty of finding Mr. Sumner, the Chairman of the Senate Committee on Foreign Relations, to inform him of the negotiations in progress, and to urge his advocacy of the treaty in the Senate.

Leutze, the artist, subsequently painted an historical picture, representing the scene at the Department. It gives, with fidelity, the lighted room, the furniture and appointments. Seward, sitting by his writing table, pen in hand, is listening to the Russian Minister, whose extended hand is just over the great globe at the Secretary's elbow. The gaslight, streaming down on the globe, illuminates the outline of the Russian province. The Chief Clerk, Mr. Chew, is coming in with the engrossed copy of the treaty for signature. In the background stand

Mr. Hunter and Mr. Bodisco, comparing the French and English versions, while Mr. Sumner and I are sitting in conference.

On the following morning, while the Senate was considering its favourite theme of administrative delinquencies, the Sergeant at Arms announced, "A message from the President of the United States." Glances were significantly exchanged, with the muttered remark, "Another veto!" Great was the surprise in the chamber, when the Secretary read "A Treaty for the Cession of Russian America." Nor was the surprise lessened, when the Chairman of the Foreign Relations Committee, a leading opponent of the President, rose to move favourable action. His remarks showed easy familiarity with the subject, and that he was prepared to give reasons for the speedy approval of the treaty.

The debate which followed in the Senate was animated and earnest, but in the end the treaty was confirmed without serious opposition. But the purchase was not consummated without a storm of raillery in conversation and ridicule in the press. Russian America was declared to be "a barren, worthless, God-forsaken region," whose only products were "icebergs and polar bears." It was said that the ground was "frozen six feet deep," and "the streams were glaciers." "Walrussia," was suggested as a name for it, if it deserved to have any. Vegetation was said to be "limited to mosses"; and "no useful animals could live there." There might be some few "wretched fish," only fit for "wretched Esquimaux" to eat. But nothing could be raised or dug there. Seven millions of good money were going to be wasted in buying it. Many millions more would have to be spent in holding and defending it,—for it was "remote, inhospitable, and inaccessible." It was "Seward's Folly." It was "Johnson's Polar Bear Garden." It was "an egregious blunder," "a bad bargain," palmed off on "a silly Administration" by the "shrewd Russians," etc.

Most of these jeers and flings were from those who disliked the President and blamed Seward for remaining in his Cabinet. Perhaps unwillingness to admit that anything wise or right could be done by "Andy Johnson's Administration" was the real reason for the wrath visited upon the unoffending territory. The feeling of hostility to the purchase was so strong that the House of Representatives would not take action toward accepting the territory or appropriate any money to pay for it.

The Russian Government courteously waived any demand for immediate payment and signified readiness to make the final transfer whenever the United States might desire. Accordingly commissioners were appointed, who proceeded to Sitka.

On a bright day in August, 1867, with brief but impressive ceremonies, amid salutes from the Russian and American naval vessels, the American flag was raised over the new territory to be thenceforth known as "Alaska."

This ceremony might be called the christening as well as the transfer. The territory had previously been known as "Russian America." During the progress of the treaty through the Senate, there were occasional discussions in the State Department and in the Cabinet as to the name to be bestowed upon it by the United States. Several were suggested as appropriate, among them "Sitka," the name of its capital, "Yukon," that of its chief river, "Aliaska" or "Alaska," derived from the name of its great peninsula "Oonalaska," and "Aleutia," derived from its chain of islands. Seward, with whom the final decision rested, preferred "Alaska" as being brief, euphonious, and suitable. The name was generally accepted with favour and began to be used before the transfer was made.

It was not until the 27th of July, in the following year, that the act making appropriation to pay for Alaska was finally passed and approved—the Chairman of the Foreign Affairs Committee of the House, General Banks, being its effective advocate. On the next day the Secretary of State made his requisition upon the Treasury for $7,200-000, to be paid to the Russian Government.

The United States at first merely garrisoned the forts at Wrangell, Tongass, and Sitka with small detachments of troops. The Russian inhabitants generally remained, but they were few in number. The Indians were peaceable and friendly in the neighbourhood of the forts, though sometimes belligerent in the remoter regions.

A shrewd old Indian chief was one day watching the soldiers drilling at Sitka. He said to the commander, "What for you work your men on land with guns? Why you no work them on water with canoes?" It was a valuable suggestion. As the Indians lived principally on fish and marine animals their villages were all on the shores of bays, sounds, and rivers. Armed vessels patrolling the waters could easily control them, while soldiers cooped up in garrison or struggling through forests would be useless. When this became understood at Washington, naval vessels and revenue cutters were ordered to Alaskan waters and rendered good service there.

My Father's Diary—and Others. One day, during his first week in the Department of State, my father requested me to get a blank book for him, remarking that as the epoch would probably be one of historic importance, he should begin to keep a diary. A suitable book was obtained and laid upon his table.

On the following morning he came out of his room with the book in his hand. In giving it back to me, he said:

"There is the first page of my diary and the last. One

day's record satisfies me that if I should every day set down my hasty impressions, based on half information, I should do injustice to everybody around me, and to none more than to my most intimate friends."

The book still remains with its one written page.

At the time, I thought his decision was a wise one, and subsequently, perusal of what purport to be extracts from the diaries of well-known public men convince me of the correctness of that judgment.

When, in 1913, I read in Mr. Bigelow's diary the story of the enormous lobby fees in connection with the Alaska bill, the question naturally occurred to me. Why should my father tell the story to Mr. Bigelow instead of telling it to me? I was with him, and in his daily confidence, knew about the bill being held up in Congress, and was quite as anxious as he was for its passage. Yet he never told the story to me at all!

Another defect of the story seemed to be: where did the money come from? The full amount of $7,200,000 was paid over to the Russian Minister, as the books of the Treasury show, and as the Treasury warrant also attests. There was no other fund to take it from. The small annual appropriation for diplomatic work, known as "the secret-service fund," would not begin to meet such heavy payments. To suppose that anyone would carry such an amount in his pockets, or keep it in his bank account, of course would be absurd.

My own conjecture is, that he told Mr. Bigelow, who had recently arrived from Paris, the sort of news that he might expect to find flying around Washington and the lobbies of the Capitol, and that Mr. Bigelow, not fully comprehending that these were *canards*, went home and set them down in his diary as actual facts.

Certainly there were plenty of such stories at that time. The air was full of them. Various rumours were afloat to the effect that some of the purchase money had been used to corrupt agents of the Russian Government, or to buy votes in Congress, or to subsidize newspapers, etc. A committee was directed by the House of Representatives to investigate the tales, and soon found that most of them were malicious and all of them absurd. This investigation is described in my memoirs of my father's life, on page 392 of the third volume. Its proceedings will be found in the *Congressional Record* of the year 1868.

The Secretary of State appeared before this committee and said:

"I gave notice to the Russian Minister that the requisition had been made, and that he could call upon the Secretary of the Treasury for the money. I assume, upon general information, that the money was paid. I do not know when it was paid out of the Treasury, nor to whom it was paid. I know nothing whatever of the use the Russian Minister made of the fund. I know of no payment to anybody by him.

"In regard to all those allegations, I have no knowledge. I thought the Alaska purchase a very good, proper, and national achievement; and out of the funds of the State Department, therefore, I subscribed for a small number of the speeches made by Mr. Charles Sumner, to be used for the information of the public and of Congress. Various persons, some connected and others not connected with the government, patriotic gentlemen as I supposed, came to give me their cordial support and co-operation in the matter; and among the rest were Mr. Sumner and Mr. Robert J. Walker. Whenever I found they were in possession of information or arguments which would be useful, such as documentary information, I received it and transmitted it to Congress, who had it published. All that I ever did, or that I ever expended, was in that way, and in no other, and no engagement was ever made with anybody for any part of the purchase-money, or any other fund.

"My impression is that the whole expense and cost to the United States Government for the negotiation, payment, and everything, did not exceed $500. As to any other fund to subsidize or propitiate the press, or any person connected therewith, I have knowledge that no fund at the State Department went to subsidize any press anywhere. But when I found there was a continued fire all along the line of the press against the Alaska purchase and the purchase of St. John's and St. Thomas, and I read how valueless these possessions were, by reason of perpetual icebergs in Alaska, and the universal cannonading of volcanoes and hurricanes down through the West Indies, I recollected the attacks of the Federal party upon Mr. Jefferson's Administration for making the purchase of Louisiana. I was familiar with that literature in my boyhood, as you all probably were, and I sent a young man—Mr. Dimon—to New York and Albany for the purpose of collecting from the Federal press (remaining in public libraries) extracts and articles attacking Mr. Jefferson in such papers. He collected and sent them to me.

"These articles were published through the press, so far as they would do it gratuitously, but in no other way. That is all I know of the influence upon the press."

He might have added that among the accusations made against him at this time was that of being an accomplice in the attempt at his own assassination.

1867.

Oriental Indemnity Funds. When a man pays us more money than we are entitled to, the simple and honest way to do, is to hand the surplus back to him. But when the transaction is between two great governments, it is not so easy. Government financial machinery is intricate and complex. And there are always political casuists to prove that the rules of ordinary morality do not apply to the case.

So, when Mr. Baker, the disbursing agent of the State Department, informed the Secretary of State that a considerable portion of the Japanese indemnity fund was still remaining in his hands, my father inquired, "How does this happen, Mr. Baker?"

The reply was that the respective claims of the various claimants had all been audited and paid, and there was still some money left.

"Why not pay it back to Japan?"

The reply to this was—"Nothing can be paid by government officers except under provisions of law, and there is no law applicable to this case."

"How was the money paid to us?"

"In Japanese gold," was the reply.

"Ask Mr. Hunter what precedent there is—how have other governments treated such matters."

Mr. Hunter was not aware there had ever been a precedent. Most governments take all they can get and seem to be rather proud of doing it.

Evidently the United States had asked and received more money than they were entitled to. The Secretary of State stated the facts of the case in Cabinet meeting, and suggested that the President, in a message to Congress, should request authority to make proper restitution of the money. This was agreed to, and the President did so.

But when the matter thus came before Congress there were debates and delays. It was urged that it would be folly to pay back the money when Japan had not asked for it. It was argued that to pay it back would be a confession that we had been in the wrong in demanding it, which would be humiliating to the nation. Then it was said that to pay it back would be to expose the Japanese

24

officials to the censures of their people, for having yielded to an unjust demand. Then it was proposed to use it for some public enterprise that would benefit both countries— a Pacific coast university—a school of diplomacy—Legation buildings—ships—forts—telegraphs, etc. Congress is not only a deliberative body, but a controversial one. So the session rolled away, and nothing was done.

Finding that there was likely to be delay before a decision could be reached in Congress, the Secretary of State now directed that the money should be invested in government registered bonds, as the best way to keep it safely. Session after session passed, the President's messages again and again called attention to it, but still Congress reached no conclusion.

Meanwhile the credit of the United States appreciated.

The bonds bought at a discount and paid for in gold rose rapidly in value. Interest accrued on them, was paid and reinvested "in like manner." So the $606,838 originally received from Japan amounted in 1869 to a much larger sum.

Here began new perplexities, and fresh debates in Congress. It was argued that even if Japan was entitled to the original amount, she was not entitled to the interest. At any rate, how could she be entitled to the additional amount which our thrifty government had earned at compound interest? And if she was paid the original surplus, dollar for dollar, in gold, what should be done with the residue?

Another similar indemnity fund had now been received from China. In this case the balance over and above the audited claims, by the same careful management, had much increased.

The two Eastern governments, with becoming sense of their dignity, looked on placidly, and declined to make any complaint or demand, saying that they left the whole matter to the wisdom and friendship of the United States Government, in which they had entire confidence.

My father directed that exact account should be kept, so that, in due time, the amounts should be turned over to his successor, to be held until Congress should finally decide.

Ultimately, after a few more years of delay, Congress found it to be both wise and right to pay the money back to Japan and China, in such manner as to convince them that we were actuated solely by desire for fair and honest dealing.   There is no doubt that the action of the United States in these matters came to the Oriental governments as an agreeable surprise, and led them to the opinion that there was one government, at least, to which they might look for friendship and justice.

Forty years have now elapsed, and Japan and China have repeatedly asked the United States for advice and counsel in governmental reforms—have employed American advisers in making such reforms, and have sent their young men to the United States to be educated in modern methods.   How much of the change that has occurred in those governments is attributable to the moral influence of these events, it is impossible to estimate.

Certainly it would have seemed, forty years ago, most unlikely that we should be dealing today with Japan as a modern parliamentary government, and China as a full-fledged republic.

1867.

The Japanese Commissioners. General Van Valkenburg, who was now, in 1867, the American Minister to Japan, wrote that the Japanese, having emerged from their long seclusion, were desirous of a better understanding with the other nations.

Commercial facilities were accordingly extended, and

diplomatic intercourse was enlarged. They manifested not only a commendable curiosity in regard to foreign ways and customs and inventions, but also a desire to adopt any that might be found better than their own.

He reported that the Government had carried out their engagements relative to the opening of ports, "in so liberal a manner, as not only to satisfy my colleagues and myself, but also to inspire me with perfect confidence." Sites for foreign settlements were selected at Hiogo, Osaka, and Yeddo, and arrangements made for the appointment of consular officers. Persecution of Christians was abandoned and Christian houses of worship were to be established.

Two commissioners were to be sent out in accordance with this new policy. They bore the sonorous names of Ono Tomogoro and Matsumoto Judayu. They were to visit navy yards, arsenals, foundries, machine shops, etc., and if possible purchase one or more ships of war.

The commissioners duly arrived by way of San Francisco, with their secretaries, interpreters, and suite. Among them were two officers of the modern navy about to be established by Japan.

They were all installed in lodgings at Wormley's. The Secretary of State received them at the Department, and in the evening they called at his house. As several of them were of such rank as to be "two-sworded men," and as it was not in accordance with Japanese etiquette to wear these ornaments into a parlour, quite a pile of swords accumulated at the door. Their costumes were of gay colours, and mostly of silk on this occasion, though they intimated that they had tried the American costume at San Francisco, and that some of them had provided themselves with frock coats and hats, "if it will not be deemed improper for us to wear them."

They regarded with polite curiosity the pictures and furniture which were novel to them, but recognized as a familiar friend a Japanese chess table which stood in the room, and seated themselves at it to show that they understood the game.

Tea was served, and when I inquired if it was at all like what they had at home, they evaded replying. They said that it was very good and they liked it, and asked of what plant it was made in this country? A small statuette of Buddha stood on the mantel. This, one of the Secretaries observed, and said that at Yeddo there was a statue of that deity sixty feet high. On my expressing surprise, they replied through the interpreter that "though he was so big they did not believe in him."

They were presented on the following day to the President. A dinner was given to them by the Secretary of State, and Senator Sumner as chairman of the Foreign Relations Committee, Baron Gerolt as Dean of the Diplomatic Corps, and Admiral Porter as head of the navy, were invited to meet them. After dinner there was an evening reception, to which many ladies came. The commissioners expressed their satisfaction at meeting them, and regretted that the customs of their country had not permitted them to bring their wives.

On the following day an officer of the State Department was detailed to accompany them in their explorations and sightseeing. He reported that they inspected all the chief public buildings with grave demeanour, and made intelligent inquiries and comments in regard to them. Then, going down Pennsylvania Avenue, they visited various shops. Rather to his surprise, the jewelry and drygoods seemed to interest them but little, but they were highly pleased with the novelties which they found in the hardware and tinsmiths' shops. The tinware especially delighted them, and they made many inquiries as to its manufacture—exclaiming "it is so beautiful and so cheap. It should be introduced into Japan."

It is needless to say that their visits to the Arsenal and Navy Yard were even more painstaking and fruitful of results. Nothing seemed to escape their observation. Subsequent events in the wars of Japan have shown that the information thus gained for their government was promptly and wisely used.

When my father and I went to make an official call on them, at Wormleys, we found Ono Tomogoro standing surrounded by his secretaries and interpreters and arrayed in his official robes of flowered satin. But his colleague, Matsumoto Judayu, came forward with evident pride, to show us that he had adopted the American costume, which we could not help thinking was not so becoming or dignified as his own. Among the subordinates, also, there were signs of the adoption of Western habiliments.

When Ono Tomogoro courteously waived us to seats, and ordered the customary tea to be brought, there was a hasty colloquy with one of his secretaries. Turning to us, he said with a smile: "In Japan we offer our visitors always tea, but my secretary informs me that the custom in America is champagne." We had some difficulty in assuring him that champagne was not the national drink which we offered to all comers.

The Commissioners remained in Washington some weeks, and were frequent visitors at the Department, as well as at the house of the Secretary. They asked the aid of the government to enable them to purchase arms with the latest scientific improvements and to build a ship of war with the latest modern appliances.

One of the chief purposes of their mission was accomplished when they purchased the *Stonewall*. This vessel, built for the Confederates, now belonged to the United States. The Secretary of State wrote to General Van

Valkenburg advising him of the purchase and saying that the *Stonewall* was fitting for sea at the Washington Navy Yard, and that Captain Brown of the Navy had been granted leave of absence, to aid in the transfer of the vessel to Yokohama. Part of the purchase money was paid down in gold by the Japanese, the rest was to be remitted from Yeddo. He added in the dispatch, "It is hoped that the Commissioners who are now crossing the Pacific on their way to Japan will carry back with them an impression of us as agreeable as that made by themselves."

China's Entry into the Field of Diplomacy. Prince Kung, the Regent of China, gave a farewell dinner to Anson Burlingame, on the occasion of his resignation and return home. It was attended by several of the high Chinese officials.

Great regret was expressed at his departure, and urgent requests made that he would, like Sir Frederick Bruce, state China's difficulties, and inform the treaty powers of the desire of the Chinese to be friendly and progressive.

China's isolated position among nations had exposed her to foreign intrigues and designs, and she had no representatives of her own to prevent or defend her against them.

During the conversation at the dinner, Wan Siang, a leading councillor of the Prince, said to Burlingame, "Why will you not represent us officially?" At first Burlingame supposed this was but an exaggerated form of Chinese politeness, but he soon learned that the proposal was seriously made. He was requested to delay his departure a few days until a formal proposition was made requesting him to act for China as ambassador to all the treaty powers. He wrote to my father:

"I thought anxiously upon the subject, and, after a consultation with my friends, determined in the interest of our country and of civilization to accept. My colleagues approved of the action of the Chinese, and did all they could to forward the interests of the mission. Two Chinese gentlemen of the highest rank were selected from the foreign office to conduct the Chinese correspondence, and as 'learners.' My suite will number about thirty persons. I shall leave for the United States by the February steamer for California."

My father received and answered this letter, with his hearty approval. He at once made arrangements for the reception of this novel legation. They arrived in Washington about the first of June. Their credentials read: "Anson Burlingame, of the first Chinese rank, Envoy Extraordinary, and High Minister Plenipotentiary, and Chih Kang and Sun Chia Ku of the second Chinese rank, associated High Envoys and Ministers, respectively, to the United States of America."

Burlingame came to our house in the evening prior to the delivery of these credentials. He desired to consult my father as to whether his becoming a Chinese Minister would interfere with his status as an American citizen. My father's judgment was, that no such obstacle existed, as Burlingame had already informed the Chinese Government that, while endeavouring to serve them to the best of his ability, he must adhere to his native allegiance.

"But, Burlingame, how about the personal audience? You are now the representative of the Celestial Empire, with which a grave diplomatic question, about 'personal audience by the Emperor,' has been pending for years. If the American Minister is not received by the head of the Government, at Peking, how can the Chinese Minister be received by the head of the Government in Washington? We must find some way of bridging that difficulty."

Fortunately it happened that the Emperor of China, at this juncture, was only a small boy, and this enabled the Secretary of State to bridge over the difficulty by this formal reply.

"It is well understood that, owing to the minority of the Emperor of China, the sovereign authority is now exercised by a regency. Reserving therefore and waiving, though only during the Emperor's minority, the question concerning the privilege of personal audience by the head of the Chinese Government, the President will receive their Excellencies the High Ministers of China, on Friday at 12 o'clock at the Executive Mansion."

On the appointed day President Johnson cordially received the new Chinese envoys. Burlingame began his address by saying that, if he had not been kindly relieved from embarrassment by the Secretary of State, his first duty on this occasion would be to "explain how it is that I, who left this capital seven years ago as a Minister of the United States to China, have now returned here a Minister from China to the United States."

He announced that the Chinese Government now accepted the system of International Law in use among the Western Powers, and was now about to open a regular diplomatic intercourse not only with the United States, but with Belgium, Denmark, France, Great Britain, Holland, Italy, North Germany, Russia, Spain, and Sweden.

The President's reply welcomed the coming of the Legation as an evidence of the growth of mutual trust and confidence, as well as of the sagacity of the Chinese government. In conclusion he said he would "build upon this day's transaction an expectation that the great empire, instead of remaining as heretofore merely passive, will henceforth be induced to take an active part in the general progress of civilization."

The Legation was installed at Brown's Hotel, in a spacious suite of rooms. The great yellow flag, bearing the Imperial Dragon, floated in the breeze from the roof of the hotel during their stay.

Needless to say that many anxious observers were attracted there for a glimpse of their faces, and cues, their caps with insignia of rank, and their gorgeous robes of flowered satin. Needless also to say that visitors were welcomed with many affable smiles, and very little English.

Mr. Burlingame kept his American name and costume. The Chinese associate Envoys were styled "Sun-Tajen," and "Chih-Tajen." Their chief was also entitled to be styled "Burlin-Tajen," the title so appended having a meaning equivalent to the European prefix of "His Excellency."

The secretaries and attachés were selected by the Foreign Office with reference to their proficiency in the various languages required. Thus two could speak French, two German, two Italian, two Russian, and two Dutch.

Now came the work on the treaty. It was elaborate, because it was hoped that the other powers might take it as a model for similar ones.

As the period was one of high political excitement over "reconstruction" and "impeachment," it was thought best, in order to avoid delay from unfriendly criticism and partisan wrangling, to admit as few people as possible to knowledge of its provisions beforehand. So the example of the Alaska treaty was followed. The ordinary course of protocols and notes and references was omitted. The Secretary of State and the three "Tajen" agreed upon the various points in verbal conference.

The treaty placed China in an entirely new attitude toward other Powers. Instead of remaining a remote, secluded empire, yielding reluctant concessions, she now gave her adhesion to the principles of Western International Law, and to more advanced doctrines in regard to personal rights than most Western nations had yet been able to adopt. The treaty guaranteed liberty of conscience, and protection from persecution on account of religious opinions. It recognized the right of man to change his home and religious belief, and also the mutual advantage of immigration and emigration, for trade, travel, or permanent residence. It pledged neutrality in war, and forbade foreign nations to carry their mutual quarrels into China. It opened public educational institutions, and gave the right to establish schools. It provided for diplomatic and consular intercourse, for international improvements and closer relations of international friendships.

A state dinner was given at the White House to the Chinese Envoys, and they received many other hospitalities. My father entertained them at Washington, and subsequently on their northern trip met them on the way, and, opening his home at Auburn, received them there. From there they went to Niagara Falls.

Chih-Tajen and Sun-Tajen took part in the verbal conferences, as well as in the drafting of the treaty. They offered no objections, but on the contrary highly approved its advanced ideas. They brought with them a bulky volume containing a translation into Chinese of Wheaton's *International Law*. Its title in Chinese literally translated read, *All Nations' Public Laws*.

They were especially solicitous not to offend by any infraction of the manners and customs of the Western nations, which they were desirous to learn and adopt. At the State dinner, Chih-Tajen inquired of me whether it would be any infraction of the rules of politeness to taste each one of the several courses presented to him. I told him that it was exactly what I should do if I went to a State dinner in China. They declined my invitation to go to St. John's Church, although anxious to witness the ceremonies, as they feared they might give offence by not knowing when to get up and sit down. I told them it would not be expected of them to conform to those usages, and even offered to take a seat at the back where they would not be noticed. But they thought on the whole it was best to abstain from going.

Mr. Burlingame frequently adverted to the aid he had received in China from four of the other Ministers at that Court, Sir Frederick Bruce of England, M. Berthemy the French Minister, and MM. Balluzek and Vlangally the Russian Envoys. A familiar phrase at the Court described the "four busy B's" as the leaders of advanced opinion, both in the diplomatic circle and among the Chinese themselves, in favour of a liberal and progressive policy between China and the Western powers.

When my father visited China in his journey round the world in.1870, among his first visitors at Shanghai were Chih-Tajen and Sun-Tajen. They announced to him the success of their diplomatic labours in Europe, condoled with him on the death of Mr. Burlingame, and thanked him over and over again for the aid they had received from him in their mission, and dwelt long and gratefully on the hospitalities which they had enjoyed in the United States.

At Peking, he had a long and interesting conversation with Wan Siang, the Minister of Foreign Affairs. Wan Siang was the master spirit who led the Chinese Government in the enterprise of entering into diplomatic relations with the Western powers. He had asked, and obtained from my father, the copy of Wheaton's *Law of Nations*, and had it translated and adopted by the imperial government. He, more than any other, was the effective mover in instituting the diplomatic mission of Mr. Burlingame.

They talked over the various questions in regard to China's action and found they were quite in accord in believing that the time had arrived for China to adopt a more just and liberal policy in her governmental affairs. He asked my father for suggestions, and, when made, said they were in harmony with his own sentiments. He spoke somewhat sadly and regretfully as to the slow progress he had made in inducing his fellow-countrymen and governmental associates to share in his ideas of a more enlightened policy.

He said: "I have attempted to procure the establishment of an Imperial college, in which modern sciences and languages shall be taught. For a while, I thought I should succeed. But the effort has failed, and has brought me under deep reproach and general suspicion."

My father replied: "This ought not to discourage you. Every wise minister at some time falls under temporary reproach and unjust suspicion. Public opinion in every country is a capricious sea. Whoever attempts to navigate it, is liable to be tossed about by storms."

Wan Siang said: "It is, as you say, indeed unavoidable. A statesman stands on a hill. He looks farther, in all directions, than the people, who are standing at the foot of the hill, can see. When he points out what course they ought to take, they are suspicious that he is misdirecting them. They cry 'Pull him down!' When they have at last gained the summit from which he points the way, they then correct their misjudgment. But this, although it may be sufficient—for them—comes too late for the statesman."

The Portrait Gallery. Grey, bent, and weary, my father was standing one evening in the parlour of his Washington home, looking at the portraits which thickly overspread its walls.

During eight years, now drawing to a close, gradual additions had increased the number until they now formed "a diplomatic gallery" of the world's sovereigns and ministers.

He pointed out to his guests those who during that time had passed from office or from earth.   Leopold of Belgium had been succeeded by his son; Frederick of Denmark by Christian IX.; Isabella Segunda of Spain, fat and fair, had been dethroned and exiled; Pius IX. of Rome, gentle old man, was shorn of temporal power; Abdul Medjid of Turkey, slender and dark, had been assassinated and followed by Abdul Aziz; Hien Fung of China had yielded the Celestial Throne to Tung Chi, a baby; the Tycoon of Japan, with his high headdress, emblematic of supreme power, had been deposed and banished by the Mikado; Maximilian of Austria was executed in sight of his army, at Queretaro; Carlotta his empress was a wanderer and insane.

Then the array of South American Presidents—their brief tenure ended by an election, or shortened by war and violence—Mosquera deposed, Cabral overthrown, Prado assassinated, Geffrard banished, and so on through a long list.

Premiers and ministers of foreign affairs had found their terms even more brief: Earl Russell, Thouvenel, Drouyn de l'Huys, Cavour, Rogier, Zuylen D' Avila, Manderstrom, Calderon, Van Schleinitz, and their contemporaries in office had all experienced the mutations of politics and of time.   Gortschakoff's placid face beamed from its frame, as a reminder that he alone of all the Ministers of Foreign Affairs with whom my father had held intercourse in 1861 was now remaining in office in 1869.   And all this had happened in the brief period of eight years!

"It is a sermon on the instability of human greatness," remarked one of the guests.

"Perhaps so," said my father with a smile; "I can only hope that they all enjoyed the prospect of getting out of office as much as I do."

1869.

The " Great Tyee " in Alaska. Two years after the cession of Russian America, my father, having retired from office, was travelling in the west.

At San Francisco, his friends made up a party to accompany him, to see the territory he had purchased for the nation.   The steamship *Active* was placed at their disposal by Ben Holliday.

They cruised along the California and Oregon coasts, explored Puget Sound, with its great forests, busy mills, and growing villages, were received with courteous hospitalities at Victoria, and then passed on through the magnificent scenery of the Inland Passage.

All there was beautiful, silent, and lonely.   Not a vessel nor a human habitation in sight.   Only an occasional canoe of an Indian fisherman.   Cautiously proceeding through waters as yet but imperfectly known, we arrived at last at Sitka.

The little town had been built by the Russians, of squared hewn timbers,—it being easier, as a townsman remarked, "to square a log than to get a board."   A high stockade separated it from the Indian huts and lodges just outside.   A medley of population walked its streets: Russians in their national dress, United States soldiers in their blue uniforms, Indians in blankets and feathers, traders and travellers in the garb of San Francisco.

Several days were devoted to points of interest, the historic castle and church, and the embryo modern enterprises.   Then, a week later, the *Active* weighed anchor and proceeded northward with my father and his party, this time accompanied by General Davis and his staff.   Some of the friendly Sitka Indians acted as pilots, and the destination was the Chilkat River, the headquarters of the formidable tribe recently engaged in hostilities with the troops.

They had expressed a desire for peace, and this visit of the *Active* would give an opportunity to treat with them. Besides, as the General laughingly told the ex-Secretary, he looked to him for valuable assistance in the negotiations. The General, in talking with the Indians, had given them news that a scientific expedition sent out from Washington to observe the total eclipse of the sun was coming among them; and also that the "Great Tyee" (or chief), who had bought the whole territory, was coming to make it a visit.

It had not occurred to him that the Indian understanding of the fact would be different from his own. But he soon found that, to their simple minds, it meant the advent of the sovereign owner of the soil. They could not understand how a great "Tyee" could buy Alaska, and then not own it. They were expecting to welcome him with great respect, and to receive favours at his hands.

As to the eclipse story, they received that with some incredulity, but thought it had some connection with the visit of the "Great Tyee."

After three days spent in traversing the various straits, channels, and sounds, the steamer anchored at the mouth of the Chilkat River.

Communication was opened with the Indians, and the next day came messengers from the Coast Survey party, inviting the "Great Tyee" and his friends to come up and visit their camp. This invitation was accompanied by one from Klakautch, the Chilkat chief, who sent canoes to aid the ship's boats in bringing the guests.

They embarked, and, pulling rapidly up the river, soon lost sight of the steamer, as she came cautiously along behind them, "feeling her way with the lead" in unknown waters.

Arrived at their destination, they were welcomed by Mr. Davidson, the head of the Coast Survey party, and the Chilkat chief, who had placed one of his great lodges at the service of the scientific party, and the other at that of the "Great Tyee" and General Davis.

Each of these royal residences was a substantial structure of hewn logs, seventy or eighty feet long. Its entrance was guarded by a score of Indian dogs, yelping and howling in chorus. Within, the house had no partitions, but formed one vast room, from the earth, which was its floor, to the roof, with an opening in the centre to let out the smoke. Hanging blankets or skins shut off one end for sleeping places, or depositing of valuables.

Here they supped on fresh fish and game, cooked at the blazing fire in the centre of the lodge, and passed a comfortable night with semi-civilized, semi-savage surroundings, wrapped in bear skins and army blankets.

The eclipse was to occur on the 7th. When Mr. Davidson commenced posting his assistants at different standpoints,—one armed with a telescope, another with a sextant, another with a camera, another with a chronometer, and another with pencil and note book, all gazing intently at the sun, and pointing their mysterious instruments towards it,—it seemed proof positive to the uneducated Indian mind that they were a sort of sharpshooters, taking aim at that luminary.

When, at the time announced, the first faint line of obscuration began to creep over the disc of the sun, stolidity and incredulity gave way to visible anxiety, and the Indians gathered more closely round the little circle of observers. When these were shifting the instruments and noting their observations, and Mr. Davidson was passing rapidly and quietly from one to another, giving directions and receiving reports, it certainly looked as if the "Boston men" were personally conducting the exhibition.

The shadow had crept about half way over the face of the sun, when the Chilkats began to expostulate. They said they were convinced of the "Boston men's" skill, but

25

they had seen enough now, and they feared bad consequences if the thing went further. But the observers were too busy to listen or explain.

The black shadow crept steadily on and on, over the sun. The weird, unusual light, which was neither day nor night, settled down over river and forest. Birds and insects were hushed and sombre silence covered the scene. On board the *Active*, when the eclipse became total, the chickens in the coop went to roost, the cow laid down contentedly for the night, and some of the Sitka Indians, who had been taught by the Russians, fell to their knees and fervently repeated the Lord's Prayer in Greek.

There were unmistakable signs and exclamations of relief when the shadow began to pass away. The Indians were convinced that the "Boston men" were taking it off as skilfully and methodically as they had put it on. The Coast Survey party were highly pleased with the successful termination of their enterprise, and general satisfaction came back with the sunshine.

Soon after, the Chilkat chief invited his guests to come to his lodge, to meet the principal people of his tribe. The assemblage numbered two or three hundred. The chiefs of greater and less degree, the warriors, the medicine men, and the women stood in grave, passive rows all round the sides of the building,—the chief Klakautch and his guests being seated in the middle.

The latter had not quite understood whether this gathering was for a formal and ceremonious greeting or for some other purpose. They were not left long in doubt.

As soon as all had assembled, Klakautch rose and uttered a few emphatic sentences, which the interpreter proceeded to translate:

"Some time ago, the Kalosh (or Sitka Indians) killed three of the Chilkats. Now the Great Tyee has come.

We have gathered to ask him, what he is going to do about it?"

So sudden and direct a demand seemed to require a categorical answer, and Seward had never even heard of the case. He asked,

"When did this killing take place?"

Question and answer were translated by the interpreter. The date was given in Indian fashion, reckoning by "suns" and "moons." It appeared that it happened nine or ten years before.

"Then it happened," Seward said, "when this country belonged to the Emperor of Russia, long before it became the property of the United States. He was a great sovereign, who listened to the Indians, and treated them with kindness. This demand should have been made to him."

Evidently this reply was not at all satisfactory. The chiefs consulted together, and presently their answer came back, through the interpreter.

"We did appeal to the Emperor of Russia, but he gave us no redress. Perhaps he was too poor. We know that he was poor, because he had to sell his land to the 'Great Tyee.' But now the 'Great Tyee' is here in his stead. And we want to know what he is going to do about it?"

Seward conferred with General Davis, and then asked:

"How many men were murdered?"

"Three," was the response.

"And what sort of redress do you yourselves desire?"

There was a visible brightening up in the faces of the Indians at this. They consulted as before, and presently came their reply:

"A life for a life is the Indian law, and always has been. But as these three Chilkats were of the chief's family, we reckon each of their lives to be equal to the lives of three common Indians. What we want, then, is the Great Tyee's permission to send our warriors down to kill nine of the Kalosh (Sitkas) in order to avenge the death of the Chilkats."

To this, Seward replied with promptness, that it was not to be thought of. No killing would be allowed. He then asked,

"Is there any other form of reparation that you think might be made?"

The faces of the Indians beamed with satisfaction, when this was translated to them. It began to look like business. They consulted as usual, and answered:

"We know that the 'Boston men' are averse to any killing except by their own soldiers. So we have sometimes consented to take pay in blankets. We think the life of each Indian is worth about four blankets. Nine times four blankets,—if the 'Great Tyee' chooses to give them to us, would be full redress, and make our hearts glad; and we should then regard the Sitkas as our friends and brothers."

"Well, General," said Seward, "there you have the conclusion of the case. I think you can afford to give thirty-six blankets, to make peace between the tribes. Shall I tell them you will send them up?"

The General was very well pleased, as this would end the last of the Indian disputes, and establish peace throughout the territory. He thought it advisable, however, to give the adjustment greater dignity and effect, by requiring the Chilkats to appoint commissioners to proceed to Sitka, and there receive the blankets, and at the same time exchange tokens of amity with the Sitkas.

This arrangement proved highly satisfactory all round. The Chilkats, who hitherto could not venture into the region occupied by their enemies, were glad of an opportunity to visit Sitka, see its wonders, and make friends with its Indians.

So the meeting broke up with mutual congratulations. The climax was added to the general rejoicing, when the

Chilkat chiefs were invited to row down to the *Active*, and dine there with the General and the "Great Tyee."

Toward evening they arrived, in their brightly coloured and gaily decorated canoes.

On board the ship, the stewards and cook had been busily at work, to meet the responsibilities imposed on them. Soon a banquet was spread, bewildering in its variety, considering the limited resources of the ship's larder, and lavish in its quantity, since all who were to partake of it were blessed with good appetites.

The cabin was too small to accommodate the whole company; but it was entirely in accordance with Indian usage that the six chiefs should sit in state at the cabin table, while their wives and attendant warriors gathered on deck round the open skylight, through which the viands were passed out to them, while they had full view of the proceedings below.

On deck there was merriment with the feasting. In the cabin all was grave and decorous, with little conversation until the principal courses had been disposed of. After the exchange of various information about the territory and government, Seward inquired if there was anything further that the chiefs would like to ask?

They consulted according to their wont, and presently answered through their interpreter, that they would like to have the "Great Tyee" tell them about the eclipse.

Seward accordingly proceeded to explain the phenomenon, in the simplest language possible, using as illustrations the cabin lamp to represent the sun, and an orange and an apple to represent earth and moon. When he had finished, he inquired if the chiefs had understood his explanation?

After conference as before, the reply came back:

"The chiefs have understood much though not all the 'Great Tyee' has told them. They understand him as

saying that the eclipse was produced by the Great Spirit
and not by men.   Since he says so, they will believe it.
They have noticed, however, that the Great Spirit generally does whatever the 'Boston men' want him to."

With this shrewd comment on ethics, astronomy, and
human nature, the feast came to an end.

1869.

The Guest of a Nation. Regarding him as the chief
defender of the Mexicans in their long struggle with the
European Powers, the Mexican Government had cordially
invited my father to visit their country, see the people
whom he had befriended, and accept their hospitalities.
Now that he was free from official cares and was travelling
so near their frontiers the invitation was renewed.

On the 30th of September, the *Golden City* was steaming
out through the Golden Gate.   My father and his party
were on board.   On the voyage down the coast, it was a
daily surprise to find how the usual discomforts of sea
travel are mitigated on the tranquil Pacific.   The great
steamer moved on even keel, over waters hardly ruffled,
and through continual sunshine.   Her spacious cabins
and airy staterooms rose in successive tiers, and were
"steady as a church."   Her decks presented an aspect
like that of a summer hotel.   Under the broad awnings
were groups of gentlemen smoking, children playing, and
ladies chatting, reading, and embroidering.   There was
no noise or hurry.   Chinese sailors, with placid faces,
moved quietly about, while the officers pacing the deck
and glancing around the horizon seemed to find nothing to
order, and nothing to alter.

Cruising along the Coast of Lower California for a couple
of days, and approaching the shores of Jalisco, the voyage
was without incident except the meeting and exchange of
news with the steamer *Montana*.   Then, crossing the gulf

and approaching the shore, they were reminded that they had passed out of a temperate climate into a tropical one, and out of a dry season into a wet one. A strong warm rain was pouring down, and it accompanied them into the harbour of Manzanillo, where they were to debark and enter Mexico.

Landing at Manzanillo at sunrise, they were received and welcomed by Señors Luis Rendon, and Jacinto Cañedo on behalf of the Mexican Government, and by Governor Cueva of the State of Colima. Citizens had come down from Colima to join in the greeting; among them some of the merchants and Dr. Morrill, the United States Consul.

Two days of driving rain kept them at Manzanillo, but they were comfortably lodged and hospitably cared for. Meanwhile a telegraphic dispatch came from President Juarez and his Cabinet welcoming my father to the country and wishing him a pleasant journey to the capital.

On the morning of the third day the sky cleared. Under the direction of the Mexican officers, five large boats carrying the national colours were in readiness to take the party and their baggage up Lake Cayutlan.

The landscape was picturesque and tropical, the lake smooth and glassy, the shores covered with dense growths of trees, among which could be seen the palm, the cypress, and the guayava. Here and there was an alligator basking in the sun or a flamingo wading in the marsh, while flocks of parrots flew screaming overhead.

Midway on the trip a pause was made for breakfast, in the friendly shade of a thicket.

Arriving at the end of the lake, stages and mules were found waiting. The afternoon was spent in a ride over muddy roads and swollen streams through luxuriant tropical vegetation. Another pause for dinner with Don Ignacio Largos, whose house, built of cane, allowed free circulation of air in every direction. Evening brought the party to the great hacienda of Don Juan Firmin Huarte.

Through the open doorway came a blaze of light and a swarm of attendants. Then followed a hearty and hospitable welcome from the owner of La Calera, a native of Old Spain, genial, polished, and enterprising.

Here Sunday was passed. Then the journey was resumed. This time it was to be only from the country to the city home of Don Juan, but this involved a climb over mountains, chasms, and torrents. Rising gradually from the coast the road wound through successive gorges. Just at nightfall, the travellers looking back had their last glimpse of the Pacific.

It was after midnight when they reached the silent deserted streets of the ancient Spanish-looking town of Colima. The watchman was crying "Dos horas y todo bueno" when they knocked at the massive gate and were ushered into the spacious court of Señor Huarte's home.

Life in Colima at Señor Huarte's was full of contrast to the scenes left behind in the United States.

One seemed to have stepped not only into another clime, but into another century. Within doors, the Moorish arches, pillars, and frescoes, the glazed tile floors, the grand salon and stairway decked with masses of bright flowers and glossy foliage, were suggestive of Seville or Granada.

Looking out from the carved stone balconies, or through the iron-latticed windows, one saw strongly built houses in mediæval style, quaint little shops, ruins of church and palace, plazas with stone seats and fountains, and passersby, peasants, priests, soldiers, and women, in costumes gay or sombre, such as were worn two hundred years ago. At every corner a group such as Murillo loved to paint. Now and then a well mounted cavalier, glittering with arms and ornaments; or a lady with her duenna, whose black dress, lace veil, and prayer-book showed her to be on the way to mass. Heavy carts and patient little donkeys plodded along with marketing or merchandise. No railway whistle, no telegraph poles, no gas-lamps, no carriages, no boy with the morning papers.

Three days were passed in Colima. There were dinners and festivities at the mansion, and a christening at the parish church, around whose doorway stood a hundred children eagerly crying "Padrino, mi medio!" in accordance with the old superstition that a sixpence from the hand of a new godfather is sure to bring good luck.

But the crowning event at Colima was a ball and banquet at the palace, in honour of Señor Seward's visit. Ballroom, corridor, galleries, and arches were brilliant with tropical plants and Oriental illuminations. Green, red, and white, the national colours, were everywhere. The flags of the United States and Mexico hung side by side. A portrait of Juarez at one end of the hall, and of Seward at the other, were wreathed with flags and laurel.

Among the ladies and gentlemen there was every type of the blended Aztec and Spanish races, the Castilian predominating. Quadrilles and waltzes were followed by the favourite national *danza*, whose music has a measured cadence and soft plaintive melody suited to a tropical clime.

At the banquet, Governor Cueva addressed "the eminent statesman who presented a barrier to the irruption of those who sought to sow in our soil the obnoxious seeds of the old continent." He closed by saying:

"I salute you in the name of the Mexican people, and offer you its friendship as sincerely as you have been a true and sincere friend to the government and people of this nation who applaud and bless you."

Seward made due acknowledgment. In his reply he said that one additional principle remained to be adopted to secure the success of the Republican system: it was that "the several American Republics, while abstaining from intervention with each other, shall become more than ever heretofore political friends."

A day or two were spent in visiting the cotton mills, and the gardens filled with palms, bananas, cocoanuts, coffee, orange, and lemon trees.

On the morning of departure the escort sent down by the government of the State had arrived, and were drawn up in line at the gate. They were a fine-looking body of one hundred cavalrymen, well mounted and armed.

As the journey for the next two days would be through the *barrancas*, which are impassable for carriages, handsome Spanish horses and sure-footed mules were brought, equipped with the comfortable Mexican saddles, for the use of each of the party. Trunks, baggage, bedding, and supplies were strapped on the backs of eighteen pack mules, under the guidance of a muleteer. Señor Huarte, whose thoughtful care for his guest extended to every detail, had provided a palanquin for Seward's use, in case he should prefer it. Several of the gentlemen from Colima accompanied him through the *barrancas* to the cities beyond. Altogether the cavalcade was about two hundred in number. Nothing could be more picturesque than its winding progress, up and down, through the passes of the Sierra Madre—the soldiers with gay uniforms, streaming pennons, and flashing arms, the cavaliers with broad sombreros and bright red sashes, belted, and armed to the teeth, and mounted on prancing steeds, the ladies, on easy pacing palfreys, whose trappings were ornamented with silver, and the long train of laden mules, climbing the steep acclivities in obedience to the muleteer's whistle. Still more like a mediæval scene it looked when passers-by from the opposite direction, travellers similarly mounted, trains of mules with merchandise, peasants and soldiers, priests and nuns, would greet them with courteous salutation or blessing, "Yaya con Dios, Caballero," "Dios guarde usted."

The wild landscape, the ancient-looking roadway, the grey walls and battlements of the distant haciendas, peering out through the glossy green foliage, all seemed appropriate accessories. When, at noon or nightfall, the bugler, at some heavily-barred, stone-turreted gateway, sounded a parley, and asked leave to enter, it was like a chapter out of Scott's novels, or a page from the adventure of Don Quixote de la Mancha.

The *barrancas* are huge valleys or gorges, formed by the action of mountain torrents. Some of them are five hundred feet deep, others one thousand or one thousand five hundred. Up and down their steep precipitous sides runs the zigzag mule path, partially paved, but needing constant repair. A dense growth of trees and vines clings to the slope, where it can find a foothold. At the bottom of the valley, a stone bridge spans the little stream, which in the rainy season becomes a roaring flood, making havoc and devastation. One of the Californians in the party likened them to "minor Yosemites," and found in the great "Barranca de Beltran" a counterpart of Church's *Heart of the Andes.*

A very considerable traffic goes through these mountain roads. The travellers met many trains of one or two hundred mules, and estimated that, in a day, they saw two thousand. They carry up from the *tierra caliente* sugar, rice, and tropical fruits, and bring down from the temperate region above, earthenware, soap, and other manufactured articles.

At Tonila, the travellers dined with the venerable Governor Vega. At night they were to sleep at the great hacienda of San Marcos, at the foot of the volcano of Colima, over whose crater hung a sluggish cloud of smoke by day—a dull red glow by night. It was after dark when they arrived there. The lighted torches borne by the soldiers, as they came up the mountain defile, were met by a similar procession from the hacienda, making a scene of wild and weird beauty. It is commonly supposed that the Castilian phrase, *Esta casa es a la disposicion de usted*, is but a hospitable flourish. But at San Marcos, and, indeed, everywhere that he went, Seward found it to be, not a mere compliment, but an actual truth. The owner of the mansion literally gave his house, with its servants, furniture, and equipage, to his guests, for them to live in, and do what they pleased with, so long as they chose to stay. At every city he visited in Mexico, Seward found "his own house" ready and waiting for him.

The last *barranca*, that of Atenquiqui, was passed on the afternoon of the 15th. A rest of an hour or two, in a cane hut by the wayside, was taken, preparatory to entering the comfortable Concord stage-coach, drawn by six mules, in which the rest of the journey was to be made. In the evening, as they approached the town of Zapotlan, they found it brilliantly illuminated from one end to the other, in honour of the festival of San José. Here was another hospitable reception; and then a leave-taking of the friends who had accompanied them from Colima, except Señor Cañedo, who had charge of the party as far as Guadalajara.

In the morning a stroll through the plaza and streets, a look at church, market, fountains, and convent ruins, substantial residences and pretty gardens.

Then on the road again, through a landscape showing the different altitude and climate now attained—the palm and sugar cane having given place to the maguey, and the mesquite to corn fields and orchards. Everywhere, lofty mountain ranges bounded the prospect; while near at hand were the cane huts, with cactus hedges, the fields of corn and beans and barley, with here and there the tree-cotton, the castor bean, and the coffee tree. Long stretches of uninhabited, uncultivated plains were covered with tall grass, or with a profusion of wild flowers—among which the travellers recognized many that, at the North, are carefully cultivated in garden or greenhouse. Calla lilies were growing in the ditches at the roadside. Zinneas, verbenas, and marigolds were weeds in the fields. Tall pink and spotted lilies, and gay striped convolvulus appeared among the grass here, as buttercups and daisies do at the North.

Only one ominous feature showed itself in the smiling landscape. Rude black wooden crosses, surrounded by piles of stones, appeared at frequent intervals; each marking the spot where some victim had met a bloody death.

The shores of Lake Chapala offered a beautiful view. It was like Lake George or Seneca, but without the houses and without the boats. In lieu of other inhabitants, there were flocks of cranes, plover, ducks, and other water-fowl, of varied and brilliant plumage.

Everywhere, the houses of brick and stone and stucco were clustered together in villages, for mutual protection. Each village had its church, its plaza and fountain, its dwellings of massive masonry, with flat roofs, broad windows, airy balconies, and paved court-yards, as if they had been transplanted but yesterday from Old Spain. Three-fourths of all the people seemed of unmixed Indian blood; the rest resembled their Spanish progenitors. But the word "Indian" in Mexico is applied to a race widely different from the savages of the United States. In Mexico they are civilized and Christian people, neat, intelligent, and industrious, kind-hearted and affectionate.

The labourers in town and country would be met on the road, contentedly trudging to market, with long wicker baskets strapped on their backs, containing their scanty produce. Many, as if to lose no time, were busy knitting, embroidering, or plaiting straw, as they walked along.

On each day's journey Seward was greeted with new and varied forms of hospitality and kindness. At Sayula he was met by a cavalcade of a hundred gentlemen, accompanied by ladies in their carriages. He was escorted into the town amid the ringing of church bells and the firing of cannon. There was a banquet with speeches, visits to schools that would compare favourably with those of New England, and churches that eclipse any that the Pilgrims would tolerate. There was a ball in the evening, and a serenade with harp, guitar, and violin. At Zacoalco there was a similar reception and welcome.

At Techaluta, a little village of cane huts, a band of Indian boys, playing the national anthem, escorted the carriage through the single street. There was not a flag in the place; but the poor people had decorated the fronts of their houses with bright-coloured blankets, shawls, and scarfs, bits of gay ribbon, and whatever finery they possessed. Each family stood in their doorway, with uncovered heads, to say "God bless you," "Vaya con Dios, Señor," "Dios guarde usted," "Mil gracias, Señor,"— "Adios."

As the carriage passed the last houses, and the musicians ceased, a tall, swarthy Indian stepped forward, threw a roll of paper into the carriage, and, with a profound obeisance, withdrew. Unrolling and reading the scroll, Seward found it was addressed "To the great Statesman of the great Republic of the North—Techaluta is poor, but she is not ungrateful!"

At Tepetitlan they arrived after dark. But the town was brilliant with bonfires, torches, and fire balls, while the air was filled with strains of music from unseen instruments, and the merry peals of chimes from all the churches. Everywhere there were addresses of welcome, long or short, but all marked by good taste and deep feeling. Everywhere, tables were loaded with the fruits and dishes of the country, of every variety, from the national *frijoles* and *tortillas*, to the most elaborate *dulces* and *pasteles* that skilled ingenuity could contrive.

Cordially as he had been invited and welcomed by the government of Mexico, Seward was hardly prepared for the warmth and depth of popular feeling which he everywhere encountered. Mexicans, of whatever ancestry or party, are intensely patriotic; and they were determined to show their appreciation of one who had stood by their country in its hour of trial.

Passing Santa Aña Acatlan, San Augustin and Sant' Anita, the drivers unharnessed the six tired little mules and put before the coach six milk-white horses, with resplendent trappings, for the entry into the great city of Guadalajara, whose white spires and towers were shining in the distance. Three miles before reaching the city, there came out a long line of carriages and horsemen, with the Municipal Council and State officials, to welcome Seward to the capital of the State of Jalisco. His entry into the city was an ovation. The streets were lined with carriages; the sidewalks crowded; windows, doors, and housetops occupied; the ladies waving their handkerchiefs; the men shouting *Vivas!* and hurrahs; and the whole scene replete with excitement and enthusiasm.

At the door of a stately house, the procession paused. The keys were presented to Seward; and he was informed that it was his own. It was thoroughly appointed and furnished; the table was spread for a banquet; and there was a corps of trained servants at command. Drawing-room and dining-room opened upon a marble-paved court-yard. As the tired travellers sat under its spacious arched and frescoed corridors, by the mellow light of shaded lamps listening to the plashing of fountains and the tinkling of guitars, they appreciated the satisfaction of Hassan Bedreddin, when, after a hard day's work, he suddenly woke up and found himself Caliph.

Seward's first act, when left alone, was to sit down and write a kindly letter of acknowledgment to the people of Techaluta, whose welcome touched him deeply.

A week was spent in Guadalajara, driving through its spacious avenues and well-built streets, and on its beautiful Paseo; looking at its majestic Cathedral with costly adornments, and its scores of ancient and modern churches; strolling through the luxuriant foliage of its Alameda, and the profusion of fruits and flowers in its markets; visiting its palaces and public offices; studying its prisons and benevolent institutions; its great Hospital of San Miguel de Belan, for the treatment of every form of human ailment; its Hospicio, where hundreds of orphans and foundlings are sheltered and trained to lives of usefulness. A day spent in visiting the public schools was full of surprises. Some of the buildings were the old convents, and replete with memories of the sixteenth and seventeenth centuries. But the schools themselves exhibited the highest progress of the nineteenth. Señor Matute, one of the chief officers of the municipal government, explained that commissioners had been sent abroad to study the schools of other countries. So Guadalajara had adopted a system combining the best features found in Boston, New York, and Philadelphia, as well as in Paris, Copenhagen, and Stockholm. Study of books was combined with training in arts, sciences, and trades. In the recitation-rooms the children showed as much proficiency as in the United States. In other rooms were four hundred boys, learning blacksmithing, carpentering, weaving, and tailoring. In the needle-work rooms the girls were sewing, knitting, and copying oil-paintings in silk embroidery. At the boys' High School was a band of one hundred musicians, all schoolboys, who had earned their own instruments. At the music hall of the girls' High School, the pupils were giving the opera of *Ernani*. Gymnasiums, art-galleries, laboratories, and libraries were among the adjuncts of the schools.

On coming out from their inspection, Seward remarked, "Why do people talk of a 'Protectorate' for a country capable of such things as these?"

Citizens, officials, and associations vied in their hospitalities to the national guest. Preparations were making for a ball to be given in his honour at the hall of the State Congress. The Academy of Sciences presented him with a certificate of honourary membership, in which he was styled "Defender of the Liberty of the Americas." He was presented also, as a memento of his visit, with the original royal proclamation of Charles II., of 1676—a parchment yellow with age, but plainly showing the signature, in a bold round hand, of *Yo el Rey*.

One evening was spent at a representation of *El Valle de Andorra*. The opera house was a spacious and handsome edifice, with massive walls, holding an audience of four thousand, and having five tiers of boxes, each box having its own distinct entrance, dressing, and refreshment-room.

"Theatres never burn down in this country?" asked one of the visitors.

"Never," was the reply of a Mexican gentleman, "how could they?"

Another gentleman remarked that he was much surprised, on his first visit to the United States, at being told not to throw a match on the floor, as it might set the house on fire. "Burn a house with a match!" said he; "I never heard of such a thing!"

With walls of thick masonry, tiled floors and roofs, with no lath or plaster, no shingling or planking, houses in

Mexican cities are practically fire-proof. It was said that the little old hand-engines were all that was ever needed; and that there was not an insurance company in the Republic, till the French invaders introduced the fashion.

The ball brought together a brilliant and fashionably-dressed assemblage of all political parties. The fine hall of the State Congress was used as a ball-room; while the tables were set in the decorated corridors surrounding the illuminated patio—a feature of Spanish architecture admirably adapted for entertainments. Spanish beauty and Aztec grace were exemplified in the Señoras and Señoritas; and in Mexico, even men dance gracefully.

It was two o'clock in the morning, when Governor Cuervo, at the supper-table, announced that the hour had come for the addresses of welcome. Señors Matute and Jones spoke in terms of enthusiastic greeting.

Seward, in his speech of acknowledgment, alluded to his hope for the North American States, and the Spanish American Republics, in the creation of a policy of mutual moral alliance, to the end that external aggression may be prevented, and internal peace, law and order, and progress be secured throughout the whole continent.

Governor Cuervo responded with hearty assent to that "Great Continental American policy," and said that, as a patriot, he should devote all his efforts to its realization.

One of the subjects under discussion by the municipal authorities, at this period, was the question of abolishing the bull-fights. The custom was linked with so many traditions of the nation and the race, and was so intrenched in popular favour, that it would be difficult to put a stop to it. Nevertheless, progressive and public-spirited men in Guadalajara were urging its abandonment. Of course, Seward heartily agreed with them. However, it was urged that he should first attend a *funcion*, see the performance and audience, and then give his unbiased judgment for or against its continuance. The great amphitheatre, packed with thousands of the people of Guadalajara, of every age, rank, and station, was a fine spectacle. Seward had assigned to him the chair of honour. The gaily dressed line of matadors, picadors, banderilleros, and *chulos*, marched up before him, to make their opening salute, in accordance with the custom, centuries old, of the gladiators, who, in the Coliseum, used to say: "Te, Caesar, morituri salutamus!"

But bull-fights and their audiences have been so often described that the scene needs no repetition here. Suffice it to say, "five valiant bulls were fought," and four "done to the death"; and that, while the audience enjoyed it as they would a circus, the American travellers found it bloody, cruel, and only less brutal than the prize-fights in their own land. Their sympathies were less moved than they expected for either the bull or his assailants, since both seemed to court the blows they received. But the poor horses, blindfolded, and forced into a combat in which they had no interest, exposed to all the danger and having none of the escapes or triumphs, were the real sufferers. It was a pleasure to learn subsequently that the progressive party in the City Council carried their humane purpose into effect by a majority vote.

At Guadalajara, Señor Jacinto Cañedo took his leave. He had accompanied the party from Colima, and they regretted to lose his cheerful companionship and guidance. He now returned to resume his official duties at Colima. Don Luis G. Bossero, the commissioner appointed by the general government, had arrived and took charge of the travelling arrangements. Formerly in the Diplomatic Corps at Washington, he spoke English fluently and perfectly. His tact, courtesy, and knowledge of affairs were invaluable. Under his care the eastward trip was

resumed on the morning of Tuesday, the 26th, in a coach
sent down from the city of Mexico, drawn by eight mules
and escorted by a large detachment of cavalry.

The incidents of the following week were like those of the
preceding ones—the same warm-hearted hospitality and
enthusiastic greetings in the villages and cities successively
visited, but with an ever-changing panorama of beautiful
scenery, and ever-varying objects of historic and poetic
interest. At the suburb of San Pedro they parted with the
Guadalajara friends who had come out so far to bid them
good-bye. At Zapotlanejo they saw the fine old church,
and the barricades and bullet-marks of the recent war.
At El Puente de Calderon they saw the great stone bridge
where Padre Hidalgo, with eighty thousand men, struck
the blow for national independence in 1811. At Jalos
they found a quaint old city, embowered with trees, with
a magnificent church building. At Venta de Los Pajaros
they spent the night at a hacienda, fortified to resist
bandits or revolutionists, and provided with a military
force of several hundred strong, mustered and organized
by Señor Perez, the owner. At San Juan de los Lagos
they saw the Cathedral—one of the finest in Mexico. The
townspeople were making preparations to celebrate the
centennial anniversary of its consecration. At Lagos, a
city of twelve thousand people, was another great church,
whose specialty was the possession of the remains of a
Saint, brought from Rome eighty years before. The road
in this vicinity passed among the numerous small lakes,
from which the town takes its name. The fields, fenced
in with the tall "Organo" cactus, had the grains and fruits
of a temperate clime. At each of these towns there was a
deputation of mounted citizens to meet Seward at the gates.
There was the house provided for his reception and use.
There were addresses of welcome, serenades, and banquets.

Like greeting awaited him at Leon. Here was the

novelty of the festival of *Todos Santos* (All Saints), the plaza being illuminated and surrounded with booths for the sale of fruits, flowers, and the curious bon-bon confections in the form of skulls, angels, devils, birds, and fishes, which are deemed appropriate for gifts and mementoes of the day. In the morning, the city, seen from the upper windows, seemed like a garden, the flat roofs of the houses in all directions being covered with a profusion of flowering plants in full bloom.

At Guanajuato they found another old and important city, the capital of a state. Resembling Guadalajara in architecture, it was widely different in site and surroundings. Built in the midst of mountains, with streets following the ascent of hills or the curve of ravines, some of its quaint and unexpected turns were suggestive of Quebec. Massive masonry and heavy embankments everywhere gave it a solid, substantial look. Its handsome residences and terraced gardens added to its beauty and attested the wealth of its silver mines, which are among the richest in Mexico.

Seward was met and escorted up to the city through the cañon of Marfil. Received and cordially welcomed by Governor Antillon and others in authority, he was shown to a new and handsome house prepared for his occupancy, was presented with the keys, and duly installed therein.

A week was spent in visiting Guanajuato's ancient Cathedral and numerous churches, its elaborate and substantial water-works, its residences and terraces, its fine theatre and busy mint, its historic castle, which Hidalgo and his Mexican followers besieged and stormed in 1810, and which the Spaniards recaptured in 1811, hanging the heads of Hidalgo and his three associates on its four corners. There they remained until the national independence was achieved in 1823, when they were buried

with the honours due to martyrs for patriotism.   Now
occupied by court-rooms and prisons, the edifice looked
new enough and strong enough to stand another siege.

Among the friends met here was Mr. Parkman, who
had emigrated in his youth from Cayuga County; and,
after various adventures in the mining region, had come
to Guanajuato, married and settled, and had become a
prosperous mine-owner.   One of his daughters accepted
an invitation to go with the party to the United States
for a visit, and subsequently joined them at the city of
Mexico.

Accompanied by Mr. Parkman and others of the owners
and superintendents of mines, Seward visited the shafts
and tunnels of some of the principal ones, some *in
bonanza*, and some *in borrasca;* was shown the various
processes of getting out the ore and of "beneficiating" or
extracting the silver from it.   One of these mines, the
Valenciano, discovered by the Spaniards shortly after the
conquest, was said to have yielded $800,000,000, and when
Humboldt visited it, he estimated that it was producing
one fifth of all the silver in the world.   A fine sight was that
at "La Serena," where the party, standing in a tunnel
four hundred feet below the surface, looked down six
hundred feet farther, to the bottom of the shaft, which
was illuminated by blazing fire balls thrown in at the top
and rushing down like fiery comets.

The day before departure there was a distribution of
premiums at the College, followed by a *soirée* and ball.

Leaving Guanajuato, the travellers proceeded along
the mountain road; pausing at midday at Salamanca, and
spending the night at Celaya, where, for the first time in
Mexico, they heard the sound of the steam whistle. It
came from a woollen factory established there.   Another
of the modern enterprises there was an artesian well four
hundred feet deep, supplying the city with pure water

thrown out in great jets, and having a temperature of 100 degrees.

On Wednesday they arrived at Queretaro, and were received at the city gate by a deputation of state and city officials and citizens. Addresses of welcome, letters, and visits were followed by a drive out to the great Rubio cotton factories standing in the suburbs, and named the "Hercules" and "La Purissima." They were encircled by a high wall, and guarded by a uniformed military force maintained by the proprietors.

The next day was a deeply interesting one. It was spent in visiting the historic spots connected with the final defeat and fall of Maximilian, and listening to the descriptions of those eventful scenes by their eye-witnesses. They pointed out the lines of fortification and siege, the field of battle, the stronghold of the old convent and church of La Cruz, where the imperial forces made their last desperate stand; the streets where the republicans under Escobedo made successful entrance, the spot where Maximilian was captured by Corona, the old monastery of Los Capuchinos where he was confined with Miramon and Mejia, the theatre where the court-martial sat, by which they were tried and condemned to death, and finally the "Cerro de las Campanas," where they were executed.

The sun was just setting as Seward ascended this hill. Standing by the side of the three black wooden crosses, which marked the spot of execution, and looking off toward the distant city, whose roofs and domes were fading into evening shadows, one could realize the feeling of the unfortunate Archduke, who here expiated, with his life, his mistake of attempted "Empire." While contemplating the scene, a carriage drove up, containing some ladies clad in deep mourning, and with them the uncle of Miramon—"Tio Joaquin"—as the three prisoners had affectionately called him in the days of their captivity. The scene was a touching and impressive one, as he stood there, with uncovered head, narrating to Seward, in low tones and with deep feeling, the incidents of the capture, the imprisonment, the trial, the farewell messages of the condemned men to their friends, their wishes as to the disposition of their remains, and their last utterances, as they stood up to receive the volley that ended their lives.

Leaving Queretaro on the following day, the coach, with its mounted escort, proceeded over valley and plain and through passes in the Sierra, till it stopped for the night at San Juan del Rio. Another hospitable welcome, with addresses and music, greeted Seward's arrival. Here was the boundary line between the states of Queretaro and Mexico.

Two days more were spent, chiefly among the rocky hills and roads that showed they were passing through the mountain chain surrounding the valley of Mexico. Here were great plantations of the maguey, in every stage of growth, and of its manufacture into the national beverage of *pulque*. The Mexicans were amused at hearing their northern guests give it the appellation of the "century plant," wondering why, since here tall stalks with white blossoms were visible every year in every field.

' At Arroyo Sarco, high up in the mountains, where the stage stopped for the night, there was a fire on the hearth, "the only one you will see, or need, this winter."

Now came the long descent toward valley and plain, sometimes almost imperceptible, as the road wound through forests and fields, sometimes quickly and rapidly down some rocky declivity, but all the while downward and downward still.

Emerging from woods and rocks, on Monday, the 15th, as the road wound along the mountainside, the travellers saw, gradually unfolding before them, one of the most magnificent panoramas of the world. The valley of

Mexico lay spread out in the mellow autumn sunshine, dotted here and there with white villages and sparkling lakes, and surrounded by the blue mountain range from which, high above the rest, rose the snow-clad cone of Popocatepetl. Far in the distance were the gleaming towers and spires of the city of Mexico. On one hand stood a steep hill crowned with the palace-like castle of Chapultepec. On the other was the clustering group of churches and chapels in Guadalupe Hidalgo.

Down from the mountain, crossing the level plain, passing cultivated fields, long causeways, and suburban villages, the stage whirled on, till suddenly confronted, some miles from the city, by a brilliant welcoming party. Señor Lerdo de Tejada, the Minister of Foreign Affairs, Señor Romero, the Minister of Finance, and Mr. Nelson, the American Envoy, were waiting with carriages and a cavalry escort, to receive and take the party to the city. At the Garita de San Cosme the carriages paused again, for there stood President Juarez, with his wife and daughter, come out to welcome the guest of the nation. The cordial greetings of old friendship were exchanged as the cavalcade rapidly went on through the streets past the old Alameda of Montezuma, and the great equestrian statue of Charles the Fourth, past stately churches, handsome dwellings and public edifices, to the corner of Alfaro and San Augustin Streets.

An open gateway led into a *patio* lined with plants and flowers, and around it were the rooms of a charming house fitted up with luxury. President Juarez, with a smile and wave of his hand, said, "Mr. Seward, will it please you to enter your house? This is your home!"

Certainly the kind friends who had prepared this home had spared no pains to give it every requisite for quiet comfort, or for social entertainment. Built in the favourite Spanish fashion, its large reception-, drawing-, and dining-rooms looked out on the ornamental courtyard, whose galleries, draped with tropical foliage, offered a choice of sun or shade. Furnished and decorated in accordance with modern European taste, it was supplied with a corps of servants and equipages to meet every possible wish. As if to remind him of home, two of Canova's statues on the main stairway were the same as those in the entrance hall of his house at Auburn.

Visitors, Mexican, American, and European, came to proffer warm greetings and kindly offices. With some, it was the renewal of old friendship begun in Washington; with others, it was the opening of a new and agreeable acquaintance. It was especially pleasant to meet again the Juarez and Romero families. The members of the Cabinet called in a body. Military and civil officers, formal deputations and private citizens, all came to welcome the national guest, and made him feel that he was no stranger, but a well-remembered friend.

A month was spent in this charming home. The city of Mexico has many places of historic interest. No day was allowed to pass by its hospitable people, without some agreeable excursion. The majestic Cathedral, the spacious Plaza, the curious Aztec Calendar Stone, the National Palace, with President, Cabinet, and Congress in the exercise of their official functions, the Museum, with its ancient Aztec memorials and bloody Sacrificial Stone, the Mint and Assay Offices, the School of Mines with its admirable equipment for educating miners, scientists, and engineers, the orderly and busy streets, the gaily ornamented shops, the massive old convents and beautiful churches, the Academy of Design, with paintings and sculpture that showed the Mexicans to have more natural taste and aptitude for the fine arts than their northern neighbours, the libraries with their treasures of rare and ancient volumes, the Monte de Piedad, whose benevolent functions have gone on uninterruptedly during a century of wars and revolutions, the public institutions, and the private dwellings, all seemed to have a welcome for the nation's guest.

Strolls through the beautiful Alameda, drives on the fashionable Paseo, and walks about the streets, with ever novel views of the distant and glistening summits of gigantic Popocatepetl, and his spouse Ixtaccihuatl, "the Woman in White," were followed by longer excursions about the city and its romantic suburbs.

One of these drives was to look at the old cypress tree, under which Cortez is said to have taken refuge, on the "Noche Triste," after his bloody and disastrous battle in the city. Another was a visit to Tacubaya with its fine country seats, and to San Fernando with its historic graves.

One day was spent in visiting Guadalupe Hidalgo, where thousands of Indians were congregated to hold their annual festival in honour of their patroness, "Our Lady of Guadalupe." A picture of the Virgin Mary, with Aztec dress and complexion, is enshrined there with reverence, as being of supernatural origin, and as commemorating her aspect at the time when she appeared to Juan Diego. The tradition has built up a great town, with churches and convents, around the spot where he saw his vision.

Another interesting day was spent in company with the Ministers of War and Finance and their families, in visiting the battlefields of Contreras, Churubusco, Chapultepec, Molino del Rey, and the Belen Gate, as well as the hacienda of La Canada, a favourite resort of Maximilian. Then there were excursions by boat up the Grand Canal, to see the monument to Guatamozin, the famous "Floating Gardens," the "Rock Piñon," the warm springs, and the lakes Chalco and Tezcoco.

One morning, as the party were passing through a hall of the National Palace, an attendant threw open a side door and invited them to look in. A large room was piled full of the dusty, mouldering relics of the dead Empire—scarlet canopies, laced liveries, jewelled swords, gold and silver cups and vases, rods and maces of court ushers, belts and caps of imperial guards, royal portraits, chairs of state, battered statuary and broken monograms, furniture from throne and banquet rooms, costly trappings and useless rubbish, all thrown confusedly together as no longer of any service. It was like the property-room of a theatre, save that here the tragedy was a real one, and its insignia were of enormous cost. No sermon on the vanity of human greatness was ever preached, half so eloquent as that silent room!

There was a round of festivities and hospitalities, public and private. There was a dinner at the United States Legation, followed by a ladies' reception. There was a dinner at Mr. Lerdo's and another at Mr. Romero's. There was a military parade of the regular troops. There was a *gran funcion* at the Circo de Chiarini, another at the Opera of *Crispino e la Comare*, and another at the Iturbide Theatre of *La Cabaña de Tom* (*Uncle Tom's Cabin*).

The 24th of November was spent with President Juarez and his family at the beautiful castle of Chapultepec, which had been fitted up with all the decorations and appliances of modern art as one of the imperial residences. The dinner was served in the great hall, and several hours were passed in looking at the state apartments, galleries, corridors and courtyards, fountains and gardens, terraces and groves, and in viewing the magnificent prospect. The golden-hued valley of Mexico stretched away in the sunshine; the white walls and towers of the city gleaming in the foreground, while in the remote distance loomed

up the snowy summits of the two mountain giants—
Popocatepetl and the "Woman in White."

On the 27th of November came a grand banquet at the
National Palace, the invitations to which were issued by
the Minister of Foreign Affairs, in the name of the President of the Republic and "in honour of William H. Seward."
Four hundred guests, including all the chief officers of the
government and the leading members of Congress, sat at
the table—Juarez and Seward together at the head. Here,
as at the other festive gatherings, music, toasts, and
speeches prolonged the proceedings to a late hour. These
were full of enthusiastic and affectionate references both
to the United States and to Seward. One of the most
eloquent of the orators was Señor Altamirano of Guerrero.
He said:

"This banquet is not to the foreign monarch, who,
leaving his throne for travel, is received with official
orations; nor to the conqueror, raising the cup to his lips
with a bloody hand. It is the apostle of human rights,
the defender of the dignity of America, and one of the
venerable patriarchs of liberty, whom we welcome in our
midst, and in honour of whom we decorate with flowers
our Mexican homes. . . . It is not merely Seward, the
great statesman of the age, Premier of the United States.
I see, and only wish to see in him, the friend of humanity,
the enemy of slavery, and the liberator of the bondsman!
His heart, his thoughts, his whole life have been consumed
in the task!"

In his speech of acknowledgment Seward adverted to
the crisis of 1861, when Slavery had taken up arms in
alarm for its life, and had organized rebellion aiming at the
dissolution of the Union:

"The statesmen of Europe, with its press almost unanimous, announced that the United States of America
had ceased to exist as one whole sovereign and organized

nation. The Emperor of France, emboldened by the seeming prostration of the United States, landed invading armies at Vera Cruz and Acapulco and overran the territories of Mexico, overthrowing all its republican institutions and establishing upon its ruins an European empire.

"With the United States in anarchy, San Domingo reestablished as a monarchy, and Mexico as an empire, it was unavoidable that republicanism must perish throughout the whole continent. . . . In that hour of supreme trial, I thought I knew, better than the enemies of our cause, the resources, the energies, and the virtues of the imperilled nation. The United States became, for the first time, in sincerity and earnestness, the friend and ally of every other Republican State in America, and all the Republican States became, from that hour, the friends and allies of the United States."

On the 9th of December, came the grand ball at the National Theatre, which closed this series of hospitable demonstrations. The theatre was brilliantly lighted, and decorated from floor to roof with flowers, and with Mexican and American flags. Three thousand guests were present. After the opening quadrilles, there were waltzes and galops, but, most frequent of all, the favourite national *danza*, with its soft, slow music, and its graceful movement—the dance of all others best adapted to a great ball, since it enables each guest to meet and exchange greetings with every other.

The street by which the guests arrived and departed seemed to have changed into a great illuminated and decorated arcade.

The time fixed for departure was now approaching. Farewell visits were made and exchanged. The day before leaving, there was a "last breakfast," at the beautiful country seat of Mr. Barron at Tacubaya. Many and warm were the heartfelt expressions of affection and regret that were exchanged with Mexican friends, on bidding adieu to them and to their historic city.

And now the mode of travel was changed. Mexico's first railway had been completed from the city as far as Puebla, and a special train was in waiting to take Seward thither. He left Mexico on the 18th of December in the President's car, and was accompanied as far as the first station by Señors Lerdo, Romero, and Mejia of the Cabinet and their families. Luxurious and easy as was the car, it had one disadvantage as compared with the stagecoach in the mountains; for it gave but passing glimpses, instead of intimate acquaintance, with the country traversed. The train whirled only too rapidly through Ometusco, Apam, San Juan, Tchuacan, and the battlefield of Cortez at Otumba.

Reaching Puebla toward evening, after a run of one hundred and sixteen miles, they were welcomed by the Governor and the local authorities, and were lodged in the Bishop's Palace—that prelate having gone to Rome to attend the Ecumenical Conference. The Palace was a spacious and stately structure, with long suites of apartments for the accommodation or entertainment of clerical visitors, as well as the keeping of valuable records and works of art. Some of the walls and ceilings had been frescoed by modern artists. One, containing the doorway to the Bishop's sleeping-room, had been painted (through some religious or artistic whim) in exact imitation of the entrance to a grated prison cell. It was said that Maximilian, who occupied the room on his last visit to Puebla, started back and shook his head with a melancholy smile on seeing this ominous presage.

Directly across the plaza was the great Cathedral, the largest and richest on the continent, and all around could be seen the towers and steeples of the churches and convents that attested the fidelity of Puebla to the ecclesiastical organization of which it had long been a stronghold. Besides these edifices, Puebla had other points of more modern interest, in its fortifications and battlefields, its buildings riddled and shattered by artillery during the war with the French. The victory won here by Zaragoza, on the 5th of May, has made the Cinco de Mayo a national holiday.

One day was devoted to an excursion to Tlascala—a city three centuries old. Here was the capital of the Indian republic whose people became the allies of Cortez, and aided him in his war on Montezuma's empire and the final conquest of Mexico. Many buildings are still standing which date back to the time of the conquest. Among them is the church built by the Spaniards in 1529—the first spot on the continent dedicated to Christian worship. The Governor of Tlascala and his staff met and welcomed Seward to the city, and taking him to the State Palace exhibited the antiquarian relics preserved with care— among them portraits of the "Conquistadores," and of the Tlascalan allied chieftains, ancient documents bearing their signatures, Aztec weapons and musical instruments then in use, and the royal banner unfurled by Cortez, faded and worn, but still nearly whole.

Another interesting trip was to Cholula, to visit the celebrated pyramid, whose origin was in some remote age before the days of historians. As the carriage approached the town, its people were seen gathering in the plaza; while a hundred church bells were chiming forth a welcome. Ascending to the top of the pyramid by the winding pathway, paved with lava, they found there the old Spanish church, standing on the ruins of the still older heathen temple devoted to human sacrifices.

The Prefecto and other authorities received Seward with addresses and a collation. One of the incidents of the feast was the appearance of a band of musicians, attired in the costumes and playing upon the ancient instruments the wild and plaintive melodies of their Aztec ancestors.

In his speech, Seward said:

"The scene around me seems like one to awaken momentary inspiration. I am on the steps of the Aztec Pyramid which is one of the most stupendous altars of human sacrifice ever erected to propitiate the Deity, in the ages when He was universally understood to be a God of vengeance. Around me lies that magnificent plain, where an imperial savage throne was brought down to the dust, and I am surrounded by Christian churches and altars.

"After a long contest with monarchial and imperial ambitions, the independence of the ancient Aztec race has been reconquered, without the loss of the Christian religion, and consolidated in a representative Federal Republic. Witnesses of towering majesty and impressive silence are looking down upon me—La Malinche, bewildering, because she is so indistinct, and the volcanoes of Popocatepetl, Ixtaccihuatl, and Orizaba, clad in their eternal vestments of snow, attest that nature remains unchangeable, and only men, nations, and races are subject to revolution."

Returned to Puebla the party were entertained at a banquet by Governor Romero y Vargas, at which forty or fifty guests were present. On the morning of the 23d they bade adieu. The Governor and his staff accompanied them as far as Tepeaca, where they stopped for breakfast. Then they proceeded on their way in a stage escorted by a detachment of the neatly uniformed Rural Guard of Puebla—the railway to Vera Cruz not being yet completed. It was fortunate for them that it was not, for then they would have missed the majestic scenery of Las Cumbres and Aculzingo, where the road descends from the temperate plateau above to the torrid plain below—six thousand feet—in ten miles. Gazing at the apparently illimitable prospect of mountains, cañons, cascades, precipices, and plains, a Californian remarked with a sigh, "Until today I thought that nothing could beat the Yosemite!"

They arrived at the quaint old city of Orizaba on Christmas eve. Horsemen and carriages were in waiting at the gates, city authorities with the ever-pleasant and welcome greeting, and a large and handsome house ready for occupancy. Ten days were spent in Orizaba, enlivened by the festivities of the Christmas season. Many usages and customs with which a devout race has surrounded it were new to the American travellers. Then there were fine old churches, handsome fruit gardens, and modern factories to be visited. Many localities were pointed out that had been the scenes of incidents of the French invasion, or of the war with the United States, crumbling fortifications, deserted camp grounds, and battered walls. The front of one church bore so many scars of battle, marks of bullets and of cannon balls, that inquiry was made "when that fierce fight occurred?" The bystander to whom the question was addressed shrugged his shoulders, and said he did not remember; "*Es costumbre del pais, señor.*" (It is the custom of the country, sir!)

Magnificent scenery surrounds Orizaba, whose prominent feature, everywhere visible, is the high, conical snow-capped peak which bears its name.

Leaving Orizaba on the 4th of January, they overtook and passed a procession peculiar to Mexico. This was a great *conducta*—a train of more than forty carts laden with thousands of dollars in specie, for export. Each cart was drawn by fourteen to eighteen mules, and the whole were guarded by a force of eight hundred government troops. The *conducta* halted and the soldiers presented arms as "the nation's guest" passed by.

The journey to Vera Cruz by way of Cordova was

through a wild and rocky region. The road passed through luxuriant tropical forests in its gradual descent to the coast. A short pause was made to look at the work on the Chiquihuite Pass—a gigantic piece of railway engineering.

Now they were in "Tierra Caliente," out of the region of grain fields, orchards, and magueys, and again among bananas, oranges, sugar plantations, and cane huts. At Paso del Macho, a train was in waiting; and in a few hours more they were in Vera Cruz. "Mr. Seward's house" was ready here also. This time it was one belonging to Mr. Schleiden, a merchant of Vera Cruz, and a brother of an old friend, formerly Minister at Washington from the Hanseatic cities. The Governor of the state of Vera Cruz, the Collector of the Port, and other federal and state officials, in full uniform, soon came to pay a visit of ceremony and tender a welcome.

Only one more week remained before departure. It was passed in rambles through the well-paved, substantial streets of Vera Cruz, visits to its historic spots, to its great Mole, and to the Castle of San Juan de Ulloa. One day was spent in penning farewell letters to the kind friends who had made the journey through the republic so memorable and enjoyable.

Besides the formal letter of thanks addressed to the Government, Seward wrote to President Juarez:

"But I could not think of leaving the country without making a more direct and unstudied acknowledgment of my profound sense of obligation to you for the attentions and hospitality with which you have received myself and family during our delightful sojourn in Mexico."

To Mr. Romero he wrote:

"It is not to renew my grateful acknowledgment that I write this parting letter, so much as it is to assure you of my profound sympathy with you in your arduous labours for the restoration of law, order, prosperity, and prestige in Mexico."

And to Mr. Bossero, the Government Commissioner who had accompanied him from Guadalajara, he expressed his thanks "for cares and attentions, which have not merely saved me from every danger and discomfort, but which have made the journey of my family and friends a constant instruction and continual pleasure."

There was no steamer from Vera Cruz proceeding directly to the United States, all the lines touching at Havana. As the change from a tropical to a northern climate in mid-winter was not desirable, Seward decided to spend a few weeks in Cuba, so as to reach home in the early spring. He embarked on the *Cleopatra*, Captain Phillips, on the afternoon of Tuesday, January 11th. Long after she had passed the Castle and out of the harbour, and had lost sight of the coast, the snowy crown of the Pico de Orizaba was glistening in the rays of the setting sun on the distant horizon. It was like a last glimpse of an old friend, and the party sat on deck in the evening watching it, and recalling their thousand-and-one pleasant memories of the journey through Mexico.

Napoleon III. and His Ministers. A Talk with M. Drouyn de l'Huys. It was after the close of our Civil War, the collapse of the Mexican Empire, and the fall of Napoleon III., that my father for the last time visited Paris. He had retired from office as Secretary of State, and had spent two years in travel. On his return from his journey round the world, he stopped in Paris to meet old friends, and to watch the growth of the young Republic. Mr. O'Sullivan, a resident there who had been connected with the American diplomatic service, describes an interview that took place between my father and M. Drouyn de l'Huys, who had been the Emperor's Minister of Foreign Affairs.   He writes:

"Knowing both these eminent men, remembering how, at the heads of the departments of foreign affairs of France and the United States, they had been pitted against each other under extraordinary and critical circumstances, and happening to visit them both on the same day, I thought they ought to come together, and mentioned it each to the other.

"'I should be most delighted to meet Mr. Seward,' said M. Drouyn de l'Huys; 'we have been opposed to each other, as athletes, but I preserve a great esteem and respect for him, and I know that he has always spoken kindly of me.   Moreover I have not forgotten some excellent cigars which he did me the agreeable honour of sending to me.'

"'M. Drouyn de l' Huys,' said Mr. Seward on the other hand, 'why, I was but yesterday thinking of how to find him and call upon him.'

"It is not therefore wonderful that the next day Mr. Seward and I alighted at the door of M. Drouyn de l'Huys, after a pleasant drive up the Champs Élysées. They met with the utmost cordiality, and manifest pleasure reflected from each countenance.   Mr. Seward explained that he, unfortunately, could not grasp and shake the hand held out to him, as he once could have done.   M. Drouyn de l' Huys is a tall, large, and powerful man, not much if at all beyond sixty, with a massive head and open countenance, a very English general appearance, a very kindly as well as intellectual expression, and manners at once cordial, frank, and simple.   He speaks English quite well.

"I need not describe Mr. Seward, with the sad traces of his cruel wounds on his face, and his arms rendered helpless: but with the same bright gleam under his bushy eyebrows, the same hearty laugh at a good point of his own or anybody else's, and the same continuous flow of bold and pleasant talk, as of old, in his better—no, not his better—but his younger days.

"I must do him the justice to say that he occupied a good three-fourths of the conversation, while neither M. Drouyn de l'Huys nor I myself could have wished it otherwise.

"An interview of about an hour and a half, in which the conversation ranged far and wide, on topics embracing politics as well as geography, no stenographer present, no notes taken, and myself the only third person present (you will forgive to my Irish origin the implication that there might be more than one 'third person'), I myself too much under the charm of the talk to think of fixing it in my recollection for narrative—how can I give you much of an account of it? But I will do my best.

"It began on the topic of his travels. I believe I started it by remarking that he was probably the only man to whom it had ever occurred, since the world was made, to have been so nearly killed by being thrown from a carriage; then, while lying helpless, to have been left for dead under the stabs of a powerful assassin; and then with advanced years superadded to all that, and strength greatly impaired by the consequences of his injuries, to have made the circuit of the globe, which he would have accomplished, as soon as he had got back home from his present journey.

"This led Mr. Seward to give an interesting account of what he had done. After his eight years of direction of the foreign affairs of his own country, he had a desire to visit the different nations with whom or about whom he had had, in various ways, to deal.

"He first went to Alaska, which he had bought from Russia with a view to marking the whole hemisphere as properly belonging to the American system up to the North Pole.

"Then he went to Mexico, whose struggle against imperialism had furnished one of the gravest questions of his term of administration.

"Then to Cuba which is a chronic source of diplomatic questions for the American Government.

"On this second journey, the present one, he took in Japan, China, India and Egypt, and now Europe.

"From Paris he was going to Berlin, and thence home by way of London.

"It had been a matter of great interest to him to meet many men with whom he had had more or less dealing as Secretary of State: the ministers as well as the sovereigns, with whom he had discussed international questions on behalf of his Government. He had paid a very pleasant visit to Lord Napier, formerly at Washington, now Governor of Madras; Lord Lyons, formerly at Washington, now British Ambassador at Paris. Another of his old friends he had great pleasure in meeting was Henri Mercier, formerly French Minister to the United States during the Mexican imbroglio, a loyal adherent to the Imperial dynasty, always cordial and friendly in his good wishes for the United States.

"M. Drouyn de l'Huys asked: 'Can you tell me anything recent about Signor Bertinatti, formerly Italian Minister at Washington, who was once a confidential and private ambassador from me to you at a grave emergency in our diplomatic intercourse?'

"Mr. Seward answered: 'Oh, yes, he is just as true and earnest and sympathetic as he was then. He is now Italian Minister at The Hague, where he writes he has just been fitting a house to receive me. I regret very much that I am unable to see him.'

"'By the way, those confidential missions formed a

very important feature in the intercourse between our governments. I early learned that the Emperor liked that way of doing business, better than the ordinary diplomatic channel. He sent several confidential messages to me by persons outside of your department. But I always made it a point that our confidential replies should pass through the hands of the Minister of Foreign Affairs. I was unwilling to be a party in keeping a secret from him.'

"The conversation then turned upon Mr. Seward's former acquaintance with the Emperor and his visit to Paris in 1859. M. Drouyn de l'Huys asked: 'What opinions did you form of the persons you met here then?'

"'Of Walewski, that he was a minister who was not possessed of the Emperor's entire confidence. Of the Empress, that she was an amiable woman, whose influence was exaggerated. Of the Emperor, that he was a man of eminent talents and sagacity; that he desired to promote social progress in France; and that he was bolder in social reform than I had anticipated from the manner in which he reached the throne.'

"'What do you think of him now?'

"'I do not allow myself, if I can avoid it, to judge statesmen any more than generals on the mere ground of their success. I was astonished when I saw the Emperor afterwards balancing so closely between the United States Government and the Rebellion, and finally throwing his sword into the scale, by his expedition to Mexico. I had seen him when he was in exile in the United States; he talked with me at Compiègne about his visit there. I could not believe it possible that a European statesman who had visited the United States would fail to see that the combination of the States was impregnable, and that the American continent should never again be the theatre of European aggression or invasion.'

"'Then you were disappointed?'

"'Yes, but hardly more so with the position taken by the Emperor than with the position which the British Government at first assumed. I told Lord Lyons yesterday, half seriously, that the three most impudent men in history are Hernando Cortez, himself and Henri Mercier: Hernando Cortez when he proposed to Montezuma that he should leave his palace, and become the hostage in Cortez's headquarters for the preservation of peace; Lord Lyons and Mercier, when, under instructions, they came together to the Department of State to announce an agreement between the British Government and the Emperor as to the course they should jointly pursue in regard to the American question. I told them that the United States were bound to hear any respectful message from either of those governments separately, but they were not bound to receive communications from those states conjointly. The two ministers assented and withdrew; and each afterwards returned, with a message from his own government, without referring to the action of the other.'

"Perhaps," suggested Mr. O'Sullivan, "you overestimated the personal capacity of the late Emperor, and that at the bottom of the Mexican expedition there were influences and motives which did not appear on the surface. M. Drouyn de l'Huys, though in the ministry during the period, where he had to treat with you the questions growing out of it, was not in it at the undertaking of the Mexican expedition, to which he had always been opposed."

M. Drouyn de l'Huys confirmed this. He said that all had been settled, the attack on Puebla made, and the engagement with Maximilian taken before he (M. Drouyn de l'Huys) came in. He added this was not the only mistake and disaster for which he was not responsible, but which he was called upon to meet, and to do the best possible for his country in a situation created by others.

Mr. Seward replied: "I can well understand this now, though I did not then. From the time of Joseph in the Court of Pharaoh, until now, it has been the hard task of a prime minister to give up all the merits of his own opinions to his chief, and to bear himself the responsibilities of all the chief's errors.

"It is the necessary condition of ministerial service. I was always adverse to that service. But in the most critical hour we ever had, my country demanded that service of me, and would accept no other. It was rendered with a full knowledge of the conditions attached. The minister's reward for such misapprehensions is to be found in the approbation of his own conscience."

Mr. O'Sullivan remarked: "M. Drouyn de l'Huys had left the ministry before the final arrangement was made for the evacuation of Mexico by the French army. He, I presume, is as desirous as I am, to elicit your version of that transaction. The world thought that you might have been a little less rough with France, at the very end,— than you were, in hurrying them out so very peremptorily."

Mr. Seward answered: "Of course the world did not know the exact situation. It taxed all the confidence which the people of the United States had in me, when I consented to take the Emperor's stipulation to withdraw the French army from Mexico in three instalments, in November, March, and the November following.

"They said the stipulation on his part was perfidious. I knew better. I knew that the Emperor had every motive to be sincere, and I trusted him; at the same time I thought that the withdrawal would necessarily be made all at once, and earlier than he had promised to complete it. As the time approached for the withdrawal of the first instalment, the Emperor found, as I had apprehended he would, that military exigencies would prevent the execution of the plan of evacuation by instalments.

"The Marquis de Montholon approached me early in the season, for the purpose of sounding me upon a proposition to delay the November evacuation. Conscious of the difficulty existing on our side, I repelled his suggestion with so much decision that he forbore from presenting me the communication from his Government, in which the proposition was made.

"At a later day he came to read to me the communication from his Government, in which it was stated that the Emperor would not withdraw a portion of the troops in November, but would withdraw the whole in the spring. When this communication was received, the session of Congress was near at hand. It was sure to be unsatisfactory to them and to the people. Our Civil War was at an end. General Grant, with the Mexican Legation urging him on one side, and a powerful party in Congress on the other, was inclined to send an army into Mexico to expel the French. I knew this was unnecessary. I knew it was easier to send an American army into Mexico than it was to get it out again. My understanding of the Monroe Doctrine is, that the United States shall maintain American republics against monarchial intervention, but not absorb them by fraud or force. I therefore hurried off a strong dispatch by telegraph to be read to the Emperor, which would arouse him to the necessity of giving us a guaranty for the execution of his project."

"Ah," said Mr. O'Sullivan, "that was the famous cable dispatch of two thousand words, I suppose."

"Yes," replied Mr. Seward, "it contained seven hundred and fifty words, but the telegraphic cipher at that time had a faculty of multiplying signs, so that I think it was given out by some of the telegraph people that it contained ten thousand words. Mr. Bigelow intimated the earnest character of the dispatch to M. Lavalette, then Minister of Foreign Affairs. The Emperor declined to hear it read, but gave the guaranties which the dispatch required, so the transaction was satisfactorily closed, without offence on either side.

"It was a pleasant experience in Mexico, to receive the thanks of the President and his ministers for my agency in procuring the withdrawal of the French army without sending the United States force to expel it."

Many were the exclamations and expressions of interest and sympathy which M. Drouyn de l'Huys made in reply to the brief account which, at his request, Mr. Seward gave of the fearful events of the assassination night at Washington.

Mr. Seward said that it had been a subject of some amusement to him, to note the European reverberations of the telegraphic accounts of that night. "At the moment when it occurred, India was rapidly coming to replace the United States in supplying the world with cotton. At Bombay they showed me two telegrams. The first was, 'London, April 15th, Lincoln shot, Seward murdered.' The next one was, 'London, April 16th, Lincoln dead. Seward not dead. Cotton a shade better.'

M. Drouyn de l'Huys expressed a hope that he might some time be able to visit the United States.

Mr. Seward said: "You must come while I am there to receive you; come while I am alive."

"Oh," answered M. Drouyn de l'Huys, "no fear of that, after all you have gone through without its preventing you from making a tour of the globe. I do not see what could ever kill you, until you may choose to die of your own accord, after all the rest of us."

And so they parted, as genially as they had met.

1869, etc.

Retirement to the Country. After my father's death, the next few years were largely devoted to gathering his correspondence, and writing the memoir of his life.

This work was partly done at his old homestead in Auburn, and partly at our new home, which I had purchased, on the banks of the Hudson River. It was a rough, uncultivated piece of ground, hardly fit for farm purposes, but possessing a fine prospect and the possibilities of natural beauty that might be developed and improved.

There was a plain substantial brick house, which would serve for a residence. My family were installed in it, and we began the operations of gardening and cultivation.

There was ample leisure for literary work, plenty of fresh air and exercise, and notable peace and quiet. Here we have lived ever since, except for the periods devoted to travel, or the exigencies of public life, when I was called to Albany or Washington or New York.

1875.

Legislative Life. In 1874 the Republicans of one of the New York City districts invited me to become their candidate for the Assembly. I was elected, and in consequence found it necessary to take up my residence in Albany again, for the winter. I rented a furnished house, very near what had once been the site of the Pearl Street Academy, where I had spent my early school days.

It was fifteen years since I had formerly resided in Albany, but the old town seemed much like home. It had grown considerably to the north, south, and westward —but its general aspect was the same. Many old landmarks were still standing, though surrounded by many new residences and places of business. The "Governor's

Mansion" of my boyish memories was gone. The historic home of the old Patroons, the "Van Rensselaer Mansion," was standing, but no longer occupied by the family. The "Schuyler Mansion" of revolutionary fame had been turned into a public institution. New churches had been erected in various parts of the city, for the use of their old congregations. The old freestone Capitol still stood on State Street Hill, though showing many signs of age and premonitions of its approaching end.

Under the astute and able management of Governor Tilden, "the Democrats had swept the State," and the Republicans were in a minority in the Legislature. But the Assembly still retained some of its veteran leaders, among them Lieutenant-Governor Alvord, ex-Speaker Husted, and L. Bradford Prince.

Shall I confess that the issues presented for our consideration seemed to me, at first, comparatively trivial, and unimportant? Certainly they did not awaken such enthusiasm in their favour, or such rancour and bitterness among their opponents, as I had been accustomed to at Washington. Yet there were some questions among them that were of high importance to the welfare of the State.

As the work of the session went on, I found that, although belonging to the minority, I received my full share of consideration. I was listened to with courtesy, though voted down on all partisan questions. Whenever I clearly demonstrated that a measure was undoubtedly for the public good, I found no difficulty in obtaining support for it. Speaker McGuire appointed me on various committees—I think eleven or twelve in all.

Among the measures of chief importance at this time were "rapid transit" in the city of New York, canal investigation and reforms, and amendments to the Constitution. I introduced two Constitutional Amendments, providing for a Superintendent of Prisons and a Superintendent of Public Works, which were afterwards adopted. I introduced also the bill for the construction of the Ninth Avenue Elevated Railroad, which was the first experiment in the way of "rapid transit." So it fell to me also to be one of the spokesmen in behalf of the advocates of the reduction of canal tolls, of the Society for the Prevention of Cruelty to Children, and of other measures, for the improvement of the Banking System, and the adoption of general laws instead of specific charters.

The Legislature supported the policy of Governor Tilden in regard to the investigations of canal frauds, and the amendments to the New York City Charter. It also elected Francis Kernan to be United States Senator, in place of Governor Morgan, and extended an honorary welcome to William C. Bryant, and passed a flood of bills of minor and local interest.

In the fall, the Republican State Convention nominated me for Secretary of State, and named several veteran Republicans as candidates for other State offices; among them Francis E. Spinner, whose signature as United States Treasurer was so well known throughout the Civil War. In the election, however, we were unsuccessful; the Democrats again carrying the State, though by a reduced majority.

1877.

A Puzzled Potentate. When the head of a government is changed, it is the custom for every diplomatic representative to wait upon the sovereign to whom he is accredited, and formally announce the fact. In accordance with this usage, our representative at the Court of one of the Barbary Powers formally announced to his Highness the Bey the accession of Rutherford B. Hayes to the Presidency of the United States.

When the formal ceremony was over the Bey signified he would like to have a little private conversation with the minister. Said he:

"What has become of General Grant?"

"He retires from his position to give place to Mr. Hayes."

"Was the fighting bloody, or long continued? Was Washington captured?"

"Oh! no, your Majesty. All was peaceable and conducted in order."

"And what proportion of the army does General Grant take with him? And what part of the public treasure is allotted to him?"

"None at all, your Majesty; General Grant simply becomes a private citizen."

"How," exclaimed the Bey, "a private citizen! Why, we have been hearing for years that this General Grant was one of the greatest military commanders of the age. And now it seems he has surrendered his Capitol, abandoned his army, and given up his revenues to his successor —all without even striking a blow. Allah il allah! God is great, but this is incomprehensible!"

The Vice-President of the Confederacy. Alexander H. Stephens was a prominent and dramatic figure in Congress, in the early days of the Hayes Administration. He was back in his old position as a Democratic leader in the House of Representatives, as before the War. But age and illness had overtaken him. He could not rise from his seat to address the Speaker. When he wished to speak, his invalid chair was wheeled down the aisle to the open space in front of the Clerk's desk, and, as he sat there, his emphatic, but shrill and enfeebled voice was listened to with marked attention by a House that seldom listened to any one else.

The Democrats had a strong majority, and many of them were inclined to oppose the President, and even to refuse appropriations for his administration, on the ground that Tilden instead of Hayes should have been in the Presidential chair.

At the instance of Secretary Evarts, I had been recalled to my old position of Assistant Secretary of State, and met again in the Department many of those whom I had left there eight years before.

One morning a message was brought me that Mr. Stephens would like to have a call from me at his rooms, where he was ill in bed.

I went down to the hotel and found him propped up in bed with pillows, and attended by a nurse. It was an attenuated form, with emaciated face. In a voice hardly above a whisper, he said: "I have something to say to you, Mr. Seward, which perhaps may be of importance, and I hoped to say it today. But I find myself too weak. I shall be stronger in a day or two, and then I would like to come up to your rooms, if you will arrange for a private interview with me there."

Of course, I promised. A few days later he was brought to the Department. I shut out all other visitors, and his wheeled chair, brought up in the elevator, was rolled into my room by a stout black man. A tall young Georgian whom I took to be his secretary attended him. To him Mr. Stephens said: "You may go now. I shall not need you any longer."

The young man bowed and retired. The black man, however, remained sitting calmly and placidly on the sofa. Looking toward him, I said, "Don't you wish him to go too?"

Mr. Stephens looked up in surprise. "That,—oh, that is George. He is always with me. I've no secrets from George."

28

So George stayed through the interview; but apparently took very little interest in it.

After a little chat over the old times before the war, when he and my father were so long at opposite ends of the Capitol, and on opposite sides of political questions, he said, in substance:

"Though always sharing in the opinions of my section, I was not in favour of disunion. When secession was first talked of, I opposed it. But I found there was no use in resisting what had become the general feeling of our people, and when my State seceded, I acquiesced in the situation. Later I accepted the place of Vice-President of the Confederacy, partly in the hope of mitigating the horrors of the war, which had become inevitable, and of ending it, whenever that could be done with honour, and with due regard to the interests of the South.

"Your father and I did not see each other again until we met in the Fortress Monroe Conference, where he with Mr. Lincoln, and I with my colleagues, made an unavailing attempt to agree on terms of peace."

Continuing, he remarked that these were now all matters of past history. Recanting none of his past opinions, which were carefully set forth in his books, he remained a Southerner and a Democrat. But he now was once more a Representative in the Congress of the United States. He purposed to accept and faithfully discharge the duties and responsibilities of that position. And so he added, "I expect and desire to die a Union man."

Then he went on to say that he should not be a supporter of the administration, and should oppose any measure that seemed to him merely Republican and partisan. But he should countenance no unpatriotic refusal to vote for measures that were for the true interests of the country and the public welfare. He should advise his colleagues not to deny or oppose any just and proper appropriations needed for the maintenance of the Government at home, and to uphold its interests and prestige abroad.

"It seemed to me that I must say this to somebody. I could not go to the White House and say it to the President without exciting talk and perhaps provoking newspaper controversy. The members of his Cabinet I have no personal acquaintance with. But I can talk with you, on the score of old acquaintance, and what I say you are at liberty to repeat to them."

The conversation was somewhat long, as he expressed himself more clearly and emphatically on these points, in more detail.

Of course the President and Cabinet were gratified to know of his views and his proposed course of action. So far as I am aware, he faithfully adhered to it during his term in Congress.

I did not see him again. His call at the State Department seemed to excite no outside remark, as many of the leading ex-Confederates—Gordon, Lamar, King, Trescott, and others—were frequent visitors at my rooms to discuss questions of foreign policy or candidates for foreign positions.

1877.

The Recognition of Porfirio Diaz. Among the diplomatic questions awaiting decision by the new administration of President Hayes, was one about which I was supposed to be especially qualified by past experience to speak. This was our policy in reference to Mexico. Of course I was familiar with all the events of the rise and fall of the French invasion, and Maximilian's Empire, and the restoration of the Republicans to power there.

When I was in Mexico with my father in 1869, we found a peaceable and grateful Republic under the benign ad-

ministration of our old friend Benito Juarez, with Lerdo as
Vice-President and Romero as Secretary of the Treasury.
We had fondly imagined that Mexico had now entered
upon a new era in her troublous history, and that constitutional Presidents, in due course of election, would
succeed each other there, as in the United States.

But in the intervening eight years President Juarez had
died. His successor, Lerdo, was driven from power; and
the Presidency had been grasped by Porfirio Diaz, whom
we had known as an able and patriotic general and presumably a supporter of the constitutional order of things.

Now he appeared in the unwelcome character of a
disturber of the public peace and a usurper of the Presidential office by revolution. We were assured that the
Mexicans approved of him, and would not, at all events,
resist his accession to supreme power.

It fell to me, therefore, to outline the policy of the
United States in regard to Mexico, as well as in reference
to other Spanish-American Republics. The rules thus
laid down have been followed ever since by the Government of the United States. In an instruction to Mr.
Foster, I wrote:

"It is the custom to accept and recognize the results of
a popular choice in Mexico, and not to scrutinize closely
the regularity or irregularity of the methods by which
Presidents are inaugurated. In the present case the
Government waits before recognizing General Diaz as
the President of Mexico, until it shall be assured that his
election is approved by the Mexican people, and that his
administration is possessed of stability to endure and a
disposition to comply with the rules of international
comity and the obligations of treaties. Such recognition,
if accorded, would imply something more than a mere
formal assent. It would imply a belief that the Government so recognized will faithfully execute its duties and

observe the spirit of its treaties. The recognition of a President in Mexico by the United States has an important moral influence which is appreciated at the capital of that Republic."

The recognition of President Diaz was therefore deferred for some months, and meanwhile he gave assurance that the treaty obligations of Mexico to the United States would be faithfully observed by him. The Mexican people also sanctioned his choice by a regular election.

He then entered upon that long career of over thirty years, in which, by successive elections, he remained the ruler of Mexico, with the consent of his people, maintaining her peace, developing her resources, and adding to her prosperity.

1877.

The Story of Samoa. One morning in 1877, while sitting at my desk in the Department of State, I was informed that two gentlemen "from some Pacific Islands" desired to see me. On entering, they introduced themselves. One was an American merchant, who had been engaged in business at Apia Harbour. The other was a tall, fine-looking, swarthy-complexioned man, in ordinary American dress, who proved to be the Secretary of State and Minister of Foreign Affairs of the Samoan Islands.

He spoke English easily and fluently, but with some quaint idioms that seemed to render it more impressive. When I asked how he had learned it, he told me that he was taught by the missionaries. Schools and text-books not being available, his chief book for study of the language had been the Bible.

His credentials proved to be all in proper form, and as the business which brought him to Washington was so important it had been deemed wise that he should come on himself, instead of entrusting it to any diplomatic or consular representative, I duly presented him to the Secretary of State, Mr. Evarts, and to President Hayes, and I was authorized to discuss matters with him on the part of our Government.

With the increase of intercourse and trade, the Samoan Islanders had perceived that they might become the object of some intrigue, or perhaps fall under the sway of some one of the maritime powers of Europe, whom they would be powerless to resist. Doubtful of their ability to maintain peaceful and stable existence, they wished the United States to recognize and protect their independence, to establish commercial relations with their people, and to assist them in their steps toward regulated and responsible government.

In short, his mission was nothing less than to ask that they might come under the flag of the United States, and become a part of our extended dominion, either by formal annexation or under a protectorate, in such form as the American Government might prefer.

Having seen Pacific islands, one after another, eagerly seized upon by some European power, and having no wish to become subjects of any such power, they had decided to offer their islands to the United States. Of course they hardly anticipated that there would be any hesitation on our part in accepting such an offer.

I explained that, while the American people had in former years been willing and desirous of extending their national domain on the continent, yet there had now come a decided change in public opinion. Extension of the national boundaries was now looked upon with disfavour.

Especially was there a strong opposition to the acquisition of any islands, near or remote, inhabited by any race but our own. The proposed treaties for naval harbours in the West Indies, and for the acquisition of St. Thomas,

Santa Cruz, and Santo Domingo, had been shelved or summarily rejected. Even the Panama Canal had been allowed to pass into the hands of a European power; and the purchase of Alaska was still a subject of reproach and ridicule, and pronounced a gigantic folly.

Having had a hand myself in the negotiation of these treaties, I could foresee the difficulties in the way of the mission he had undertaken. Of course I believed this dread of national expansion was a passing phase and an unreasonable and unnatural one. But, while it lasted, it had to be reckoned with.

The Samoan proposals were laid before Secretary Evarts, and by him laid before the President and Cabinet. Both President Hayes and Mr. Evarts believed that my father's policy in this regard had been wise and judicious. But they saw also that it would now encounter the same opposition that it had during the administration of President Johnson and subsequently under that of President Grant.

The Navy Department warmly favoured the Samoan proposition, as it had always desired the establishment of naval outposts in the Pacific. In fact, tentative steps had already been taken by naval officers for obtaining a port in the Islands for coaling and repairs.

The leading members of the Foreign Affairs Committees in Congress, and the leading Republicans in both Houses were sounded. There were differences of opinion among them, but practically all were agreed that the times were inauspicious for the consideration of any such project. The Senate would not consent to any treaty that involved expense or obligation, and the House, in which there was an anti-Administration majority, would vote it down as a matter of course. It seemed to be considered a mark of patriotism to oppose any addition to our own country.

The Samoan Envoy listened gravely and sadly to the

recital of these adverse conditions. Finally, he said that
I might draw up the treaty in any form I thought best,
and he believed his people would agree. They would give
us their best harbour, that of Pago-Pago, which fortunately was as yet unoccupied, and in return would ask
nothing, except our assurances of peace and friendship.

I drafted a treaty, and then another and yet another,
endeavouring to meet the various Congressional and
popular objections. It seemed as if the Senate might be
induced to consent to the acceptance of a harbour, provided
the country was not to pay anything for it, or even to
agree to protect or defend it.

So, at last, the treaty was put into that form. Even the
phrases tendering our good offices in case of disputes
with other powers were objected to, but were finally
allowed to stand. The treaty was signed and sealed by
the Secretary and Mr. Mamea, the Samoan Envoy. It
was sent to the Senate, and in due time was confirmed.

The press and the public seemed to regard the matter
with indifference, and the House refused any appropriation for a coal yard for Pago-Pago, which remained
deserted and unused.

The Diplomatic Corps of course took note of the
Samoan affair. Some of them were amused and others
puzzled by it. For a nation of "landgrabbers" as we were
called in Europe, we seemed to be very slow and reluctant
to take steps for our own aggrandizement.

When I mentioned to the British Minister, Sir Edward
Thornton, that the Samoans might perhaps ask Queen
Victoria for a protectorate, in case their negotiations with
us should fail, he smiled and said, "Well, I suppose we
should take them, but I do not think we should care to
enter into any quarrel about it."

A few months later, Dr. von Schlozer, the German
Minister, came into my room in very cheerful mood.

"Aha!" said he. "Also we have a harbour in Samoa. Not the best—no, you have the best. You have Pago-Pago. But we have the next best."

"What one have you, mein Herr?"

"Apia—Apia Harbour. It is a good harbour. It is where the people are, and the trade. We shall use our harbour now. You do not use yours—no. But you will, some day. Some day, you will."

And in so saying the cheery Envoy proved himself a prophet.

A Night Move against a Mob. It was in the summer of 1877. Washington was sweltering in the heats of July. The dry and dusty streets were deserted by all who were not obliged to face the blazing sunshine. Congress and the Courts were gone. Officers of the Departments were having their usual summer vacations. President Hayes was living out at the Soldiers' Home. The Secretary of State, Mr. Evarts, was up at his country place, at Windsor, Vermont, and I, as Acting Secretary, was in charge of the Department of State. The Secretary of War, Mr. Mc-Creery, was out in Iowa, and the Adjutant-General was in charge of the War Department.

Four o'clock in the afternoon was at hand, and the clerks were putting up their papers and locking up their desks,—when a messenger came over from the War Department. Sudden and disquieting news was coming in by telegraph, requiring immediate conference between the Acting Secretaries of State and War.

The conference was held at once; and we found ourselves confronted with a serious situation. There had been some weeks of railroad troubles, growing out of the business depression, and augmented by the lack of harmony between their managers, a war of rates, and hasty and sweeping reduction of wages. Strikes and riots had resulted, beginning in Maryland, and spreading to Pennsylvania.

Now had come information that the troubles had culminated in riots o grave proportions in Pittsburg. Merchants, mechanics, the local press, and many citizens, having their own reasons for discontent, had, at the outset, largely given their sympathies to the strikers. But they speedily found they were rousing a power they could not control. Crowds of the unemployed thronged to the scene of disturbance "to aid the strikers." Thieves, criminals, and lawless outcasts saw their opportunity to pursue their nefarious plundering, while posing as "friends of the working man," and loudly proclaiming a "war of Labour against Capital." A hundred thousand men were said to be involved in it. Trains were stopped. Business was paralysed. Riot, arson, murder, and pillage had begun. Affairs in Pittsburg were rapidly assuming the shape of anarchy. The police were inadequate. The civil authorities were powerless. The State soldiery were more or less disaffected, many of them fraternizing with the rioters. Peaceable citizens were helpless. The Governor was out of the State travelling at the West. His Adjutant-General was sending militia from Philadelphia, but it was said they would be overborne, or join the mob. As one of the organs of the strike sympathizers exultingly declared, "The Lexington of the Labour Conflict is at hand!"

The Governor, hastening homeward, had telegraphed to Washington for aid from the General Government. No other power could stop the destruction of life and property at Pittsburg but "Uncle Sam." And "Uncle Sam's" hands were tied!

The promoters of the "Labour War" had laid their plans with shrewdness and cunning. They had taken advantage of the political situation. Congress had adjourned in March without passing the Army Appropriation bill,—so the soldiers would be left without pay. Furthermore, the stringent legislation adopted at the instance of the Southern States had provided that no United States troops should be moved into any State until after a formal request for them should be made by the Governor, and not then until after the President had issued his proclamation, calling upon the disorderly elements to desist and return to their homes "within twenty days." So it looked to the Pittsburgers as if their city was likely to be at the mercy of the rioters for at least three weeks. And it looked so to the rioters too! With the Federal troops kept out, the mob would have full sway.

The General Government practically had no Army available. There were no United States troops anywhere within reach, that would be at all adequate to cope with any formidable force. There were a few scattered garrisons at Carlisle Barracks, Cleveland, Philadelphia, and elsewhere, from which squads or detachments might be drawn. But that was all. And there was no time to lose.

We summoned our clerks back to their desks, and prepared for a night's work. The Acting Secretary of War answered the Governor of Pennsylvania, by advising him to make his formal request for troops at once, and to make it by telegraph. He instructed the commanders of the different garrisons to equip detachments, and hold them in readiness to move at daybreak.

Meanwhile I sat down at my desk to prepare the necessary Proclamation for the President to issue, and sent a messenger out to the Soldiers' Home, to ask President Hayes not to retire until it should come to him for his signature. Then I sent over to "Newspaper Row," to invite the correspondents of the leading journals to assemble at the State Department at midnight, as there would be important news, which their papers would desire to put in their morning editions.

The whole military force that we could muster would be but inconsiderable. But there was a potent moral influence on which we thought we could rely. That was the latent patriotism of the people. Ever since the close of our Civil War, profound respect and even reverence had been shown for the National flag and the National authority. There was no one now, who would willingly care to fire on the "Stars and Stripes," or to lift his hand in open conflict with the "Boys in Blue." Even the mail waggons of "Uncle Sam" were not molested by the rioters. So we determined that "Old Glory" should wave in Pittsburg streets, even if borne there by only a corporal's guard, and that the country should see whether it was respected or defied.

Everything was done with dispatch. When midnight arrived, our responses had all been received, and our documents were ready. Our messenger had found the President reclining on his lounge, awaiting the proclamation. He had read, approved, and signed it. The seal and attestation were appended. The Governor's call for troops had been received, acknowledged, and filed. The commanders of the troops reported their men in readiness to move at daybreak. The newspaper offices would hold back their presses, if need be, for the proclamation. The correspondents had assembled and had been furnished with the copies prepared for them, and with information of the "movements of troops."

Next morning, at their breakfast tables, the people of Washington, Baltimore, New York, Philadelphia, Harrisburg, and Pittsburg read in their newspapers the proclamation of the President, and the news that the United States Army was on its way to Pittsburg, and that its advance-guard would reach there early in the day.

The leaders of the rioters now held their hurried consultations. Only a few squads of United States soldiers would arrive, but resistance of these involved a principle, and would mean a struggle thenceforward with the whole civil and military power of the United States. They decided that discretion was the better part of valour, and that rioters' proceedings should be postponed to a more favourable time. Pittsburg subsided at once into the quiet suitable to a summer's morning in a loyal town, even before the "advance-guard" arrived.

A day or two later, President and Cabinet reassembled around the Cabinet council table at the White House and took the situation in charge. General Hancock was summoned to command, and authorized to use the whole Division of the Atlantic to restore law and order. When he arrived, with his little force of six hundred "Regulars," they were as welcome in Pittsburg as the first regiments of volunteers had been in Washington in 1861. Peace prevailed at once. Rioters dispersed, and criminals slunk to their hiding places. Strikers returned to duty, and business was resumed as usual.

1877.

The Outcome of a Fugitive Slave Case. Attorney-General Devens came into my room one day and said, "Do you remember the case of 'Thomas Sims' in Boston?"

"Of course," said I. "Wasn't that the one that stirred Boston so greatly? When chains were said to have been put around the State House and Faneuil Hall, and the church bells tolled as for a funeral, while they were taking the fugitive under military escort down to the wharf—amid the execrations and curses of the mob?"

"Yes," said he, "that was the one, and I was the marshal of the United States Court at that time. Much as I disliked the law, I considered it my official duty to execute it, in spite of the resistance of the mob. I sent 'Sims' off in charge of his owner. But I determined then to keep track of him, and to see if I could not get him released from slavery.

"I found the place where he was taken, and raised the money to buy his freedom. When Mrs. Lydia Maria Child proposed to raise a similar fund, I wrote her a letter requesting her to return the sum she had collected for that purpose and that she allow me the privilege of paying the whole sum myself. But our efforts were fruitless, and the owner refused the offer.

"Then the war came on and I went into it, as you may remember, in '61."

"Yes," said I, "you entered as a Major of Massachusetts Rifles and ended as a Major-General in command of a Corps in '64, at Richmond."

"Well," said he, "the war and the Emancipation Proclamation liberated 'Sims'—and when you call to see me at the Attorney-General's office, you will find him on duty there."

I did so and found the celebrated ex-slave smiling and respectful, and highly pleased with his position under the United States Government.

I told General Devens that my recollections went even farther back than his—that I happened to be in the Senate chamber when Senator Mason rose in his place, next to John C. Calhoun, and read the provisions of the Fugitive Slave Law that he was about to offer. They were so drastic and vindictive, with pains and penalties, in commanding every man and woman in the North to become slave catchers, that I wondered at them.

I was then only a law student, and I wondered that a grave Senator of the United States should not foresee that such an enactment would goad people to frenzy, and precipitate the very evils of disunion and civil war which

FREDERICK W. SEWARD'S RESIDENCE AT MONTROSE-ON-THE-HUDSON, NEW YORK

he professed to dread—for Mason, at that time, was not an avowed disunionist. I was then an ardent Whig, but three years later I saw the collapse of the Whig Party, which, as a cynical critic remarked, "died of an attempt to swallow the Fugitive Slave Law."

1879.

Country Life.   When I retired from office in 1879, my house in Washington was taken by the Swedish Government for its Legation. The Swedish Minister, Count Leuwenhaupt, was calling to see me.

"And so you are expecting to go to live in the country, Mr. Seward? What will you do in the country?"

"Oh, I don't know. Raise cabbages, probably."

"Ah, yes,—that is the conventional phrase—raising cabbages. It reminds me of our Queen of Sweden. One day, she said to her ladies-in-waiting: 'Oh, I am so sick and tired of these endless formalities and ceremonies of Court life! I think sometimes I would like to go to live in the country and raise cabbages.'

"But, your Majesty," said one of the ladies, "is it not sometimes lonesome,—this living in the country, and raising cabbages?"

"'No, indeed,' said the Queen; 'whoever has energy and independence enough to go to live in the country and raise cabbages,—can always find somebody to come and eat them.'"

1881.

President Arthur and the Yorktown Centennial.   Among the long line of Sophomores, which we Freshmen were eagerly scanning on our first morning in the College Chapel at Schenectady in 1845, my attention was drawn to a tall fine-looking young man directly opposite. On inquiring who he was, I was told that he was Chester A. Arthur, the son of a clergyman. He had diligently prepared for

college, and had eked out his scanty funds for the purpose
by teaching school at the same time. We became acquainted, and, having many tastes in common, became
members of the same college society.

Arthur was a popular class-man of pleasing address,
fond of a joke, but a creditable student, and was especially
active in college "politics," as we used to call our contests
for elections. Three years were spent together at Union.
He graduated in 1848, and then we drifted apart to different places of residence. But I occasionally heard from
him, first as a law-student, then as a successful lawyer in
New York, and then as the head of his firm. And always
as an active Republican.

One evening in 1860, just before his inauguration,
Governor Morgan called at Mr. Weed's to consult him
about the composition of his Military Staff, and desired
to offer me a position on it. While I declined the honour
for myself, I was glad to perceive that he had on his list
the name of my former college friend, Arthur. He was
to be Quartermaster-General.

It was supposed that in time of peace this would be
merely an honorary appointment. But with the outbreak of the Civil War, soon afterwards, it became a
highly important position, and General Arthur's services
were invaluable in forwarding troops to the front, and in
providing for their needs.

After the war, when General Grant appointed Arthur
to be Collector of the Port of New York, the appointment
was generally regarded with favour. He occupied the
post for about six years.

It is needless to recount here the discords which subsequently arose in the Republican Party,—the unsuccessful attempt to renominate General Grant for a third time,
and the Compromise in 1880 by which Garfield was
nominated for President, with Arthur for Vice-President.

They were elected, but had only a brief tenure of office, when the country was again horrified by the news of the assassination of President Garfield, by a madman.

It was one of the ironies of fate that Arthur, always desirous of honourable distinction in politics, should have had the highest office in the land suddenly thrust upon him by the hand of an assassin.

To a lady who came to greet him, soon after his accession, he replied: "No, madam, it is anything but a subject of congratulation. It was a hideous crime that I would have given worlds to prevent."

In 1881, it was thought proper in Washington to celebrate the centennial anniversary of the Battle of Yorktown, the last great victory by which the colonies had assured their independence of Great Britain. Due preparations were made. Naval vessels were ordered to Chesapeake Bay. Troops were marched to the old battlefield. Localities of the old siege guns used by Washington and Lafayette were marked, and high officials of the Government were expected to take part in the ceremonies.

It was pre-eminently fitting to invite the French Government to participate in this celebration, as the success of the Americans in the struggle and the victory had so largely depended upon the aid given at that time by their French allies.

The French Government heartily responded to President Garfield's invitation. It was announced that a delegation had been appointed at Paris to proceed to Yorktown. Among its members were several bearing such well-known historic names as Lafayette and Rochambeau, De Grasse and Steuben, who were the descendants of the illustrious heroes of the Revolution. General Boulanger was named as the head of the delegation.

As the French delegates would doubtless sail by one of

29

the French liners, to New York, it was also suggested that a Commission be appointed by the State of New York to receive them on landing, and finally to speed them on their way to Washington.

It seldom happens that elaborately arranged festivities take place in the order intended, without some break or casualty. The tragic note in life too often reasserts itself at such times. While the European visitors were on their way to the joyful occasion, the President who had invited them was lying mortally wounded, on his death bed. The Capitol, which had expected to greet them with a round of balls and dinners, was plunged in deep grief, rendering the idea of hilarity an unsuitable mockery.

When we of the New York Commission met, we were confronted with this new and changed situation.

Among our members were John A. King, John Austin Stevens, Colonel William Jay, General James B. Varnum, General Francis Barlow, Cornelius Vanderbilt, Robert R. Livingston, W. W. Astor, and Lispenard Stewart.

An unofficial message from the Secretary of State at Washington was received, intimating that the longer the stay of the French delegates in New York could be protracted, the greater would be the relief experienced at Washington, in this unexpected season of gloom. Accordingly, we did our best to make their visit an enjoyable one. A handsome suite of apartments was prepared for them at the Fifth Avenue Hotel, and various projects for their entertainment were planned that would occupy two or three weeks. Fortunately there was no lack of co-operation in these efforts on the part of State and City authorities, local organizations and societies, and the general public. "The Spirit of '76" was again aroused. Revolutionary and patriotic emblems and pictures and traditions and memories were the fashion of the hour.

The Commission went down in a body to welcome the

French visitors when the steamer *Canada* bearing them was telegraphed. A steamboat took us out to meet her, and her progress up the bay was greeted by salutes, displays of the Tricolour with the Stars and Stripes, and complimentary addresses of welcome.

At the Battery the Seventh Regiment was drawn up in line to escort their carriages up Broadway to the hotel amid the cheering crowd. Visitors, of course thronged there to greet them.

A day or two later, Governor Cornell ordered a review of the First Division of the National Guard, which they witnessed from a stand erected near the Worth Monument. A notable feature of this review was the fact that the regiments were drawn up in alternate cross streets, so as to fall into line in due succession. As each regiment had its band, the discord between these would have been bewildering, but for the happy idea that all should play the *Marseillaise* at the same time.

On another day we invited our guests to make an excursion to West Point. Two frigates were furnished by the Government, the *Vandalia* and the *Kearsarge*, of which the nominal commands were given to John A. King and myself respectively. The day was a fine one and we pointed out to our guests the various historic localities on the way. In Haverstraw Bay we gave them a collation, and at the close of it called them up on deck to show them the "King's Ferry." This, I told them, marked the real beginning of the Yorktown campaign, since it was at this point the French and American armies joined forces, and crossed the river, prior to beginning their march through New Jersey, Pennsylvania, and Maryland, toward Yorktown. At General Hancock's suggestion the engine was stopped, and the National Anthems of France and America were played, as we drifted by the ancient ferry. At West Point they were welcomed by General Howard, who was then in command there. A review of the Cadets was followed by evening festivities.

Next in order was a trip to Niagara Falls. The Vanderbilts furnished a well appointed private car for the French guests, which waited there for them and brought them back after two or three days' sojourn. Part of the Commission accompanied them.

The others remained in town in order to welcome Baron Steuben, who was coming on the German steamer, with other German officers. They were duly installed at the hotel. A dinner to them was followed by a review at Union Square of the various German organizations. In this Mayor Grace took part. The societies numbered several thousand, and some of the German regiments were bearing the tattered flags of the Civil War.

By the time the French delegation had returned from Niagara, preparations were well under way for the great ball which was to close the series of entertainments in New York. Needless to say that this was brilliant and well attended. So also was the banquet given by the Chamber of Commerce.

Meanwhile the Washington preparations for the celebration at Yorktown were making progress. But now arose a new complication, or the expectation of one. The whole Diplomatic Corps were of course to be invited to attend. But would the British consider it any courtesy to be invited to attend ceremonies based on the discomfiture of their own nation? Would they not rather be left out? Or would they consider it a slight to be left out on such an occasion? The Secretary of State thought this was a time for a private diplomatic interview with the British Minister. He was politely asked whether he would prefer to have an invitation or not for his legation. He took it very good-humouredly. He said: "I suppose the British were there, one hundred years ago, or you would have had nothing to celebrate. Yes, if you will invite us, we will all come, and we will listen, or not listen, with such equanimity as we can, to your recital of the misdeeds or misfortunes of our ancestors."

Not to be outdone in courtesy or magnanimity was the action of the President. After all the speeches had been made and the ceremonies performed and concluded, President Arthur, from the desk of the flagship gave the order for the British ensign to be raised to the mainmast and saluted by every vessel of the fleet, saying: "In recognition of the friendly relations so long and so happily subsisting between Great Britain and the United States, in the trust and confidence of peace and goodwill between the two countries, for all the centuries to come, and especially as a mark of the profound respect entertained by the American people for the illustrious sovereign and gracious lady who sits upon the British throne."

So closed the Yorktown celebration.

Taxation in New York. Andrew H. Green was so long prominent in the history and government of the city, and so wise in administrative measures, that he had earned the title in his later years of the "Father of Greater New York."

My last interview with him was a year or two before his tragic death. He was then, I think, about eighty-seven years old, and, though stooping and emaciated, was alert and active.

We talked of old times and people, of the many men, in both parties, with whom he had been associated,—of the vast improvements that had taken place,—of the careless or corrupt methods of finance,—of the spasmodic attempts at reform,—of the unrivalled advantages that the city possessed, and above all of its marvellous growth.

A newspaper lay on the table before us, the whole of

one of its broad pages being filled with the annual report
of some insurance or other Company.

"Tell me, Mr. Green," I said, taking up that big paper,
"something which you can comprehend, but which I
confess I cannot.   Here is this great corporation which,
by its report, shows it is well managed and profitable and
pays all its own expenses.

"Now, the city of New York is a corporation which has
vastly more property and more resources, in the way of
real estate, streets, franchises, docks and wharves, buildings, rents, licenses, powers and privileges, than any other
corporation possibly can have.   And yet it cannot pay its
own expenses! It has to ask the individual taxpayer to go
down into his pockets, and take out of his personal earn-
ings a yearly contribution, in order to keep this gigantic
corporation on its feet.   Why should not the city of New
York pay its own expenses?   Why should the individual
taxpayer be called upon at all?"

He looked keenly at me, as I spoke, and then said: "Mr.
Seward, you are right.   The problem is one that I have
worked over many years.   The city of New York has
given away more then enough to pay its expenses many
times over.   But the citizens of New York don't see it.
Either because they are too careless, or too ignorant, or
too unpatriotic, or don't care—whichever it is, the fact
remains they don't correct it, or don't want to."

Here occurred an interruption.

A clerk touched his arm and said: "Mr. Green, those
Rapid Transit gentlemen are in session now, and they
want you to come around there this afternoon! What
shall I tell them?"

Mr. Green turned to me and said, "There is an instance
of what I was just saying.   Yes! I will come round and
try to do my best to stop the waste, but I don't know
whether I can accomplish much."

VIEW FROM FREDERICK W. SEWARD'S RESIDENCE ON THE HUDSON RIVER

July, 1902.

Alaska Revisited.   The Inland Passage.   Here we are
once more in Alaska!

We are on board the steamer *Spokane*, and steaming
through the waters of the famous "Inland Passage."
Thirty-three years have passed since we were here before.
What are the changes that time has wrought?   Certainly,
the evergreen forests on the shores come down to the
water's edge just as they used to do.   The "everlasting
hills" are the same.   The distant ranges of snow-capped
mountains have not changed in the least.

The first change that we notice is that a "solemn still-
ness" no longer "broods o'er the scene."   There are now
indications of the bustle of commerce.   Propellers and
passenger steamers meet and salute us with steam whistles.
Some vessels are passing every hour.   Buoys and beacons
show that the channel has been surveyed and is no longer
unknown.   Our decks and spacious "observation room"
are occupied by our passengers eager to observe the
scenery of which they have heard so much.

We have cruised all day through the waters of British
Columbia, and have now traversed the "open water" of
Queen Charlotte Sound.   Before us looms up the "Dixon
Entrance" admitting us again to the territory of the
United States.   No especial landmark shows where the
boundary is, but we gather on the hurricane deck, to
salute the flag and give it three cheers, in token that we
are once more in our own country.

Captain Lloyd notified us that if we have any letters to
mail there is an American post-office at Ketchikan where
we shall stop in the evening.   This is another novelty.
There was neither post-office nor village here thirty-three
years ago.   Several new buildings are pointed out as
"salmon canneries."

Our Passengers. Our party consists of eleven persons, guests of our old friend Mr. Samuel R. Thayer. Mrs. Seward, Miss Barnes, and I joined the others at Minneapolis. They were: Warner Miller and his daughter, Mr. and Mrs. George W. Thayer of Rochester, Mr. Rufus H. Thayer of Washington, Mr. Rodman and Mr. Bradstreet of Minneapolis. Mr. and Mrs. Samuel Hill joined us at Seattle. To Mr. James J. Hill's courtesy we are indebted for the special car, which brought us over the Great Northern Railroad.

On board the *Spokane* there are about a hundred other passengers from the East and from California—tourists, pleasure seekers, and business men. It sounds odd to have the latter speak glibly of different points in Alaska, and down the Yukon Valley, to which they are bound. When we recall that the whole territory was a vast unexplored region only thirty-three years ago, it is difficult to realize that these towns and villages have a real existence.

Wrangel. Here is Wrangel! "Fort Wrangel" it used to be, but there are no signs of the frowning guns that once guarded "The Passage" at this point. Instead there is a substantial dock and a neat village along the shore. We land, and Mr. Thayer and I set out to explore the place. Meeting a well-dressed man on the street, Mr. Thayer inquires "Are you a resident here?"

"Yes," is the reply, "and have been for several years."

"What has become of the old Fort?"

"It used to be out there, on the promontory, but the Government abandoned it sometime ago, not needing it any longer."

"And the Indian lodges, what became of them?"

"Oh! after the Fort was abandoned, the Indians came away too; they all moved into town."

"Rather an unruly lot, weren't they?"

"Yes, but that was when they were uncivilized; they are all good citizens now."

"What do they do?"

"They all have their various trades. The children go to school, and they to church. Bible classes and Christian Endeavour are favourite occupations with them now. Some of them are very well to do."

"Where do they live?"

"Oh, everywhere. That double cottage with a rose vine over the door belongs to an Indian. That motor boat, in the bay, belongs to another."

Much enlightened, we resume our voyage.

Sitka. Sitka! This is indeed familiar ground. The towering mountains, the magnificent harbour with its clustering islands, are all that they used to be. We identify Mount Edgecumbe and others. But the town itself has spread along the shore in both directions. And where is the Indian village?

"That is it, along the north shore."

A row of neat white houses like those of a New England village has taken the place of the old lodges and wigwams.

We land, and proceed up the well remembered streets, with the Greek Church at the head of one. We inquire for Governor Brady's house. We find he is not at home, but we make the acquaintance of Mrs. Brady and her sister. The Governor is making his usual summer tour at the north. The ladies invite us in, and then sally out with us, to show us the changes that have come over Sitka in thirty-three years.

The Baranoff Castle on the high rock is gone, and in place of it stands a modern structure which we are told is the Agricultural College. There are numerous churches,

Presbyterian, Episcopalian, Swedish, and others, with industrial and other schools attached to nearly all of them. A large edifice is the Museum, founded by Dr. Sheldon Jackson, whom we are sorry not to see, as he is gone, like the Governor, on a trip to the north connected with his educational and missionary work.

In this Museum are many interesting carvings of the Hydahs, implements and weapons of the Thlinkets, the Kalosh, and the Chilkats, canoes of the several tribes, *baidarkas* of the Esquimaux, and a reindeer sledge like those of Lapland. It is fortunate that the Doctor had the foresight to commence this collection while it is still possible, for the Indian relics will be rapidly disappearing with the progress of time. We could spend hours in this Museum, if we had them, but our time is limited in Sitka now.

Out in the streets again, we find some of the old Russian houses, built of squared logs, are standing; but all the new buildings are modern frame structures. There are several tasteful country residences, which are occupied by their owners or visitors from the south. Mrs. Brady takes us out to a park, in the suburbs, which the authorities have decorated with the tallest and most massive of totem poles. We notice that the roads are straightened and that there are no animals running in them, improvements due, as Mrs. Brady tells us, to the efforts of the Village Improvement Society.

On our way back, we come across the school children, of whom there seem to be several hundred. They are neatly dressed, and for the most part with air and complexion like other school children in the northern States, though occasionally the darker hue of some of them denotes their Esquimau or Indian parentage.

We stopped to converse with some of them, and to recall some of the phrases of the Chinook jargon, which we took

some pains to learn several years ago, as it was then the
only mode of communication in vogue in the Territory.
The youngsters look at us with open eyes and shake their
heads. One of the missionary teachers laughingly says:
"They know good English, and do not know the Chinook
jargon,—some have not heard of it, and those who have,
consider it 'low down talk.'"

Pausing in front of a Russian house, I say: "This is Mr.
Dodge's house, where we spent a fortnight thirty-three
years ago. It is still standing, though I do not know its
present occupants. Let us consider it our 'old homestead'
in Sitka, and take a photograph of it and ourselves."
While engaged in this, several townspeople gather around
us and I interrogate them: "Were any of you here, thirty-
three years ago? I want to see the oldest inhabitant."
But no one would own to such long residence. One man
says: "I came here twenty-eight years ago and I thought
I was the oldest inhabitant."

At the Greek Church we found everything looking as
of old, except that it was newly renovated, cleaned, and
repaired, which the custodian added was due to the Bishop
and the Government at St. Petersburg. He displayed with
pardonable pride the gorgeous vestments worn by the
dignitaries of the church.

He furthermore informed us that he claimed the distinction of having neither been born nor naturalized in
the United States, but was nevertheless a citizen. He had
been transferred by the treaty of purchase of the Territory,
which contained a clause saying that any Russian who
chose to remain should thereby be considered entitled to
the privileges of American citizenship.

An hour or two was spent at the Governor's looking at a
collection of water-colour pictures of Alaskan localities,
and chatting over the changes and prospects of the Territory. We noted that the flowers that were brought us

in profusion, from different gardens, were much like those of our own garden at home.

On our way to the steamer we found some of our fellow passengers bargaining with a group of Indian women, blanketed as of old, who were selling curios. Here were neat and pretty little totem poles, canoes and carvings, and weapons fresh and newly painted, but all of miniature size,—in fact, convenient for packing in trunks or dress-suit cases. Evidently these were for tourists, not for Indian use. The story was told, but we do not vouch for the truth of it, that the supply from Indian sources being insufficient to meet the demand from travellers, an enter-prising firm in Connecticut had taken the manufacture in hand, and sent them on to Alaska for the Indians to sell.

Glaciers. The tossing cakes of ice around us this morning are of a brilliant blue colour, a phenomenon that no one seems able to explain. These are from the Taku Glacier. We inquire if we shall see the Muir Glacier. The captain says, "Yes, but not too near, as the falling masses of ice sometimes make it dangerous for a vessel in the vicinity." But we get a fine view of it.

Then the much mooted question comes up: whether the glaciers, on the whole, are receding or not? The general opinion appears to be that some certainly have receded, while others apparently have remained unchanged.

The Tredwell Mine. The steamer comes to a pause, in the midst of a deafening din from the shore, at the next landing. The captain shouts out that this is "Douglas Island," and that the noise we hear is made by the trip-hammers of the "Tredwell Gold Mine."

We debark to look at the machinery of the stamp mill from a respectful distance. We are told that this is the largest stamp mill in the world. Although the ore is of low grade, the company is said to be satisfied if they can get three or four dollars in gold from a ton. Yet sometimes it yields two or three times as much.

Already they have thus pulverized a considerable part of one mountain. But there look to be plenty more mountains of the same sort standing close at hand.

Juneau. "It is a pity that we shall get to Juneau in the middle of the night," say we. But the middle of the night turns out not to be dark, or even dusk, in Alaska at this season. As the steamer makes the landing at eleven o'clock, the town is revealed to us in very good daylight; the townspeople muster on the wharf to inquire for news, or to greet friends.

We, the passengers, are equally eager to see the town. So we proceed up the street, and find places of business open, and people going to and fro as if it were noon instead of midnight. We ramble through various streets, one of which we are informed is "Seward Street," and some of which seem to be built on piers or piles in the water.

This is a growing town, and its transition state is somewhat bewildering to the observer. All of the buildings are frame edifices, and some of them have been very hastily erected. The townspeople, however, have great expectations, and high hopes. They say that here was the first discovery of gold. They confidently look forward to its becoming the capital of the Territory.

Skagway. Skagway is the *ultima thule* of our navigable voyage. As we approach it up the broad reaches of the Lynn Channel, we see its long piers pushing out into the water. Signs of business activity on them prove it to be a commercial port of importance.

Here begins the White Pass Railroad, the first in the Territory. We land and walk up the street and find the rails laid in the centre of it.   Freight and passenger cars are standing on the track.

We recall how within our own remembrance there was no trail over the mountains and into the wilderness. Klakautch, the Chilkat Chief, was then asked about it, and we learned from him that there were Indians on the other side of the mountains, who held intercourse and traffic in furs with the Chilkats, but who were not allowed to come down to the coast.   He made a map of the trail in Indian fashion, on a bearskin, indicating the trail by two rows of footprints running over the mountain.

"Is Klakautch still living?" is inquired.

"No," is the answer, "but his family are well known, and his son has a position in the Custom House, yonder."

The White Pass Railroad.   Was there ever such a daring piece of engineering as this White Pass Railroad?   Beginning on the level of the street, and running smoothly for a mile or two, it gradually climbs the side of the mountain. Then it speeds toward precipitous cliffs, around dizzy curves, and on the edge of unfathomable abysses, until you imagine the train cannot possibly find a foothold among the jagged rocks that beset it on every side.   The train comes to a sudden stop in the midst of this chaotic scene.   We are looking where to jump and wondering whether there is anything to jump on, when the conductor blandly informs us, "It is all right.   We always stop here, in order to give the ladies an opportunity to take a snapshot with their cameras."

Resuming our tortuous course and steadily going on, and up, at last we reach a level plateau, and are told this is the summit of the Pass.   It is also the boundary line between Alaska and British America.   Two little custom houses, one for Great Britain and one for the United States, mark the frontier, each surmounted by its national flag.

Looking off toward the north, we see the ranges of mountains gradually diminishing in height, until the valley of the Yukon is reached.   Some of our passengers who have business at Dawson, or are expecting to take one of the steamboats down the Yukon River, now continue on the railway.   We go back on our train, and on the way Mr. Brackett points out the old wagon road, which was made at great trouble and expense, in the time of the first rush of miners and prospectors.   Now it is abandoned and superseded by the railroad.   The railroad is said to be highly prosperous, having now a practical monopoly of the traffic to and from the gold region.

The Alaska Boundary Dispute.   If it be true that the Americans for many years remained singularly incredulous and indifferent to the value of the great Territory that we purchased from Russia in 1867, it cannot be said that our Canadian neighbours have shared in that feeling.   From the first, they have shown an appreciation of it, and once or twice the restless and reckless element of their people have manifested a covetous desire to get hold of a part of it, and add it to the Canadian Dominion.

In 1902, when visiting Alaska, we found some of the inhabitants of Skagway seriously alarmed lest they should be practically "gobbled up" by the Canadians, who were putting forward a claim to own their harbour and a considerable slice of their Territory.

Returning home, I found that the movement had taken such definite shape, that maps were prepared and spread abroad from Ottawa, by which it appeared that we not only had no claim to Skagway or Dyea, but that Canada rightfully owned all of the mainland on the Lynn Canal, and that our boundary only took in part of the islands of the sea!   I wrote a letter to the *Tribune*, calling public attention to the fact, as follows:

"A MENACE FROM CANADA

"*Mr. Seward Believes that the Alaskan Boundary Dispute Endangers International Good Feeling.*

"Very few people either in England or the United States seem to comprehend the 'true inwardness' of the so-called 'Alaska Boundary Dispute.' That is unfortunate, for it contains the germ of a grave national danger. The average newspaper reader supposes it to be a dispute over a few acres or square miles of wild land, perhaps frozen, on either side of an imaginary line. But it is not a boundary dispute of that sort. The boundary was established years ago by treaties in which both nations took part. What the Canadian schemers are pushing for now is 'an outlet to tidewater' by means of a harbour on the Lynn Canal.

"What is the Lynn Canal? It is a great estuary, broad and deep, like the lower Hudson or the Delaware. It traverses Southern Alaska and is the chief artery of commerce. It is the thoroughfare by which all traders, miners and travellers reach the valley of the Yukon, unless they make a two-thousand-mile voyage around by the ocean.

"What is the harbour that the Canadian schemers covet? It is one of the most important strategic points on our Pacific Coast. It is a deep, wide, semicircular basin, safe in all weathers, open to navigation all the year round, with easy access to the sea, large enough to float not only trading craft, but the cruisers and battleships of the British navy. It is surrounded by mountain heights which, when fortified, would render it impregnable. In a word, what they want is to establish a naval and commercial port for Great Britain, resembling Gibraltar or Aden—and to establish it in the heart of an American Territory, at the head of its inland navigation! The power owning such a stronghold might well claim to dominate the North

Pacific. It would cut Alaska Territory in two parts, with British forts and custom houses between, controlling their intercourse with each other and with the outside world. Compared with such a stronghold Esquimault or Halifax is of minor consequence. That port is the objective point that Canadian schemers are working for. That is what they hope to extort from us by threats or cajolery. They know what they are about; apparently we do not; at least they hope so. So they muddle the question with specious pretences of harmless purpose, by which to 'outwit the Yankees.'

"When this monstrous demand, without a shadow of foundation, was first put forward it brought to a sudden check the work of the Joint High Commission to settle questions between Canada and the United States. If persisted in it will do more than that. It will tend to break up the present era of good feeling between the two branches of the English-speaking race—an era so full of promise for both nations and for the whole civilized world.

"The whole 'claim' is so preposterous and absurd that it would hardly be credible if we did not know how silly and blind to their own interests great governments may sometimes be. The Canadian 'statesmen' who are pressing it are blind leaders of the blind. They are like children playing with fire. They do not realize the far-reaching consequences of the conflagration they are trying to kindle. For it is not to be believed that the American people, when roused to an understanding of the question, are ever going to acquiesce in the construction of a Gibraltar in their own waters by any foreign power. American patience is great and American good nature is proverbial, but even these have limits.

"FREDERICK W. SEWARD.

"Montrose-on-Hudson,
    November, 1902."

30

This letter was widely copied and commented upon, especially in the northwestern States. Soon the subject became one of general discussion by the press. Ultimately it became a topic of debate in Congress. Both Governments perceived that it would be necessary to take action in regard to it.

A semi-official answer was published by the Government at Ottawa, arguing that, as there were conflicting claims between Great Britain and the United States, the subject would be a proper one for arbitration. To this I prepared an equally elaborate reply.

The *Tribune* said: "Three noteworthy contributions to the Alaska boundary discussion have recently appeared in our columns. These were a brief statement of the American case by Mr. Frederick W. Seward, a reply by Mr. F. C. T. O'Hara, and a rejoinder by Mr. Seward. These letters were weighty with authority, for Mr. Seward, the son and official aide of the Secretary of State who negotiated the Alaska purchase, is a past master of the American side of the controversy, while Mr. O'Hara, as Secretary to a Canadian Cabinet officer, may be supposed to be an adequate exponent of the Canadian side. Between the two, our readers will doubtless have judged for themselves. That the decision of the vast majority of Americans is on Mr. Seward's side, is beyond doubt."

Frequent conferences were now held between Secretary Hay and the British Minister at Washington. The final outcome of their deliberations was the agreement to hold a "Joint Alaska Boundary Commission" during the coming season.

The Commission was duly held—its official title was, "The Alaskan Boundary Tribunal." Six members composed it, three for each side. The American members were ex-Secretary Elihu Root, and Senators Henry Cabot Lodge and George Turner. Two Canadians, Sir Louis

Amale Jette, Lieutenant-Governor of Quebec, and Allen Bristol Aylesworth, one of his Majesty's Counsel. The British Government reserved to itself the right to appoint the third member, and it selected for that place Lord Alverstone, Lord Chief Justice of England, a jurist of such wide experience and unimpeachable integrity that it was felt no one could question his impartiality.

The sessions were held in 1903. The case for the United States was very elaborately prepared by Mr. John W. Foster, ex-Secretary of State, and the chief argument for it was presented by Elihu Root.

When the Tribunal rendered its decision, in October, Lord Alverstone took the same ground as the Americans, that the true boundary was that laid down in the Treaty of Purchase in 1867. The two Canadian members adhered to their claim, but the decision of the majority of four to two was in favour of the American side.

Perhaps my comment on the decision may have interest enough to warrant its insertion here:

"THE ALASKAN DECISION

" *F. W. Seward Says Both Nations are to be Congratulated.*

"Both nations have reason for congratulation.

"The Americans are to be congratulated that their title is reaffirmed and no longer disputed as to the region which they bought from Russia, and which has been held and occupied by them and the Russians before them ever since the day of its first discovery.

"The British are to be congratulated that they did not win their contention, nor even stubbornly insist upon it to the point of a 'deadlock.' Their wisdom, tact, and statesmanship were manifested through the Lord Chief Justice, though his two Canadian associates seem to have been unable to follow him. To have obtained possession of a harbour and town built, owned, and occupied by

Americans for thirty years would have been to England a most unprofitable victory. Skagway would then have been between Great Britain and the United States what Strassburg has been between France and Germany, a perpetually rankling thorn. It would have put an end to that international friendship on which both nations are building such high hopes.

"It was natural, perhaps, that the provincial ambition of the Canadians should have been captivated by the fancy of getting one of our harbours for their outlet from Klondike to the sea, and, perhaps, natural that they should be blind to the consequences of their own project. But the idea was largely a fanciful one.

"During long centuries it has been the habit of nations to hold on to whatever they could grasp by fair means or foul until compelled to disgorge by force or the fear of it. It has been reserved for two nations which are but two branches of one great race to lift international dealing to a higher plane and to seek to decide questions in accordance with justice and equity, regardless of national sentiment or prejudice. We have proved it thrice. In the *Trent* case, the *Alabama* Claims case, and now in the Alaska Boundary case, we have shown that we can afford to relinquish to each other anything not justly belonging to us, whether prisoners, land, or money. Two nations actuated by this disposition, and ready to carry it into practical effect, can hardly be dragged into war, since they themselves are their own high court of equity. The Alaska Boundary decision seems, therefore, a guarantee of perpetual peace between Great Britain and the United States, and that is a step onward in the march of progress and civilization worthy of the opening of the twentieth century.

"FREDERICK W. SEWARD.

" Montrose-on-Hudson,
    October 21, 1903."

Hudson Centennial Celebrations.   When one hundred years had elapsed after Hudson's discovery of the river, the people of the province of New York did not hold any celebration.   They were too much absorbed in their own doings and those of their Colonial Governors, to bestow much thought on those of Henry Hudson.

But when a second century had rolled by, New York had become an independent State and a part of the Federal Union.   Then the anniversary of the discovery was deemed worthy of celebration.   Under the auspices of the then newly organized Historical Society, orations were delivered at the City Hall, a banquet followed at the City Hotel, at which Governor Tompkins presided and Mayor DeWitt Clinton was an invited guest.   Especial stress was laid upon the fact that to Henry Hudson they also owed the best dishes of the feast,—the oysters and fish that he discovered in the river, the wild ducks and pigeons that he found flying over it, and the Indian corn and "succotash" that he found growing on its banks.

Simeon DeWitt, who was then Surveyor-General, proposed the toast:

"May our successors, a century hence, celebrate the same great event, which we this day commemorate."

When Simeon De Witt offered that toast, he was a true prophet.   But his foresight did not extend as far as to know that the next anniversary would be a double one, and that the hero who would divide its honours with Henry Hudson would be the young artist-inventor, Robert Fulton, who married the niece of his friend Chancellor Livingston, and who had just devised a new-fangled craft to go without oars or sails, but belching fire and smoke! Indeed, it was one of the jests at the dinner table, that a frightened farmer, looking over the edge of the Palisades, was asked what it was that he saw.   He said he did not know, but he believed "it was the Devil on his way to Albany, on a saw-mill!"

When the next hundred years had rolled away, the tricentennial "Hudson-Fulton Celebration" of 1909 occurred. There is no need to relate here who organized and conducted it, or to recount its sayings and doings. Are they not all fully and faithfully set down, recorded, and illustrated in the two large volumes of the Report to the Legislature, prepared by Dr. Edward Hagaman Hall, the Assistant Secretary of the Commission? Suffice it to say that the celebration was a memorable one, a hundred and sixty miles long, and sixteen days broad,—and that it was worthy of the great events it commemorated. Many thousands participated in it, and millions witnessed it from the banks of the historic stream.

EPILOGUE

History and Memory. Napoleon at Saint Helena was reading over a file of newspapers, just received by an English ship.

"Las Cases," said he, to his secretary, "we have always supposed that history was the record of past events. I perceive it is not so. It is only a compilation of the statements given out concerning those events."

This philosophic truth is worth bearing in mind, by readers of history, and writers of it. But what then? Oral tradition is discredited, because human memories are deemed unreliable, unless corroborated by some sort of documentary evidence. If the documentary evidence cannot be relied on, what can?

The simple fact seems to be this. Memory supplies us with successive pictures of past scenes. Like the photograph she aims to be exactly truthful, and, like the photograph, her pictures are often more impressive than the reality, because minor details and outside surroundings are excluded. But that is Memory's limit. Of dates and names she is proverbially careless, and her worst errors are made when she tries to reconcile her own vivid impressions with somebody else's hearsay testimony.

Let whoso would write or read reminiscences, govern himself accordingly.

471

INDEX

A Selection from the
Catalogue of

G. P. PUTNAM'S SONS

❦

Complete Catalogues sent
on application

Secret Diplomatic Memoirs

By

Count Hayashi

Late Ambassador to Great Britain; Foreign Minister and Minister of Commerce and Agriculture
at the Court of Japan

8°. $2.50

In this volume the veteran Japanese diplomat
traces some of the great consummations of
recent Japanese diplomacy. The author, as the
Ambassador from the Mikado's Empire to the
Court of St. James's, had a large measure of
responsibility for the shaping of the Anglo-
Japanese alliance. His verbatim account of
the diplomatic play of forces gives a very clear
impression of the conduct of this important
affair of state.

Of especial interest to American readers are
also the chapters in which the author discusses
the Americo-Japanese Convention of 1909, and
reviews the foreign policy of Japan.

G. P. Putnam's Sons

New York   London

DATE DUE

GAYLORD			PRINTED IN U.S.A.